SPECTRE OF INVASION

By the same author

Steam Yachts at War:
The Naval Deployment of British & American Armed Yachts 1898–1918

The Petrol Navy:
British, American and Other Naval Motor Boats at War, 1914–1920

The Harwich Striking Force:
The Royal Navy's Front Line in the North Sea 1914–1918

British Naval Trawlers and Drifters in Two World Wars

The Power and the Glory:
Royal Navy Fleet Reviews from Earliest Times to 2005

Battle in the Baltic:
The Royal Navy and the Fight to Save Estonia and Latvia, 1918–1920

Southern Thunder:
The Royal Navy and the Scandinavian Trade in World War One

Bayly's War:
The Battle for the Western Approaches in World War One

Securing the Narrow Sea:
The Dover Patrol 1914–1918

Blockade:
Cruiser Warfare and the Starvation of Germany

Formidable:
A true story of disaster and courage

The Coward?
The Rise and Fall of the Silver King

The Scapegoat:
The Life and Tragedy of a Fighting Admiral and Churchill's role in his death

www.steverdunn.com

Spectre of Invasion

The Royal Navy and the Defence of Britain's Coast, 1900–1918

STEVE R DUNN

PUBLISHING

For Vivienne, with love

Copyright © Steve R Dunn 2025

First published in Great Britain in 2025 by
Seaforth Publishing,
A division of Pen & Sword Books Ltd,
George House, Beevor Street, Barnsley S71 1HN
www.seaforthpublishing.com

British Library Cataloguing in Publication Data
A catalogue record for this book is available from the British Library

ISBN 978 1 3990 3990 1 (HARDBACK)
ISBN 978 1 3990 3992 5 (EPUB)

All rights reserved. No part of this publication may be reproduced or transmitted in any form or by any means, electronic or mechanical, including photocopying, recording, or any information storage and retrieval system, without prior permission in writing of both the copyright owner and the above publisher.

The right of Steve R Dunn to be identified as the author of this work has been asserted by him in accordance with the Copyright, Designs and Patents Act 1988.

Pen & Sword Books Limited incorporates the imprints of Atlas, Archaeology, Aviation, Discovery, Family History, Fiction, History, Maritime, Military, Military Classics, Politics, Select, Transport, True Crime, Air World, Frontline Publishing, Leo Cooper, Remember When, Seaforth Publishing, The Praetorian Press, Wharncliffe Local History, Wharncliffe Transport, Wharncliffe True Crime and White Owl

Typeset and designed by Ian Hughes, www.mousematdesign.com

Printed and bound in Great Britain by CPI Group (UK) Ltd, Croydon, CR0 4YY

Contents

Introduction   9

1	This Precious Stone Set in the Silver Sea	13
2	The Fear of Invasion	37
3	Sir John Fisher's Navy, 1904–1910	60
4	Coastal Defence and the Road to War, 1911–1914	79
5	The Defence of Britain, 1914	95
6	The Auxiliaries, 1914	120
7	The East Coast Under Attack, 1914	135
8	A Troubled Island, 1915	165
9	A Concerted Plan: The Attacks on Lowestoft and Great Yarmouth, 1916	186
10	But What If They Come? 1916	204
11	'Shoot and Scoot', 1917	218
12	Last Knockings, 1918	240
13	The Invasion of the Air	250
14	Defending the Shores	269
15	Coastal Defence Afloat and Science Ashore	277
16	In Conclusion	294

Author's Notes   304

Appendices

1	The Major Saxon Shore Forts (late fourth century AD)	305
2	Cinque Port Benefits	306
3	The Henrician Castles	307
4	Major Unit Distribution by Station c. 1898	308
5	The Home Defence Squadrons in 1900	309
6	Types of Gun Recommended by the Owen Committee	310
7	UK Coastal Artillery, 1914	311
8	Comparative Naval Expenditure, 1900–1913	313
9	Fleet Distribution 1907, 1909, 1912, Heavy Ships only	314
10	Distribution of Destroyers and Submarines, 1909	316
11	Guard Ships Deployed as at January 1915	317
12	The Consolidated DORA Act of November 1914	318
13	Chapter I of Convention No 9, Second Hague Conference	320
14	Days Lost to Industrial Action in Britain, 1914–1918	321
15	Sites of Indicator Loop Systems	322
16	British Communities Attacked from the Sea by German Naval Forces	323

Notes and Sources   324
Bibliography   334
Index   340

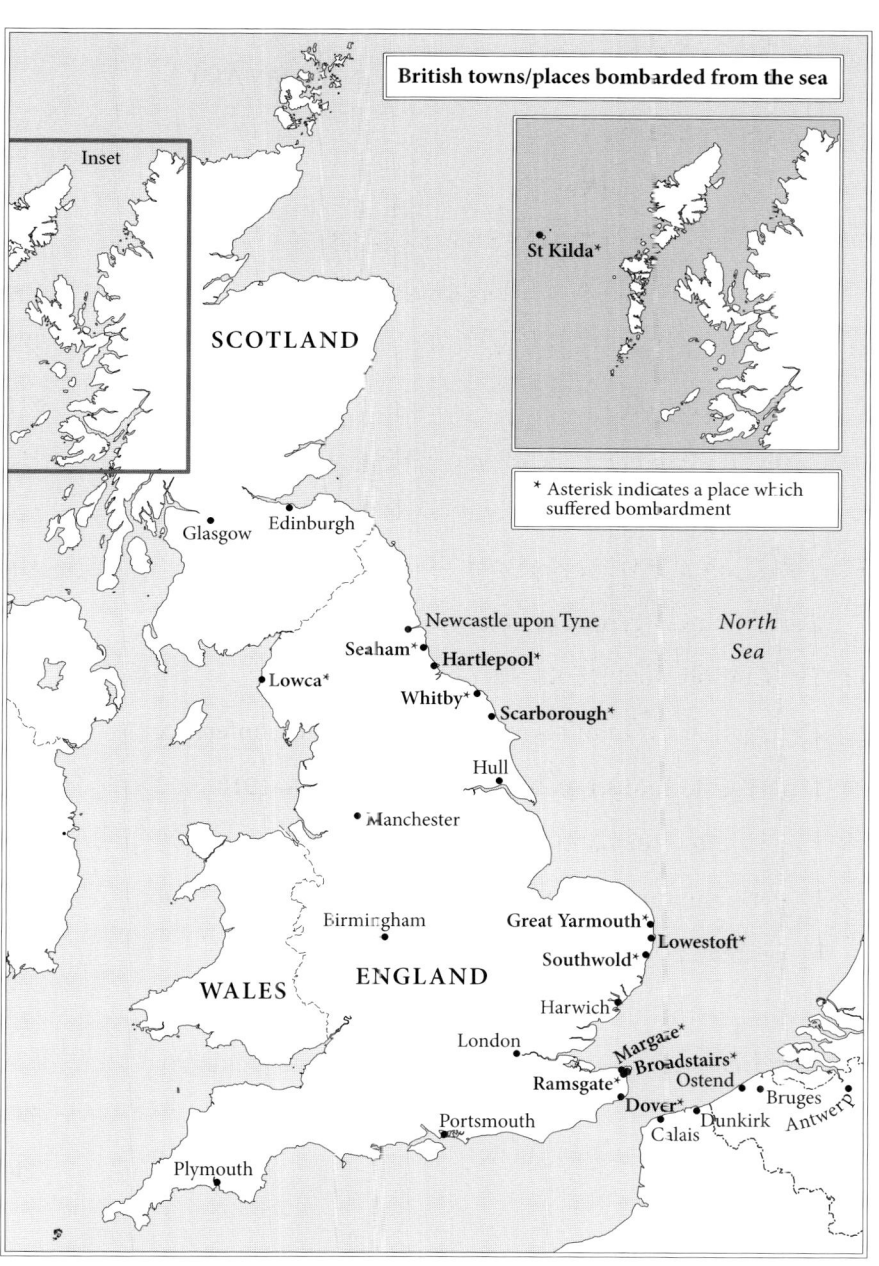

'Our navy is one of the chiefest defences for the preservation of us and our realm against the malice of any foreign potentate'.
Queen Elizabeth I in 1588, quoted in Martin, Parker, *Armada*, p 74

'This England never did, nor never shall,
Lie at the foot of a conqueror'.
W Shakespeare, *King John*, Act V, Scene VII, 112–113

'What shall we do to be saved in this world? There is no other answer but this, look to your moat. The first article of an Englishman's political creed must be that he believeth in the sea'.
Charles Montagu, Marquess of Halifax, 1694

'I do not say, my Lords, that the French will not come.
I say only they will not come by sea'.
Admiral of the Fleet John Jervis, 1st Earl of St Vincent (letter, 1801)

'The man who has nothing for which he is willing to fight, nothing which is worth more than his own personal safety, is a miserable creature and has no chance of being free unless made and kept so by the exertions of better men than himself'.
John Stuart Mill, *Principles of Political Economy* (1848)

What! Wrench the Sceptre from her hand,
And bid her bow the knee!
Not while her Yeomen guard the land,
And her ironclads the sea!
Alfred Austin, *To Arms*

'The German Emperor is ageing me; he is like a battleship with the steam up and screws going, but with no rudder, and he will run into something some day and cause a catastrophe'.
Sir Edward Grey, November 1908,
quoted in Herwig, *Luxury Fleet*, epigraph

Introduction

An island archipelago, Britain has ever been susceptible to invasion from the sea. The Roman and Norman ones are well known but there were many others, some invited, most not.

As a result, there has always been a clamour for coastal defence. Castles, fortified emplacements, redoubts and trenches were built from earliest times, with coastal artillery being added as it became available. During the French Revolutionary Wars, Martello towers dotted the landscape and many volunteer organisations, such as the Sea Fencibles, were formed to defend the littoral. Even the creation of Belgium in 1831 can be seen in terms of protecting the English Channel coastline and oceanic access.

In one of many French scares, a Royal Commission recommended the expenditure of £11.8 million on fixed defences between 1859 and 1863. Dover and Deal, Portsmouth and Plymouth still exhibit signs of all these historical works, as do scores of other locations. Despite this, in 1887, French Admiral Hyacinthe Aube advocated the bombardment of British coastal towns as a legitimate tactic in any war with the old enemy.

Quite who was accountable for coastal defence was a moveable feast. In 1771 it was decided that it was the Royal Navy which held the primary responsibility for preventing invasion and in the late nineteenth century, the RN was being described as 'Britain's Sure Shield in Peace and War'. By 1900, the reality was more complex. The Royal Artillery manned the fortifications, the Royal Engineers were responsible for the remotely-controlled mines and the Brennan torpedo harbour defence system, and the navy guarded the seaways.

However, it was becoming clear that technology was overtaking the existing methods of defence. Naval gunnery range and accuracy had increased considerably since Napoleonic times and the muzzle-loading rifled cannons mounted in the coastal fortifications were outranged and outweighed by the latest ships and weaponry. Moreover, existing plans did not take into account the risk of attack on British harbours by the recently developed torpedo boats and submarines.

Additionally, as the new century dawned there was a freshly-minted great fear of invasion, not from traditional enemies such as France, but from Germany, across the North Sea and increasingly bellicose. This terror was driven by books from authors such as Erskine Childers and H G Wells, and fanned by newspapers, especially Alfred Harmsworth's *Daily Mail*. This rampant fright led to the Committee of Imperial Defence commissioning General John Owen to produce a report on the state of Britain's land/sea defences, which was released in 1905. It proved to be damning and recommended an immediate upgrade in weaponry, based around breech-loading 9.2in, 6in, 4.7in QF and 12pdr QF weapons. Coastal defence therefore became a battlefield for public money between the army and the navy, each wanting increased expenditure for more resources and in part using coastal defence to justify their positions.

At around the same time as Owen, First Sea Lord Sir John Fisher, naming Germany as the likely foe, and committed to reducing the cost of the navy, scrapped 150 outdated vessels and reorganised the fleets, concentrating his heavy ships in home waters and clustering the best and newest ships where they were well placed to protect Britain's southern and eastern coasts. However, between 1905 and 1907, Fisher began to recognise the dangers to his heavy units posed by small torpedo-carrying craft operating in the North Sea, constricted and often shallow. Instead, he developed the theory of Flotilla Defence, whereby the battlefleet would not patrol in the North Sea but smaller vessels would take the responsibility. In 1912, the naval part of this system on the east coast came under the command of a newly created post, Admiral of Patrols, although the static guns were still manned by the Royal Garrison Artillery and the recently installed searchlights by the Royal Engineers. This was the position when war came in 1914.

With war declared, the Defence of the Realm Act gave government unprecedented dictatorial powers, which were especially exercised in coastal areas, controlling citizens' movements, restricting access to beaches, prohibiting street lights, etc. In addition to naval and static defences, ports and harbours were now protected by the simple expedient of blockships, sunk in existing channels to deny access, such as the old HMS *Hood* at Portland, or ancient cargo vessels at Dover. Booms and nets were positioned across harbour mouths to prevent access except when opened.

Minefields and mining became a key part of coastal defence and the navy's minelayers were out in all weathers laying new fields. Soon the whole of the eastern seaboard of Britain was a long continuous minefield with narrow gaps to allow egress and access, and a swept War Channel along the littoral was created which ran from Dover to the Firth of Forth.

The Royal Navy had nowhere near enough resources to deal with all the wartime tasks that now devolved to it. Motor pleasure craft were taken on to patrol harbours, steam yachts to monitor the seaways, and trawlers to sweep the path through minefields and operate boom defences.

But the system proved fallible. Major coastal raids were made by the German fleet on such east coast towns as Dover, Lowestoft, Great Yarmouth, Scarborough and Hartlepool; and to the west the Cumbrian coast and even St Kilda in the Hebrides were attacked. Running battles were fought with these attacking forces and both ships and lives ashore were lost. The coastal artillery was unsuccessful in driving off such raids; and the naval resources were overstretched. One reason was that so much naval capability, especially light cruisers and destroyers, was tied up with the battle fleet at Scapa Flow. Unforgivably, the site chosen as the fleet's wartime home was completely undefended when war came. Admiral Jellicoe, commanding the Grand Fleet, had to improvise protection and use Royal Marines to man guns taken from warships and mounted ashore.

From the outset of war, the Royal Navy had been given the responsibility of protecting the coast and London from Zeppelin attack, another scare driven by the imagination of authors, such as Wells and his book *War in the Air*. Ill-equipped RNAS aircraft flew night sorties against the giant gas bags, and monitors were positioned in the Thames to shoot at them. The navy even took charge of the anti-aircraft guns ringed around London, a situation which lasted until 1916 when the army took back what should always have been its role.

Invasion fear reared its head again in 1916 and a squadron of pre-dreadnought battleships was moved from Scapa Flow to Sheerness to add its guns to the defence of the south-east coast. They would have had a short life up against the German High Seas Fleet, but could have value fighting an invasion force.

Science was called in to help with coastal defence. The great physicist William Bragg Snr was recruited to work on underwater detection. Bragg loops, for detecting submarine movement near harbours, and (eventually) hydrophones were the fruits of his labours. The navy developed the Y-system of wireless listening posts along the east coast and a long line of acoustically magnifying giant 'earphones', manned by civilian volunteers. Both of these creations were intended to give warning of German Zeppelin and ship/submarine movements.

This book tells the story of the defence of the British coast from attack or invasion, primarily in the years leading up to, and during, the First World War. It is based on the particular perspective of the Royal Navy and the navy's role, actions, successes and failures are detailed and examined. It is a tale little told and one of considerable interest now, as the world comes to terms with the fact that such assumed givens as security of food and energy supply, sanctity of borders and freedom of the seas, are not as inviolable as politicians would give us to believe. The first duty of government is surely to protect its citizens; maybe ministers should recognise this rather more than they seem to.

The narrative that follows is not necessarily in chronological order but rather structured by topic. Naval ranks are given as at the time of the actions described. The 24-hour clock is used throughout for clarity; where ante or post meridian was given in the original documents, the time has been converted. A date in brackets after the name of a ship is the year in which it was launched. In the period covered by the book, the War Office was responsible for the army and the Royal Flying Corps and the Admiralty for the navy and the Royal Naval Air Service. After 1 April 1918, when the air arms were merged, the War Office had responsibility for the combined force.

Finally, it may be useful to note that all Conservatives were Unionists but not all Unionists were Conservatives. Joseph Chamberlain and his Liberal Unionists were driven to combine forces with the Conservative party by Gladstone's first Home Rule bill of 1886. Between 1895 and 1905 these two political entities ruled as a coalition, with Chamberlain joining Prime Minister Salisbury's Cabinet. In 1912 the two wings of unionism formally merged as the Conservative and Unionist Party. The Liberal Party won the General Election of 1906 with an overwhelming majority. However, in the elections of 1910 they lost many seats and as a result were not the largest party in the House of Commons. They remained in power only through the support of the Irish Nationalists, backing given in exchange for an Irish Home Rule bill. This led to many on the right suggesting that they were not a legitimate government as they remained in power despite not having a parliamentary majority and refused to submit their key policy (Irish Home Rule) to the electorate.

1

This Precious Stone Set in the Silver Sea

So wrote William Shakespeare in 1590, putting the words in John of Gaunt's mouth in his play *Richard II*, and going on to add that the waters around Britain were 'a moat defensive'. An accident of tectonic plate movement, successive ice ages and the flooding effect of glacial meltwater had gifted Britain with a superb defensive wall. Once joined to Europe by a land bridge that linked the Weald in Kent to the Boulonnais in the Pas de Calais, Britain exited the Pleistocene as a group of islands surrounded on all sides by water.

But this sea-girt position was not only a protection, it was also a road, a route for invasion and settlement. The first invaders arrived in dribs and drabs, but in 55 BC the Romans and their legions came, crossing the Channel under Julius Caeser and establishing a client state which persisted until 43 AD when the Emperor Claudius staged a full-scale invasion, with subjugation of the local tribes (except those in Scotland) complete by the 80s.

However, Roman occupation did not bring safety from other aggressors; Picts, Franks, Scots and Saxons all troubled the shoreline and during the third century AD a series of forts sprang up along the southern littoral, under the overall command of 'The Count of the Saxon Shore', whose task it became to protect the coasts of Britain and Gaul from the attacks of the Saxon pirates and their like. Originally built with the control of shipping and trade in mind, these fortifications found greater use in the protection of Roman Britain from seaborne invasion by marauders from across the North Sea. The Saxon Shore Forts were placed at strategically important coastal inlets and estuaries, and safeguarded key Roman settlements, from the Wash in northern Norfolk round the east and south coast of England down to Portchester Castle in Hampshire (see Appendix 1).

But as Rome came under attack at home, soldiers and resources were withdrawn from Britain and by 401 AD most had been removed. The ocean road now facilitated Saxons, Jutes, Danes and Vikings to sail over the North Sea or down the English Channel and settle Albion's pleasant shores, without as much let and hindrance as before. The invasion of Britain by multiple opportunists began; and as one wave of incomers established their power, it was challenged by the next wave of *soi disant* settlers. It became evident that to stop the newcomers, naval force might be an advantage.

Himself the product of a previous invasion, Alfred 'the Great' (King of

Wessex from 871–c 886 and King of the Anglo-Saxons from c 886–899) saw the benefit of a fighting navy to protect against, or repel the incursions of, rampaging Norsemen. Around 896 he had ordered the construction of a flotilla of longships to his own design, all having sixty oars, which made them twice the size of the Viking longships and thus able to carry double the number of fighting men.[1] He appreciated the doctrine of sea power and command of the sea. If enemy fleets could be intercepted before they landed, he might save his kingdom from despoliation. In practise his ships proved difficult to manoeuvre, but the tactical intent was important and served for future naval thought. Notwithstanding the unwieldiness of his ships, Alfred won important naval victories, perforce close to the littoral or in river estuaries, such as that of 896 when his nine new ships intercepted six Viking vessels and inflicted 120 casualties, at a loss of only half that number among his own forces. Unable to put out to sea through lack of manpower, the Norse ships were wrecked on the coast (possibly at Selsey Bill) and the survivors hanged at Winchester.

Another early monarch to recognise the benefit of a fighting sea force was also of Anglo-Saxon descent, King Edgar (ruled 959–975). At his coronation he allegedly summoned six client kings to Chester, including the King of the Scots and the King of Strathclyde, and made them pledge their word that they would be his liegemen on sea and land. Later chroniclers made the number of kings into eight and have them all plying the oars of Edgar's state barge on the River Dee as an act of obeisance. With Edgar, the union of England under one dynasty became more firmly established. Highly conscious of the importance of sea power, the king was said to have built up a navy of 3,600 ships by the time of his death, which were deployed to guard England's coasts from the incursions of the Danes. There will, of course, be an element of exaggeration in this account, but even if halved the number of ships he could call upon if necessary was formidable.

Indeed, defence of the coast by naval means seems to have been the default position in the time before the Norman Conquest. 'The emphasis seems to be almost entirely naval. Edward the Confessor defends his people by sailing out from Sandwich every summer, and is appeased by a gift of a great gilded warship.'[2]

Then came, by sea of course, the Norman Conquest. The Normans' goal was to acquire land and once it was gained they built castles to defend it. Despite being descendants of seafaring Vikings, after the conquest 'is to enter a world dominated by cavalry and castle ... indeed when ships were needed in 1066, they have to be borrowed or built from scratch'.[3] And when William the Conqueror, now William I, was himself threatened by Danish invaders, instead of sailing to meet them, he despoiled the crops and fields inland from their likely landing places, so they would have nothing to live on. Despite this, the idea of seaborne defence did not die.

The Cinque Ports

One reason the concept did not fade was the creation of the Cinque Ports. From the Old French for 'five harbours', the Cinque Ports had their origins in the reign of Edward the Confessor (1043–66). In return for certain privileges, some south-eastern ports undertook to supply men and ships for the king. Hastings, New Romney, Hythe, Dover and Sandwich (later joined by the so-called Ancient Towns of Winchelsea and Rye) undertook to provide fifty-seven ships for 15 days' service annually, each port taking a portion of the responsibilities. (For a summary of the benefits they obtained, see Appendix 2.)

If more than the defined term of service was requested, there was no obligation to provide it. 'The aristocracy of the Cinque Ports were ... bound to assist ... but their obligations were not infinite ... the Portsmen were required to turn out for only two weeks. The king might appeal ... for longer, either in return for payment, or simply as favour, but his appeal might fall on deaf ears.'[4] When the famously warlike King Edward I was battling Llywelyn ap Gruffudd for control of Wales in July 1277, 'courtesy of the men of the Cinque Ports, Edward was able to dispatch some 2,000 soldiers across Conway Bay and the Menai Strait'[5] to achieve a famous victory. The contribution of the Cinque Ports to naval defence would continue throughout the thirteenth and fourteenth centuries with their final naval service being to meet the threat of the Spanish Armada.

Naval Kings and Queens

Edward I was a ruler who understood the importance of sea power in the defence of his realm. Threatened with a French invasion in 1295, he created a great fleet; 'his new galleys – fighting ships with 120 oars a piece – were now ready under the command of William Leybourne, who was duly accorded the newly coined title of "Admiral of the Sea". They were backed up by teams of paid men patrolling the shoreline.'[6]

Richard I had granted the first charter for the town of Portsmouth in 1194. The fortifications that can still be identified in parts of the city have their origins in the fourteenth century. With England almost continually at war with France, Portsmouth bore the brunt, supposedly being burned down four times between 1338 and 1380. The result was to build walls around the city, shortly followed by the Round Tower, which could fire at enemy ships making their way up the Solent. Henry VII built the Square Tower, to further fortify the entrance to the Camber area, and constructed the dockyard. Henry VIII also helped design Southsea Castle.

Indeed, Henry VIII established a more formal naval force than had hitherto existed, the 'Navy-Royal', and was also responsible for the creation of the supporting anchorages and dockyards. He also built land fortifications to prevent foreign invasion, the so-called Device Forts, also known as Henrician Castles, a series of artillery fortifications constructed to defend the southern coast of England, the largest coastal defence programme since the Saxon Shore. The defences ranged from earthen bulwarks, through small blockhouses and artillery towers, to state-of-the-art fortifications influenced by the latest Italian designs. Henry took a personal interest in the military engineering techniques of the time, and approved and amended the designs himself.* They were ruinously expensive, costing £376,000 in 1546 money, much of it raised through the Dissolution of the Monasteries, for thirty castles, earthworks or blockhouses (see also Appendix 3).

By the late sixteenth century, the largest and richest empire in the world was that of Spain. British naval forces successfully played their part in repelling a Spanish attempt at invasion in 1588. A great Spanish fleet sailed from Lisbon in late May under the Duke of Medina Sidonia, with orders to sail up the English Channel, link up with the Duke of Parma in Flanders, and escort an invasion force that would land in England. The objective of the exercise was regime change: to overthrow Elizabeth I, reinstate Catholicism in England, end support for the Dutch Republic in its struggle with Spain, and prevent attacks by English and Dutch privateers on Spanish interests in the Americas.

But it was those very adventurers and privateers – men such as Frobisher, Drake and Raleigh – who led an English fleet which sailed from Plymouth to defend the nation. Faster and more manoeuvrable than the larger Spanish galleons, they were able to attack the Armada as it came up the Channel. Medina Sidonia was advised to anchor in the Solent and occupy the Isle of Wight but he refused to deviate from his instructions. Although the Armada reached Calais, while awaiting communication from Parma it was attacked at night by English fire ships and forced to scatter, and then suffered further at the Battle of Gravelines. Only a change in the wind saved the Spanish great ships from running aground, allowing them to escape into the North Sea. Pursued by the English, the Spanish ships returned home via Scotland and Ireland. Some eventually got home, but twenty-four ships were wrecked along the way. Aggressive naval assault of the type favoured in the past by Alfred the Great and Edward the Confessor had saved England from the ravages of Spanish landings.

---

* Although built to defend England during Henry's reign, many of them were used in the English Civil War and were refortified at various times during the Napoleonic Wars, and the First and the Second World Wars.

From the Plantagenet age onwards, the cost of the *ad hoc* naval protection provided by the state was met (at least in theory) by the levy of 'Ship Money', a tax on the inhabitants of coastal areas of England and one of several taxes that English monarchs could raise by royal prerogative, without the approval of Parliament. Under the Plantagenets (ruled 1154–1485), littoral towns and cities could commute the demand to supply ships and men in time of war or danger through the payment of a cash sum. Over time and in different reigns, this payment became an established tax, Ship Money, and an important source of income for the crown, whether or not it was spent on naval protection. As late as 1619, James I was able to extract £40,000 of Ship Money from London and £8,550 from other maritime towns. It was the attempt by Charles I, desperately short of money and reluctant to ask for more from Parliament, to levy Ship Money during peacetime from 1634 onwards, and to extend it to the inland counties of England without Parliamentary approval, which provoked a backlash from the monied middle class and became one of the key issues which fomented the Civil War. Only when his son Charles II came to the throne was the navy established on a proper basis and funded more from general taxation.

Indeed, Charles II was very naval minded, as was his brother, the future James II. Charles saw the need to protect sea borne commerce as a paramount mission for the navy. From early on in the restored monarchy the brothers publicly declared their determination to support and protect trade. Convoy was introduced in time of war, with merchant vessels escorted by the navy, and ships were stationed out in what came to be called the Western Approaches to meet and escort incoming merchantmen from the Mediterranean or the Atlantic. This is exactly the same problem and solution found by Admirals Lewis Bayly and Max Horton in the Western Approaches during the First and Second World Wars respectively.

The Seven Years War

In 1756 came a new war with France and Spain, a war fought for global domination as the French strove to emulate the Spanish and the British to stop them. Another invasion of England was planned and again the Royal Navy would prevent it. Bottled up by a close blockade of their coasts, the French finally attempted a breakout in late 1759: and Admiral Edward Hawke was waiting for them. In the Battle of Quiberon Bay, 20 November 1759, Hawke demolished the French invasion fleet off the coast at St Nazaire, which had consequences for Britain that surely compare favourably with all that Nelson would achieve later in the seas off Cadiz. Hawke destroyed six and captured one of the twenty-one ships that he faced. The invasion was abandoned, through magnificent British seamanship and bravery; and William Boyce and David Garrick wrote *Heart of Oak* in Hawke's honour!*

The French Revolutionary and Napoleonic Wars

Invasion by, and conflict with, France once again threatened in the early nineteenth century. Between 1797 and 1815 Britain was held in constant dread of an incursion from France; indeed, one landing was made near Fishguard – by the 'Black Legion' – but was driven off by the locals. By 1803, Napoleon was assembling invasion fleets at Boulogne and Flushing. In response, Home Secretary Charles Philip Yorke passed a Defence of the Realm Act, which required all counties to submit a full report on all able-bodied men aged between 15 and 60, classifying those in the volunteer regiments, those willing to serve, to drive waggons or act as guides, as well as the details of waggons, boats, horses, cattle, food and forage. The task of these levies, which emulated the French *levee en masse* by raising a huge number of volunteers, was to harass and wear down the enemy if he landed. The French were to be denied the means of living off the land by the burning of all corn and other crops as they disembarked. Farmers would be given chits to indemnify them for losses, and these tickets would be redeemable once the war was over.

Fear of invasion was rampant and Thomas Hardy used this in his novel *The Trumpet Major* (1880), where the threat of foreign dominance permeates the work and one underlying theme is that of the defence of the realm. However, to be successful, France had to have command of the Channel and the Royal Navy denied her this boon, a feat sealed by Nelson's destruction of a combined French and Spanish fleet at Trafalgar in 1805. Nonetheless and hurriedly, a large fort was built at Eastney Point and redoubts constructed at Eastbourne, Dymchurch and Harwich. The Royal Military Canal in Kent was created as a barrier to advancing French troops and the landscape suddenly became dotted with Martello towers.

These were small defensive forts, built across the British Empire, mainly in coastal locations. Up to 40ft high and set out on two floors, Martellos typically had a garrison of one officer and 15–25 men. Their round structure and thick walls of solid masonry made them resistant to the cannon fire of the time, while their height gave a good platform for a single heavy artillery piece, mounted on the flat roof and able to traverse and fire around a complete circle. Some had moats or other batteries and works attached for extra defence. A total of 103 Martello towers were built in England between

---

* Hawke was given an annual pension of £2,000 by Parliament, but not the immediate peerage such exploits usually attracted. He disdained to ask for the honour and it was not conferred on him until just before his death in 1781.

A cutaway drawing of a Martello tower. (Author's collection)

1804 and 1812, set at regular intervals along the coast from Seaford in Sussex to Aldeburgh, Suffolk. A few were also constructed in Scotland and Wales. Many towers remain today as a mute memorial to past invasion threats.

Belgium

It may seem odd to claim a foreign land as part of the defence of British coasts; but the ports of Ostend, Zeebrugge and Antwerp are so placed as to represent a clear and present danger to British trade and control of the English Channel and southern North Sea if held by a power inimical to British interests.

During the French Revolutionary Wars, all three were taken by France. At the conclusion of the conflict the Congress of Vienna (1815) portioned out Europe, led by Britain, Austria, Prussia and Russia. They decided that the Netherlands and the Southern Netherlands (the latter approximating to modern-day Belgium) would become a united monarchy, the United Kingdom of the Netherlands, with the House of Orange-Nassau providing the king. This placed Ostend, Zeebrugge and Antwerp under control of this new polity, which Britain saw as the best option on the table at the time to protect her interests.

But this new creation lasted only 15 years, for the outbreak of the Belgian Revolution in 1830 led to the de facto secession of the southern part of the state, leaving a rump which refused to accept the split, and a minor civil war ensued. This situation was only rectified in 1839 when the Treaty of London was signed, fixing the border between the two states and guaranteeing Belgian independence and neutrality as the Kingdom of Belgium. The Treaty of London officially recognised the independent Kingdom of Belgium and the five great powers of Europe (Austria, France, Prussia, Russia and Britain) also pledged to guarantee Belgium's neutrality. This was entirely what Britain wanted – with the three ports held by a neutral power, whose neutrality was guaranteed by the so-called Concert of Europe, Britain's coastal defence was substantially reinforced.

In 1866, the French had held exploratory talks with Prussia as to the possibility of France acquiring Belgian and Luxembourg. On 25 July 1870, just after the Franco-Prussian War commenced, *The Times* broke the story. Britain immediately insisted on a double treaty, one with France and one with Prussia and the North German states, which obliged the British to intervene militarily if either combatant invaded Belgium. Parliament approved a bill to increase military and naval forces by 20,000 men at the same time. As Prime Minister William Gladstone said of the situation, 'we have an interest in the independence of Belgium which is wider than that which we may have in the literal operation of the guarantee'.[7] Disraeli made the same point; 'It has always been held by the government of this country that it was for the interest of England that the countries on the European coast extending from Dunkirk to Ostend to the islands of the North Sea, should be possessed by free and flourishing communities ... and should not be in the possession of a great military power.'[8] When Germany invaded Belgium in 1914 and occupied the coast and harbours, Britain's security was threatened, as the progress of the war demonstrated when Zeebrugge and Ostend became German U-boat bases.

France Again

In 1848, King Louis Philippe of France was forced to abdicate the throne. He tried to pass the crown to his nine-year-old grandson, also Philippe. The National Assembly of France initially planned to accept the youngster as king but a strongly opposed public opinion made that impossible. The ex-king fled to England, disguised as 'Mr Smith', and on 26 February, the Second Republic was proclaimed. Louis Napoleon Bonaparte, nephew to the great emperor himself, was elected president on 10 December 1848. Three years later, on 2 December 1851, he declared himself president for life and subsequently Emperor Napoleon III in 1852.

Britain was worried about anyone named Napoleon; and the more so because 'the new Bonaparte had high ambition to remake Europe and

Stack Rock Fort near Milford Haven, photographed in the early 1920s. (Author's collection)

The French ironclad *La Gloire* was the first ocean-going ironclad, launched in 1859. She was developed after the Crimean War in response to new developments of naval gun technology, which had resulted in rifled guns and explosive shells, giving increased destructive power against wooden ships. (Author's collection)

extend French power around the world, to restore the glory of the first Napoleonic era. But before he did this, the French Navy had to neutralise Britain by exerting the maximum pressure on British home waters'.[9]

The French upgraded and completed new defences at Cherbourg, a few hours steaming from Portsmouth, making the port its first battleship base in the Channel and an arsenal for a potential invasion of Britain. It was an obvious danger to British military planning and an overt threat to her sovereignty of the seas. Britain's response included building new fortifications, such as the one at Stack Rock, off Milford Haven, which was constructed between 1850 and 1852 to offer increased protection to the Royal Dockyard at Pembroke. As built, it housed three 32pdrs as well as a 12pdr. The garrison comprised an officer and thirty men. Then, in 1859, the French Navy launched *La Gloire*, an armoured frigate capable of firing explosive shells.

Technological Change

British coastal defence batteries were largely dependent on the guns developed for the Royal Navy. Thus, as ships became better protected, the relationship between ships' armour and the increasing gun power required to breach it also meant that existing coastal defence artillery became less effective. The coastal defence guns of 1840 were primarily the 24pdr and 32pdr smoothbore guns which had changed little from the Napoleonic Wars. The later development of 8in and 10in shell guns proved effective against wooden ships, particularly their rigging. However, the introduction of *La Glorie*, and the prospect of more armoured ships like her, meant that the old smoothbore guns were unable to penetrate the armour of new vessels.

HMS *Warrior* photographed off Plymouth, probably during the later 1860s. She appears to have her original short bowsprit, which was replaced in 1872–5. (US Navy History and Heritage Command NH 71191)

These developments triggered panic amongst the political and chattering classes in Britain and this in turn produced three immediate responses. Firstly, the launch of the Royal Navy's iron-hulled warship, HMS *Warrior*, completed in 1861, secondly, the advent of rifled breech-loading cannons, designed and manufactured by the Armstrong Company,* and thirdly, a Royal Commission, under the chairmanship of Royal Engineer Major General Henry ('Harry') David Jones, was established in 1859 to inquire into the state of Britain's defensive fortifications and protection for its dockyards and arsenals.

The 1859 Royal Commission

On 7 February the following year, the Commission's report recommended a huge programme of fortification to defend the country's arsenals and naval bases. The Commissioners concluded that the fleet, standing army and volunteer forces, even combined, did not provide sufficient defence against invasion. Furthermore, the coastline which they considered to be at risk, the 700 miles from the Humber to Penzance, could not feasibly be completely fortified and therefore they recommended that 'the fortifications of this country should be confined to those points ... whose possession would give him [the enemy] sure bases for operations'. A detailed plan and costing was produced for each location which required protection, resulting in a massive programme that would cost around £10 million (maybe a billion pounds in today's money).

Coastal batteries were recommended, to provide protected positions for heavy artillery which would be able to engage enemy warships and troopships. In some places, for instance high on a cliff, the guns could be mounted in a barbette or open gun pit. Where close to the shoreline and could thus be engaged directly by enemy gunfire, each heavy gun was mounted in a casemate, a vaulted chamber with an embrasure for the gun which was pierced through an armoured shield. As being mounted in an enclosed space limited the traverse of the gun, casemates were arranged in a long, curved row in order that the guns of the battery could track the progress of a passing enemy ship, each weapon engaging it in turn. Some were completely circular, enabling defence on all sides. Other fortifications were uprated. Stack Rock, mentioned above, was one gaining sixteen 10in and seven 9in rifled muzzle-loaders.†

---

* The Admiralty, however, was initially ambivalent about switching to breech-loading guns. Rifling, however, was accepted and many of the ships of this period were fitted with rifled muzzle-loading weapons, despite Armstrong's rifled breech-loader of 1858.
† Stack Rock was rearmed again in 1902 with just four 12pdr QF guns. A small number of men manned the fort between 1914 and 1918, by which time only two 12pdrs remained.

A newspaper etching from 1881 depicting external and internal views of Admiralty Pier Turret at Dover. (Author's collection)

The largest coastal gun to be installed in Britain was the Admiralty Pier Turret at Dover. This was an enclosed armoured turret constructed in 1881 on the western breakwater of Dover harbour. It housed two Fraser rifled muzzle-loading 16in 80-ton guns, the largest ever installed at that time. The turret had a frame of wrought iron clad with three layers of 7in armour with 2in layers of iron and wood between them and its weight, including the two guns, was 895 tons. It revolved on thirty-two rollers. By 1909, the weaponry had been further enhanced by the addition of two 6in BL guns on top of Admiralty Pier Fort, either side of the turret. Searchlights were fitted to the pier and a battery command post was added, using the top of the contiguous, disused, lighthouse. Admiralty Pier Turret remained the largest static guns to be part of coastal defence until 1921.

Land forts were also constructed to prevent an enemy force, which might have landed at an undefended beach, from marching overland and attacking a dockyard from the rear. These forts were built in a polygonal style and sited such that each could support its neighbour with artillery fire. Construction of some landward forts at Portsmouth and Plymouth had already begun in the 1850s. Building of such defences was still taking place in 1875, when work commenced at Chatham.

Meanwhile, at sea, before *Warrior*, the Admiralty had responded with even bigger and better ships of the line. HMS *Agamemnon* was ordered in

HMS *Agamemnon* (1852) depicted in the watercolour *Laying the Atlantic Telegraph Cable in 1858, A Whale Crosses the Line,* by Robert Charles Dudley.
(MET 92.10.68, Metropolitan Museum of Art, New York)

1849 and completed three years later. Of ninety-one guns, she was the first British battleship to be designed and built from the keel up with installed steam-powered engines as well as a full square rig on three masts. And HMS *Duke of Wellington*,* launched in 1853, was twice the size of Nelson's *Victory* and mounted 131 guns. It took 76 acres of trees to build her.[10] At the time, she was the most powerful warship in the world, although the design process which created her had started in 1841 and was not finished until she had been cut in half on the stocks in January 1852 to be lengthened to receive steam engines and screw propulsion.

---

* She had been first named HMS *Windsor Castle*; but on the day of her launch the Duke died and she was renamed in his honour.

Not to be outdone, the French built ten new wooden steam battleships and converted twenty-eight old ones. In turn, Britain built eighteen and converted forty-one. It was a naval arms race which prefigured that between Britain and Germany in the last years of the nineteenth and the early twentieth centuries.

But the Royal Navy had made *La Glorie* obsolete. HMS *Warrior* was the first armour-plated, iron-hulled warship.* She was not intended to stand in the line of battle but was designed as a forty-gun armoured frigate, the precursor to the cruisers of later times. Conceptually, she was faster, better armoured and harder to hit than her rivals and superior to any extant naval warship. *The Times* reported that '[she] will be at once fire and shot proof – the largest man of war afloat in the world'. Her armour, made from 4.5in of iron backed by 18in of teak, was safe against any gun of the time. *The Times* noted '[her] monstrous slabs of armour are formed from scrap iron with a certain amount of puddled bar iron . . . they were fired at by 69 pounders [*sic*: actually 68pdrs] at a point blank range of 200 yards. The massive shot . . . failed to penetrate the iron, though they have dinted it to the depth of one and a half inches.'[11] She was the biggest warship in the world at 420ft long, and the fastest at 17.5 knots under steam and sail. One onlooker when *Warrior* started sea trials with a line of wooden three-deckers said that 'she looks like a black snake among the rabbits'.[12] With her launch, the Admiralty stopped the construction of all new wooden ships of the line, barring those already earmarked for conversion. From now on it was iron and steel all the way, and other navies followed suit.

En passant, we might note that *Warrior*'s gunnery lieutenant was John Arbuthnot 'Jacky' Fisher, who would later revolutionise battleship design with the launch of HMS *Dreadnought* in 1906. *Dreadnought* made a generation of warships immediately out-of-date, as did *Warrior* in her time. Indeed, Fisher wrote of her that 'it certainly was not then appreciated on board *Warrior* . . . that this, our first armour clad ship of war . . . would cause a fundamental change in what had been in vogue for something like a thousand years. For the navy that had been founded by Alfred the Great had lasted till then without any fundamental change till came this first ironclad battleship.'[13] So, once more, Britain had upgraded her coast defences and her navy in the face of fear of aggression from abroad.

The Volunteers

The Royal Navy was assisted in the duty of coastal defence by various volunteer organisations. The French Revolutionary Wars precipitated the formation of the first volunteer movement to have a name and degree of

---

* *La Glorie* had a wooden hull, clad with iron plates.

organisation – the 'River Fencibles' and the 'Sea Fencibles'. Created in 1798, they mostly comprised professional sea or river workers; fishermen, watermen, longshoremen, and sometimes retired naval ratings. Their purpose was the defence of the coast and rivers from the land or by use of small sailing craft. 'They distrusted the navy, believing that if they went on board men-of-war they would be pressed into long and distant service.'[14] Indeed, one of their privileges was freedom from impressment. They served mainly at home, although they picked up a few French vessels in coastal waters, and resisted calls to take up service afloat. When in 1801 Horatio Nelson, at that time in charge of defending the English Channel to prevent invasion, asked for the Fencibles to man floating batteries, offering the view that 'the place to defend England was at sea',[15] they refused. But the Fencibles did play a part in the rout of the Black Legion at Fishguard. With the threat of invasion gone, the Fencibles were disbanded in 1813.

No attempt was made to introduce another body of volunteers for over 30 years. Then, driven by the same fears which eventually produced the 1859 Royal Commission and *Warrior*, a Manning Committee was set up in 1852 under Admiral Sir William Parker to study the problem of crewing the navy's ships and the Admiralty's part in coastal defence. The outcome was the formation of the Royal Naval Coast Volunteers (RNCV); 5,000 to 6,000, but not more than 10,000, seafaring men who would be given a guarantee that their service, when requested, would not be more than 100 leagues (150 miles) from the home coast. Volunteers would be free of all compulsory naval service, training would be organised to avoid the fishing seasons and they would be instructed in the use of the coastal artillery.

In 1856, control of the RNCV passed from the Coastguard Service to the Admiralty and steam blockships with heavy guns were placed for training purposes at Leith, Hull, Harwich, Milford Haven, Liverpool, Greenock, Kingstown and Queenstown. However, the navy rather lost interest in the RNVC with the formation of the Royal Naval Reserve (RNR) in 1859, and it faded gradually away, being replaced in 1873 by the Royal Naval Artillery Volunteers (RNAV). 'Only those at least moderately well-to-do could really afford to serve their country in the RNAV' and as a result membership was targeted on 'rowing and yachting gentlemen of good social standing'.[16] This organisation bore many of the hallmarks and tenue of a yachting or gentlemen's club and was disliked by the regular naval officers and the Admiralty, which starved it of support, not least because the RNAV was not governed by the Naval Discipline Act. There was some rejoicing when the Admiralty succeeded in getting the RNAV suppressed in 1891. Nonetheless, the groundwork had been laid for future volunteer organisations which would play a very necessary role in coastal defence when war came in 1914.

The View From the Year 1900

So far, this chapter has tried to sketch out how coastal defences developed over a thousand years of invasion history and scares, and which left their mark on the landscape and the country's naval forces. As the Victorian century drew to a close, what then was the state of Britain's protection from invasion?

AT SEA

It was a key part of late Victorian British military thinking that because she was an island, Britain could use her naval power to prevent direct invasion. To avoid defeat in war, she must maintain free access to the resources of her empire, and to other overseas trade as necessary. Accordingly, no matter whether a war was purely European or not the defence of Britain herself was inextricably linked with the defence of the empire. The destruction of the empire would impoverish Britain and make her vulnerable to any great continental power. A large navy was essential to provide the necessary protection, and so the Royal Navy grew in stature and size during the nineteenth century. It was a wonderful thing to be an admiral, a sailor, a member of the Senior Service. The navy was our 'sure shield in peace and war'.[17]

To the public it became their navy, and admirals became stars as sportsmen are today. The entertainment industry took up the strain and songs and verse praised the Royal Navy and its ships with lyrics such as 'Stand by to reckon up your battleships, ten, twenty, thirty there they go. . .', words to a popular song of the time by Henry Newbolt and Charles Villiers Stanford.* People responded to and copied the navy's tropes, *inter alia* beards and, perhaps the most toe-curling, the sailor suits which little boys and girls were forced into. Cigarette packets and matchboxes† carried images of ships and sailors. Cigarette cards featured admirals and ships. Jolly tars danced across biscuit tins and advertising posters.

To be an admiral was to have authority over thousands of men, many thousands of pounds of weaponry, and the life and death of both friend and enemy lay in his hands. He made and unmade careers from the lowest sailor to the highest-ranking subordinate. He was possessed of plenipotentiary powers and when abroad on service represented the monarch and government. In the far-flung corners of the world, away from communication with London, flag officers made and unmade foreign policy. He was the Supreme Being wherever he went, so much so that Admiral

---

* Sir Charles Villiers Stanford, *Songs of the Fleet*, opus 117, iv *The Little Admiral*.
† Such as Players Navy Cut cigarettes and tobacco, introduced in 1883 and which bore an increasingly debased likeness of Able Seaman Thomas Huntley Wood from the 1882 battleship HMS *Edinburgh*.

Algernon Charles Fieschi 'Pompo' Heneage* refused to kneel for divine service in his naval uniform, as a British admiral did not recognise a superior. Pompo always changed into civvies for such events. Flag officers had personal servants, their own barges and crews, a suite of officers to fulfil their every desire or order and untrammelled authority over their ships and captains. Their orders were unquestionable, divine writ, omniscient and omnipotent, and if no admiral was present then this mantle of greatness fell to a commodore or the senior captain afloat.

The British flag flew over 20 per cent of the earth's surface and 25 per cent of its people; and the size of the Royal Navy meant that Britain could project its power wherever it chose to. However, there were problems both of *materiel* and of men. All this pomp masked a sad truth. The navy had become a hidebound organisation, fossilised in the past, rigidly hierarchical and obsessed by petty rules.

Ships were not assessed on their ability to fight but more on how spick and span they were. They had to positively gleam and sparkle. As Admiral Percy Scott related,

> it was customary for a commander to spend half his pay, or more, in buying paint to adorn HM ships, and it was the only road to promotion. A ship had to look pretty; prettiness was necessary to promotion, and as the Admiralty did not supply sufficient paint or cleaning material for keeping the ship up to the required standard, the officers had to find the money for buying the necessary housemaiding material.

Scott added that 'the prettiest ship I have ever seen was the [Duke of Edinburgh's flagship] HMS *Alexandra* (1875). I was informed that £2,000† had been spent by the officers on her decoration.'[18]

Gunnery practice was abhorred (and often ignored) as it made the ship dirty. Many captains, sent to fire off practice ammunition at sea, simply threw it overboard. When at sea, manoeuvres were balletic and formal, unreflective of the sort of fighting that modern warfare would call for and devised top down by the admiral in charge. Absolute adherence to the admiral's plans was required and formation sailing was the rule. Orders were gospel and not to be questioned. The admiral knew best and initiative was completely discouraged. Captains followed orders religiously and likewise ships' officers obeyed their commanders' orders without question.

---

* Commander-in-Chief, Pacific Station in 1887 and Commander-in-Chief, The Nore, in 1892.
† Over £255,000 in today's money, according to the Bank of England.

Percy Scott noted that

> the rule was that the senior officer made out a fixed routine which all ships had to follow, irrespective of the time they had been in commission. What exercises the ships are to perform; what clothes the officers and men are to wear; what boats the ships are to use; what awnings the ships are to spread; when the men are to wash their clothes; when and how the washed clothes are to be hung up, and when they are to be taken down. All these are matters over which captains of ships have no jurisdiction; they are settled by the senior admiral present.[19]

Historian Arthur Marder noted that 'although numerically a very imposing force, it was in certain respects a drowsy, inefficient, moth-eaten organisation'.[20]

There were 165 Royal Navy warships present at Queen Victoria's Diamond Jubilee fleet review in 1897, out of 212 in active commission and 451 in total. At her Golden Jubilee review ten years earlier, 134 had taken part. But whilst some of the ships present at the Diamond review were a significant advance on those at the Golden Jubilee, Captain Lord Beresford wrote that 'the fleet of 1887 was in no way adequate to our needs at that time and many of the ships assembled for review could not have taken their places in the fighting line'. But even now, the glittering array of ships hid some problems. Beresford noted that 'of the older ships that figure in the

The battlefleet lined up at Queen Victoria's Diamond Jubilee review at Spithead, 26 June 1897. On the left of the royal yacht, HMS *Renown* leads the line of *Majestic*-class battleships. Captains' barges can be seen heading to their reception on *Victoria and Albert*. From a painting by Charles Dixon. (National Maritime Museum BHC0645)

1897 review, the *Inflexible* and the *Alexandra*, armed with muzzle-loading guns . . . and the armoured cruisers *Black Prince*, *Agincourt*, *Minotaur* and *Northampton* also armed with muzzle loaders, . . . are quite useless and all seven of the muzzle loading ships in this review are of no value as fighting ships while so armed.'[21] These ships had all been groundbreaking in their time but were now almost practically obsolete. *Alexandra*, of 1875, a central battery battleship, was the second most massively protected ship at the review, with 12in of armour amidships, and the flagship of the First Reserve Fleet until 1899; she was broken up as late as 1908. *Inflexible* had 24in of iron at its thickest point.

Naval theorists, and the majority of the public, regarded the navy as the bulwark against invasion and of home defence. As long as the Royal Navy controlled the seas, Britain was safe from invasion or conquest. Such beliefs were known as the 'Blue Water' school, after (primarily) the writings of Vice Admiral Philip Howard Colomb (1831–99). But a blue water strategy assumed that, if it came to a crisis, Britain could stand against any combination of foes. Although this had sometimes been possible, it came at a high price and required a huge navy. Some sort of land-based intervention was usually necessary. As William Pitt (the elder), Britain's grand strategist in the Seven Years War said 'those who talk of confining a great war to naval operations only speak without knowledge or experience'.[22]

Moreover, as Britain industrialised through the nineteenth century, she became more and more dependent on imported foodstuffs, creating a situation whereby if any hostile power were able to mount a successful blockade of British ports, they would not need to conquer on land, for the country would have to capitulate for want of food. Even if Britain's home army defeated an invasion force, this would spare the country only weeks under blockade. The Blue Water adherents used this weakness to argue that it would be better not to have a home army, because the funds would be better utilized by building more ships which would command the oceans and approaches to Britain.

But despite the fact that the navy was regarded as the key part of home defence, the majority of its heavy ships were located in the Mediterranean, which was seen as the plum command for any admiral. Here they were supposed to keep watch on Britain's traditional enemy, France, and guard the Suez Canal approaches thus protecting the sea route to the jewel in the British crown, India. The ships of the Royal Navy were allocated to a number of geographic stations but only those in the Mediterranean were described as a fleet. These distributed commands, intended to police imperial trade routes and 'show the flag' were: Mediterranean Fleet, East Indies Station, China Station, Australian Station, Cape and West Africa Station, North America and

West Indies Station, South America Station and Pacific Station (see also Appendix 4). Few fully operational warships were stationed in Home Waters. They were spread between the three traditional home commands: Nore Command, Plymouth Command, and Portsmouth Command, all of which faced the Channel, the Western Approaches and France.

A small force of battleships made up the Channel Squadron, which could be reinforced by the older battleships and cruisers of the Coast Guard. Those ships on Coast Guard duty were distributed around the ports of the United Kingdom as guard ships, certainly a visible but possibly not very effective presence (see also Appendix 5). There was clearly a disconnect here between the perception (or at least the opinion held by the public) that the RN was the first line of defence against invasion and the reality of its distribution.

ON LAND

What about the shore defences? In 1898 there were 99,000 regular soldiers stationed in Britain (about the same number of RN sailors in total). In India, there were 75,000 British soldiers together with 148,000 native troops. Another 41,000 British soldiers were maintained abroad.[23] Again, there

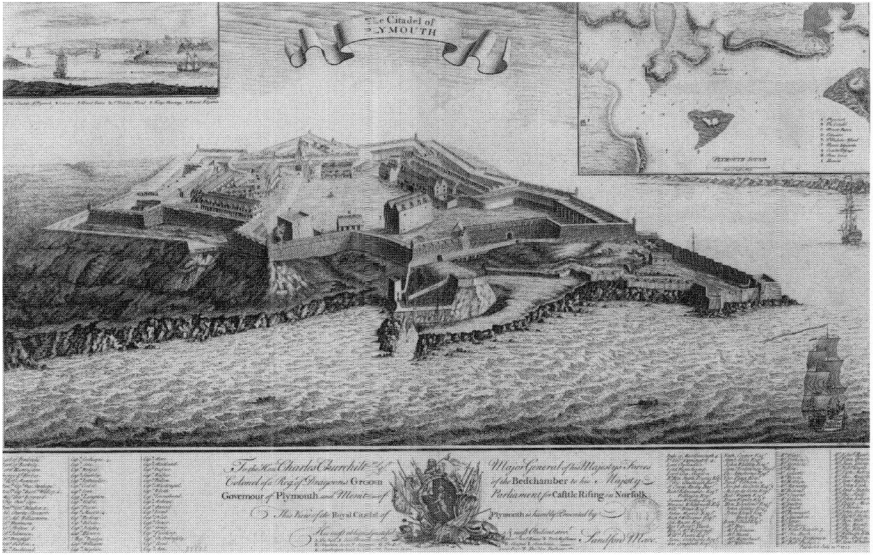

The Royal Citadel, Plymouth, as seen in 1737. During the Dutch Wars of 1664–7 King Charles II decided that it was necessary to recognise and improve the defences of Plymouth as an important Channel port. A new fortress was constructed, which was known as the Royal Citadel, and which incorporated an earlier construction designed by Sir Francis Drake. Possibly due to Plymouth's support for the Parliamentarians in the Civil War, the guns of the fortress were so configured as to be able to fire on the town as well as to seaward. (Author's collection)

RGA soldiers on guard duty at the Royal Citadel in 1905. For over 100 years, the Royal Citadel was considered to be one of the most important British static defences, with its 70ft high walls, and was regularly strengthened, reaching a peak during the 1750s when it boasted 113 guns. In 1860, the Royal Commission on the Defence of the United Kingdom recommended the construction of a new ring of forts to defend Plymouth from a greater distance, the so-called 'Palmerston Forts'. But the Citadel was still considered to be of value and use and on the formation of the Royal Garrison Artillery, it was put to work as the RGA centre for training and instruction. (Author's collection)

seems to be a difference between the perception and the reality of the forces available to defend the homeland.

Prior to 1899, the coastal defence batteries of guns were manned by the Royal Artillery (RA). The officers of this branch of the military tended to look down their noses at garrison artillery (which included coastal defence) and a posting there was often the 'reward' for poor performance or failure to fit in with the self-image of the RA. But as more advanced guns and technology became available to gunners, a reorganisation was conducted in 1891 which had as its objective the desire to better equip the officers and men to master these scientific advances. At this point, twenty-two companies of garrison artillery were created based in Britain, which compared with twenty-four in India and twenty-one in other colonies. Then, on 1 June 1899, recognising the different skills set needed for garrison gunnery, the RA was split into two distinct parts, the Royal Artillery (which comprised horse and field gunnery) and the Royal Garrison Artillery (RGA), which had its training centre at the old Plymouth Citadel. Coastal defence guns formed 80 per cent of the new RGA.

For the provision of extra manpower in times of need, Militia and volunteer artillery companies had existed since the Napoleonic Wars. In 1899 these were merged into a new body, the Royal Garrison Artillery Volunteers. Those who were based in coastal areas trained at the coastal defence batteries contiguous to their home.

However, the weapons themselves were not of the best. As Colonel Maurice-Jones noted; 'The situation at the turn of the century as regards coast defence guns was chaotic. Both at home and abroad, the ports and harbours were defended by a medley of breech and muzzle loaders, some very modern, some very old, but mostly very old.'[24] Despite the general acceptance that rifled breech-loaders were the best form of weapon for modern gunnery, in 1881 the majority of guns equipping RGA stations were either smoothbore or muzzle-loading or both. At Portsmouth for example, out of a total of 437 guns, 85 were rifled muzzle-loading, 233 smoothbore weapons converted to rifled muzzle-loading, and 119 were smoothbore. At sea only breech-loading rifled guns were now being used on the latest ships; *Barfleur* (1892), had four 10in breech-loading (BL) guns, and one of the most recent cruisers, *Immortalité* (1887) had two 9.2in BL and ten 6in BL.[25] So coastal defence was certainly not at the cutting edge of gunnery practice or technology at this point.

Guns were not the only defences deployed at Britain's ports and harbours. Brennan torpedoes were a device patented by Irish-born Australian inventor Louis Brennan in 1877. They were propelled by two contra-rotating propellers that were spun by rapidly pulling out wires from drums wound inside the torpedo. Differential speed on the wires connected to a shore station allowed the torpedo to be guided to its target, up to 2,000 yards away, at speeds of up to 27 knots. They could only be used from a land

Royal Garrison Artillery drilling with a 5in gun at the Royal Citadel, Portsmouth. The 5in dated from 1880 and was more commonly used in coastal fortifications as a mobile weapon on a carriage. It was replaced by the 4.7in QF and was obsolete by the time of this 1905 photograph. The circular object right of centre is possibly a range clock.
(Author's collection)

Aiming tube practice with 6pdr Hotchkiss guns at The Citadel, Plymouth. The Ordnance QF Hotchkiss 6pdr gun Mk I and Mk II were a family of naval guns introduced in 1885 to defend against new, small and fast vessels such as torpedo boats and later submarines. (Author's collection)

base and were difficult to deploy at night. In 1891 it was intended to build fifteen such stations but it seems only eight were completed.[*] Four Brennan installations were added to existing fortifications at Fort Albert on the Isle of Wight, Cliffe Fort on the Thames, Garrison Point at the entrance to the Medway and at Fort Ricasoli at the entrance to the Grand Harbour at Malta. Curiously, although the torpedo was clearly a naval weapon, the Brennans were manned by the Royal Engineers (RE), introducing yet another player into the world of coastal defence. The RE were also responsible for static minefields (known as 'observation minefields') at the entrance to some harbours, which were electrically detonated from a post on land when an enemy ship was near or over the location of a mine.

* * * * *

In summary, the defence of Britain's coasts seemed a lot less certain than it might at first appear. For although the landscape was studded with defence batteries and stations, both old and new, and the Royal Navy was of great size and preponderant in numbers, old weapon systems still dominated the arsenal and older ships still made up the naval ship count. And the resources deployed at home was considerably less than those based overseas. Moreover, responsibility for home defence was split over a number of discontinuous organisations. But did anybody in the general public know or care?

---

[*] Thames (Cliffe), Medway (Garrison Pt), Portsmouth (Cliff End/Fort Albert), Plymouth (Pier Cellars/Cawsand Bay), Cork Harbour (Fort Camden), Malta (Tigné and Ricasoli) and Hong Kong.

2
The Fear of Invasion

If the public was complacent about Britain's safety from invasion, they were soon to be jolted out of their apathy by the rise of a new genre of fiction – that of invasion of their country by various foreign actors, but in particular Germany. This threat was expressed primarily in two ways; invasion by force or uprising from embedded foreign nationals.

Invasion

The 'father' of this type of writing might justifiably be said to be Lieutenant Colonel George Tomkyns Chesney. In 1871, *Blackwood's Magazine* caused uproar by publishing his story *The Battle of Dorking*. Chesney believed that Britain was unprepared for an armed invasion from Germany, especially after its victory in the Franco-Prussian War of 1870–1. His intent was to awaken the nation to the danger and to the (in his view) meagre number of troops in the British Army, and the likelihood that Britain would be unable to defend herself should she need to. The story is told in retrospect from 50 years in the future. A soldier recounts to his grandson the terrible events that befell the country. Using a powerful new weapon (called only 'fatal engines') the German navy destroys the British fleet and soldiers land at Harwich. They march upon London and the final battle is at Dorking in the Surrey Hills. The British army is defeated. Germany takes control of Britain, and the Empire is disbanded. There was an immediate outcry from the public and press, not least because a booklet of the

One of the books that sparked the invasion panic, Chesney's *The Battle of Dorking*. (Author's collection)

tale was published in Britain and Europe which sold over 10,000 copies. The government of the day had to reassure the public that all was well. Chesney's fable inspired a host of imitators and publications such as *What Happened after the Battle of Dorking* (1871), *The Siege of London* (1871), *The Invasion of England* (1882) and *The Battle off Worthing: Why the Invaders never got to Dorking* (1887) followed from a variety of hack pens.

Terrorism also reared its head shortly afterwards; George Griffith introduced his terrorist organisation, the Brotherhood of Freedom, in *The Angel of the Revolution* (1893). The organisation finances a British inventor to create a fleet of super-airships, and when war breaks out between a Franco-Russian alliance and Britain and Germany, the terrorists come in on the side of Britain. With their fleet they defeat the Franco-Russian alliance and subjugate the rest of the world.

Full-scale war was also envisaged – without the terrorists but with the 'Yellow Peril' – by M P Shiel[*] in *The Yellow Danger* (1898) in which an army of 180 million Chinese conquer Asia and Europe with only Britain holding out. The United States remained neutral until the final battle. The Chinese threat is countered, *inter alia*, by an early version of germ warfare.

A common theme of the genre was that if the Royal Navy was to be defeated Britain would fall. Albert Charles Curtis was one of the originators of this form. In his *A New Trafalgar* (1902), he imagines a lightning German naval strike against Britain in the absence of the Channel Squadron; fortunately, the Royal Navy has a lethal new battleship in reserve which wins the day. A Tasmanian reviewer noted;

> First, we have an encounter between the British and German fleets in the North Sea. Germany has planned a raid upon England in the absence of the Channel Squadron on its usual autumn cruise at Gibraltar, so that the first brunt of the storm falls upon a British battle line of nearly obsolete ships. The skilful, nay, daring handling of the submarines, however, stands the British admiral in good stead, with the result that the German navy is practically wiped out – but at fearful cost. In this extremity, France and Russia fall upon Britain, and then, indeed, begins the tug-of-war. Later on, Spain joins the allies, cripples Gibraltar, the so-called key to the Mediterranean.[1]

Colonel Lionel James' *The Boy Galloper* (1903) took the genre to the young adult market when following invasion Jack Montmorency, his schoolboy

---

[*] A pseudonym of Matthew Phipps Shiell, primarily a science fiction and horror writer and later a convicted child molester.

hero, has to leave the prefects' room and don his Cadet Corps uniform to take on the Germans.

1903 also saw the publication of one of the masterworks of the genre – Erskine Childers' *The Riddle of the Sands*. Here, sardonic Foreign Office civil servant Carruthers accepts an invitation from a college friend, Davies, a shyly intrepid yachtsman, and joins him on a sailing holiday in the Baltic. There, amidst the sunshine, fog and myriad coastal creeks, they discover a German plot to invade England. Childers was himself an excellent yachtsman (and indeed was employed during the 1914–18 war as a navigator of the North Sea coasts by the Royal Navy and RNAS) and the book benefits from his detailed knowledge and lively writing style. Published as invasion fear was reaching a critical point, it was hugely influential and 'was credited with highlighting Britain's poor military presence in the North Sea'.[2]

But the book that really took invasion fear to boiling point was William Le Queux's *The Invasion of 1910*.* In this bestseller, Le Queux imagines a successful invasion of England by a 40,000-strong German army followed by such horrors as 'The Battle of Royston' and 'The Bombardment of London'. The story was made all the more potent because it was serialised before publication in Lord Northcliffe's (born Alfred Harmsworth) *Daily Mail*. Northcliffe, a keen advocate of both increased military spending and British conscription, used the narrative to further his causes, to wit those of pressurising the government and furthering the sales of his newspaper. To the latter end, he had the author redraw the original route of his fictional German invasion so that it passed through towns with large potential *Daily Mail* readerships and thus allowed 'the Hun to terrorise every major town in England from Sheffield to Chelmsford'.[3]

With Germany now clearly fingered as the sole potential attacker, H G Wells joined the fun

And one of Le Queux's offerings; *The Great War in England in 1897*. (Author's collection)

---

* Which was a follow-up to his earlier *The Great War in England* in 1897, published in 1894.

with *The War in the Air* (1908) in which European civilization is 'blown up' by bombardments from airships, leaving only 'ruins and unburied dead, and shrunken yellow-faced survivors in a mortal apathy' while Germany dispatches 'a huge herd of airships', some as big as 2,000ft long, in a surprise bombing raid against New York City. 'No place is safe . . . Quiet people go out in the morning and see air fleets passing overhead, dripping death.'

Even the best short story writer of his generation, Saki (Hector Hugh Munro) took up the baton with *When William Came; a story of London under the Hohenzollerns* (1913). Here his hero, Murrey Yeovil – 'bred and reared as a unit of a ruling race' – returns from Asia to find a vanquished Britain 'incorporated within the Hohenzollern Empire . . . as a Reichsland, a sort of Alsace-Lorraine washed by the North Sea instead of the Rhine', with Continental-style cafés in the 'Regentstrasse' and on-the-spot fines for walking on the grass in Hyde Park. But he finds himself deserted by his Tory contemporaries, who have fled (along with George V) to Delhi, leaving behind a despicable crew of collaborators which includes his wife and her Bohemian friends, petty bureaucrats and the 'ubiquitous' Jews. This picks up several of Saki's tropes for he felt Britain had gone soft, was an anti-Semite, and – as a homosexual – was suspicious of women.*

Sir Arthur Conan Doyle followed, almost immediately before war broke out, with a short story for *The Strand* magazine in July 1914. It was billed as 'the amazing story of England's peril and how our naval supremacy was challenged by a few submarines'. In Conan Doyle's tale he has an enemy naval officer make this speech;

> Of course, England will not be caught napping again in such a fashion. Her foolish blindness is partly explained by her delusion that her enemy would not torpedo merchant vessels. Common-sense should have told her that the enemy will play the game that suits them best – that they will not inquire what they may do but they will do it first and talk about it afterwards. The opinion of the whole world now is that if a blockade were proclaimed one may do what one can with those who try to break it and that it was as reasonable to prevent food from reaching England in war time as it is for a besieger to prevent the victualing of a beleaguered fortress.

He accurately prefigured what would transpire and how Britain was nearly overcome by unrestricted submarine warfare in 1917.

---

* Munroe volunteered to serve in the coming war at the age of 43 and was killed in November 1916.

Spies and Infiltration

The second thread to the fearmongering was that of the Germans already in Britain. Such anxiety directly led to the internment of many German workers and residents of Britain as war broke out and the various spy phobias that gripped the nation. Many Germans had settled in Britain before the war and were especially prominent in occupations such as restaurant waiters and hairdressing.

Headon Hill wrote *The Spies of Wight* in 1899, the first full-length account of German spies at work in Britain and a very early pointer that Germany was perhaps the more likely enemy in any coming war than France. E Phillips Oppenheim's *A Maker of History* (1905) picked up this theme; his 'Captain X', the head of German intelligence in London, opines 'there are in this country 290,000 young countrymen of yours and of mine who have served their time, and who can shoot . . . Clerks, waiters and hairdressers . . . each have their work assigned to them. The forts which guard this great city may be impregnable from without, but from within – that is another matter.' And in Walter Wood's *The Enemy in our Midst* (1906) there is a 'German Committee of Secret Preparations' covertly laying the foundation for a takeover in London.

A J Dawson's* *The Message* (1907) also sees Britain lose the war because of the enemy within. While pacifists demonstrate for disarmament in Bloomsbury, a German waiter tells our hero: 'Vaire shtrong, sare, ze Sherman Armay.' It transpires that he and thousands of other German immigrants have been acting as pre-invasion intelligence-gatherers, ensuring that 'the German Army knew almost to a bale of hay what provender lay between London and the coast'. And Captain Henry Curties' *When England Slept* (1909) depicts London occupied overnight by a German army which has entered the kingdom by stealth over a period of weeks. It was certainly true that there were many Germans in Britain. A large German community had settled north of Oxford Street in London and Schmidt's delicatessen and restaurant† on Charlotte Street was always full at lunch times. The streets of London were filled with itinerant German music makers and some 53,000 Teutons were estimated to live in Britain.

Meanwhile David Couper Thompson serialised *Spies of the Kaiser; Plotting the Downfall of England* (also 1909), again by Le Queux, in his *Weekly News*, preceded by advertisements offering readers £10 for information about 'Foreign Spies in Britain'. Le Queux claimed that 'England was awash with a vast army of German spies'.[4] Many influential people

---

* Alec John Dawson, adventurer, writer and army major in the First World War.
† Reputed to have waiters described on a spectrum from 'curt' to 'the rudest in the world'.

A painting by W H Wyllie of an exercise staged for the colonial Prime Ministers' Conference on 3 May 1907, in which a mock invasion of Whale Island was enacted by an attacking White Force dressed in white duck uniforms and the defending Blue Force, dressed in blue serge. The Whites came from seaward, hauling ashore 12pdrs and 4.7in guns, covered by the fire of a squadron of gunboats. (National Maritime Museum PAE 1016)

agreed with him. In 1907, for example, Major William Thwaites, head of the German section at the War Office, was convinced 'there was much truth in newspaper reports that German intelligence officers were at work in Britain', as was the Director of Military Operations, Major General John Spencer Stuart, who believed Germany was pouring 'hosts of agents and spies' into Britain.[5]

Fear from Abroad

Foreign authors also picked up on the invasion genre and added to the flames. In America, Frank R Stockton believed future wars would take advantage of new technology. In *The Great War Syndicate* (1889) a group of industrialists fight a war against Britain on behalf of the American government.* Their weapons include rocket-powered bombs and mini-

---

* War between Britain and America was not an unimaginable event at the time. In 1895, the USA sent a diplomatic note seemingly threatening war over a territorial dispute between Venezuela and British Guiana. Prime Minster Lord Salisbury ignored it for four months and then sent a rather dismissive reply. The USA once again seemed to threaten conflict and the Royal Navy was put on readiness. In January 1896, a war seemed possible. Wiser counsels eventually prevailed and the original matter was settled by arbitration.

submarines that sabotaged shipping, demonstrating Stockton's prescience. In France, writer, politician, and army officer Emile Cyprien Driant wrote *La Guerre de Demain* (1889) in which France and Germany clash once more; manned balloons feature prominently. Driant would become the first high-ranking casualty at the Battle of Verdun in 1916. And French artist and author Albert Robida focused on the inevitable horrors of a future war, which involved advanced and as yet unavailable weaponry, in *La Guerre au Vingtième Siècle* (1887). A worldwide war starts in 1945, and is fought using armed blockhouses, tanks, submarines, aerial bombing and chemical warfare, an accurate prefiguring of what was indeed to come.

Germans too took up the theme, generally putting Germany on the winning side. Karl Eisenhart's *Die Abrechnung mit England* (1900) imagines Britain, defeated in the Boer War, being attacked by France. Accurately predicting what would come to pass, he has Britain imposing a naval blockade and ignoring the rights of neutral shipping. This brings about war between Britain and Germany. A German secret weapon (the electrically-powered battleship!) settles the war in their favour, and the Germans take over British colonies and Gibraltar. And in August Niemann's *Der Weltkrieg* (1904), Russia, France and Germany wage war against Britain. Niemann imagined 'the armies and fleets of Germany, France and Russia moving together against the common enemy . . . who with his polypus arms enfolds the globe'. The French and German navies defeat the Royal Navy at the Battle of Flushing and an invasion force lands at the Firth of Forth. German jealousy of Britain's empire and global reach, which Kaiser Wilhelm II so resented, is evident in both these tomes.

Then there was Rudolf Martin, a civil servant who had been dismissed from his position in the German Imperial Statistical Bureau for publicly forecasting the imminent collapse of the Russian Empire. In 1907 Martin had written a novel called *Berlin-Bagdad*, which foresaw a German empire of the air. On 11 July 1908, the *Daily Mail* published an interview with him in which he predicted that Germany could conquer Britain by airlanding troops in waves of 350,000, delivered by thousands of Zeppelins.

Such literary works as described above are of course an open target for satire and P G Wodehouse provided the poniard of humour in his novel *Swoop!* (1909) in which a fictional boy scout, Clarence MacAndrew Chugwater, manages to save Britain from a fiendish concatenation of invaders; Germans in Essex, Russians at Yarmouth, the Swiss Navy at Lyme Regis, China at Lgxtpll in Wales, Monaco at Auchermuchty, Moroccan brigands at Brighton and the dark-skinned warriors of Bollygolla at Margate!

Concerns

The Second Boer War, fought between 1899 and 1902, was eventually won by British forces but not before it had revealed serious deficiencies in the command, equipment, training and men of the regular army. The loss of confidence in Britain's military power caused further exacerbated fears over the ability of the nation to defend the homeland, and had also made considerable demands on the exchequer. Improvement and financial efficiencies were necessary.

Even within the military, there was concern that Britain's homeland defence was inadequate if the country found itself at war with Russia and France (who had formed an alliance by the agreements of 1891–4). In August 1901, Colonel Edward A Altham, of the Directorate of Mobilisation and Intelligence, wrote that the threat did not require an increase in an army for home defence; 'due to the strength of the navy, it would be folly to lay upon the nation the financial burden of an enormous army adapted to meet a contingency which will not arise'. But other actors reasoned that if Britain were at war and the army was away fighting in India or in central Asia, 'if she [Russia] could acquire naval superiority in the Channel for ten days or a fortnight, there would be nothing to prevent her from attempting an invasion of England'.[6]

The uncertainty generated by this combination of imaginary and real military problems led to uncomfortable questions in Parliament and the press. The debate became one of whether or not the navy could be relied upon to defend the coast and prevent invasion, or was a larger army (backed perhaps by conscription) necessary. Unsurprisingly, the latter cause was fuelled, overtly or at least behind the scenes, by military men such as the eventually victorious commander of the army in South Africa, Field Marshal Lord Roberts.

The nature of the probing was reflected in one of the many questions raised in the Houses of Lords and Commons through the first decade of the new century. Francis Richard Charteris, 10th Earl of Wemyss, was concerned in 1902 that the navy could not defend the country from invasion without suffering in other parts of the world. His failure in the House of Lords to get a straight answer from the First Lord of the Admiralty, William Palmer, 2nd Earl of Selborne, led him to sound off:

> My Lords, I have to ask the indulgence of the House while I endeavour to adduce reasons for the motion which stands in my name on the paper, and which results from the answer I received to two questions in reference to national defence which I put to the First Lord of the Admiralty immediately before the Easter recess. It would appear to

the ordinary unofficial mind that those questions required the simple answer 'Yea' or 'Nay.' But they did not appear in that light to the mind of the First Lord of the Admiralty. The questions which I asked the noble Earl were; whether in the case of this country being at war with one or more European Powers, he could rely absolutely upon the navy alone for protection against invasion; and, further, whether by relying upon the navy for security against invasion, its general power and its effectiveness, the world over, would not be *pro tanto* lessened by the necessity of retaining in our home waters a sufficient naval force for the protection of the United Kingdom. Instead of giving me the answer I expected – a simple 'yea' or 'nay' – the First Lord of the Admiralty replied to me as follows. 'With very great respect to my noble friend who has asked me these questions, I hope he will allow me to say that I do not clearly see what public service is going to be gained by putting these conundrums. Nor do I consider it my duty to supply formulas to answer questions which contain material for debate for all the debating societies in London for years to come.'[7]

Balfour's Dilemma

In 1902, the swirling fears of invasion were part of a general climactic coming together of problems for the government of new Prime Minister A J Balfour, who had replaced Lord Salisbury (by now old, tired and prone to falling asleep in meetings) in July of that year. Particularly, these included a worsening financial position due to the expenditure of the Boer War* and a general agricultural depression from around 1880, a manifestly inefficient military system, and ongoing tension on India's North-West Frontier. Balfour became convinced of the need for some overseeing body which could coordinate the various defence demands. In December 1902 he formed a new Cabinet committee† whose remit was 'to survey as a whole the strategical military needs of the Empire',[8] and which morphed into the powerful Committee for Imperial Defence (CID). Chaired by the prime minister, members were usually Cabinet ministers, the heads of the military services, and key civil servants. prime ministers from Dominion countries became *de facto* members of the committee. Eventually, a powerful secretariat was developed under first Captain George Sydenham Clarke and then Maurice Hankey, a Royal Marine officer, which was tasked with

---

* 450,000 British and Empire troops had fought in the war, which had cost £223 million.
† This was not a completely groundbreaking move as Lord Salisbury had formed such a Cabinet body (the only one such) on returning to power in 1895. However, it was ineffective. The Duke of Devonshire complained that it 'has met rarely, and generally without a definite agenda. No minutes have been kept' (Bogdanor, *The Strange Survival of Liberal Britain*, p 39).

ensuring that the decisions made by the CID were implemented.

One of the first concerns the CID attacked was that of home defence and the issue of whether the navy alone could defend Britain from invasion. The problem, as ever, came down to money. Both soldiers and sailors wanted more of it. For the army, it was argued that the navy could not do the job of homeland defence alone and therefore a larger budget for more soldiers was required; for the navy, conscious that it had traditionally taken the lion's portion of military expenditure, the Admiralty wished to demonstrate that its budgets could not be cut and that it could carry out the responsibilities which were expected of it.

Arthur James Balfour, Prime Minister of Britain 1902–05, photographed at the beginning of his period in office. (Library of Congress, LOC ggbain02758)

In January 1903, the War Office asked of the Admiralty for an appreciation of 'the possibility of a lightly equipped force of say 20,000 men being landed, in the absence of the fleet, at any spot on the southern coast'.[9] This was a variation on the so-called 'bolt from the blue' theory, which in essence stated that with new technology allowing a rapid mobilisation (i.e. steam ships and railways), a hostile army could land on British soil before the Royal Navy could intercept it. A conscript army from the Continent might cross the sea in a sudden *coup de main*, evading the navy and brushing away the small British army.

Director of Naval Intelligence, Captain Prince Louis of Battenberg, replied that he could not conceive that 'the fleet would leave the Channel unguarded' or that 'the fleet would be temporarily absent'.[10] This did not suit the army's objectives, as its reply conveys with suitable irony; 'It is understood that the navy will entirely suffice to protect the United Kingdom from attack or invasion in considerable strength ... and that it is therefore unnecessary to provide troops for home defence.'[11] Both sides thus held the positions they had occupied for some time and were in violent disagreement as they attempted to protect their financial claims.

The War Office did not accept that the Admiralty could deliver on its promises, and that a volunteer home defence force which acted as a backup to naval might would allow for naval deployment across the empire, without tying the navy to the British coasts. They, and their supporters, maintained that Britain would be vulnerable across its trade routes and colonies if the navy was constrained to stay in the Channel because no suitable armed force existed on land.

The CID had to cut through this Gordian knot and Balfour applied his supple mind to the impasse. In order to frame a response, he asked the War Office for an estimate of the smallest invasion force it thought credible. The reply was 70,000 men plus equipment, a number which the Admiralty felt confident of detecting and interdicting. Thus, on 8 July 1903, the CID noted that a restructuring of the army could be considered under the assumption that 'an invasion in force of these islands need not be taken into account'.[12]

As the War Office considered that any body of troops less than 70,000 strong could not successfully subdue the nation, the issue, Balfour stated, was that of dealing with smaller raiding forces of, say, 5,000 or 10,000 men and it was on this basis that the army should plan.

Balfour thus circulated a memorandum in November 1903 which gave as its conclusions that the navy was responsible for preventing invasion and that the military provision to resist a major invasion was a waste of money. Instead, the home defence force, primarily of the Militia and volunteers, should only be strong enough to take on and defeat raids of 5,000–10,000 enemy.

This memo was accepted, one assumes grudgingly from the army side, in a joint response for the War Office and the Admiralty of 26 March 1906. They added the caveat, however, that 'in view of the fact that in peace time our coasts are virtually undefended from sudden attack, the General Staff attach great importance for defensive measures being taken as soon as a state of tension with a maritime foreign power exists' and emphasised the need for the politicians to issue the 'precautionary telegram' which would put the armed forces on alert as soon as possible.[13]

Meanwhile, in the House of Commons in 1904, Balfour was being suavely evasive on the issue. Colonel Sir Howard Vincent, MP for Sheffield Central, sought to understand 'the numbers of the land forces necessary for the protection of Great Britain and Ireland against the possibility of invasion, and of the numbers it is necessary to have available at home for the strengthening of the land forces in India, Canada, Australasia, South Africa, or elsewhere in the Empire in a time of stress'. The reply no doubt failed to enlighten him: 'It seems to me that the problem put by my hon friend is not really capable of definite numerical solution. The number of troops required to defend our shores must evidently depend, and depends very largely, upon the character of those troops.'[14]

In April 1905, Balfour again dodged the issue in reply to a question from Sir William Cremer, MP for Shoreditch Haggerston, who responded to a statement from the prime minister to the effect that invasion was considered impossible; '[as you] are clearly of opinion that invasion of these islands in such force as to inflict a fatal blow or threaten our independence is impossible, [does] he propose to prepare any scheme for repelling invasion'. The reply was non-committal. 'I have already indicated to an hon and gallant friend that I should favour all questions on this subject being put off until after the debate on the vote . . . which I propose to bring on at no distant day after Easter.'[15]

In the Lords, the Earl of Wemyss was still on the warpath, returning to his theme in 1905, and now pressing for a larger army, when he rose to propose the motion:

> that in the opinion of this House, it would be a danger to the realm, and limit the power of the navy as an offensive force in war, to trust to it alone for home defence, and, inasmuch as it is admitted that the navy cannot guarantee us against so-called hostile raids, it is the more needful that our land defences should at all times be such that no nation would ever attempt in any form a hostile landing on our shores.[16]

He was still grinding this axe a year later. By now Balfour's government had been replaced by that of the Liberal Party's Henry Campbell-Bannerman, but in May 1906, Wemyss rose to call attention to the question of home defence and of compulsory service in the Militia within the United Kingdom.

> My Lords, on the Front Bench to the right of the Woolsack there always sit some distinguished members of your Lordship's House who form part of the government of the day. Now, what, my Lords, would you say was the most important duty that falls to the government? I hold that their most important duty is the defence of the Empire at large, and the safety of our hearths and homes in this country. I put some questions on Friday night to my noble friend the Under Secretary of State for War to endeavour to ascertain whether or not this duty is attended to by His Majesty's government, and the answer I got was anything but satisfactory, though I am bound to say it was the answer I had every reason to expect.[17]

The Owen Report

Responding to the growing tide of concern regarding invasion, in 1904 the CID had commissioned 65-year-old General John Fletcher Owen to chair a committee to enquire into the state of readiness and appropriateness of Britain's coastal defences, with particular reference to the suitability of the weaponry in place given the rapid strides forward taken in warship armament. Owen was a Royal Artilleryman who had seen action in the Zulu War of 1879 and had served, *inter alia*, as Commandant of Military Forces, South Australia, and President of the Ordnance Committee from 1902 to1904. At the same time, he was also requested to produce a separate report on the defences of Empire ports and coaling stations overseas. Owen's methodology was to ask the Admiralty what warships they thought the enemy would commit to attack each port and then decide on a level of armament appropriate to fight it off. Class A ports such as Portsmouth were believed to be subject to attack by battleships, class C, on the other hand, described as 'commercial ports', were deemed targets only for light cruisers.

Following investigation, the 'Report of a Committee on Armament of Home Ports' was presented to the CID in 1905. It was highly critical in some areas, especially with regard to the large number of rifled muzzle-loaders and rifled breech-loader guns of an obsolete type still to be found in the defences and recommended that they should be replaced as soon as possible as 'they were useless against modern warships and absorbed large numbers of men to man them'.

Instead, Owen recommended a standard fit-out of four types of weapons only, stating that 'the only guns really suitable for employment in coast defences were the 9.2in breech loader (BL), the 6in (BL), the 4.7in (QF) and

An example of a 9.2in gun, as recommended by the Owen Committee for coastal defence. (Author's collection)

the 12pdr quick firer (QF)'.[18] Appendix 6 gives further detail. The quick-firing 12pdrs were to be located on harbour moles to deal with fast-moving torpedo craft. The heavier 6in and 9.2 in guns were sited in batteries on land. The committee also submitted detailed lists of alterations and fit-outs required to existing structures.

The weapons selected represented something of a compromise. The committee recognised that the 9.2in gun would probably be no match for the latest battleships and that the 4.7in might not deal with a modern light cruiser, but should be able to handle a blockship. But the important point was that they were currently available or could be quickly manufactured. Owen urged that production ought to be concentrated on these weapons and rearmament of coastal defences, not just in Britain but across the Empire, should begin as soon as possible; and indeed it was with these guns that the coastal artillery was equipped when war finally broke out.

Another issue to be addressed was how to target a fast-moving warship, especially at night. A Depression Range Finder and a Position Finder were invented by a Royal Artillery officer named Captain H S Watkin, the information from which could be electronically transmitted to the guns, alleviated this problem. They worked on the principle that if the observer was at a height above the waterline, this became the base of a measuring triangle and a simple reading of the angle of depression to the target would give the range.

A Royal Engineers' Defence Electric Light (DEL) detachment, showing the searchlight projector with its generating car in the background. (Author's collection)

Prior to the use of electricity, finding a ship to shoot at in darkness was tricky. Searchlights ('defence electric light' or DEL) were recommended to be added and where this was done, they came under the purview of the fortress Royal Engineers. They were able to either follow a moving target with a dispersed beam of illumination or used to light up a patch of water through which a torpedo boat intent on attacking a harbour would have to pass. Some were designed to be quickly transportable around the battery. The committee further proposed that the Brennan torpedo units were to be handed over to the Royal Navy, as were the electronically operated minefields (known as 'Observation Mines'). The majority were subsequently scrapped.

Owen believed that such defences as he recommended would allow the coastal gunners to fulfil four fundamental objectives; close the passage of a river or channel; protect a town or dockyard from bombardment; deny use of an anchorage; and defend a landing place.

There were some deficiencies in the report. For example, the 'Owen committee made no provision for defences at Cromarty or Scapa Flow'.[19] Later, and despite the Admiralty having requested it and the War Office having drawn up plans, the Government rejected them on grounds of cost. And curiously, the committee seemed to pay little heed to the growing German threat. On the east coast, Harwich was downgraded to a 'C' port, indicating low military importance; and the Humber, also classified as 'C', lost most of its guns. But overall, the report was accepted and work put in hand. By 1914, the defensive static positions were armed as shown in Appendix 7.

The importance attached to keeping the situation under review is demonstrated by the formation of a permanent standing subcommittee of the CID in 1906, the 'Home Ports Defence Committee', whose chair was secretary to the CID, at this time George Clarke. In the context of the army versus navy debate on home defence, it should perhaps be noted that Clarke was not unbiased. He had published a book on defence in 1892 which maintained that large-scale permanent fortifications built in peacetime were a waste of money and that the Royal Navy was Britain's primary defence against invasion.

More Volunteers

In both the War Office, and to a lesser extent in the Admiralty, it was thought necessary to reform the system of home defence volunteers. On the naval side of things the First Lord of the Admiralty, the Earl of Selborne, invited his one-time fag at Winchester Sir Edward Grey, Liberal MP and foreign affairs spokesman, to chair a Manning Enquiry. The findings affirmed the need for naval reserves to be not only adequate in size and training but also to be increased to match the growth of foreign nations, especially Germany.

Chapter 1 noted the demise of the RNCV and RNAV, both of which were actively opposed by the Admiralty. But the concept of a volunteer force had some powerful supporters. One such was Hugh Oakeley Arnold-Foster,* who shared a barge-yacht with W L Wyllie, the well-known marine painter. In 1900 he became parliamentary secretary to the Admiralty under Selborne, from which position he was able to agitate from within. He gained agreement to the formation of a committee to study the issue of a volunteer organisation. With the support of individuals such as the Marquis of Graham (James Graham, later 6th Duke of Montrose), who held a master mariner's certificate, and C E H Chadwyck-Healy QC, who had been a lieutenant in the RNAV and had an honorary commission in the RNR, pressure was brought to bear which the Admiralty fought hard against.

There were at least three reasons for the Admiralty's historical opposition to the volunteers. Firstly, they espoused the view that it took years to make a sailor and that there was a particular knowledge and skill set which could only be learned with years before the mast. But the demise of sailing ships made this argument specious. Secondly, there was a special cachet to being a Royal Navy man in the late nineteenth century; the volunteers were seen as trying to 'cash in' on this public adulation without putting in the 'hard yards' and this was resented. And thirdly, all of the volunteer bodies to date had not been governed by the Naval Discipline Act – the regular navy had no power to control and punish such men. When the volunteers' representatives on the investigating committee offered that the new organisation would willingly be subject to the Act, there was no longer a viable ground for Admiralty resistance. The Naval Forces Act of 1903 amended the 1859 Royal Naval Reserves Act and the Admiralty was authorised to 'raise and maintain a force to be called the Royal Naval Volunteer Reserve'. The RNVR was born.

In a very class-conscious regular naval world, the RNVR came to be tolerated, mostly because they were 'gentlemen'. There was a popular saying in the pre-1914 navy; Royal Navy – gentlemen and seamen; Royal Naval Reserve – seamen but not gentlemen; Royal Naval Volunteer Reserve – gentlemen trying to be seamen. But when war came, the navy would be glad of both the RNR and RNVR. The volunteers received no payment for attending drills but a contribution towards travelling expenses was made when joining RN ships for sea training. Headquarters and drill sheds were also not provided by the Admiralty and each division (based on a town or city) had to find and fund their own. So, for example, Clyde received support

---

* Later, Secretary of State for War between 1903 and 1905.

from Glasgow corporation in the form of a gratis new building, while Bristol took over an old wooden man-of-war. London was granted a 14-year-old composite sloop, *Buzzard*, and at Brighton and Hove the volunteers gave concerts to raise money for their funds. The volunteers also had to pay for the upkeep of their premises and officers had to purchase their own uniforms. The Admiralty did, however, supply practice guns, rifles and cutlasses. Overall command was exercised by the Admiral Superintendent of Coastguards and Reserves. But one clearly had to be keen, or wealthy, or both, to join the RNVR.

Finally, it should be noted that since 1901, under an Order in Council of 13 May, the so-called 'Emergency List' had existed, comprising RN officers who had resigned their commission but who volunteered to serve again in an emergency. Such officers would bear the date of their original seniority, but would not receive pay or pension or promotion.

On land too, volunteer forces were regularised, and the old Militias, Volunteers and Yeomanry were done away with.* Following his reorganisation of the regular army, which reconstituted it as an expeditionary force of one cavalry and six infantry divisions kept in constant readiness for deployment abroad, 150,000 men strong, in March 1907, the Liberal Secretary of State for War, Richard Burdon Haldane,† delivered his Territorial and Reserve Forces Bill to Parliament. Under this legislation, the Volunteers and Yeomanry would be transformed into the Territorial Force administered by County Territorial Associations. Meanwhile, the Militia would be disbanded and its depots used for a new, all infantry, Special Reserve which would contain men who had not served in the regular Army but agreed to be liable for service with the regular forces in wartime.

The new Territorial Force (TF) was to consist of fourteen infantry divisions, fourteen cavalry brigades, and a large number of support units, all raised, organised and financed by local organisations but liable for service under War Office command. New extra manpower was available on land as well as at sea. It was to number around 315,000 officers and men. Such a figure was derived from estimating the force needed to deal with an invasion by 70,000 enemy; as noted above, the CID considered that such a force would find it impossible to evade the Royal Navy's attention and was the minimum size necessary for the invasion task. At a meeting of the CID on 22 October 1908, the report of the subcommittee, which had been meeting

---

* A commission under the chairmanship of the Duke of Norfolk had concluded in 1904 that the Militia and Yeomanry were incapable of taking the field against regular troops.
† In introducing his bill to the House of Commons, Haldane revealed himself as a Blue Water supporter, remarking that 'the first purpose for which we want an army is for overseas war. The fleet defends our coasts' (quoted in Longmate, *Island Fortress*, p 396).

since the previous year* to consider invasion, it was confirmed that 'so long as our naval supremacy is assured against any reasonably probable combination of powers, invasion is impractical' and that further any likely attack would be by the aforesaid 70,000 men. The TF was to 'be sufficient in numbers and organisation not only to repel small raids, but to compel an enemy who contemplates invasion to come with so substantial a force as will make it impossible for him to evade our fleets'.[20] In July 1909, H H Asquith, now prime minister in succession to Campbell-Bannerman, announced to the House of Commons that the 'margin of force for maintaining home defence should be one capable of dealing with an invading force of 70,000 men'.[21]

As to the impact on coastal defence, the TF now provided a Home Defence Army organised in field divisions and coast artillery units, which were appropriately located close to defended ports or naval bases so as to be able to man the coastal defences without delay. The Territorial gunner enlisted for four years, and had to undertake an initial forty-five drills and then twenty per annum and be capable of taking his place alongside the regular RGA soldiers. He only received pay when attending the yearly 15-day training camp. Like the RNVR, it required dedication to want to participate, although in war the RGA volunteer would be liable for home service only. Altogether, by 1914 the RGA coastal artillery units of the Territorial Force numbered eighty-one companies in seventeen divisions.

Are We Happy Now?

So, it had been made clear that a major invasion was neither expected or planned for; raids of up to 10,000 men aimed at destroying docks, ports, or civilian morale might be feasible but the navy would detect and prevent anything larger; the newly-founded Territorial Force would take the responsibility for what army home defence needs were envisaged, even an attack by 70,000 enemy, freeing the regular army for use overseas (which to most politicians meant India and its borders); and the coastal artillery positions were to be re-armed and defended. Moreover, these policies and beliefs, embedded under Balfour's Conservative-Unionist administration, did not materially change with the resignation of Balfour's government and the advent of the prime ministership of the Liberal Party's Henry Campbell-Bannerman in December 1905.† CB, as he was known, went on to win the

---

* This subcommittee had been formed after Lord Roberts persuaded Balfour to write to Campbell-Bannerman asking if recent German armament programmes had made reconsideration of the invasion issue necessary. The prime minster reluctantly formed a group with Asquith in the chair.
† He would resign in 1908 for reasons of health and was replaced by H H Asquith.

election of 2 January to 8 February 1906 with a landslide gain of 216 seats.

The focus of the Liberals was social reform;* they were not at first seen as being reliable on martial matters. Captain George Clarke, secretary to the CID, wrote privately to Haldane in 1905 that 'you will, I know, forgive me for saying that in matters bearing on national defence, a Liberal Government would not, on taking office, command great confidence'.[22]

They were initially content to let the sleeping dogs of war lie, although, as seen earlier, Haldane's army reforms and the creation of the Territorial Force happened within a year of their coming to office. Haldane had got his army reorganisation through despite some fierce opposition. Several groups opposed his approach, such as the National Service League (NSL), founded in 1902, led by Field Marshal Lord Roberts and *The Times* Defence Correspondent, Charles à Court Repington, and backed by retired senior officers, Lord Northcliffe, Lord Lovat, and some Conservative MPs. They argued that auxiliary forces would be ineffective against Continental armies and that a conscription based standing army was necessary. They also maintained that a 150,000-man regular force was too small. But at the other end of the spectrum of dissent, the radicals in the Liberal Party, and organised labour, generally opposed any increase in military strength which might lead to a large standing army, which could be used as an instrument of repression.

But the NSL kept the debate very much alive. In February 1907, for example, Simon Joseph Fraser, 14th Lord Lovat (not a disinterested observer, as a founder of the NSL), rose in the House of Lords,

Field Marshal Frederick Sleigh Roberts, 1st Earl Roberts, a highly vocal agitator for conscription and a large standing army. (Library of Congress LC-DIG-ggbain-17848)

---

* Campbell-Bannerman's election address committed the government to 'secure those social and economic reforms which have been too long delayed' (Bogdanor, *The Strange Survival of Liberal Britain*, p 488).

to call the attention of the Under-Secretary of State for War to the number of efficient fully manned British battleships on active commission in home waters on 13th February, 1907; to ask him, in view of the naval conditions obtaining on that date, whether the possibilities of foreign military invasion of these isles must necessarily be confined to a raid of 10,000 men; and to move that facts and figures be produced and laid on the table of the House to substantiate the contention of the Under-Secretary of State for War on 10th December, 1906, that the supremacy of the fleet guaranteed the British Isles from invasion by any force greater than that of a raiding party of 10,000 men.[23]

The NSL contained those who were all for national service and conscription, and those who did not believe that the Royal Navy could, at all times and in all places, be the defensive shield that Britain required. Roberts himself, speaking in the House of Lords, stated that 'our sea power was not won altogether upon the sea . . . and it cannot be maintained solely by the navy', adding that 'a proper army reserve, a body of trained men able to move to the front line at a moment's notice'[24] was necessary. And in 1908 Roberts made a major speech in which he stated that a successful German invasion of Britain was feasible and called for a greatly enlarged army.

The position of this group was cogently expressed by *The Spectator* magazine in 1909.

> If we wished to chop logic with Mr Asquith, we should draw attention to the fact that he makes his conclusion that sea power, and sea power alone, can save us . . . By doing so he leaves out of account the temporary loss of the command of the sea which might result from a great naval action between fleets of more or less equal strength, in which both fleets would be so much injured that till repairs were effected the command of the sea might be nobody's or anybody's. Again, for strategic reasons the fleet might have to leave home waters and cause a temporary or local loss of sea power, and thus tempt a reckless enemy to make a dash for our shores. Mr Haldane, so to speak, let the cat out of the bag when he talked about the defence of our coasts 'by the fleet in such a fashion as to give the Territorial Force time for maturing,' and of our fleet 'being particularly attentive to our coasts for the short time that was necessary to put the Territorial Forces into proper condition.'

Indeed, *The Spectator* went on to question the whole role of the Royal Navy.

In such a demand for our fleets to cuddle our coast and soothe the fears of our old women of both sexes lies a very real danger, and we are sorry indeed to see it encouraged by Mr Haldane. We dare not let the fleet be the nurse of the army. The fleet must go where the higher strategy at the beginning of a war demands that it should go, and nowhere else. This is very unlikely to be our own coastline.

In other words, command of the sea required the navy to have a global presence, irrespective of who the enemy was.

The RN should be free to operate anywhere, asserted the writer;

though we yield to none in our belief that our navy must be our first line of defence, and that unless we keep the command of the sea we are undone, we hold it to be vital that the male population of this country shall be trained to the defence of their liberties and homes. The result will be not only to set the fleet free for its supreme function of securing the command of the sea by the destruction of the enemy's fleet (which work, and not coast defence while the Territorial Force is maturing, is its duty), but also to free us from unworthy panic, and to give the manhood of the nation their full rights of citizenship – the ability to bear arms in their own defence.[25]

The conscription debate refused to die down. As late as 1913, two bills were tabled in Parliament. The first, proposed by George Sandys MP (Conservative member for Wells) in the House of Commons, sought conscription to bring the Territorial Force up to strength. The second, raised in the House of Lords by Lord Willoughby de Broke, harked back to the days of knights in shining armour, by calling for the conscription of only 'gentlemen', meaning men of education or high income. Neither bill passed.

Spies

Meanwhile, concerns regarding German spying activities in Britain continued to fester. The Germans had, in fact, established an espionage organisation in 1901. But, unbeknown to the British, this organisation – under Gustav Steinhauer, Head of German Admiralty Intelligence Service – was focused on naval sources.

Such counterespionage as there was in Britain was originally the purview of a branch of the War Office under William Melville. By 1906, he believed he had identified a group of German spies in Epping who were reconnoitring invasion routes. Secretary of State for War Richard Haldane was another who became convinced that Britain was threatened by spies. In

March 1909, he established a subcommittee of the CID to consider the nature and extent of espionage in Britain. The report of this group led to the establishment of a dedicated counterespionage organisation, named the Secret Service Bureau (SSB), under one Reginald Kell, which also incorporated an Admiralty representative, Mansfield Cumming, who would later take overall responsibility for espionage overseas as the legendary 'C'.

The operational brief agreed by the War Office at the establishment of the SSB gives a clear indication of the worries of the time. According to Cumming, they included 'organise an efficient system by which German progress in armaments and naval construction can be watched' and 'to obtain any information of any movement indicating an attack upon this country'. By the end of 1909, Cumming had three agents abroad whose specific purpose was 'to warn of sudden attack by Germany'.[26]

Home Secretary Winston Churchill was an enthusiastic supporter of Kell and ordered chief constables to assist him in building a register of suspicious Germans and other foreigners. Later, he also gave Kell the authority to open the mail of any suspects. And Kell's first formal report of March 1910 stated that German espionage was 'linked to plans for a German invasion'.[27] This did nothing to dispel the growing invasion paranoia.

There was also (yet another) volunteer body which preoccupied itself with espionage abroad. One of the more quixotic organisations to emerge during the early years of the century was the Legion of Frontiersmen, founded in 1904 by Henry Roger Ashwell Pocock. Pocock had served in the Northwest Mounted Police in Canada, tried missionary work with indigenous peoples in British Columbia and had participated in the Second South African War in an irregular band of scouts.

In 1904 Pocock was sent by the *Illustrated Mail* to Russia to report on the effects of the Russo-Japanese War. He returned with information and photographs, and some skilfully drawn plans of a naval base. This aroused the interest of Prince Louis of Battenberg, the Director of Naval Intelligence, and convinced Pocock that he should found a paramilitary force that would serve the empire both as an irregular scouting force in time of war and as an intelligence network through its 'frontier' connections. In this he received the support of Field Marshal Lord Roberts and Robert Baden-Powell. Although the organisation's global membership reached 10,000 by 1914, the Legion's requests for official recognition were rejected and the Ruritanian nature of its uniforms caused public mockery. As for Pocock himself, by 1909 his behaviour had become so eccentric that he became the unwilling victim of spy mania and 'was ousted because of suspicions that he himself was a German agent'.[28] In 1915, the Legion was subsumed into the army as the 25th Royal Fusiliers and served in the German East African campaign.

The National Reserve

It was perhaps for the reasons expressed in the *Spectator* article above, and 'the insistent and earnest warnings of the late Lord Roberts [which] awoke some of the public to the real meaning of the German peril'[29] that yet another reserve defence force was called into being in 1910. This was the 'National Reserve'. Its avowed purpose was as a means of retaining the option to call on the services of ex-military personnel to augment the regular and auxiliary military forces of the United Kingdom in the event of a major war. In reality it was little more than a register of trained officers and men who had no further obligation for military service, and the object was to enable an increase in military resources in the event of imminent national danger. The register was maintained by the County Associations which also administered the Territorial Force and they would frame their own rules for organising the reserve within their area. Membership was open to any retired military personnel, both officers and other ranks, including ex-naval or RNR men who could not, however, enrol until over age 55 or 60 dependent on service. Enrolled men were categorised into three classes of which Class I and II contained the more physically able.

The government refused to grant it any funding and National Reservists were not required to undertake any definite liability. They were invited to sign an honourable obligation to present themselves for service when required. If mobilised, they would receive a gratuity of £10 (for officers, warrant officers and men of Class I) or £5 (Class II) provided they were found fit and accepted for service. They would receive army pay from the point at which they were accepted for service in accordance with the pay warrant for their rank and branch of the service. And so, a Militia by any other name was conjured back into existence and the concept of 'a nation in arms' lived another day.

* * * * *

But before we go further, we need to consider what was happening in Royal Navy circles, and the impact that new naval thinking and *materiel* had on the defence of Britain's island coasts.

3
Sir John Fisher's Navy, 1904–1910

Following her humiliating defeat in the Franco-Prussian War of 1870–1, the France of the Third Republic endeavoured to make colonial gains as part of rebuilding her self-confidence and world status. But relations with a unified, Prussian-led Germany were such that in 1887 France looked to Russia for support. In concluding the so-called Reinsurance Treaty with Germany in 1887, Russia insisted on maintaining for France the same conditions that Germany had stipulated for its ally, Austria. France and Russia were now bound together by mutual agreement. And they possessed the second and third largest naval fleets on the planet.

Perhaps unsurprisingly, this led in Britain to considerable agitation for increased naval expenditure as well a sustained political campaign aimed at both raising awareness of the Royal Navy and reforming its perceived weaknesses. For example, on 10 May 1888 a notice headed 'strictly non-political – Great Britain's danger' appeared in *The Times*. Placed there by a group of naval officers and city businessmen led by Captain Lord Charles Beresford and Admiral Sir Geoffrey Phipps Hornby, it asked 'Englishmen of all classes and politics' to consider whether or not the Royal Navy was adequately equipped and funded to protect Britain and its trade in time of war. This question was followed with a dire warning: 'a great war may at any moment burst upon us, in which we may have to fight for our very existence.' The two basic assumptions underlying the notice – that war was imminent and the country unprepared – formed the underlying theme of discussions relating to national defence of the British Empire.

A major meeting to consider such issues was advertised and many serving officers choose to speak, attacking the system of 'government by party' which, they claimed, had left the navy in such a poor condition. Public agitation grew and Queen Victoria added her voice, berating her Prime Minster Lord Salisbury in December 1888 about the concerns raised. Salisbury promised to act.

Early the following year, Salisbury was able to redeem this pledge. Money was going to be spent on improving the navy. A huge new building programme under the Naval Defence Act would be set in place. It would 'put your majesty's fleet in a completely commanding position'.[1] In a speech

HMS *Royal Sovereign*, seen here as flagship at the Coronation Review of Edward VII. (National Maritime Museum N00432)

at the Guildhall he stated that 'in a sensitive commercial community like ours, alarm is almost as destructive as danger and what we have to provide is not only safety for our citizens but a sense that safety exists'.[2] In other words, it was necessary to ensure that Britain retained sovereignty of the seas to protect her trade position.

Salisbury persuaded the Cabinet to support a new Naval Defence Act* which would spend an extra £20 million† on the Royal Navy over the following four years. Since the Battle of Trafalgar, Britain had been content with having a fleet which gave a one-third advantage over the world's next largest (usually France). Henceforth, the yardstick would be the 'Two Power Standard' by which the Royal Navy was always to be kept 'to a standard of strength equivalent to the next two biggest navies in the world'. As First Lord of the Admiralty Lord George Hamilton later recalled, 'it was deemed impolite to mention either France or Russia by name'.[3] But nonetheless these were the enemies that Britain's Two Power Standard would be measured against, and the Royal Navy was thus committed to keeping a superiority over the combination of both the French (Britain's traditional enemy) and

---

* Which received Royal Assent on 31 May 1889.
† About £2.5 billion at today's prices, according to the Bank of England.

the Russians (a source of worry throughout the nineteenth century due to her agitation on the northern borders of India, and ambitions for Turkish and Persian territory and other eastern gains) fleets.

The Act called for ten battleships, thirty-eight cruisers, eighteen torpedo gunboats and four fast gunboats; it represented the greatest ever peacetime expansion of Britain as a naval power. The new *Royal Sovereign*-class battleships provided for by the bill would be the most powerful ever constructed. 'With a navy thus augmented, it was hoped that the Franco-Russian combination could be faced down, the empire's communications protected, the Mediterranean fleet made a match for the Toulon fleet, French invasion fears dispelled and the Jingoes silenced.'[4]

Indeed, the *Royal Sovereign*s were the harbingers of a new age of battleships. With their high freeboard and turrets, and improved armour protection, they were the template for every country's future battleship developments. By the beginning of the twentieth century, all battleships were of around 15,000 tons, heavily armoured and boasted a primary battery of four 12in guns* (or larger) in two turrets and an impressive secondary battery. Such a fleet came at significant cost. By 1900, Britain was spending £30 million per annum on its navy, which was a source of considerable budgetary contention.

Jacky Fisher

Jacky Fisher (eventually Admiral of the Fleet Sir John Arbuthnot Fisher, First Baron Fisher of Kilverstone) was the man who created the modern navy. The fleet which served throughout the First Word War was his legacy.

Fisher was the son of a Ceylonese tea planter, from a poor background, a man who rose to high rank through ability, not connections or his position in society. He was volcanic in temperament, Old Testament in expression, intolerant of fools or anyone who disagreed with him, and a compulsive and skilful dancer. Appointed First Sea Lord in 1904, for good or bad Fisher created a revolution.

In this he had form. From May 1891 to February 1892, Fisher was Admiral Superintendent of the Dockyard at Portsmouth, where he concerned himself with improving the speed of operations. *Royal Sovereign* was built in two years rather than three under his watch. As Third Sea Lord, Fisher developed the modern torpedo boat destroyers, soon abbreviated to just 'destroyers', intended to sally ahead of the battlefleet and deal with the emergent torpedo boat threat before they could attack the larger and big

---

* The *Royal Sovereigns* had initially been intended to carry four 12in guns, but this was uprated to four 13.5in. They had a secondary battery of ten 6in.

gunned ships. In 1892, he ordered the development of this new type of ships, equipped with novel water-tube boilers and quick-firing small calibre guns. Fifty-two were under construction at the time of Queen Victoria's Diamond Jubilee Review of 1897.

Appointed Second Sea Lord in 1902, together with First Lord of the Admiralty Lord Selborne, he changed the system of naval recruitment and education, improving the status of engineering officers. All cadets were to receive instruction in science and technology as it related to life on board ship, as well as navigation and seamanship. Physical education and sport were to be taught, not only for the benefit of the cadets but also for the future training of ships' crews which were expected to produce sporting teams on goodwill visits in foreign ports. Entrance by examination, which biased the intake to those who could obtain special tuition, was replaced with an interview committee tasked with determining the general knowledge of candidates and their reaction to the questions as much as their answers. After four years, cadets were posted to special training ships for practical experience before being posted to real command positions. The results of the final examination affected the seniority allotted to each cadet and the chance of future early promotion.

Finally, in 1904, Fisher walked through the doors of the Admiralty as First Sea Lord (and thus executive head of the navy) and set about reshaping the service, whilst promising his political masters that he could reduce the cost of the fleet.

Admiral Sir John Fisher, painted by Sir Hubert von Herkomer.
(Library of Congress LC-B2- 3330-5)

Who Was the Enemy?

It has already been noted that Britain's force orientation posited France and Russia as her most likely naval and military opponents. Three separate events would change this viewpoint.

Firstly, the Anglo-Japanese Treaty of 1902 provided Britain with a strong Asian ally that could assist it in the struggle with Russia on several fronts. The Japanese were likewise pleased, for the treaty ensured that Russia would be partly isolated in the case of a conflict with Japan.* Prior to the agreement, if Britain were to face a Franco-Russian enemy in the Pacific, she had just four first class battleships and sixteen cruisers in Chinese waters, whereas Russia and France between them had seven first class and two second class battleships and twenty cruisers. First Lord of the Admiralty Selborne insisted that Britain should 'look to diplomacy and alliances to help us out'[5] of this position and the alliance was the result. It specified that if either party became involved in war against any two powers, the other would come to their aid. A secret codicil stated that between them, Britain and Japan would maintain naval forces in the 'extreme east' jointly superior to those of any third power. Now, with Japan as a partner against Russia, Britain no longer needed to court German aid against the Russian threat. To this extent the alliance was also the removal of a barrier to the next key event – the French *Entente* of 1904.

King Edward VII loved France and was fluent in its language. He enjoyed the people, the food, and the freedom he had found there as a younger man. When he became king, he took it as a personal mission to rebuild British relations with France. As his biographer Jane Ridley has written, 'he was ... responsible for making possible the *Entente Cordiale* with France'.[6] In May 1903, Edward personally arranged to visit Paris in what was possibly the most important political intervention that he made during his reign. When he arrived, he was booed and the crowd shouted '*Vivent les Boers*'. On his departure, after a round of dinners, opera, horse racing and bonhomie, they shouted '*Vive le Roi*'. 'In a little over twenty-four hours, the English milord had conquered Paris,' noted Ridley.[7]

Edward's intervention paved the way to a formal compact, generally known as the *Entente Cordiale*, a series of agreements signed on 8 April 1904 between Britain and the French Republic which saw a significant improvement in Anglo-French relations. In particular, the concordats granted freedom of action to the UK in Egypt and to France in Morocco. This pleased the French who had imperial ambitions in North Africa. For the British it eased France out of Egypt where the Suez Canal, and the route to India that it provided, remained a paramount foreign policy concern. And it turned an old enemy into a (sort of) friend.

The final event was the Russo-Japanese war of 1904–05 in which Russia was decisively beaten and almost her entire navy destroyed in the Battle of

---
* The treaty would be renewed in 1905.

the Yellow Sea (1904) and the Battle of Tsushima (1905).*

As a result, once a great naval power, Russia dropped from the third largest in the world to sixth or seventh place and would endure marginality for decades to come. In a note to Secretary of State for Foreign Affairs Henry Petty-Fitzmaurice, 5th Marquess of Lansdowne, Arthur Henry Hardinge, Minister General in Persia, wrote that the battle 'eliminated the Russian threat for the foreseeable future'.[8] Such weakness drove her into the arms of Britain, and the Anglo-Russian Entente of 31 August 1907 was the result, a pact in which Britain and Russia settled their colonial disputes in Persia, Afghanistan and Tibet. The agreement delineated spheres of influence in Persia, stipulated that neither country would interfere in Tibet's internal affairs, and recognised Britain's influence over Afghanistan. It eventually led to the formation of a triple *entente* between France, Russia and Britain.

Sir Edward Grey, Foreign Secretary 1905–16, still the longest continuous period of service in the position. (Author's collection)

Thus Russia and France were taken off the board. Who was the enemy now? Fisher was convinced it was Germany. Admiral Alfred von Tirpitz (State Secretary of the Imperial Navy Office), with the enthusiastic backing of Kaiser Wilhelm II, was creating an Imperial German Navy designed to raise his country to first-class naval status. With other factors, including violent anti-British feeling during the Boer War and the German government's refusal to consider an alliance except on terms that guaranteed Germany a free hand and hegemony in Europe, Fisher was convinced that Germany was now the most probable foe. His political master, Lord Selborne, certainly agreed with him. In a memo to the Cabinet of 26 February 1904, Selborne noted that 'the great new German navy is being built up from the point of view of war with us'.[9]

Soon to be Foreign Secretary, Sir Edward Grey wrote to Selborne in the summer of 1904 that the North Sea would 'probably be the scene of a naval

---

* A battle which not only proved the worth of long-range gunfire but also was a portent of the future, with mines and torpedoes all playing a part and which showed that battleships could be vulnerable to these new weapons in a war zone.

conflict with Germany and I adhere to my opinion that we have at any rate to consider the probability'.[10] And two years later, Sir Charles Hardinge, Permanent Under-Secretary at the Foreign Office noted that 'Germany ... if once decided in her intention to make war on England would select the most favourable moment for making a sudden attack with her full naval strength, possibly accompanied by a descent on the British coast'.[11] Fear of invasion was still writ large. As historian Andrew Lambert has written, 'by early 1906 the centre of naval effort was shifting from the Mediterranean to the North Sea; Germany was not only the most likely but also the only realistic enemy. Russia was no longer a naval power and the French navy had collapsed.'[12]

Fisher's Revolution

Amidst considerable public controversy, in 1904 Fisher quickly sold off ninety obsolete and small ships and put a further sixty-four into reserve, describing them as 'too weak to fight and too slow to run away',[13] and 'a miser's hoard of useless junk'. This, of course, also did away with the sinecure of commanding them too. Five battleships were withdrawn from the China station in 1904. The standing South American, North American and Pacific squadrons were abolished. Not everyone agreed with these changes and Fisher made lasting enemies as a result.

But these actions freed up crews and money to increase the number of large modern ships in home waters. The Naval Estimates for 1905 were reduced by £3.8 million on the previous year's total of £36.9 million despite new building programmes and greatly increased effectiveness. Naval expenditure fell from 1905 to 1907, before rising again (see also Appendix 8).

But this was not the end of his reorganisations. On 14 December 1904, Fisher created a new entity by renaming the Home Fleet as the Channel Fleet, to be based at Sheerness, where easy access to the North Sea and the German coastline could be obtained. The pre-existing Channel Fleet was renamed the Atlantic Fleet to be based at Gibraltar. Fisher stripped the Mediterranean, Atlantic and old Channel Fleets of battleships and cruisers to make up this new force and backed it up with ships from the reserve.*

As Admiral William Jameson noted:

> In December 1904, less than two months after his arrival in Whitehall, a memorandum was issued ordering a major reorganisation of the fleet. France was no longer our enemy. Japan was an ally. America was a friend. The threat which had for years been centred in the

---

* The name 'Home Fleet' was used again from 1907 when such an entity was created.

HMS *Dreadnought*, the ship that changed the naval world. With ten 12in guns in five turrets and turbine engines, she made all other battleships obsolete overnight. (US Naval History and Heritage Command NH 61017)

Mediterranean was now in the North Sea. The old Channel Fleet, renamed the Atlantic Fleet, was moved to Gibraltar where it could reinforce either home or foreign waters. The Home Fleet, renamed the Channel Fleet, was increased to ten battleships in full commission supported by other ships in reserve, but now with nucleus crews. Men for the extra ships and nucleus crews could only be found by reductions elsewhere. Fisher took the drastic step of paying off no less than 174 [*sic*] of the very large number of smaller ships on various foreign stations abroad.

A howl of protest greeted these changes, but Fisher was undoubtedly right. Many of the ships on distant foreign stations were obsolete and very little use as men of war, and naval distribution abroad had been little changed in nearly 100 years in spite of vastly altered political requirements.[14]*

Fisher was determined that the decisive force would be concentrated in the decisive area. In 1904, nearly all the modern battleships had been stationed in the Mediterranean. Now two fleets, Atlantic and Channel, were in place

---

* Fisher had inherited nine squadrons or fleets in 1904. Their distribution was based on the old needs of sailing ships and trade.

to protect Britain and its environs. The journey to concentration in the key area can be seen in Appendix 9.

* * * * *

Next, one year into his post, Fisher revolutionised the battleship. HMS *Dreadnought* was Fisher's new conception of what a modern battleship should be, and he got her built in record time. Laid down in 1905, she was launched in February the following year and commissioned in December 1906. King Edward VII officiated at the launch. Wearing a bicorne hat and the full-dress uniform of an Admiral of the Fleet, Edward had to twice swing a bottle of Australian wine against the ship before it would shatter and christen the latest battleship for the navy. He then took up a hammer and chisel made from the timbers of HMS *Victory* and severed the last cord holding her in place; and touched off a revolution. She sported, for the first time on any battleship, an all-big-gun armament of ten 12in guns in five turrets, virtually no secondary armament, turbine engines, and even moved the officers' accommodation forward, breaking a long naval tradition. And at 21 knots she was faster than any battleship afloat.

At a stroke, her armament destroyed several naval shibboleths. Throughout the late nineteenth century British gunnery prize shooting had

The armoured cruiser HMS *Drake*, which would be sunk by *U-79* on 2 October 1917 near Rathlin Island. (Library of Congress det.4a19535)

HMS *Indomitable*, an *Invincible*-class battlecruiser, one of Fisher's greyhounds of the sea. (US Naval History and Heritage Command NH 60003)

been at 2,000 yards and battle practice was only 3,000 yards in 1904, the year that accurate fire had been made at 18,000 yards during the Russo-Japanese War. British Admirals still expected to close the enemy and pepper them with quick-firing weapons, in the Nelsonian tradition.

It was for this reason that all RN battleships such as the *Royal Sovereign*s carried a limited number of heavy guns and a preponderance of quick-firing weapons, usually 6in. So did the latest cruisers, such as the *Drake* class of 1900 which mounted two 9.2in guns and sixteen 6in. The larger weapons were intended to serve as 'hull-crackers'. The idea was that they would 'crack' the enemy's armour plate in order that the smaller side mounted guns could pour in a broadside.

Worse, ships carried mixed armaments. This made rangefinding impossible as no-one could tell the splashes apart at distance. Gun smoke made it even more difficult. Individual gun captains were expected to sight and fire their own guns and each gun fired when ready, exacerbating the aiming and ranging problems. *Dreadnought* solved this problem, having no smaller-calibre weapons, although later ships mounted anti-torpedo boat armament. Fisher actively promoted improvements in gunnery, including centralisation of gunnery control in director towers, high above the ship (and giving British warships a distinctive profile with their tripod masts). Overnight, *Dreadnought* made all other battleships obsolete and sparked a rush to build Dreadnought-type vessels which spread across the globe.

Not content with such a fundamental change, Fisher next rendered the armoured cruiser redundant. He ordered three new 'Dreadnought Cruisers', *Indomitable*, *Invincible* and *Inflexible*, all laid down in 1906. They were the logical next extension of Fisher's battleship ideas, ships that could catch anything that they could fight, and quickly withdraw from any ship too well armed to engage. Fisher called them his 'new testament' ships, 'greyhounds to catch hares'. Each carried eight 12in guns and sacrificed armour protection for speed – 'speed *is* armour', claimed Fisher.[15] Four screws and steam turbines drove them at 25 knots.

The first of the breed, *Indomitable*, crossed the Atlantic in 1908 with the Prince of Wales (the future George V) on board. For reasons best known to themselves, both he and his private secretary worked a shift in the stokehold. On the return journey she averaged a fraction below 25 knots, almost equalling the record for the voyage of 25.08 knots set by RMS *Lusitania*. Prince George, a former naval officer, told Fisher (whom he actually disliked), 'she is indeed a grand ship and the finest steamer I have ever seen'.[16]

In the light of the odium heaped upon the class after the loss of three of their type at Jutland in 1916, it should be noted that Fisher had not intended them as 'line-of-battle' ships. They were originally to lead a cluster of light cruisers, which would act as their 'eyes', sweeping the seas for enemy commerce raiders and sinking them. Thus, their initial appellation was 'Dreadnought Cruisers'; they were only christened 'battlecruisers' by Admiralty order on 25 November 1911, not least so that the fleet of capital ships would seem, for public consumption, to be larger than it was.

Germany Builds a Fleet

Germany began to build up its navy in 1898 with the first of Admiral Alfred von Tirpitz's *Flottengesetze* (Fleet Laws), of which five were passed in total, devoting more and more expenditure to create a large, battleship-heavy fleet. Between 1900 and 1910, for example, annual German naval expenditure grew over two and a half times (see also Appendix 8).

Kaiser Wilhelm II had long wanted a large naval force to help Germany attain what he believed she deserved – 'a place in the sun'. A large German navy could assist in German attempts to attain colonies. But in particular he wanted to develop a navy that could match the Royal Navy, of which he was insanely jealous. In his autobiography, *My Early Life*, he noted that 'I had a peculiar passion for the navy. It sprang to no small extent from my English blood. When I was a little boy . . . I admired the proud British ships. There awoke in me the will to build ships of my own like these someday, and when I was grown up to possess a fine navy as the English.'

The German battlefleet had been developed on the principle, first adumbrated by Admiral Tirpitz, of *Risikoflotte*, risk fleet. In essence this posited that, if the *Kaiserliche Marine* (German Imperial Navy) reached a certain level of strength relative to the Royal Navy, the British would try to avoid confrontation with Germany. The belief was that if the two navies fought in opposition, the German Navy would inflict sufficient damage on the Royal Navy such that Britain would lose its naval dominance and sovereignty of the sea, crucial to maintaining control over the British Empire. And if a powerful battlefleet that broke out of the North Sea and attacked British shipping and colonies could inflict significant harm, it would cripple Britain's ability to intervene on the Continent, perhaps for the crucial period of decisive battle.

Britain could not afford, given its fears of German Continental domination and invasion, to let this new competitor for oceanic power grow unchallenged. Thus, as the German fleet increased, financed by successive German Fleet Laws and championed by Kaiser Wilhelm II personally, Britain responded in kind.

Many were inflamed by Germany's presumption. Foreign Secretary Sir Edward Grey noted that the German dreadnoughts were 'not the least necessary for the protection of her oversea commerce, which latter is the proper function of cruisers'[17] and he told the German ambassador that 'our object was to maintain such complete command of the sea in our home waters that even with the small army we maintained, we should be safe from invasion'.[18] This sentiment he repeated in Parliament stating that 'our navy to us is ... a matter of life and death'.[19] The 'crunch' for Britain came in 1909.

'We Want Eight and We Won't Wait'

Herbert Henry Asquith had become Prime Minister of Britain in April 1908. He and his Chancellor of the Exchequer, David Lloyd George, were set on a redistributive policy which would allow for the introduction of old age pensions and a number of other socially reforming policies.

In a major speech in December 1908, Asquith announced that the upcoming budget would reflect this agenda, and a so-called 'People's Budget' was submitted to Parliament by Lloyd George the following year. This greatly expanded social welfare programmes. To pay for them, the budget significantly increased both direct and indirect taxes. These included a 20 per cent tax on the unearned increase in value in land, payable at death of the owner or sale of the land. There would also be a tax of a halfpenny in the pound on undeveloped land. A graduated income tax was to be imposed, and there were increases in imposts on tobacco, beer and spirits. The proposed budget divided the country and provoked bitter debate through the summer of 1909.

The focus on social spending ran counter to a widespread belief that more money was needed for the navy to fund expenditure on Dreadnought-type warships, in competition with the significant German building programme which now included such vessels. On 8 December 1908, First Lord of the Admiralty Reginald McKenna had recommended to the Cabinet a new ship building programme of six Dreadnoughts for 1909–10. This would have brought the navy's strength of these vessels to eighteen in 1912; but Germany was thought to have plans to build seventeen (possibly twenty-one) by then – the Two Power Standard would not apply, and indeed Britain might be outnumbered.

Winston Churchill (President of the Board of Trade) and Lloyd George opposed increased spending, proposing only four such ships, and a public battle broke out with navy supporting sources calling for at least eight ships to be laid down – the 'we want eight and we won't wait' campaign, led by the Navy League. It became a bitter argument, with proponents of increased social spending set against those who argued that old age pensions were less important than a strong navy. Both Foreign Secretary Grey and First Lord of the Admiralty Reginald McKenna threatened to resign from the government if increased Naval Estimates were not approved. Eventually, not six but eight were agreed upon, across two years; but the two-power standard was quietly consigned to the history books. And of course, the Russian defeat at Tsushima and the French agreement of 1904 made it easy to do so. The only enemy to focus on now was Germany.

Flotilla Defence and Coastal Defence

Fisher was a supporter of new naval technology, especially the submarine, which he had driven forwards to such an extent that before the First World War submarines were often dismissively referred to as 'Fisher's toys'. Indeed, he wrote that 'I don't think it is even faintly realised . . . the immense impending revolution which the submarine will effect as a weapon of war'.[20] This statement was contained in two papers which he prepared for Prime Minister Arthur Balfour on 24 January 1904, one of which looked at the submarine as an offensive weapon and one which examined its defensive possibilities, especially in relation to the protection against invasion. He recognised before most that new technology meant that he could organise the navy to better exploit the opportunities such advances presented. Instead of continuing to build battleships and cruisers, his vision was to create a navy built around the battlecruiser and the newly developed submarine. As historian Nick Lambert has written, 'the battlecruiser was to serve as the blue water, multi role warship for imperial defence. Submarines were to form the cornerstone of Britain's naval defence against invasion.'

According to Lambert,

> Fisher developed a new theory of sea power – the concept of 'Flotilla Defence'. This was a sea denial strategy intended to protect the British Isles from the possibility of invasion in the absence of the main fleet, thus restoring to the Royal Navy the ability to project naval force in distant waters without fear of a bolt from the blue from another European power when the surface fleet was on foreign service.[21]

Fisher hoped that his new system would enable Britain to maintain its naval strength relative to other great powers in spite of its growing financial weakness.

Under international law, close blockade of an enemy's ports was legal but the closing off of large areas of the seas to them was not. This close blockade had been the Royal Navy's traditional strategy. But Jacky Fisher foresaw that the submarine, the torpedo and light inexpensive craft which could deliver them, made the shallow and confined North Sea unsuitable for the battleships and other large vessels of the navy's battlefleet. Nor, in any case, could warships stay close to the Continental coastline, as in the days of the Nelsonian frigates of old. They were too vulnerable to underwater attack and too dependent on regular refuelling. Instead, he strongly advocated a distant blockade in which the North Sea was sealed off at either end and patrolled only by light craft, with the battle fleet held out of harm's way to the north.

As the contemporary historian Julian Corbett noted, 'torpedoes, wireless telegraphy and submarines have produced changes of strategical conditions . . . and the chief importance is that they practically destroy the old system of blockade . . . close blockade . . . is now impossible'.[22] *

If the ability to deploy formations of large surface ships was denied to both sides then neither Britain or Germany (or anyone else) would be able to convoy an expeditionary force across the Channel. 'Strategically, mutual sea denial would be much more advantageous to Britain because it left the Royal Navy free to protect the trade routes and defend distant colonies with armoured ships that would otherwise have been tied to home waters',[23] and invasion would be prevented.

---

* In this concept there is a faint echo of the French *Jeune École* school of the late nineteenth century, which 'proclaimed the obsolescence of the battleship and the conquest of maritime supremacy by torpedo boats which, swarming in large numbers from their bases, would protect the coastline and prevent blockading actions' (Stanglini and Cosentino, *The French Fleet*, p 6).

The 'River'-class destroyer HMS *Kale* (1904). Armed with a 12pdr, five 6pdrs and two torpedo tubes, a fit-out increased by three further 12pdrs in 1906. She was one of the class whose build contracts were cut back by Fisher. (Naval Photograph Club)

HMS *Gadfly*, a turbine-powered destroyer launched on Empire Day 1906. She was the first of new coastal destroyers to be commissioned and had a contract speed of 26 knots. Picture from *Black and White* magazine, 2 June 1906. (Author's collection)

The Admiralty's dispositions and orders for new craft reflected this thinking. Desperate to extend his coastal forces quickly, Fisher cancelled a contract for thirteen 'River'-class fleet destroyers almost as soon as he took office, and instead ordered vessels he called coastal destroyers. These were short-range yet seaworthy craft, designed for operations in the Channel and which could be delivered at half the price of a 'River'. Between 1905 and 1907, the Admiralty contracted for thirty-six coastal destroyers, the last of which was delivered in 1909, and only twelve fleet destroyers.

The coastal destroyers were not a homogenous group, for six shipyards were involved in their construction and the boats differed in detail as each shipbuilder was allowed to build to their own plans, modifying their designs for the later batches. However, all had two funnels and sited one of their three torpedo tubes on the stern. They resembled the earliest 26-knotter torpedo boat destroyers (TBDs) of 1892–3, having turtleback forecastles, and carried a minimal armament of two 12pdr guns. Oil-fired, they could achieve 26 knots, displaced 247 tons and had a crew of thirty-nine. Originally, they were given names but in October 1906, these were replaced by numbers, *TB-1* to *TB-36*, and categorised as first-class torpedo boats. Experience proved that whilst they were well adapted for coastal waters as intended, they really were not strong enough for oceanic operations.

The 'C'-class submarine HMS *C-35* (1909). She was scuttled off Harmaja on 5 April 1918 to avoid capture by advancing German forces. (Author's collection)

As early as 1903, Fisher had foreseen the submarine as an anti-invasion tool. His protégée Captain Reginald Bacon wrote in May of the that year that the submarine could replace the fixed minefield in helping to prevent invasion. And in December 1903, Fisher wrote a paper for Balfour in which he asserted that 'the submarine boat had made invasion impracticable and this being so the army needs to be reconstituted because invasion has apparently been hitherto a governing condition in arranging its strength'.[24] Consequently, the Admiralty built more relatively cheap 'C'-class coastal submarines, even when larger and more effective craft could have been obtained. These were the last class of petrol-engined submarines of the Royal Navy and marked the end of the development of the Holland type. Thirty-eight were constructed between 1905 and 1910. With limited endurance and only a 10 per cent reserve of buoyancy over their surface displacement, they were poor surface vessels, but their spindle-shaped hull made for good underwater performance compared to their contemporaries. With a complement of sixteen, they were equipped with two 18in torpedo tubes and could make 5–8 knots submerged. Fisher saw the submarine primarily as a coast defence vessel at this stage, operating even as a sort of intelligent minefield. So, clearly, Fisher was going for quantity, not necessarily quality, and for protection of the littoral. Although, as one of his biographers has noted, 'the submarine's ability to prevent invasion is, of course, much exaggerated; but during his term as First Sea Lord, Fisher would supply only too tangible a demonstration of his belief in this capability by his excessive

Seen here at the 1909 Royal Fleet Review, the last pre-dreadnought battleships built for the Royal Navy. HMS *Agamemnon* (front) with *Lord Nelson* were commissioned in 1908, two years after *Dreadnought* had made them obsolete. To their rear is the *Bellerophon*-class dreadnought HMS *Temeraire*, commissioned in 1909. (Author's collection)

orders for small coastal types which were virtually useless in the Great War'.[25]

Dispositions reflected this strategy too. By 1909, Fisher's last full year in post, nearly all the destroyer and submarine resource of the navy was concentrated in home waters (see Appendix 10). Coastal defence was to be by the navy.

Fisher and the Army

Before the Haldane reforms, Fisher was no fan of the army. Writing to Lord Esher* in 1903, he observed that 'The military system is rotten to the very core, you want to begin *ab ovo*', going on to aver that 'the best of the generals are even worse that the subalterns, because they are more hardened sinners'.[26]

Fisher was on the side of those who believed that the Royal Navy was sufficient for the prevention of invasion. 'The foundation of our policy is that the communications of the Empire must be kept open by a predominant fleet, and *ipso facto* such a fleet will suffice to allay the fears of the "old women of both sexes" in regard to the invasion of England or the invasion of her Colonies.'[27] And if Britain lost command of the seas, Fisher thought that there was no need to fear a foreign landing: 'it's not invasion that we have to fear if the navy is beaten, it's starvation'.[28] Lack of food would induce the country to surrender.†

He was an opponent of a large standing army and certainly of a Continental commitment. Apart from anything else, he saw the need to transport a great standing army as a strain on Britain's key resource – its merchant and naval fleets.

> Every soldier that you raise or enlist, or recruit . . . unless he is absolutely part of a Lord Lieutenant's Army, never to go out of England and only recruited, like the Militia – that splendid force – to be called up only in case of invasion . . . every soldier that is recruited on any other basis means so much tonnage in shipping that has to be provided, not only to take him to the Continent; but it's got to be kept ready to bring him back, in case of his being wounded, and all the time to take him provisions, ammunition, stores.[29]

Of course, there was also an element in maintaining the lion's share of defence funding for the navy in Fisher's position. 'Fisher was haunted, by 1903, by the spectre of a general demand for an army large enough to repel a major landing.'[30]

---

* Reginald Baliol Brett, 2nd Viscount Esher from 1899.
† In 1914, imports accounted for 80 per cent of wheat requirements and 40 per cent of beef and mutton.

Instead, Fisher argued that the British army should be 'a projectile to be fired by the navy. The navy embarks it and lands it where it can do the most mischief . . . instead of . . . ineffectually opposing the vast continental armies, we should be employing ourselves in joint naval and military manoeuvres.'[31] In this he was supported by many who saw only disaster if Britain became embroiled in a European land war, a group which included many of the ruling Liberal Party politicians. At an August 1907 Cabinet meeting, Sir Edward Grey repeated Fisher's views, which he endorsed, that the army 'was a weapon essentially necessary to give effect to the activity of the fleet, a projectile to be fired by the navy',[32] and 'Loulou' Harcourt,* Colonial Secretary, was aghast in a 1911 CID meeting to discover that it had been decided to land British troops in Northern France 'to assist a French army on the Meuse', an act he considered 'criminal folly'.[33]

A cartoon from *Punch* magazine of 20 May 1914, depicting Territorials on manoeuvres. 'Thank 'ivin we've got a nivy.' (Author's collection)

Meanwhile, Esher, commenting on the increasing levels of naval expenditure, noted that 'whatever the cost maybe, it is cheaper than a conscript army and any entangling alliance'.[34] And ex-Prime Minister Balfour, writing in March 1911, averred that 'even if the army continued as it was [i.e. small] the British Isles were not imperilled, but if the navy ceased to be strong, we perish'.[35] The purpose of the army, Balfour believed, was to protect the British Empire, by which he meant India. The strategic battle lines were still being drawn, three years from the coming war.

* * * * *

Admiral of the Fleet Sir John Fisher, First Baron Fisher of Kilverstone, stood down from the post of First Sea Lord in January 1910. The fleet that would fight the coming war was largely his creation.

---

* Lewis Vernon Harcourt, 1st Viscount Harcourt from 1917.

4
Coastal Defence and the Road to War, 1911–1914

1911 was a pivotal year in the history of coastal defence and how and why Britain would fight if she had to. The incident which defined it was German aggression over Morocco, the so-called 'Agadir Incident', which might have led to war.

This was a crisis triggered by the deployment of a large force of French troops to the interior of Morocco in April 1911 to put down a rebellion against the French-backed ruler. France and Germany had agreed on 9 February 1909 that while France would have exclusive political control, the two nations would uphold each other's economic interests in Morocco. However, in 1911 France forced the sultan to approve a new treaty wherein he promised not to sign any other treaties without French approval.

Germany did not necessarily object to France's expansion but wanted territorial compensation for herself. Berlin threatened war, sent the gunboat *Panther* to the port, followed by the cruiser *Berlin*, and roused German nationalists to bellicosity. Negotiations between Germany and France resolved the issue: but the British government, in the person of Chancellor

SMS *Panther* (1901), an *Iltis*-class gunboat, armed with two 10.5cm (4.1in) and six 3.7cm (1.5in) guns. (Author's collection)

SMS *Berlin* (1903), a *Bremen*-class light cruiser armed with ten 10.5cm (4.1in) and ten 3.7cm (1.5in) guns. (US Naval History and Heritage Command NH 64262)

of the Exchequer Lloyd George, made it clear that Britain would not stand idly by if Germany threatened French or British interests. 'If Britain is treated badly . . . as if she is of no account in the cabinet of nations, then I say emphatically that peace at that price would be a humiliation intolerable for a great country like ours to endure,' Lloyd George thundered in a speech at the Mansion House on 21 July.[1] The speech was interpreted by Germany as a warning that she could not impose an unreasonable settlement on France without incurring British enmity.

The British government was nonetheless alarmed at Germany's aggressiveness toward their French ally. Relations between Berlin and London became even more strained and Prime Minister Asquith called for a presentation of war plans by the army and navy to the Committee of Imperial Defence.

If one man could be fingered as the one who did most to take Britain's army into a murderous war in France, and away from Fisher's precious 'bullet to be fired by the navy' concept, it was Director of Military Operations at the War Office General Sir Henry Wilson. He had spent his holidays cycling around the likely battle grounds in France and had been in secret and private communication with the French military authorities. With information from them, Wilson had worked out a strategy for the deployment of the British Expeditionary Force into Northern France in the event of war with Germany, and had been in covert conversations with the French army brass since December 1905. Now called in front of the CID on 23 August, he presented well, and in detail, his plans. The navy, represented by Admiral Sir Arthur Knyvet Wilson VC, First Sea Lord, performed comparatively badly in a presentation proposing that five divisions guard Britain whilst one land on the Baltic coast, or possibly at Antwerp. Additionally, the navy would establish a close blockade of the German ports, destroying or sealing off the German High Seas Fleet. Wilson also proposed amphibious assaults against the islands of Sylt and Wangeroog to establish advanced bases for further

General Sir Henry Wilson.
(Author's collection)

attacks against Wilhelmshaven, Bremerhaven, Cuxhaven and Kiel. This amphibious pressure, Wilson argued, would draw vast numbers of German troops away from the United Kingdom's allies, as 'even if no actual success is gained, the mere fact of keeping the field army in motion must tend to exhaust their resources'.[2] In this he reverted to the discredited tactic of close blockade, precisely what Fisher had argued so cogently against. This bumbling performance, which 'in this battle of the Wilsons, the grim old First Sea Lord was no match for the witty and debonair Director of Military Operations',[3] demonstrated that the army and navy had different and mutually exclusive plans. The blame was placed by Asquith and others on the lack of a naval staff, a function which had been resisted by Fisher and his successor Wilson but had been imposed on the army in Haldane's reforms. The navy's political master, McKenna, supported his admiral and by the October both had been fired as a result, McKenna being replaced by Winston Churchill. Also, Asquith and his Foreign Secretary, Grey, winked at Henry Wilson continuing his *sub rosa* joint planning with the French, without informing the rest of the Cabinet. Proposals for dispatching an expeditionary force to France's aid in the event of war with Germany had begun in secret and unofficially in January 1906. Now they had the tacit imprimatur of senior government ministers.

It may be justly said that it was at this point that Britain became joined to a land-based, rather than a sea-based, war plan, etched out by an arch schemer, Henry Wilson, who was also a supporter of conscription and of a large standing army. Britain, which ruled the waves and commanded the oceans with its dominant navy, became the more or less willing slave of a continental strategy, rather than a maritime one.

Further Concentration

Winston Spencer Churchill took up his new position as First Lord of the Admiralty with almost unseemly delight and gusto. With Fisher, now retired, whispering in his ear as an *eminence gris*, he continued the latter's policy of concentration towards British waters. On 18 March 1912, Churchill announced in the Naval Estimates that, in a major reorganisation of the Royal Navy's Mediterranean forces, the ships based at Malta would redeploy to Gibraltar, from where they could project power both into the eastern

Atlantic and the Mediterranean Sea. Then, in mid-year, he informed Grey that Britain would have to pull out the battleships presently in the Med to increase the numbers in home waters, in the face of continued expansion of the German fleet and in order to maintain local superiority. Finally, in November Britain and France concluded a secret naval agreement in which the Royal Navy promised to protect the northern coast of France in the event of German naval attack, while France concentrated her fleet in the western Mediterranean and agreed to defend British interests there. Specifically, the British fleet would ensure the defence of the Pas-de-Calais, with the support

The armoured cruiser *Duke of Edinburgh* (1904), pictured in New York in 1909. She was the name ship of her class of two, and mounted six 9.2in and ten 6in guns when launched, together with twenty 3pdrs and three torpedo tubes.
(Library of Congress, LC-DIG-det-4a16120)

of French torpedo boats and submarines based at Calais, Boulogne and Dunkirk, while the French navy would watch the western approaches to the Channel backed by British cruisers. In the Med, the RN would leave sufficient force to contain the Austro-Hungarian fleet should it depart the Adriatic, and protect the Suez Canal. France was thus able to guard her communications with her North African colonies, and Britain to focus more force in home waters to oppose the German High Seas Fleet.

Churchill's intention to largely withdraw from the Mediterranean drew much criticism, especially from the Foreign Office and in order to placate his decriers, the 1st Cruiser Squadron was ordered to be based at Malta in January 1913. The Royal Navy's Mediterranean representation was thus reduced to four armoured cruisers (*Defence*, *Black Prince*, *Duke of Edinburgh* and *Warrior*), to which were added the 2nd Battlecruiser Squadron (*Inflexible*, *Invincible*, *Indomitable* and *Indefatigable*) in August. But now Britain was also, at least morally, bound to come to France's aid and protect her Channel coasts.

War Plans

How were the navy's plans for defence of the North Sea evolving immediately pre-war? Until Fisher's time, the strategy of the navy in response to war with France or Germany was that of close blockade and observation of the enemy's fleet movements from close up to their bases. Under international law, such close blockade of an enemy's ports was legal but the closing off of large areas of the seas to them was not.* This approach had been the Royal Navy's traditional strategy. But, as noted in Chapter 3, Fisher foresaw that the submarine, the torpedo and light inexpensive craft which could deliver them, made the shallow and confined North Sea unsuitable for the battleships and other large vessels of the navy's battlefleet. Nor, in any case, could warships stay near to the continental coastline, as they were too vulnerable to underwater attack and too dependent on regular re-fuelling. Instead, he strongly advocated a distant blockade in which the North Sea was sealed off at either end and patrolled only by light craft.

In April 1912, Admiral Sir George Callaghan, CinC Home Fleet, was informed that any blockade by the fleet of the whole German coast on the North Sea should be considered as cancelled. And on 16 December, he was

---

* The Treaty of Paris (1856, and subsequently re-ratified at the Hague Conventions of 1899 and 1907) gave legal basis to the concept of blockade. The agreement, among other things, permitted 'close' but not 'distant' blockades. A belligerent was allowed to station ships near the three-mile limit to stop or inspect traffic with an enemy's ports; it could not simply declare areas of the high seas comprising the approaches to the enemy's coast to be off-limits.

further instructed that in time of war he should base himself at the Firth of Forth and sweep the North Sea, without going more than halfway across. When in 1913, Winston Churchill pressed a madcap scheme for the close blockade of the Heligoland Bight and the capture of the island of Borkum, Callaghan was dismissive, stating that such an approach was no longer a viable plan.

Accordingly, as the likelihood of conflict with Germany grew, Scapa Flow was earmarked as the potential main battlefleet base. The Firth of Forth was developed for naval purposes at Granton, Invergordon and Rosyth. The Nore command, which included Chatham and Sheerness Royal Dockyards gained in importance. It might be noted that Britain ignored international treaties in determining that its strategy against Germany would henceforth be based on a distant blockade.

But this posed a problem for the Admiralty planners. For the strategy of distant blockade, shutting off the north and south exits to the North Sea and English Channel, ran the risk that important hostile movements would not be reported and intercepted in the early stages of evolution.

Confining German torpedo boats to their own coastal waters had been a key facet of previous British planning, as doing so would enable the fleet to traverse the North Sea without fear of a surprise torpedo attack. But this was no longer possible: and so the movement of the British fleet in the North Sea would become increasingly hazardous. Furthermore, coastal ports and towns, and their associated light naval forces, would become vulnerable to German gun, torpedo, mine and submarine attack, as warships would be able to make the passage across the North Sea unseen. Moreover, the annual fleet manoeuvrers of 1912 and again in 1913 showed that the attacking fleet could in fact invade Britain. In 1912, the 'Red Fleet' successfully landed 28,000 men in Yorkshire without interception, and in 1913 upwards of 60,000 troops were landed.* The coastal defence flotillas disappointed; they disrupted one landing but were defeated in the other attempts. Unsurprisingly, the results were hushed up.

The Admiralty War Staff addressed this problem by recommending patrols of the mid-North Sea but this was not seen as a sustainable tactic. Strategies were developed to restrict German movements by means of mines and to use the navy's newest submarines on observational patrols. But mainly the authorities were obliged to persist with patrols of the North Sea as the only currently possible plan. As Chief of the War Staff Henry Jackson put it in 1913, the battle fleet would be unable to interrupt coastal attacks and thus the country would have to 'trust to our flotillas and shore batteries to inflict much damage to them during the raid'.[4]

---

* These numbers were, of course, theoretical, as assessed by the umpires.

Nor had army-navy cooperation shown much improvement. The QF guns Owen had recommended were in short supply and deliveries did not take place until a few months before the outbreak of war. And it transpired that the War Office had no plans to protect the principal Royal Navy ordnance depots at Chattenden and Lodge Hill. The Admiralty had to pressure the War Office to mount two 6in howitzers apiece at these magazines. Finally, in April 1913, it was 'stated that these guns were in a position to open fire without delay'.[5]

Perhaps as a result of this dilatory arming of a key point of vulnerability, the Admiralty became exercised about coastal defences generally and, in particular, the defence of the east coast and its ports. In May 1913, Churchill drafted a note which proposed that the Admiralty take complete responsibility for the east coast batteries north of Sheerness and 'man them adequately both in peace and war'.[6] Marines and naval reservists would be used to resource them, possibly together with territorial RGA volunteers. He further suggested that the Admiralty would construct any new batteries necessary in eastern Britain, paid for out of the 'Navy Vote' (the Naval Estimates).

The note also put forward that 'the Admiralty wish to take over the whole business of coast watching on the Sheerness – Shetland line and to organise under Admiralty control whatever means exist. Whether on the sea by their patrol flotillas, or along the coasts by their coast guard and wireless stations, or by territorial cyclists or by the police, in order to report any hostile landing as quickly as possible.'[7] All coast batteries and other defences should be under the local control of a naval or marine officer.

This was a major 'power grab' and something of a slur against the War Office by suggesting that the army was not taking coastal defence seriously enough or, at least, the defence of ports for the local coastal flotillas. For, as Churchill goes on to state, 'the paramount need of having the patrol flotillas permanently protected in their harbours at all times . . . would appear to require complete unity of control throughout the aforesaid services'.[8]

As a sop to the army, Churchill suggested that the navy would 'organise four naval and marine brigades out of surplus reservists . . . until these men are required for naval service the Admiralty will hold them at the disposal of the military commander in chief for the general defence of the United Kingdom . . . [they] shall be administered by the Admiralty and controlled in all movements absolutely by the War Office'.[9]

The debate was resolved by the end of the year with the War Office taking responsibility for the land defence of Dover, Sheerness, the Tyne and the Forth, whilst the Admiralty agreed to protect Harwich, Hartlepool, the Humber, the Tees, the Tay, Aberdeen and Cromarty.

What Sort of Invasion Might Britain Face?

According to a paper circulated by Churchill in 1913, Britain faced the threat of three potential invasion scenarios.

The first he termed 'Bolt from the Blue', with the objective of preventing the expeditionary force being sent to France and incidentally damage naval dockyards and arsenals. This would be a surprise attack, without warning and in force. The likely target ports for such action were stated to be Harwich, Newcastle upon Tyne and Balta Sound in the Shetland Islands.

The second, 'Bolt from the Grey' envisaged a situation where the navy was on a war footing and the expeditionary force had been despatched to some overseas destination. Here 'the only adequate objective of the enemy in this case would be invasion in such force as to overcome the comparatively feeble military establishment in the United Kingdom'.[10] Harwich, Newcastle upon Tyne, Firth of Tay, Balta Sound, Oban or the Firth of Clyde were all thought of as likely landing sites.

The final set of circumstances envisaged war with Germany had begun, the 'Bolt from the Black', in which the enemy would conduct minor raids to destroy naval facilities and armament depots. They might also seize bases for their own flotilla use (in Shetland, for example) or attempt to invade in force to distract or divide the British fleet. Newcastle or Blyth, the Clyde, Barrow and Balta Sound were all considered possibilities here.

The paper went on to illustrate how Germany could send troops to British shores. 'Driblets' was one possibility, in which single ships evaded RN patrols to land at unfrequented spots. Alternatively, in another scenario, one, two or three detachments might be sent in pre-prepared transports simultaneously, as part of a major naval effort to land at different locations, thus dividing any response. Churchill went on to note that the Shetlands were of high strategic importance and totally undefended and ungarrisoned. The same was true for the Orkneys, Edinburgh, Glasgow, Newcastle, Hull and Harwich.

Finally, he made the point that 'the Admiralty cannot guarantee that individual vessels will not frequently slip through the cruiser squadrons patrolling the wide areas of the North Sea' and that there 'is a very good chance of an indefinite succession of individual transports reaching the British coast without being intercepted by the patrolling cruiser squadrons'.[11] It was hardly a ringing endorsement of the position that the navy was a sure shield against invasion.

Meanwhile, Director of Naval Intelligence Captain Thomas Jackson had been called before the CID 'Invasion Committee' in March 1913. Despite the establishment of the SSB and Mansfield Cumming's role in overseas intelligence, he stated that he 'could not undertake to say that the Germans would find it impossible to embark 20,000 men without our knowing of it' as we had no espionage 'organisation that could promise to give timely warning of such movement'.[12] However, he claimed that there had been an increase in the number of agents abroad to whom the promise of significant reward was held out if they could alert the authorities to an imminent embarkation.

* * * * *

In May 1912, there had been a further reorganisation of the Home Fleets. The Commander in Chief Home Fleets (Admiral Callaghan) took direct command of the First Fleet; and a Vice Admiral (Sir Frederick Hamilton, succeeded by Sir Cecil Burney in December 1913) was responsible for the Second and Third Fleets. Each of the three fleets represented a different level of availability. The First Fleet was composed of ships in full commission; the Second Fleet of ships with 50 per cent manning levels (called 'nucleus crews'); and the Third Fleet with ships laid up in reserve under Care and Maintenance parties.

Admiral of Patrols

As noted above, the sea patrolling of the east coast of Britain was now in the hands of the various destroyer and submarine flotillas dotted along the littoral. But there was no overall command of them as each was under the control of different port admirals. This led to problems of communication

HMS *St George* (1892), flagship of the Admiral of Patrols in 1912. She was armed with two 9.2in and ten 6in guns. (Author's collection)

and consistency of tactics and training. So on 16 April 1912, a new position of Admiral of Patrols was announced, to be based at the Admiralty. On 1 May, Rear Admiral John Michael de Robeck hoisted his flag in the protected cruiser HMS *St George* (1892) at Harwich and took up the post. His command encompassed the 5th, 6th, 7th and 8th Destroyer Flotillas, formerly the 3rd, 4th, 5th and 6th Flotillas of the 3rd and 4th Divisions of the Home Fleet. This resource, however, only amounted in 1913 to four obsolete cruisers, seventy-four destroyers and eighteen submarines.

De Robeck's assistant was Captain Walter Cowan. Both men were passionate fox hunters and sportsmen (de Robeck would become President of the MCC in 1925) and their responsibilities were sufficiently light for them to indulge their interests. 'We had an old cruiser for flagship, *St George*,' Cowan later recalled, 'but we were very seldom in her except when John de Robeck wanted to give a dinner-party. We soon learnt to combine business with pleasure – we were both very fond of playing golf and hunting the fox.'[13]

But coast defence was still weighing heavy upon the naval mind. There was concern that wide-ranging patrolling would leave the coast open to attack and allow for the small vessels involved to be picked off by German forces. In early 1914, the Board of Admiralty ordered the Admiralty War Staff to devise a better form of organisation for the east coast patrol flotillas and First Sea Lord Prince Louis of Battenberg directed that the doctrine of patrol was to be replaced by that of coast defence. 'They should be regarded no longer as patrol flotillas but *défenses mobile*, or simply coast defence flotillas', which to his mind meant a different organisation of resources and command more suitable 'to their restricted and local spheres of action'.[14]

The War Staff contemplated the use of fifty aeroplanes, equipped with wireless equipment, capable of searching up to 100 miles distant from their bases, as part of a solution, but suitable aircraft were not yet available to them. So the coastal destroyers and submarines were retained but with a clear emphasis on local defence, which would now also fall to the Admiral of Patrols position, and Captain George A Ballard, considered to be a 'brain' within naval circles, replaced de Robeck on 1 May 1914 with the rank of commodore (first class). There was now a single command covering the insular defence of the coastline nearest to Germany.

To War, 1914

On 28 June 1914, at around 1030, a 19-year-old Bosnian Serb named Gavrilo Princip fired the shot which started the First World War. His assassination of Archduke Franz Ferdinand of Austria, Heir Presumptive to the throne of Austria-Hungary, and his pregnant wife Sophia, lit the fuse which would eventually blow Europe apart. Austria-Hungary was spoiling for a fight with Serbia to reassert its dominance in its own back yard. This was the *causus bellum* she wanted. Despite Serbia giving in to most of the reparations and guarantees demanded of her, Austria-Hungary began to mobilise. The Germans gave a not one but two 'blank cheques' to the Austrians to deal with Serbia as they wanted. Germany did nothing to rein in her ally and the Austrian tail wagged the German dog as both led the world to war.

Russia ordered mobilisation on 30 July in response; on 1 August, the German Government began a general mobilisation and declared war on Russia; the French commenced their own general mobilisation in reply. In Britain, a Royal Fleet Review had been arranged for 20 July, with manoeuvres by the combined First, Second and Third Fleets to follow. Post these exercises, it had been planned that the navy should return to peacetime status. On the weekend of 25–27 July the fleet was meant to disperse and reservists return to their homes and families. The First and Second Fleets were to assemble at Portland for a flag officers' conference and the Third Fleet to sail to their home ports to pay off their crews.

Now, as the global situation worsened, and with First Lord Winston Churchill away from his office and at the seaside building sandcastles with his wife and children, at 1600 on the 26 July Admiral Prince Louis of Battenberg, First Sea Lord, issued the instruction that 'no ship to leave harbour until further orders' to the CinC Home Fleets. And on the 29th, the Admiralty issued the 'preparatory for war' telegram, the day after the First Fleet, now the Grand Fleet, sailed for Scapa Flow.

What imperatives drove a Liberal government, its Cabinet largely opposed to war, and a prime minister whose focus was social reform, to take the country to war? For the defence of little Belgium and the Treaty of London? Not really.

There were economic, strategic and political motivations. 'Before 1895, Britain appeared both secure and supreme, the world's only global power. Now her supremacy seemed under threat . . . The global challenge was not only diplomatic but also military, from the autocracies of the Continent, and difficult for Liberal policy to combat.'[15] Economically Germany had drawn ahead of Britain in the manufacture of many goods and her navy was now a significant challenge to Britain's own.* Moreover, Grey and his Foreign Office advisors feared that if Germany defeated France and Russia, Britain would be next on the list.

---

* In 1870 Germany produced half as much steel as Britain; by 1914 she made twice as much as Britain did. German GDP overtook that of Britain in 1910. Britain ran a trade deficit with Germany in goods, but a surplus in 'invisables', such as shipping and insurance.

According to historian Niall Ferguson,

> the Liberal government went to war for two reasons: first because they feared the consequences of a German victory over France, imagining the Kaiser as a new Napoleon bestriding the Continent and menacing the Channel coast. That may or may not have been a legitimate fear but if it was, the Liberals had not done enough to deter the Germans, and the Conservatives had been right to press for conscription.[16]

Moreover, the Liberals could credibly have either a commitment to defend France AND conscription, or a policy of neutrality and no conscription. The combination they preferred – the French commitment but no conscription – was to prove fatal. As Secretary of State for War Lord Kitchener acidly remarked in 1914: 'No one can say my colleagues in the Cabinet are not courageous. They have no army and they declared war against the mightiest nation in the world.'[17]

Certainly, Britain could not afford to allow Germany to dominate the French coast or the Low Countries, for reasons visited in Chapter 1. And to defend France she would have to become a military as well as a naval power, for France could only be defended on land. But Asquith also had political considerations in mind. His government was divided and possibly about to collapse. Until 2 August most of the Cabinet favoured staying out of the war, as did the majority of Liberal MPs. Asquith and Grey threatened resignation if Britain did not take France's part while ten other minsters said they would quit if Britain did join the war. Also on the 2nd, the Conservative and Unionist opposition leader, Andrew Bonar Law, wrote to Asquith and declared that Britain must stand by its allies, stating 'it would be fatal to the honour and security of the United Kingdom to hesitate in supporting France and Russia at this present juncture'.[18] That same day, John Burns (President of the Board of Trade), resigned from the Cabinet.

Foreign Secretary Grey spoke in the House of Commons on 3 August. He talked compellingly, arguing if Belgium fell there would be a game of dominoes. France would follow, then Denmark then Holland and Germany would finally hold the entire Channel coast and have Britain at its mercy. But the navy would, he believed, defend Britain. 'For us, with a powerful fleet, which we believe able to protect our commerce, to protect our shores and to protect our interests, if we are engaged on war, we shall suffer but little more than we shall suffer if we stand aside.'[19]

Additionally, during the 3rd, Grey was authorised to tell the French ambassador that Britain would not allow Germany to use the English Channel for action against the French coast. This led to the resignations of John Morley

(Lord President of the Council), Sir John Simon (Attorney General) and Lord Beauchamp (First Commissioner of Works).* However, the following day Simon and Beauchamp were persuaded to withdraw their letters of resignation.

Germany declared war on France on the 3rd; on the 4th she invaded Belgium. Also on 4 August, the eight aging *Edgar*-class cruisers of the 10th Cruiser Squadron sailed for the Shetland Islands to shut off the northern end of the North Sea, while the Dover Patrol bottled up the Channel. Britain issued an ultimatum to Germany that same day, to expire at midnight, Continental time. There was no response. In fact, at that moment, and expecting a short war, British intervention did not worry Germany since Britain's army was so small. Indeed, the German Admiralty was told in August not to risk its ships trying to stop the transfer of the expeditionary force.

Given their failure to avert war, it can be argued that the entire Cabinet should have resigned. However, they dreaded the return of the Conservatives and Unionists to power. 'They went to war partly to keep the Tories out.'[20] And eventually, most of the Cabinet convinced themselves 'that if a war was necessary, they must ensure that it was fought according to their [Liberal] principles'.[21] 'Poor little Belgium' salved the Liberals' conscience following a reversal of the principles they held most dear.

Readiness

The navy was ready. The coastal flotillas were in place. So was the fleet. In August 1914, Britain had twenty dreadnought-type battleships in commission with a further fourteen either under construction or planned for completion by 1916. She also possessed nine operational battlecruisers. In contrast, Germany had fifteen dreadnoughts in service and an additional four scheduled for operations in 1916. Six battlecruisers were operational or near completion, with another two due for sea duty by 1917.

As a result of the proposals made by Churchill regarding coastal defence noted above, in January 1914 newspapers had reported much discussion about whether the Royal Navy should take over responsibility for coastal defence artillery and what would happen to the Royal Garrison Artillery if it did. Such proposals were overtaken by events and coastal defence gunnery remained the responsibility of the RGA throughout the war. Historian Colonel Maurice-Jones noted that, 'The RGA companies in the coast defences at home and abroad were well led, well trained and of high morale'.[22] The volunteer units were available too; but the Territorial Force was 67,000 men short of its hoped for 314,000.

---

* Charles Trevelyan, Parliamentary Secretary to the Board of Education, resigned on the issue as well, but not until the 10th.

How were the garrisons organised for war? Each coastal artillery emplacement was part of an overall 'fortress' under the command of the senior Royal Artillery officer. They were complex bodies. 'Every naval base or defended port, together with its coast defences, landward defences, establishment etc... was organised as a self-contained coast fortress.'[23] There were many moving parts. The RGA were responsible for the landward and sea-facing guns. There were also mobile guns under their control. Infantry battalions or detachments manned the ramparts and guarded outer walls. The Royal Engineers were responsible for communications, maintenance and the DEL system. Additionally, 'within the fortress the Royal Navy, which was not under the fortress commander but worked in close cooperation with him, was responsible for obstructions by sea, such as mines and booms protecting the entrance to the harbour.'[24] Moreover, every naval base or defended port had a Port War Signal Station, manned by the RN, to identify approaching warships as friend or foe. They communicated with the fortress guns through a 'Selected Military Officer' who could give the order to open fire.

Nonetheless, the army displayed a certain testiness with regard to the navy's role in the land defence and rejected Churchill's 'power grab'. 'Broadly, the War Office claimed the sole responsibility not only in regard to naval ports and vulnerable points of all kind, even those of an exclusively naval interest. The navy were to confine themselves to the protection of the coast.'[25]

Strategically, Britain had the advantage of occupying an insular position. 'By having its entire frontier with the sea, England has little or no reason to fear a surprise attack so long as the Royal Navy controlled the adjacent narrow sea.'[26] In contrast, 'the German strategic position in the North Sea was inherently much weaker than that of Great Britain because both exits to the open waters of the Atlantic were controlled by the Royal Navy'.[27] But nonetheless, 'no matter how tight the blockade was,

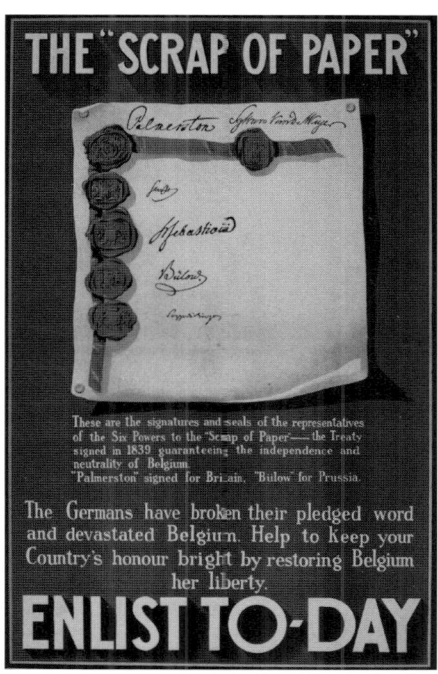

'Enlist To-day', a recruiting poster which plays upon the plight of Belgium. (Author's collection)

the British still needed direct defences of shipping and coastline behind the lines'.[28]

* * * * *

The pieces were on the board. The players had begun their moves. In the London suburb of Chelsea, the well-connected Georgina Lee, wife of the legal secretary to the Archbishop of Canterbury and mother to a nine-month-old baby son, started a diary for him to read in later life. In August she wrote 'for a hundred years we in this island have been living immune from danger thanks to our fleet and to the power of our nation, though this power has been dearly bought'.[29] Could the navy fulfil its commitments, and the public's expectations?

5
The Defence of Britain, 1914

And so the Royal Navy sped to its dispositions. But the bases that awaited it were far from ready or, indeed, properly equipped. Scapa Flow had been selected as the main fleet anchorage because 'the use of Ellis Island by the Japanese in their war with Russia in 1904–05 impressed naval opinion in England and persuaded the Royal Navy to use less frequented but spacious bases such as Scapa Flow . . . [which] was chosen because a fleet based there was able to control the northern approaches to the North Sea'.[1] But Scapa was completely undefended. The Owen committee had made no provision for defences at Cromarty or Scapa Flow, the latter because the concept did not then exist. For Cromarty, after further enquiry by the CID, it was decided that the floating dock and workshop there should be protected by defences conceived on an 'inexpensive scale'.[2] These were old naval guns and manned by Royal Marines. The works were completed by the end of July 1914.

With regard to Scapa, the Admiralty had asked, and the War Office had drawn up plans, for its defence but the government rejected them on the grounds of cost. Because of navigational difficulties, it was apparently not considered to be attackable. 'Consequently, it was decided that it would be sufficient on the outbreak of war to improvise defences.'[3] This for the base of the Grand Fleet!

Despite having been nominated as the fleet station in 1903, the intended new base at Rosyth was incomplete (which, according to Maurice Hankey, indicated 'the unsatisfactory working of the Parliamentary system in relation to defensive preparations').[4] In any case, there 'were not enough mines (a weapon the British had neglected as unseamanlike) to protect sufficient water to contain the whole Grand Fleet',[5] and 'plans for the defence of a war anchorage in the Humber, prepared by the Home Ports Defence committee and approved by the CID were hardly begun when war broke out'.[6]

As Arthur Marder put it:

> To sum up, the base situation was shocking. The only fully equipped first class base on the east coast at the outbreak of war was Chatham. Harwich was the base for the torpedo craft. Rosyth, officially described as the principal base of the fleet, and Cromarty had some artillery defence against surface attack but were quite open to

submarine attack. The construction of the dockyard at Rosyth had only just begun. Scapa Flow was an unprotected war anchorage with no provision for fleet repair and maintenance work.[7]

And the only two first-class southern bases, Plymouth and Portsmouth, were too far from the new naval centre of gravity, the North Sea. As will be seen, it was not a propitious start.

The Home Front

The declarations of war moved the invasion panic amongst public and politicians another notch higher. And some of the previous planning went out of the window. On 5 August, Asquith appointed Lord Kitchener as Secretary of War. A *bona fide* public hero who distrusted politicians and was used to getting his own way, Kitchener immediately disregarded the war plans articulated by General Wilson and the CID. And he was worried about invasion; 'I am only prepared to rule out the feasibility of invasion,' he frequently intoned, 'if I learnt that the Germans regard it as an impossible operation'.[8] Indeed, 'invasion preoccupied and alarmed'[9] the Secretary of State.

Consequently, instead of sending all six divisions of the Expeditionary Force to France, he retained two for home defence. 'There was no reason to distrust his judgment; it was well known that the Germans had at least 250,000 troops disposable for such an adventure [invasion].'[10] Or at least, that was what was supposed. The 3rd Battle Squadron of twelve pre-dreadnought battleships was stationed in the Forth, just in case.

All across Britain, a new militia sprang into life, unaided by official assistance, as citizens formed themselves into 'Drill Clubs', 'Rifles Clubs', 'Home Guards' and 'Village Guards' (amongst the most common names), all of which came to be popularly known as the

A humorous postcard of c1914 depicting the Kaiser dreaming of destroying St Paul's cathedral. 'The DOOM of St Paul's; And then he woke up'. (Author's collection)

An illustrated postcard 'The Doorway of England' extolling the virtue of defending the Kent coast. (Author's collection)

Volunteer Training Corps (VTC). Ernest Cooper was adjutant to one such organisation. He noted that many people thought that there was no one left in Britain to defend her.

> The bulk of the Territorials were sent overseas, the militia had been destroyed by Lord Haldane and the only protection for our coast, after the navy, was the home service men of the TA and the Kitchener armies in training. Once more the dread of invasion led to a popular impulse in favour of a Volunteer Force whereby the men over age or unwilling to enlist or service overseas, might be trained to take their place in the scheme of home defence.[11]

One of the more unlikely volunteer organisations to form was the United Arts Force (UAF), a home defence unit composed entirely of artists, musicians, actors, architects and writers who were generally too old to enlist in the armed forces. The UAF boasted 1,600 members by the end of October 1914, amongst them being some of Britain's most distinguished artists such as Edward Poynter, William Nicholson, John Lavery and George Frampton.

The volunteer groups fortified their villages or patrolled the coasts in company with the TF. The VTCs even formed a Central Association whose military adviser was General Sir Garrett O'Moore Creagh VC, who had succeeded Kitchener as Commander-in-Chief, India, until his retirement in

1914. Baden-Powell summoned his scout movement to take part in home defence. They assisted the coastguards, ran messages and guarded railway junctions, amongst other duties. And the press had a field day, with invasion scare stories making a regular appearance in daily and weekly editions.

The legal position of these VTCs was dubious. The Hague Convention was decisive against the legality of 'resistance by individual civilians'; and the Germans had shown themselves most willing to kill so-called *francs-tireurs* in Belgium. 'Lawyers argued while the coastguards and local bank managers with their "special constable" brassards and whistles peered anxiously into the cold mists of the Channel.'[12]

The army tried to pretend they didn't exist. 'Far from this patriotic movement receiving any official support, it was snubbed and discouraged in all directions, the heads of the War Office did not want to be bothered with volunteers.'[13] Nonetheless, at its height the VTC movement boasted 500,000 members, who were required to be under 18 years old or over 38 (later 41). For this reason, their detractors called them the 'Grandfather Scouts'.

Spy mania ran riot. A small number of spies employed by the German navy had been active in pre-war Britain. But between August 1911 and July 1914, the War Office's counter-espionage department, which would later morph into MI5, arrested just ten suspects. Come the war, and Home Secretary Reginald McKenna announced that twenty-one German spies had been arrested on 5 August 'all over the country . . . chiefly in important military or naval centres'.[14] This was in fact to jump the gun as seven of them were still at large. From the 8th, all Germans still in England had to report themselves to the police. Everywhere, there was spy fever, with many innocent people suffering temporary arrest. Waiters were sacked, strangers shadowed and interrogated. Theodore Kroell, manager of the Ritz Hotel since 1909, was dismissed due to his Germanic origins. Thousands of imaginary acts of espionage were reported to a credulous police force and the military authorities. Great interest was shown in the Channel Island of Herm which had been leased from the British government and used as a residence by Prince and Princess Blücher since 1889 (the princess was the English-born Evelyn Stapleton-Bretherton, who had four brothers in the British army and three brothers-in-law in the Royal Navy). It was inspected and occupied by British troops.

The fear of spies ran through all strata of society. Basil Thomson, Assistant Commissioner at Scotland Yard and in charge of the Special Branch,* noted

---

* The Special Branch had been formed in 1884 to counter the threat posed by Irish Republican bombers. Basil Thomson was an interesting character. Born the son of the Provost of Queen's College, Oxford (and who was later the Archbishop of Canterbury), he spent the 1880s as a colonial administrator and was briefly Prime Minister of Tonga. He was a novelist, read for the London Bar, and became governor of Dartmoor Prison, before joining the Met.

in 1914 that 'spy mania assumed a virulent epidemic form which . . . attacked all classes indiscriminately'.[15] Many British artists were confronted, interrogated and even arrested on suspicion of spying for sketching or painting outdoors, amongst them being John Lavery, Augustus John and Laura Knight. Every pigeon was suspected of carrying messages to Germany; Thomson felt that 'it was positively dangerous to be seen in conversation with a pigeon'.[16] Pigeon fanciers were required to obtain a permit to keep their birds. Even the staid and disciplined Maurice Hankey, secretary of the CID, was moved to join a friend in digging up an empty London garden owned by a German millionaire, on suspicion that it concealed a weapons platform.[17]

As the BEF began its move to France, the 5th Battle Squadron of pre-dreadnought battleships was based at Sheerness in case of German naval intervention. But in fact, Kaiser Wilhelm had instructed the Imperial Navy not to interfere, and the German High Command preferred to have the small British army where they could see and defeat it – in France.*

After initial defeats and the near loss of Paris, in the first two weeks of September the German advance into France was stopped at the Battle of the Marne, and there now began a series of attempted flanking movements across Belgium and the north of France. This is now known as 'The Race for the Sea' but at the time it was called 'The March to Calais' by the popular press.[18] Calais, it was feared, if captured would become the launching point for an invasion.

Once the Germans seized Calais, claimed the *Daily Mail*'s correspondents, mines would be strewn across the Channel, which would create a protected corridor for the Germans to ferry their invasion fleet to Dover.[19] Additionally, the *Daily Mail* and *The Spectator* both reported that the new German campaign route was 'Antwerp-Calais-Dover-London . . . the course of Great Britain's impending doom'.[20]

For the navy, the loss of Antwerp and the Belgian coast to Germany would be a disaster. The Germans assigned a force of five divisions of mostly reserve forces and 173 guns to its capture, and began a bombardment of the outer south-eastern forts on 28 September. Fearing the city's loss, and its use as another potential invasion route and warship base, First Lord of the Admiralty Winston Churchill was sent by the Cabinet to Antwerp to report on the situation, and some British troops intended for the Western Front were despatched to assist the Belgians.

Churchill was in his element. He left London on his personal train at 0300 on 3 October promising Asquith a report as soon as possible. With his

---

* German army Chief of the Great General Staff Moltke informed the Imperial Navy that 'he desired no action in the Channel preferring instead to mop up . . . the Expeditionary Force along with the French army' (Herwig, *Luxury Fleet*, p 148).

naval secretary, Rear Admiral Horace Hood, at his side, he spent three nights within the fortifications. On 4 October, Churchill reported that Belgian resistance was weakening with morale low. It was clear that the city was unlikely to hold out much longer. It was now that Churchill persuaded his colleagues that he should send his newly formed Naval Division into the breach.

In addition, in an act of more than usual ambition, he telegraphed Prime Minister Asquith on 5 October to say that he wanted to resign his post, take the rank of Major-General and command the troops in Antwerp himself. It was rash and Asquith could hardly control his mirth in declining the offer. But the Royal Naval Division,* comprising mainly of RNVR volunteers with little equipment over and above rifles and pistols, leavened with a force of Royal Marines, was nonetheless sent on 4 and 5 October, with German troops already amongst the outer forts of the city.

It was a disaster. The Naval Division went into action, arriving on the outskirts of the city in the small hours of the 6 October. In the early evening of the 8th, orders were given for them to retire from the city. In the confusion of the withdrawal most of the 1st Brigade, the Hawke, Benbow and Collingwood Battalions – 1,500 men in total – crossed the Dutch frontier and were interned at Groningen for the rest of the war; a further 1,000 men were captured by the Germans. Only the Drake Battalion got away, having left the city early. Amongst those who did escape was the poet Rupert Brooke who had signed up to the RNVR only weeks earlier. On 10 October the city surrendered.

Many observers were critical of Churchill for throwing away naval resources and, to a point, of Admiral Hood for not effecting some form of restraint whilst with him in the war zone. Vice Admiral Sir David Beatty, for example, thought that Hood had proved 'unable to control Churchill'. He went on, 'WC must be mad if he thinks he could relieve one of the most modern fortresses by putting 8,000 half trained troops into it',[21] and Captain Herbert Richmond, Assistant Director of the Operations Division at the Admiralty, confided to his diary 'the First Lord is sending his army there; I don't mind him sending his untrained two-penny rabble but I do strongly object to 2,000 invaluable Marines being sent to be locked up in a fortress and become prisoners of war if the place is taken . . . it is a tragedy that the navy should be in such lunatic hands at this time'.[22] Antwerp damaged Churchill; the action came to be seen as evidence of his lack of judgement and impulsiveness. Asquith, on hearing of it from his son Arthur (who had

---

* Churchill had first conceived the idea of a Naval Brigade in 1913, as noted in Chapter 4, when he suggested he could raise an army of 20,000 men from 'surplus reservists'.

joined the RNVR), wrote of 'the wicked folly of it all'.²³

The Times' Repington fuelled the invasion fire after the fall of Antwerp;

> We must expect to be attacked at home, and must not rest under any comforting illusions that we shall not be assailed. As an attack upon us can have no serious object unless the intention is to land an expedition in England for the purpose of compelling us to sign a disastrous peace, it is well that we should look the situation calmly in the face, and reckon up not only Germany's power to do us harm, but also our power of resistance and means for improving it.²⁴

The newspaper went on to suggest 'the necessity of an able commander to take command of defensive operation as Lord Kitchener will have enough to do at the War Office. The German fleet is intact and is expected to emerge and engage our fleet, while an expeditionary force starts from somewhere, perhaps Antwerp, and slips through.'²⁵ But others saw the threat of coastal raids differently, perhaps as a trap for the navy. 'A raid, intended to cause panic, or to inflict local damage, or as a trap to draw our fleets on to a minefield, cannot, even now, be dismissed as out of the question.'²⁶

Meanwhile, a subcommittee of the CID under Herbert Samuel, President of the Board of Trade, considered how to stop an invading army. It recommended a scorched earth policy on British soil. All transportation in the vicinity of an enemy landing, including motor vehicles, bicycles, horses and boats, was to be evacuated or destroyed to prevent their seizure by the enemy. Roads, bridges, railways, power stations, telegraph stations, sluices, petrol stockpiles and piers were suggested for demolition. Cattle would be slaughtered and granaries burned.²⁷ To many, it all seemed very draconian.*

Although quite who would defend the country, other than the navy, was now a moot point. The BEF had been decimated in battle. Kitchener had been forced to send the two retained divisions of the Expeditionary Force, and then a further twenty-two TF battalions as well. By mid-October, only four battalions of trained regulars were still stationed in Britain. They would have stood little chance of arresting an invading force, as Hankey estimated that the Germans had 289 ships that could transport troops, totalling upwards of one million gross tonnes. He calculated that if every ship was employed, the Germans could move six army corps, consisting of roughly 300,000 men. The CID concluded the Germans would not employ such a force but did raise the pre-war estimate of a maximum invasion force from 70,000 to 135–160,000 men.²⁸

---

* The precautions strangely echo those of 1803, see Chapter 1.

Moreover, the Grand Fleet had retreated, as a result of the scandalous lack of preparation at its Scapa Flow base. On 1 September, a U-boat had been spotted in the anchorage. On 17 October, Admiral Stanley Colville, Vice Admiral Commanding Orkneys and Shetland, reported another German U-boat inside Scapa Flow; two destroyers claimed to have been attacked, without result, and a vigorous hunt had produced no perpetrator.

Captain Charles John Wintour was Captain (D) of the 4th Destroyer Flotilla (4DF) in HMS *Swift*. His ships had been the first to arrive at Scapa Flow on 30 July 1914. By October, he thought that the fleet at Scapa was suffering from near-hysteria over U-boats. Everyone was 'rattled over their [German] submarines. No one can talk of anything else. If two men, whether officers or ships' cooks, get together, the one topic of conversation is "submarines". I have suggested that the word be tabooed except on the bridge, or it will be fatal to morale.'[29]

Amongst those who were 'rattled' was Grand Fleet Commander-in-Chief Admiral John Jellicoe. He had already asked for defensive nets and guns to be put in hand for Scapa, but these had not been forthcoming. Now extremely concerned about the safety of his fleet, the day following the alleged U-boat incursion he began to move to new anchorages, primarily Lough Swilly on the north coast of Ireland, to escape the submarine threat. The North Sea was empty of Royal Navy capital ships. On 19 October, 4DF joined the general exodus. 'Scapa is abandoned as a base,' wrote Wintour.[30]

Vice Admiral David Beatty, commanding the Grand Fleet's battlecruisers, was extremely disturbed by the position that the great ships found themselves in. He had been Churchill's naval secretary and the two men respected each other. Thus, Beatty felt emboldened to bypass the chain of command and write to Churchill directly. On 10 October, he sent a missive by hand of officer, from his flagship HMS *Lion*, then at anchor at the Isle of Mull.

'We have no place to lay our heads', Beatty wrote.

> We are at Loch [blanked out] Isle of Mull. My picket boats are at the entrance, the nets are out and the men are at the guns waiting for coal which has run low ... At present we feel that we are working up for a catastrophe of a very large character ... the menace of mines and submarines is proving larger every day and adequate means to meet or combat them are not forthcoming ... we are gradually being pushed out of the North Sea.

This was effecting the efficiency of the fleet; 'We have no base where we can, with any degree of safety, lie for coaling, replenishing, and refitting and repairing'.[31]

Beatty pleaded with Churchill to redress the situation;

> At Portsmouth, Devonport, Clyde, Pembroke and Queenstown we have local defence flotillas; if others are not forthcoming, these should be robbed to supply the same at Cromarty, Rosyth and Scapa ... with the aid of submarine nets, torpedo nets, piles and concrete blocks, sunken ships, wire hawsers, booms and mines, as passive defence supported by well-placed guns manned by trained artillerymen ... harbours defended thus would free the coastal forces to be out in positions were they can cut off minelayers and locate submarines at a distance, instead of being tied to protect a base which should be quite capable of protecting itself.[32]

He was also worried about an invasion.

> Can I sum up the situation as it appears to me? We are driven out of the North Sea because of the menace of enemy submarines and mines ... but aren't we giving up too much by evacuating the North Sea and permitting their fast craft to lay mines and cut up our patrols *ad lib*, and if they think it desirable, cause a panic by rushing 10,000 men

Saving the Crew of Audacious, a painting by W Wyllie, depicting her as she sinks after striking a mine, 27 October 1914. There are two incorrect features on this artwork. Firstly, *Audacious* is shown with her gun tompions in place, though she was out on a gunnery exercise when she hit the mine. Second, she still has her jack staff in place (at the bow) but this was removed on the outbreak of war. (National Maritime Museum PW1831)

across [note Balfour's number again], which under the circumstances would be quite possible.³³

Beatty was fed up with waiting for others, presumably the War Office, to provide the necessary defences; given the right materials, they would do it themselves. 'You might be told that this idea of making the entrances secure is chimerical. This is not so. I guarantee that if the fleet was instructed to defend the entrances of the ports named, and was provided with material, they could and would [do it].'³⁴

In a final postscript, Beatty proved that spy mania was not confined to the press and general public; 'if we ever use Scapa again, I trust that some steps will be taken to deal with the spies that exist there, which are a serious danger. Martial law of a fortress is the best and only real method.'³⁵

Even this flight to safety and away from Scapa Flow was not without misadventure. As part of the dispersals, the 2nd Battle Squadron had been despatched to Loch na Keal on the Isle of Mull. From here the squadron departed for gunnery practice off Tory Island, Ireland, on the morning of 27 October when the new 13.5in-gunned battleship HMS *Audacious* (1912) struck a mine at 0845, one laid a few days earlier by the German auxiliary minelayer SS *Berlin*. Her captain, Cecil Dampier, thinking that his ship had been torpedoed, hoisted the submarine warning; in accordance with instructions the other battleships left the area, leaving the smaller vessels behind to provide assistance. She sank, exploding in the process, at 2100. A major unit had been lost without firing a shot.

In order to obtain the necessary floating dock (later known as AFD5 and which Jellicoe himself had initiated when Controller of the Navy) the CinC had one towed from Portsmouth to Invergordon in the Cromarty Firth. Otherwise, the fleet would have had no nearer dockyard than Chatham. And it took months before Scapa was even adequately protected. Churchill had to authorise a special force of Royal Marines to do so. The work was completed in early 1915. Blockships were placed across the narrower channels; boom defence drifters marshalled the larger ones, and various batteries of 4in and 6in gun emplacements commanded the entrances, manned by a mixture of marines and the volunteer Orkney Royal Garrison Artillery.

The North Sea Problem

When war came, the Admiralty had concerns that the Germans would immediately lay mines in the shipping lanes of the North Sea to disrupt British trade, despite the fact that the mining of 'automatic contact mines off the coast and ports of the enemy, with the sole object of intercepting commercial shipping' had been forbidden under Convention VIII relative to the Laying of Automatic Submarine Contact Mines of the Hague Treaty of 18 October 1907, article two.

Their concerns were justified. The converted passenger ferry *Königin Luise* had been requisitioned by the *Kaiserliche Marine* on 3 August 1914 to serve as an auxiliary minelayer. Immediately on the declaration of war she sailed from Emden carrying 200 mines to sow close to the major trade artery of the Thames Estuary. A perfunctory attempt at disguise had been made with a coat of paint, which was applied overnight, giving an impression of a Harwich–Hook of Holland ferry of the Great Eastern Railway Company.*

Captain Cecil H Fox of HMS *Amphion*, depicted in one of the 240 'Cinderella' stamps issued in 1915 by the Lord Roberts Memorial Fund for Disabled Soldiers and Sailors. (Creative Commons)

Whilst in the act of mining, the German was spotted by a trawler, and a radioed warning message reached Harwich about the same time that *Königin Luise* observed the patrolling British destroyers of the 3rd Destroyer Flotilla. At 1030 she sheared off to the north to try to escape them, desperately unloading her mines as she went. But this took her nearer to the scout cruiser HMS *Amphion* (1911) and her flotilla of 'L'-class destroyers.

Amphion's commander, Captain Fox, having signalled 'good hunting' to his brood, took up the chase. Pursued by *Lance* and *Landrail*, *Königin Luise* was brought to action around 1100; when *Lance* fired the opening shell from one of her 4in guns it was the first British shot of the war. As *Linnet* and *Lark* came up, the German was steaming at a much-reduced speed. Shells were pumped into her, the disengaged gun crews crowding the engaged side and cheering every shot. At 1215, the enemy's crew began to abandon ship, although the engines continued to run and she slowly maintained her progress until turning on her side and sinking.

---

* The usual paintwork of the company's steamers consisted of black hulls with a yellow band; white uppers with brown houses; and funnels of buff with black tops.

The 'L'-class destroyer HMS *Lark* (1913), in a painting by W J Sutton. She took part in the sinking of the German minelayer on 5 August and later in both the Battles of Heligoland Bight and Dogger Bank. (Author's collection)

Out of the minelayer's complement of 140 men, forty-three were picked up, twenty of whom were taken into *Amphion*. The destroyers stayed out all night and on the following morning began to return to Harwich. Fox thought that he knew where the mines had been dropped and steered some seven miles away from the spot. But he miscalculated. At 0635, *Amphion* struck one of the eggs laid the previous day by *Königin Luise*. There was a violent explosion under the fore bridge and every man on the foredeck was killed, as were eighteen of the rescued German prisoners. Her keel was cracked and the fore of the ship was on fire. HMS *Linnet* attempted to tow her to safety but a deep rent appeared across her deck and curved upwards. It was clear than *Amphion* was finished. Fox and his bridge team were badly burnt on the hands and face but managed to organise a calm abandonment. She settled by the head, her sides turning black from the raging internal fires, but within 15 minutes the accompanying destroyers had taken the survivors aboard.

As the fires reached the magazine, *Amphion* exploded; quantities of wreckage shot into the air and fell on the destroyers, injuring some sailors; a shell landed on *Lark*, killing two ratings and one of the German survivors, and in *Linnet* a gunner was severely injured when struck by a flying hatch cover. In total 147 British sailors and one officer, Staff Paymaster Joseph Gedge* who had been in the coding room below the bridge, lost their lives.

---

* Gedge, a Freemason, was the first British officer in either service to be killed in the war. In 1929 the Royal Navy instituted the Gedge Medal, the first medal for professional merit inaugurated for the paymaster branch of the Royal Navy. Gedge was further commemorated when his old school, St John's, Leatherhead, named a science block in his memory, paid for by a fund that was supported by, amongst other, Admiral Jellicoe.

HMS *Amphion* became the first Royal Navy warship to be sunk in the war and the first ever to be sunk by a contact mine. Hubris and Nemesis had already struck and the war was only one day old.

British opinion was outraged by the incident. Rather than send her fleet out to do battle, the German policy seemed to be to deploy minelayers and U-boats into the North Sea to wreak havoc in international waters. This was strictly against international law, as most recently expressed at the Declaration of London in 1909. As the navy's Official History later noted 'such was the immediate success of the policy of mining in international waters which Germany had chosen to adopt. The indications were that the minefield had been laid between 3 degrees E long and the Suffolk coast – that is, right in the fairway – regardless of neutrals and of all the time-honoured customs of the sea. It was the first opening of our eyes to the kind of enemy we had to deal with; and yet so inhuman did the practice appear in the eyes of our seamen that as yet there was no thought of retaliation in kind.'[36] The *Daily Mail* of 6 August called the mining 'a monstrous crime against the laws of nations'.

Eight days after the sinking, minesweeping trawlers from Harwich had swept and buoyed a clear channel inshore of this field. But all through September and October, minelayers of the Royal Navy placed minefields along the east coast to protect the entrances to ports and estuaries; while the Germans dropped mines in the same areas to attempt to sink British ships as they left harbour. In no time a confused mass of minefields littered the eastern coast of England. A channel was swept inshore with exits and entrances to the sea beyond, which were kept clear by constant sweeping. This channel was extended over the next months, in the face of repeated mining of the east coast ports, into a fairway known as the 'War Channel'. This was a marked traffic lane, which eventually extended from Dover to the Firth of Forth, and was swept daily for mines, mainly by trawlers based at the Nore, Harwich, Lowestoft, the Humber, the Tyne and Granton. Soon the war channel was being swept each day by up to eighty minesweeping trawlers and patrolled at night by drifters, often armed with nothing but the White Ensign, to deter minelayers. Moreover, the Germans indiscriminately sowed floating mines in open water and mines whose moorings had parted added to the chaos at sea.

The indiscriminate and prolific mining of the North Sea gave the Admiralty the excuse it needed to close down the opportunities for transit through it. This was foremost an attempt to ensure that merchant vessels passing through the North Sea were not carrying 'contraband' goods. Accordingly, on 2 November 1914, the British government declared the North Sea a prohibited area. All neutrals were warned that unless their ships complied with the regular routes laid down by the Admiralty (and also generally submitted to being searched for goods intended to aid the enemy – contraband – as part of this process) they sailed at their own risk. Only in the designated swept channels would they be safe, and these were only known to the navy.

As *The Spectator* magazine put it;

> All merchant ships are warned of the danger they will run if they enter the North Sea – now a mined area – except under Admiralty directions. This 'closed area' is not, of course, closed in the literal sense. Neutral ships have a right to enter it. But they are advised not to do so without accepting the highest degree of safety that the British Navy can guarantee them. For this purpose, the military area is defined as being bounded on the north by a line drawn from the northern point of the Hebrides, through the Faroe Islands, to Iceland. Ships entering the North Sea, should come by the Straits of Dover. Then they will be given sailing directions so that they can avoid the minefields.[37]

But there was a second consideration too. For fear of invasion drove a surprising set of orders to naval officers, also issued on 2 November. 'The Commanding Officers of His Majesty's Ships meeting with enemy transports, which there is a reason to believe are carrying troops to British Territory, are enjoined to sink them at once by torpedo or gun fire . . . No parley with, or surrender by, a transport on the high seas is possible.' Such a 'sink on sight' instruction was unprecedented. It might even be construed as a war crime under Hague Convention rules. The instructions went on to state that 'officers will be held responsible that the enemy gains no advantage by any exercise of humanity'. The Admiralty later distributed a memorandum justifying their orders which alleged that there had been reports of fake surrenders by the German Army on the Continent and also asserted as fact that the German naval signal for 'Close to Torpedo Range' was said to be a white flag.[38]

Churchill's reasons for the issue of such a signal are not clear, but pressure from Kitchener was probably the reason. At Cabinet on 21 October, the Secretary for War had insisted that the Admiralty should take more specific precautions against a German landing. Churchill had retorted that the fleet's role was to strike and destroy the enemy's High Seas Fleet, but Kitchener was not mollified.[39]

The panic was further increased when it was reported that tides on Britain's east coast would best suit a German landing on either 17 November

Two images of HMS *Hood* (1891), four 13.5in, ten 6in, sunk as a blockship at Portland in 1914. (Author's collection)

or 20 November. Under pressure, Jellicoe returned the Grand Fleet to the North Sea to be on hand, if still rather far away in Scapa. The level of tension amongst ordinary citizens reached a new height around this time. On 19 November, Georgina Lee, separated from her baby son to attend to her ailing father in Wales, wrote in her diary 'I have been anxious about a possible invasion of England by the Germans while I was away. I would then not be able to get back to you in London because of the railway being taken over for moving of troops.'[40]

CID studies had averred that the Germans would try to seize a British port to disembark their invasion force and it had become the practice to enforce a 'lights out' policy in coastal towns from September. Now the navy commenced a programme of preparing major and minor ports for demolition, should a landing occur, and blockships were sunk in harbour entrances, leaving only limited navigation and forcing any potential intruder into clearly defined and restricted passages.

Amongst those vessels given up as blockships was HMS *Hood* (1891, a modified *Royal Sovereign*-class pre-dreadnought battleship which was scuttled in Portland harbour to block the Southern Ship Channel, a potential access route for U-boats or for torpedoes fired from outside the harbour. Another was SS *Montrose* (1905), famous for being the ship on which Dr Crippen and his inamorata were captured in 1910, now used as a blockship at Dover. Admiralty figures show that forty-nine civilian vessels were purchased for use as blockships at a cost of £424,249.[41]

Other harbours were protected by booms. A typical defensive boom was a series of 40ft-long timber baulks chained together and stretched across a harbour or river mouth to deny access to enemy surface craft. When any friendly vessel needed to pass through, the attending Boom Defence Vessel (BDV) had to draw the obstruction aside and, after passage, replace it in position. It was heavy, repetitive and hard work, usually conducted by pairs or more of boom vessels. Hired trawlers often served in this role. Many of these vessels did not have commissioned status and operated under the Red Ensign. Other were fitted with armament in their dual function of protecting the fleet anchorages.*

There also began a redistribution of naval resources to the east coast. Old pre-dreadnought battleships and aging cruisers were allocated one to a port as guard ships. The wartime career of the pre-dreadnought battleship HMS *Illustrious* (1896) gives an indication of how these guard ships were deployed and used. When war was declared she was placed in full commission to take up guard-ship duty at Loch Ewe on 23 August 1914, transferring to Loch Na Keal on 17 October, to the Tyne in November 1914, and to Grimsby on the Humber in December 1914. She remained on guard-ship duty on the Humber until November 1915, when she paid off to be used as a disarmed harbour ship and then an ammunition storeship (see also Appendix 11). Also – much against Jellicoe's wishes – half a flotilla of Grand Fleet destroyers was redeployed for coastal defence. But still there were insufficient forces to be strong everywhere, every time. As a result, in the event of invasion, the Admiralty exhorted the coastal flotillas and the antiquated

---

* By the end of the war, there were 125 BDVs in use at Scapa Flow alone.

battleships to 'proceed without further orders to attack the raiding force regardless of its strength'.[42] Their presumed sacrifice would buy time for the Grand Fleet to arrive.

Fortifications

At the same time as the navy was deploying more resources, a trench network began to appear around Britain's coast, especially in Kent and the Humber. Kitchener ordered the mobilisation of another 300,000 largely untrained men and ancient artillery pieces were sent to those areas without an existing RGA unit. Old Martello towers were taken back into use as static defences and the first pill boxes sprang up like dragons' teeth.

The area around Maidstone, Kent, was especially well entrenched, with anti-invasion lines stretching eventually between Detling to the Swale and Sheppey crossing, then along the north coast and high ground of Sheppey from Sheerness to Shellness. Barbed wire, buried strongpoints and machine-gun positions were all incorporated.

Lines of defensive works were established at likely invasion points in Norfolk, Essex and North Kent and bicycle battalions were created to provide a mobile force capable of reacting quickly. The areas between London and the coast were given fixed defensive lines of trenches with gun positions. To the north and east of the city were three lines, including the Maidstone-Swale Line where eight miles of anti-invasion trenches were dug by Royal Engineers.

'For King and Country', a 1914 postcard with the British Lion and its navy defending the Kent coast. (Author's collection)

During the invasion scares of the first decade of the twentieth century, Harwich was considered to be a prime target for attack. The Eastern District Defence Scheme, as amended in 1904, envisaged that Harwich would be the most important fortress on the east coast due to its closeness to the Continental ports,* which rendered it liable to naval attacks, or an assault with the object of seizing Parkeston Quay for use as a disembarkation place for an invading army. It was thought that the most likely form of incident would be a naval demonstration in support of landings elsewhere on the coast, with a view to capturing its fortress from the rear. But a raid on Harwich in August 1914 would have met little armed resistance. Territorial RGA gunners were manning the fort and a company of soldiers was sent from Colchester pending the arrival of the Essex Infantry Brigade (TF) who were in annual camp at Clacton and had suddenly to pack up and march to the port. There they were set to making trenches and redoubts. Additionally, the army began to commandeer houses, turning out the owners, and requisitioning barbed wire from stores and farms. Buildings were demolished to clear firing lines, or loopholed for rifles. Outposts were established and it is said in Harwich that some of the first shots of the war were fired by these Territorials, who mistook some cows for Germans.

A recruiting poster for a bicycle battalion. Cycle-mounted troops allowed a faster response to an enemy landing than on foot. (Author's collection)

Further north, on the Humber, two large forts (Haile Sand and Bull Sand) were called for in 1914, to protect the sea entrance to the estuary. They were to be 59ft above the water with a diameter of 82ft and accommodation for up to 200 soldiers and 6in guns. Started in May 1915, they took more than four years to build, and construction was not finished until December 1919, rather too late.

---

* Harwich is 126 miles by sea from the Hook of Holland and 296 miles from Wilhelmshaven.

As the campaign on the Western Front degenerated into trench warfare, there was an urgent need for RGA gunners to be sent there. WO Instruction No 248 of October 1914 ordered that the TF coastal gunners were now considered well enough trained to take over many of the duties in the coastal defences, releasing regular RGA gunners for service in the field.

Up and down the eastern coastline, there was a rush to fortify and entrench. And the coastal defences were manned by the part-time volunteers.

DORA

It has been noted above that government was able to extinguish street lights and take over citizens' land or buildings without due process. How was this possible? The answer is DORA – the Defence of the Realm Act, the biggest curtailment of civil liberties since the days of Oliver Cromwell's military dictatorship. DORA authorised the promulgation by the Privy Council of hundreds of defence regulations covering most facets of economic and social life on the Home Front.

The legislation was first enacted on 8 August 1914, and it gave the government wide-ranging powers during the war, including the ability to requisition buildings or land needed for the war effort,* and to make regulations creating criminal offences. Authoritarian, not to say dictatorial in nature, the act introduced Britain to the notion of the state-organised society and enabled the government to quash anything 'calculated to jeopardise the success of the operations of any of His Majesty's forces or assist the enemy'. The armed services were now handed sweeping powers, many of which were quickly enforced due to invasion anxiety. Section 1(c) of the August legislation, for example, empowered the armed services to 'prevent the spread of false reports' that could harm the war effort. The act allowed the military and naval authorities to requisition all buildings and supplies for defence, order their evacuation or destruction if necessary, as well as to use any public and private land for the construction of fortifications. In reporting these new powers, the *Daily Mail* described them as 'Defence Against Invasion'.[45] Britain became largely governed by a civil-military *junta* with little parliamentary involvement.

As well as censorship of press and mails, the act and its successors, particularly the DORA consolidation legislation of November 1914 (see Appendix 12), made it an offence to, *inter alia*:

---

* The government also awarded itself the power to pay only minimal compensation to property owners whose assets were so requisitioned on an ex gratia rather than an ex lege basis.

- talk about naval or military matters in public places
- fly kites
- whistle for a cab
- spread rumours about military matters
- buy binoculars
- ring church bells
- trespass on railway lines or bridges
- melt down gold or silver
- use invisible ink when writing abroad
- buy brandy or whisky in a railway refreshment room
- light bonfires or fireworks
- give bread to horses or chickens

Additionally, the act gave government the power to:

- take over any factory or workshop
- try any civilian breaking these laws
- take over any land it wanted to

And under DORA section 14b, the right to detain people of enemy origin as expedient.

The government introduced British Summer Time under DORA in May 1916, to give more daylight for additional work, especially in agriculture. Opening hours in pubs were cut and beer was watered down. Chancellor of the Exchequer Lloyd George had a particular animus against alcohol consumption. He persuaded King George V to abstain from alcohol for the duration as an example to the public; and in October 1915 he forced through under DORA laws a 'no treating order' which forbade the buying of rounds in a pub or bar. A drink could only be supplied to the person paying for it. It became illegal to ask 'what's yours' in the name of (allegedly) reducing alcohol consumption, with such an invitation punishable by six months in prison.

Continuing the attack on booze, Atkinson and Son's brewery in Carlisle (where there were ammunition manufactories) was purchased by the state's Liquor Control Board, later the Carlisle and District State Management Scheme, in 1916. The government wanted to control drunkenness so that workers were not impaired by drink and could labour more effectively, and Atkinsons was to be the guinea pig for state beer ownership. The only beer to be served in the area was that brewed by this local, government-owned brewery and it was made at a lower level of alcohol than the norm. The brewery was not sold by the government until 1971!

Bread was also regulated; fines were issued for making white flour instead of wholewheat and for allowing rats to invade wheat stores. DORA was used to control an assumed drug-taking problem. The use of morphine and opium was widespread among the wealthier classes by 1914 and narcotics could be purchased over the counter at any pharmacy. Private use of morphia, supplied to front-line troops for pain relief, fuelled the problem amongst serving men. Eventually, on 28 July 1916, the government used DORA regulation 40b to forbid the possession of opium or cocaine by any but authorised persons.

DORA had an immediate and particularly deleterious effect on the lives of the ordinary citizens in port and naval base towns such as Dover

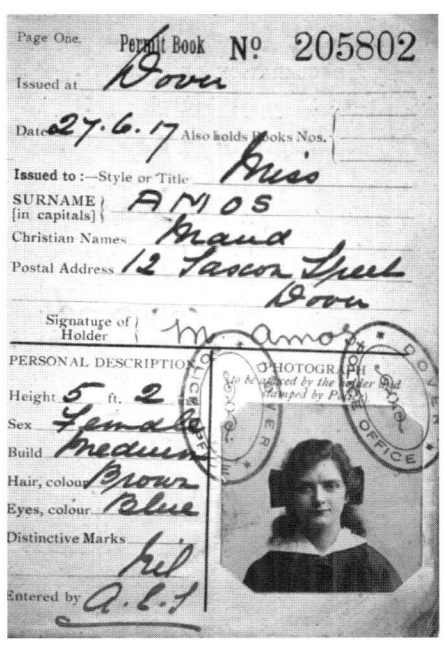

A Dover resident's pass (dated 1917), used to gain both entry and exit of the town.
(Courtesy of Dover Museum and Bronze Age Boat Gallery)

and Harwich. Dover town was immediately declared an armed camp and the Borough of Dover, became part of Dover Fortress. This meant that the military was in charge but, although public elections were suspended, councillors continued in office. Mayor Edwin Farley was re-elected by his

The harbour at Dover in wartime. It demonstrates the high level of congestion which made entry and exit difficult for the Dover Patrol.
(Courtesy of Dover Museum and Bronze Age Boat Gallery)

colleagues in November 1914, 1915, 1916, 1917 and 1918! Unlike some Dover citizens, Farley never left the town during the war. An army garrison of 10,000 men was maintained, with its HQ at the castle and from 1916 the Municipal Borough of Dover and much of the Rural District of Dover was designated a Special Military Area; residents were required to show an identity card/pass to enter the town and armed checkpoints were established at all routes of entry and exit.

Residents' lives changed immediately and completely. Many private and public buildings were taken over by the armed forces for the duration. The navy co-opted the waterfront. The beautiful Georgian and Regency villas off Marine Parade became offices for the three successive Dover Patrol admirals (no 42), Admiralty offices (nos. 40 and 18) and Paymaster's department (no 16). Sidney Terrace, equally architecturally distinguished, housed the 6th Destroyer Flotilla's HQ and officers' quarters, whilst East Cliff gave shelter to HM Naval Depot (no 23), the office of the Harbour Superintendent (no 22), the supply office and the RNAS officers' quarters (nos 9&10). Likewise, the rowing club and the Admiralty, Prince of Wales and Promenade piers became exclusive naval properties. Ratings were put into Oil Mill Barracks (a 1914 conversion). All the elementary schools in the town were taken up for military use. A central messing area was created in the sports grounds of Dover College and the isolation and smallpox hospitals became military-only. Dover resembled nothing less than a

The Great Eastern Hotel, Harwich, pictured before the war.
(photo; David Whittle/Harwich Society)

gigantic armed forces depot. On the establishment of the military regime, public entertainment and public houses were severely curtailed. Pubs closed at 2100 and servicemen were not allowed to enter them before 1700. Theatres and shows had to end by 2200.

A similar situation obtained at Harwich. Harwich became a garrison town; after war was declared residents needed passes to travel in and out of the town, or to get to their work or homes. Called a 'Defence of the Realm Permit Book' this allowed access into the 'Harwich Special Military Area'. No one was permitted to leave this area after 1800. Out-of-town visitors needed passes and had to register at the police station. Thousands of sailors and soldiers thronged the streets and the locals were prohibited from visiting the seafront. Pubs (there were sixty) had to close at 2100 and street lighting was turned off; domestic lights had to be obscured by 1900. The Royal Navy took over the harbour and Parkeston Quay and the Great Eastern Hotel, both of which were owned by the Great Eastern Railway (GER), the latter immediately becoming the garrison hospital.* A harbour boom was put in place.

Not only did the GER lose its hotel and quay, but some of its ships were also taken up by the navy too. The Admiralty requisitioned eight of the Great Eastern Railway's Harwich-based vessels. Among them were the cargo ships, *Clacton* and *Newmarket*, which were turned into minesweepers while the passenger ships *Munich* (renamed the *St Denis*) and *St Petersburg* (renamed *Archangel*) became hospital ships.

Of course, Britain still needed to import goods to keep both the Western and Home Fronts supplied and Harwich continued to operate as a commercial port as well as a naval one. Harwich's quays were used as an offloading point for large quantities of merchant shipping, bringing in supplies which had been sanctioned by officialdom, and this was the case until the Admiralty declared the town a 'closed port' in May 1916. Its residents became used to the daily wail of ships' sirens that summoned officers and men back to their vessels and the next mission at sea. Every cruiser in harbour, following the flagship's lead, sounded off three times, each for three minutes.

Further north, from July 1916, the whole of the Highlands of Scotland north of Inverness was designated a Special Military Area because of its naval importance, with bases and harbours all around the coast in constant use by elements of the Grand Fleet. To limit the ability of spies to penetrate or move around the area, local passes were produced and had to be shown at any military or police request, especially at railway station and ports. Anyone

---

* Additionally, 'The Grange', a large house on Hall Lane was requisitioned as a hospital, as was 'The Cliff Hall' on Marine Parade. There was also an isolation hospital at Dovercourt.

coming into the Highlands from the south could apply for a pass at their nearest police station. Permits were also issued, both for non-residents and residents, for permission to indulge in various restricted activities such as sketching or taking pictures in a prohibited or restricted area.

DORA was used in tandem with another Act of Parliament rushed through at the beginning of the war, the Aliens Restriction Act of 5 August 1914, which gave government *carte blanche* to impose constraints on aliens and make such provisions as appeared to be necessary putting such restrictions into effect. These included specifying where aliens might live and where they could travel.

DORA was far from popular; but as it allowed for no criticism through censorship and the repression of dissent, most people had to grin and bear it. And still no invasion came.

The Police

The police were allocated a key role in Home Defence and in the enforcement of DORA regulations. They also had particular duties in the organisation of any evacuation that might be required from coastal areas. But they were numerically too few to deal with such responsibilities. The answer was the recruitment, under DORA powers, of special constables. Historically, special constables were recruited at times of civil disturbance and had specific powers to assist in the keeping of the peace, and for a limited period only. But with the threat of invasion looming, these new specials were assigned two roles. Firstly, to assist the chief constable and the regular police; but secondly, they were to support the lord lieutenant and the Central Emergency Committee in the evacuation of the county in the event of invasion.

Once sworn in, specials were issued with a warrant card, armlet and truncheon and were enrolled from those men who were too old or unfit for military service. They did not have uniforms, only armbands, and were equipped with a length of rope to use as handcuffs. It was 1915 before they were issued with torches. They were liable to service for a minimum of three hours out of every 24 if required, and to give services free of charge.

One such and probably typical 'special' in Essex was Herbert Gripper, owner of two ironmongery shops near Chelmsford, a town councillor, keen golfer, and instrumental in building the public baths and golf course. He commanded a small team which patrolled locally, looking for spies, strange behaviour and any sign of treachery or treason, as well as petty crime. Less typical was a special constable seen pounding the streets of Hampstead in North London, for in the autumn of 1914, the composer Edward Elgar joined the force.

A group of Hertfordshire special constables in 1914, proudly sporting their brassards. (Photo: Herts Past Policing)

The number of specials grew rapidly. For example, in Southend there were 120 men in the special constabulary in 1914, and 571 in 1915.[44] And in Southwold, Suffolk, Town Clerk Ernest Cooper swore in thirty special constables on 25 November 1914.[45] Nonetheless, it was indeed a thin blue line.

6
The Auxiliaries, 1914

Volunteerism was a significant factor in the temperament of the British public of the time, and it has been noted above with regard to the TF, RGA and RNVR and the multitude of quasi-militias. The Royal Navy too became heavily dependent on amateur sailors as volunteers for, at the start of the conflict, it had neither enough men or ships to defend the British coast and exercise command of the sea. Small vessels, destroyers, light cruisers and minesweepers, were in short supply and the navy list contained far too few for the war that had broken upon the world. In particular, there was little or no provision for minesweepers and nowhere near enough patrol vessels to deal with the previously little-regarded menace of the torpedo-armed submarine. Every harbour, estuary, creek and bay potentially could shelter an enemy, and patrol of them was impossible with the resources of the regular navy, especially as so much of it was with the Grand Fleet at Scapa Flow.

To make good the lack, the navy turned to civilian craft and their crews and owners. Anything that could float, and some craft that proved they couldn't, was fair game to be pressed into naval service, under the generic title of 'Naval Auxiliaries'. By far the most numerous were converted fishing vessels – steam trawlers and drifters.

The Fishing Boats

Small, hardy, used to long voyages at sea and equipped with net-handling equipment which could easily be converted into minesweeping use, trawlers had been recognised from around 1910 as a potential reserve for naval purposes – although the number required had been vastly underestimated. Vessels were available, Britain was after all a fishing nation. What about men?

The Royal Naval Reserve (RNR) was created by the Naval Reserve Act of 1859, itself a product of the invasion scare of the same year. For one month a year, merchant sailors and fishermen were given gunnery training on drill ships stationed around the coast. When war was declared they were liable to be drafted to the fleet or reserve ships. By the turn of the twentieth century, membership was drawn from professional officers and ratings of the mercantile marine, the fishing fleet and ex-naval ratings.

In 1910, it was decided to expand the naval reserve through the creation of a special reserve for fishermen, the Royal Naval Reserve – Trawler Section. The first skipper to join the RNT(T) signed on in Aberdeen on 3 February 1911 and approval was given to recruit 1,278 ranks and ratings to man 142 trawlers.[1] By April 1912, forty-two were ready; Commander Reginald Plunkett RN noted that 'in war we shall have 140 trawlers available [for minesweeping]'.[2] This proved to be a marvellously insufficient estimate of the requirements.

Trawlers taken up by the Admiralty in time of need usually came complete with their pre-existing crews. Skippers were given warrant officer rank. Crewmen signed on under a T-124 agreement whereby they consented to serve under Admiralty rules (specifically it bound them to the Naval Discipline Act) in any commissioned vessel but retained certain aspects of their civilian pay and benefits. The ship's complement was supplemented by the addition of a signals rating and/or W/T operator and sometimes a regular navy sub lieutenant or other officer.

Once at war, financial incentives were provided. Wages were based on normal expectations for the fishing trade less 20 per cent; but a sum of £200

The Lowestoft-registered hired drifter *John Mitchell* was taken up in February 1915 and fitted with a 3pdr gun. She was typical of the drifter type, used mainly for anti-submarine net management. She was sunk in November 1917 in a collision off St Alban's Head, Dorset (Author's collection)

Steam drifter *Inverboyndie*, originally from Banff, was built in 1910 and hired in 1916. She was fitted with a 6pdr gun and used as a net vessel. (Author's collection)

was offered to any trawler or auxiliary vessel which sank or captured a U-boat. This was raised to £1,000 in January 1915; at the same time £200 was awarded for damaging a U-boat and a bounty of £5 offered for each mine destroyed.³ Salvage and prize money were sources of additional income for trawler crew. Over 400 trawlers received such payments during the course of the war.

Initially, there was no uniform provided; but concerns grew that men captured in such a state of undress in time of war would be executed as pirates. It was agreed that a badge would be produced which identified the fishermen as part of the Royal Navy. This comprised the letters RNR above the letter 'T' embroidered in red or gold onto a dark blue rectangle all surmounted by a gold and red crown.* For skippers, as Lieutenant Maitland Walter Sabine Boucher, navigating officer of the Lowestoft trawler depot ship and torpedo gunboat *Halcyon* noted, 'enough officers' uniforms could

---

* For a Second Hand. There were many variations, such as the letters embroidered in red on a blue ground and no crown for crewmen.

not be produced at short notice for so many skippers. Each therefore was given an officers' cap and a set of uniform buttons, which he was told to sew onto his best suit.'[4]

Throughout the war, recruitment into the RNR(T) continued. By the end of the conflict, the strength was 39,000 skippers and ratings, about a quarter of whom were employed on minesweeping duties. 'The institution of the Trawler Reserve,' wrote the author of an official post-war report, 'will always rank as a monumental achievement in naval administration and the scheme devised three years before the war stood the test of rapid expansion to a degree far beyond expectation at the time of its inception.'[5]

What of the vessels themselves? In 1909, the Admiralty entered into negotiations with the Board of Agriculture (Fisheries Department), the local Fisheries Boards and trawler owners to agree terms for the hire of their vessels. Those owners who accepted the terms offered had their vessels entered on a 'specialist list' which rendered them subject to release on request by the Admiralty. Lease terms were based on the boat's tonnage. The hull and outfit were valued at £18 for each unit of gross tonnage and at £40 per each unit of nominal horsepower. The value so calculated was depreciated for every full year of the trawler's age. The hire then paid was 12 per cent of this annual valuation. The Admiralty had the right of inspection at any time and the owners could withdraw vessels from the list, subject to notification of the authorities. Vessels needed to be less than ten years old and able to steam 1,000 miles at 8 knots. One hundred and forty-six trawlers were covered by these agreements when war came. For war purposes, trawlers would be formed into groups of six, each unit to be placed under the command of a (previously trained, see above) RN or RNR officer, the latter holding a master's or mate's 'Foreign-Going Certificate'.

The navy's first priority had been to secure hired vessels. But the need for these hardy fishing vessels had outstripped all possible calculation and by mid-1916 it seemed that all those trawlers suitable for naval work had been gathered up. As a partial remedy, the Admiralty built their own vessels, the so-called Admiralty trawlers. Between 18 August and 26 September, a series of conferences and meetings with trawler operators resulted in a recommendation on 26 October for three classes of Admiralty trawler. By the end of the war 453 were commissioned, either purpose-built, purchased from foreign sources or taken as prizes.

The major fishing ports of Hull and Grimsby contributed heavily to the cause; from the two combined, 9,000 fishermen and 829 hired trawlers served.[6] Lowestoft and Aberdeen were also large suppliers with approximately 300 fishing vessels each. In total, 1,372 trawlers were requisitioned by the navy.

The Admiralty had not initially considered the mobilisation of drifters in their agreements with the fishing industry and owners. But the drifter proprietors proved anxious that the navy should take the boats off their hands after they found themselves precluded by the needs of war from their most productive fishing grounds. It was perhaps just as well, for the humble herring drifter was to play a significant role in the Great War at sea as well. Some 1,372 were requisitioned during the conflict and additionally the Admiralty, as with trawlers, built their own to provide sufficient numbers, constructing 318 drifters, both wooden and steel.

Trawlers and drifters were given armament, slowly at first as a shortage of suitable weapons prevented universal arming. Old decommissioned guns from stores or from scrapped vessels were quickly sought out. Large ships demounted their smaller weapons. Anti-submarine and patrol trawlers were given priority for arming but it was not until August 1915 that the hired minesweepers and drifters could be armed in quantity. When obtained by the trawler, guns were mounted aft over the engine casing or in the bow; this latter position was initially less common as it required reinforcement and the building of a gun platform. However, experience demonstrated that the forward siting was much the better and guns became pervasively mounted in the prow of the ship, on the forecastle, commanding a good field of view but somehow looking aesthetically unbalanced. Minesweepers were fitted with 3pdrs and then 6pdrs, patrol and anti-submarine (A/S) trawlers with (mainly) 6pdr and 12pdr weapons (when they became available), as the smaller guns were inadequate to inflict serious damage on a U-boat. Enterprising skippers 'acquired' machine guns and other unofficial armaments.

Not all senior RN commanders were convinced as to the trawlers' utility, or that of their crews. Vice Admiral David Beatty wrote that 'judging from what I have seen and heard of the force of trawlers in northern latitudes in Orkney and Shetland, they are practically valueless because they are undisciplined and uncontrollable. They receive high wages and are always drunk.'[7] Vice Admiral Lewis Bayly, newly appointed to the Coast of Ireland Command in July 1915, wrote of the armed trawlers he commanded 'even as escorts they are of little use . . . I had no idea what poor things the armed trawlers were . . . to catch submarines they are wanting'.[8] Later he noted,

> our method of defence by trawlers [against submarines] does not seem to me to be a serious one, except where they are situated near the coast . . . and in ordinary weather. On the open sea it is doubtful that they are much use; few have W/T and what there is, is weak. Their speed is absurdly slow; their gun is easily seen from a considerable

distance so that they are easily recognised and avoided. I should imagine that they are bad gun platforms.[9]

But they were, in fact, all he had, so desperate was the shortage of, and need for, destroyers – most of which were assigned to the Grand Fleet at Scapa Flow.

Commander Plunkett shared Bayly's concerns. In December 1914 he wrote 'hitherto the menace [of U-boats] has only been met by ultra-defensive measures on the part of the coastal patrols. These measures have met with so little success that the large number of vessels so deployed have not justified their existence ... the enemy submarine roams round our coasts absolutely undisturbed.'[10] Admiral Beatty wrote in mid-1915 that 'the outer trawler patrols ... on account of their slow speed ... can only be considered defensive craft ... with very limited offensive power'.[11] But they were all that there was! And in the end, they and their volunteer crews acquitted themselves well.

Motor Boats

The next set of volunteers to defend their native land were men of a different cut; gentlemen with a leisure interest in sailing and owners of the recently developed and increasingly popular petrol-powered motor boats.

After the Agadir incident, there was rising concern at the growth of potential flashpoints for war. Two Balkan Wars in 1912 and 1913 threatened to pull the major powers into conflict, and many people saw the clouds of war gathering on the horizon.

These threats caused some boating enthusiasts to consider how they might be of use to their country if war came. Representing 3,000 members, the British Motor Boat Club (BMBC) approached the Admiralty in 1912 and an Admiralty committee was formed under the chairmanship of Vice Admiral Sir Fredrick Samuel Inglefield, at the time Admiral Commanding Coastguards and Reserves, to study the potential role of the motor pleasure craft. 'This officer reported in November 1912 that motor boats would be able to patrol and carry out examination service in estuaries and harbours, detect hostile submarines ... act as despatch boats and so on.'[12]

As a result of this favourable conclusion, the Admiralty proposed that a motor boat reserve be created, affiliated to the Royal Naval Volunteer Reserve in the same manner as the RNR(T) was to the RNR, and the Royal Naval Motor Boat Reserve (RNMBR) was born. When war came, the call went out for boats, and men arrived from far and wide, bringing their motor craft with them. Vessels of between 3 to 65 tons were taken. Their owners were given a commission in the RNMBR, the boats were painted grey with a white identifying numeral on the bow, equipped with a White Ensign, and a rifle or other small arm, and sent off to harbour duties or local patrol functions. The Admiralty paid a charter fee and owners enrolled their own crews, who were supplied with a service certificate. These crewmen were known as 'motor boatmen',[13] and their service number had the suffix 'MB'.

The duties of the RNMBR were officially defined as 'for services during the war, for patrol and despatch work, etc, or such duties as the Admiralty may from time to time direct'.[14] Typically, apart from working with patrol groups of trawlers, motor boat undertakings might include 'patrolling in the roadsteads, estuaries, off harbours, examining shipping, controlling traffic, taking out orders to trawlers and checking they were on station, putting pilots aboard and so on'.[15] By October, their tasks had been formalised as being 'for the purpose of examining the coast, harbours and inlets and denying the use of these places to the enemy'.[16] They were defending the coast of Britain.

The motor boats and crews of the RNMBR were long on enthusiasm and courage but short on practicality. During the first winter of the war, it became clear that 'many of the motor boats could not keep the sea in bad weather'.[17] The larger ones, of 20 to 30 tons, could at least patrol bays and exposed areas such as the mouth of the Humber. But the smaller craft proved useless except for picket work, patrolling harbours, pilotage or carrying despatches.

Seven of these RNMBR pleasure boats were lost in war service, three of them to fire, one to a mine, and three in the sinking of the ship bearing them to Cardiff. By early 1915, it was clear that their limited capabilities were of little use in the war against the growing menace of the submarine. U-boats sank 749,000 tons of British merchant shipping (out of total British losses of 855,721grt) in the whole of 1915.[18] The country needed small, capable, anti-submarine vessels, faster and better armed than the Auxiliary Patrol's trawlers, more durable than the motor pleasure boats.

Motor Launches (MLs)

The replacements for the pleasure motor craft were the American-designed, Canadian-built motor launches, known as MLs, from the Elco company of New Jersey. Fifty were originally ordered and by 1 May 1915 Elco had the frames of the first boat erected. That was the same day as the *Lusitania* set out on her fateful voyage; a week later she was sunk by a U-boat with staggering loss of life including 128 Americans. This disaster prompted the Admiralty to up the order – to an additional 500 vessels. Elco were contracted to provide 550 motor launches for delivery by 16 November 1916 for a total of $22 million dollars or about £8,400 per boat (perhaps £890,000 in today's money).

ML-524 depicted in 1918. She appears to have a non-standard canvas roof to the wheelhouse. (Author's collection)

ML-463 alongside, probably at Aberdeen in late 1916 or 1917, with seemingly disinterested civilians. (Author's collection)

The contract specification called for a minimum speed when fully loaded of 19 knots, combined with a cruising radius which required a fuel capacity of 2,000 gallons. The boat should be able to maintain station in any weather and have the facility to carry a deadweight of 20,000lbs (which was equivalent to the weight of the guns, ammunition, water and supplies of a patrol). Simplicity and standardisation were the key to producing the boats quickly and so the design details were uncomplicated; for example, there was no double planking of the hull for strength. In order to transport the vessels to Britain, the agreement specified that the boats had to be of a size to fit four at a time on the deck of a steamer for transit across the Atlantic.

Built of wood, primarily yellow and Oregon pine and white oak, there were two batch designs with slightly different dimensions. *ML 1–50* measured 75ft in length, 12ft in beam and had a draught of 3ft 8in. *ML 51–500* were slightly larger, being between 80–88ft long,* 12ft 2in across and drew 3ft 10in. All were powered by Standard Motor Construction Company engines. Each ML was fitted with two of their six-cylinder petrol engines which could together produce around 450hp and drive the craft at about 19 knots. Range at a cruising speed of 15 knots was 1,000 miles which doubled at 11 knots. A feature of the technology was that there was no reverse gear – the motors were connected directly to the propeller shaft. To start the engines required a blast of compressed air, carried in bottles on board. The motors could be initiated either ahead or astern but to transition between the two meant stopping the engines, operating a small hand lever to change the direction of the air blast, and then starting them again. This could be tricky to do when the crew was under pressure.

Coming into service from October 1915, the MLs were predominantly armed with a 3pdr gun and later, with one or two depth charges. Machine guns were also carried. They were almost entirely commanded and crewed by volunteers. The officers were RNVR, often from a sailing background, the crewmen a mixture of the original motor boat crewmen, RNR and RNVR members, fishermen, mechanics, and other volunteers. To give but two examples, Geoffrey Alfree was a professional artist and amateur yachtsman who commanded *ML-247*; and Edward Conor Marshall O'Brien was a professional yachtsman and boat builder and amateur gun-runner for the Irish nationalists, who skippered a number of MLs and then an armed yacht.

The little craft gave valuable service as escorts, A/S vessels, minehunters, even minelayers. As Vice Admiral Bacon of the Dover Patrol (which boasted

---

* To give a frame of reference, at an average 80ft the length was 1.2 times the length of a cricket pitch, wicket to wicket, or 1.3 times the distance between a baseball pitcher and the batter.

thirty-one MLs at the end of 1917) wrote, '[they] were useful for most purposes for which they were not originally intended. What a gallant little flotilla they were.'[19]

However, for all their versatility, the MLs were uncomfortable and wet boats to sail in. Amateur yachtsman and author Gordon Maxwell wrote of patrolling 'towards midday the wind abates a little, but not so the cold, and oilskins give place to duffel coats – thick wool, yellowy-brown coats with hoods, and which, if worn with these up and baggy trousers of the same material, give the appearance of a ship manned by giant teddy bears'. Eating in them was next to impossible; 'meals on an ML are "movable feasts," where the right hand never knows what the left hand may be doing, for while the latter is conveying food to the mouth the former is probably chasing the plate across the table or picking up a chop from the seat. No meal on patrol is ever dull.'[20]

The Steam Yachts

The final component of the volunteer coastal forces assembled in 1914 were the steam yachts. The steam yacht was a largely late nineteenth-century phenomenon, a brief flourishing of remarkable beauty and privilege. They were the epitome of wealth and the symbol of standing, the Learjets of their

Steam yacht *Rona* moored on the River Dart, with Kingswear in the background. She later became the armed yacht HMY *Gossia*. (Alice Wood Collection)

day. Hugely expensive to build and run, fitted out like waterborne palaces, they gave their owners privacy, the ability to travel wherever they pleased without let or hindrance, and membership of an exclusive stratum of society.

When war came, steam yachts were volunteered for naval service by their owners or requisitioned from them by the Admiralty. In both cases, promises were made to return the vessel in a decent state and in the latter case, a lawful transfer of ownership or hire was arranged. According to First Lord of the Admiralty Winston Churchill, the 'intention of the Admiralty is to obtain the vessels which they require on conditions as little onerous to the owners as possible'.[21]

At first many yachts were offered up free of charge, with the Admiralty paying all equipment and running costs. If at the end of three months, the yacht was still required for naval service, she was hired by the Admiralty at a fee of £1 per ton per month. Boats were donated or taken from members of all the major yacht clubs. The prestigious Royal Yacht Squadron, for example, provided no less that thirty-eight vessels. By the end of the war, a total of 159 yachts had been enrolled by the Admiralty. Some others also served as hospital ships. Once an owner had agreed to lend his yacht for the duration of the war, his vessel was taken to a naval dockyard – usually Portsmouth or Devonport – to be fitted out for war service. Names were sometimes changed and the prefix HMY – His Majesty's Yacht – applied.

Steam yachts had been designed for comfort, luxury and sometimes speed – but certainly not for war. Substantial modification was required to fit them for war service. Furniture and decorations were removed; the mahogany, teak and oak panels were taken down and replaced by mountings for small arms. The hulls received coats of grey paint; storm shutters replaced plate glass in the portholes and viewing panels. Crews were required to improvise sleeping berths. Yachts with sails had their masts shortened or removed and canvas-screened platforms or crow's nests erected. Galleys were enlarged to feed a different sort of catering requirements to their intended purpose. The bows, quarterdecks, and fantails now mounted guns, depth-charge racks, and other equipment of war which required the strengthening of bulkhead and decks, the fitting of additional supports and the firm screwing down of the gun mountings.

But their basic deficiencies remained. They had no armour, were not necessarily constructed for constant use and heavy seaways, and were often less manoeuvrable than their likely adversaries. 'Many of the steam yachts were only single screwed', wrote Edward Keble Chatterton, who himself served in the Auxiliary Patrol, 'extremely unhandy . . . and anything but ideal for anti-submarine work.'[22] An anonymous contributor to *Yachting Monthly* magazine noted that 'as a patrol flagship or an executive headquarters, the modern steam yacht is certainly well adapted but one must recognise the type's commercial inadaptability when in competition with, say, steam trawlers or drifters'. The same writer went on to note that 'steam yachts ... are the most costly of craft and, apart from their engines and boilers, contain little that is usable for rough work. They are incapable of sustained speed in heavy weather and I should put 10 knots as their working average speed.'[23]

In many cases, the original peacetime crew was 'volunteered' with the yacht. Where men stayed on, they were required to sign a T-124Y form. This protected their 'terms and conditions' of remuneration etc, but made them subject to naval discipline and orders. Generally, they were enlisted as members of the MMR – the Mercantile Marine Reserve. As their civilian pay was likely to be better than the rates for a regular RN sailor, this was a considerable benefit. And so another group of volunteers joined the conflict, and rich men's playthings went to war.

Organisation

The trawlers and drifters intended for minesweeping duty on the eastern coast 'belonged' to the Minesweeping Division, headed from 4 September 1914 by Rear Admiral Edward Francis Benedict (Ned) Charlton, as Admiral of Minesweepers, with his flag in the hired yacht *Zarefah* (ex *Maretanza V*),* armed with two 3pdrs. Charlton was succeeded at the end of 1915 by Rear Admiral the Hon Edward Stafford Fitzherbert.† However, it was only in October 1917 that strategic minesweeping responsibilities for the whole British coast came under one officer, when Captain Lionel Preston was appointed to the Admiralty as firstly Superintendent, and then Director, of Minesweeping.

The minesweepers were locally organised under a Senior Naval Officer (SNO), known as the Port Minesweeping Officer (PMSO). And the force was a diverse collection of vessels. Apart from the trawlers and drifters, paddle steamer pleasure craft, cross-Channel ferries, motor launches and other shallow draught craft would eventually join the Royal Navy's original ten minesweepers (which were in fact converted torpedo boats) and, in time, specially designed naval vessels.

Patrol anti-submarine civilian vessels were the responsibility of the Auxiliary Patrol, which until late 1915 came under the aegis of the Admiral of Patrols.‡ On 20 December 1914, defence of the coast of Britain was

---

* She had been built in 1905 for Sir John Pender, was hired by the Admiralty in 1914, purchased by them in 1916 and was sunk in 1917.
† Later 13th Baron Stafford.
‡ With the abolition of this post, the Auxiliary Patrols vessels came under the command of the local admiral responsible for their port.

organised into twenty-seven patrol areas, each under a senior naval officer, often a 'dug out' (a retired senior officer recalled to duty) with a shore base and all under the command of the local SNO. A random assortment of vessels were entered into this organisation; trawlers, drifters, tugs and motor launches. And to this mix, the Admiralty added the steam pleasure yachts, initially as command vessels.

From 1914, hunting patrols, based on these Admiralty patrol areas, sought the foe. They generally comprised an armed yacht, furnished with wireless, four more-or-less armed trawlers or drifters and possibly a motor boat or two.

As examples of the organisation of such vessels, consider Area I (Stornoway) where on 1 January 1915 there were five yachts, twenty trawlers and five motor boats; or Area XII (Portsmouth) which boasted twenty-six trawlers, nineteen drifters and twenty-five motorboats. Even in 1917 there were 150 such Auxiliary Patrol groups, now made up of one yacht and up to six armed trawlers. The latter were often equipped for minesweeping as well and generally had 6pdr or 12pdr guns. One or more of the trawlers were also fitted with radio and named as second and third leader. Armed yachts were also formed into specialist yacht squadrons, where their speed, superior to a trawler, might be more useful in fixing an enemy. By 1 January 1919, the Auxiliary Patrol would have no less than 3,773 vessels in the command, all taken up from civilian life, and many confined to the British littoral.

And so, a vast network of patrol and sweeping vessels, manned by pre-war civilians arose to keep the seaways clear, the harbours safe and the coastline protected.

Other Locally-Based Resources

There were, of course, flotillas of regular naval ships around the coast. Most of the modern destroyers had been allocated to the Grand Fleet (and Admiral Jellicoe was always bemoaning the fact that he didn't have enough, even then) but there was a strong force of light cruisers (generally between four and six) and 'L'- or 'M'-class destroyers based at Harwich (around twenty). Dover had the 6th Flotilla (The Dover Patrol) with eighteen, largely 'Tribal'-class destroyers, and there were small numbers of destroyers at east coast ports such as Tyne, Humber, Grimsby and Yarmouth.

Local defence flotillas were largely equipped with older vessels, including Fisher's thirty-six coastal destroyers, reclassified as torpedo boats (see Chapter 3). On 1 November 1914, Admiralty 'pink lists' show that twelve older destroyers were at the Nore with twenty torpedo boats (TBs). Portsmouth had six and seventeen respectively. Devonport, four destroyers

The 'Tribal'-class (or 'F'-class) destroyer HMS *Saracen* (1908). She served in the Dover Patrol as part of the 6th Destroyer Flotilla. 'Tribals' were armed with five 12pdrs and two 18in torpedo tubes. Oil-fired and turbine-driven, they could achieve 33 knots but had a limited range. (Author's collection)

and eight TBs; Pembroke four TBs, Queenstown also four, and Portland six TBs and a seaplane carrier.

Merchant Shipping

Merchant shipping was not immune from finding itself under Admiralty control. Any British-registered merchant ship was legally liable to be taken up for war work and the government announced on the day war broke out that the Admiralty was authorised to exercise its powers of requisition upon any such ship in British or adjacent waters.

Larger vessels were taken for troopships, while other speedier ships were converted to armed merchant cruisers (AMCs). Successive generations of Cunard's top liners, for example, had been constructed to Admiralty specifications for such use if required but generally proved too large, cumbersome and heavy in fuel consumption to be of use in that guise. Instead, the burden fell on smaller liners, such as Cunard's *Carmania* which sank the German *Cap Trafalgar*, and faster cargo vessels such as banana boats. A large proportion of tramp steamers were taken up to act as colliers and supply ships, some 30 per cent of the overall British tonnage by 1916. Short-distance ferries and excursion boats were requisitioned for use as mine sweepers and tenders. Cosens and Co of Weymouth, one of the larger operators of such pleasure boats, had their entire fleet under requisition by 1918. Later on in the war, the practice of taking up civilian vessels spread to those owned by neutral nations, under the law of Angary, by which a state at war, in time of need, might seize or destroy the property of a neutral country.

* * * * *

On all these different categories of vessel rested the defence of Britain's coast and littoral seaways, the sure shield against invasion or starvation. And all were almost completely commanded and manned by volunteers. As Julian Corbett wrote in the navy's Official History of the war:

> After the outbreak of war the system developed so rapidly that soon the auxiliary vessels far outnumbered those on the Navy List. The armed merchant cruisers rapidly multiplied; trawlers, drifters and yachts were taken up in scores for minesweeping and anti-submarine patrols, and steam-craft of all kinds for the examination service which controlled the flow of trade in our Home Waters. There had been nothing like it since the distant days when the mercantile marine was counted as part of the navy of England – nothing to equal it even in the heyday of privateering or in the days of our floating defence against Napoleon's Invasion Flotilla.[24]

7

The East Coast Under Attack, 1914

The Royal Navy achieved some limited success during 1914. German commerce raiders had largely been eliminated. The Battle of Heligoland Bight of 28 August was regarded as a great victory by the British public, with 712 German sailors killed, 530 injured and 336 taken prisoner. Three German light cruisers and one torpedo boat were sunk; three light cruisers and three torpedo boats suffered damage, all for only thirty-five British deaths. In reality, it was a melee of confusion, combining poor communication and planning, and in which RN losses could have been much greater had Beatty and his battlecruisers, not part of the original plan and sent by Jellicoe at the last minute, not made a significant intervention.

But the German U-boat arm had gained considerable success against RN warships in the early months of the war. On 5 September 1914, the scout cruiser *Pathfinder* was torpedoed off St Abbs' Head with the loss of most of its 270 crew; and on 22 September three old cruisers – known officially as Cruiser Force C but unofficially as the 'live bait squadron' – were patrolling off the Dutch coast when first the *Aboukir*, then *Hogue*, then *Cressy* were all torpedoed in the space of 45 minutes. Sixty-two officers and 1,397 men died.

Rather than blame this latter disaster on poor Admiralty planning and the removal of a destroyer screen due to bad weather, many attributed it to German spies. Member of Parliament and retired admiral Lord Charles Beresford was one such. At a rally on 2 October, he claimed that 'three cruisers were lost by information given from this country to the German admiralty. The British people should insist that the Home Office prevent the army and navy being stabbed in the back by assassins in the shape of spies. All alien enemies should be locked up.' Attorney General Sir John Simon supported him; 'I do not think it open to doubt that there are a large number of people in this country who have been making treacherous communications.'[1]

Then the old cruiser *Hawke*, part of the 10th Cruiser Squadron, was sunk on 15 October, costing 524 sailors their lives, and on 31 October HMS *Hermes*, a seaplane carrier attached to the Dover Patrol, was torpedoed and sunk with the death of twenty-two crew. But the biggest naval disaster of the year was the loss of Rear Admiral Sir Christopher 'Kit' Cradock and his two old armoured cruisers, *Good Hope* (1901) and *Monmouth* (1901), on

All Saints' Day at the Battle of Coronel off the coast of Chile. Over 1,600 men died at the hands of Vice Admiral Maximillian von Spee's German East Asia squadron, as a result of Churchill's meddling, misleading signals from the Admiralty, and Cradock's decision to fight an unwinnable battle against overwhelming odds.

Seventy-three-year-old Admiral Jacky Fisher had returned to the Admiralty as Churchill's First Sea Lord two days earlier.* He took decisive action, taking three battlecruisers from the Grand Fleet. Two, *Invincible* and *Inflexible*, he sent to the South Atlantic. The other, *Princess Royal*, went to the Caribbean Sea, to prevent the East Asia Squadron from using the Panama Canal. *Invincible* and *Inflexible* did the job they had been designed for and sank *Scharnhorst* and *Gneisenau*, Spee's two modern armoured cruisers, and scattered or destroyed his smaller vessels. German dead totalled 1,871 sailors, including Spee and his two sons.

After the Battle of Heligoland Bight, the Kaiser had ordered that the High Seas Fleet should not sail far out of the Bight itself and its commander, Admiral von Ingenohl, should in future ask for permission before engaging in a fleet action.† But the Germans knew that the Grand Fleet was temporarily weakened by the absence of these three battlecruisers. German naval strategy from the start of the war had quickly evolved to one of trying to reduce the numerical superiority of the Grand Fleet. To aid this aim, the *Admiralstab* (the German Imperial Admiralty Staff) sought to engineer a situation whereby a portion of the Royal Navy's capital ships could be isolated and overwhelmed by a larger German force, or drawn over minefields and U-boat concentrations. The time seemed propitious for an attempt to do so.

Great Yarmouth

Before the war came, the town of Great Yarmouth was chiefly famous for the fishing trade. Scottish fishermen and their accompanying wives and 'herring girls' followed the shoals of herring around the coast of Britain, from Stornoway to Lerwick, then to Peterhead and down the east coast to Yarmouth. Here, in the autumn, there were large camps of Scottish fisher-lasses set up on the quayside, gutting and packing the 'silver darlings'. The port was packed with fishing vessels and the town was prosperous. Next

---

* Fisher's predecessor, Prince Louis of Battenberg, had resigned. He was troubled with gout, frustrated by Churchill's constant interference in his work, and had been the subject of a vicious press campaign against him on account of his Germanic origins, despite him being a naturalised British citizen.

† Expecting a short war, Kaiser Wilhelm, his chancellor and his naval staff were already arguing that the fleet should be maintained as a bargaining counter at the peace table rather than (as Tirpitz wanted) be 'hurled against either the British cross-Channel troop transports or Scapa Flow' (Herwig, *Luxury Fleet*, p 147).

door to the south, Gorleston, once a fishing settlement too, had become an Edwardian beach resort, with golden sands, a theatre and a pier. But in November 1914, the fishing had largely ceased, the fishermen had gone to war and it was late in the year for the tourist trade. Neither town was defended but naval vessels were often based in the area.

Across the North Sea, on 2 November, a squadron of German warships under the command of Admiral Franz Hipper* sailed from the Schillig Roads. It comprised the battlecruisers SMS *Seydlitz*, *Von der Tann* and *Moltke*, the slightly smaller armoured cruiser *Blücher* and the light cruisers SMS *Strassburg*, *Graudenz*, *Kolberg* and *Stralsund*. Their objective was to lay mines off the coast of Yarmouth and then shell the town to attract British ships to the newly-sown field in the hope of causing one or more sinkings. Behind them, two squadrons of German battleships of the High Seas Fleet, and their attendant cruisers and destroyers, stood guard, with the intention of catching Royal Navy ships drawn to the action.

There were three British ships off the East Anglian coast and between the Germans and their target; HMS *Halcyon* (1894), an old gunboat converted to a minesweeper, stationed at Lowestoft and occasionally used as a depot ship for armed trawlers, which was then working near Smith's Knoll; and the small destroyers *Lively* ('B' class, launched in 1900, armed with a 12dpr, five 6pdrs and two torpedo tubes) and the 'C'-class *Leopard* (1897, with the same armament).

Just before 0700, *Halcyon* suddenly saw huge battlecruisers emerge from the morning fret, made the recognition signal, and was disconcerted to find 11in shells dropping and exploding all around her. Her captain, Commander George Norman Ballard, at once turned away to the south-west and radioed that he was under attack. Able Seman Joe Spiers was on deck at the time. He wrote to his mother 'we made the challenge and they answered with a broadside . . . I thought well goodbye Old England'.[2]

Halcyon raised steam on all boilers and ran for port 'at 24 knots, a speed which the ship had never done before',[3] according to Spiers. This had an understandable element of exaggeration for her design speed when built was only 19 knots! The splashes from the shells falling around her washed over the ship and Joe Spiers 'got nearly drowned' by it.

Two miles to the south-east, Lieutenant Harold Baillie-Grohman in *Lively*, recognising the acute danger that the minesweeper was in, dashed towards her and steering a parallel course began to make smoke between *Halcyon* and the onrushing German flotilla. For 15 minutes both vessels came under a sustained fire, as did *Leopard* to the east, but the smoke and

---

* He became von Hipper in 1916 when ennobled by the King of Bavaria.

the fact that all the battlecruisers fired at the same time, making fall of shot difficult to spot, meant the British vessels were not fatally harmed.

Halcyon sustained damage, but not a major hit. The steering engine broke down and they had to use the aft manual wheel. A yard was carried away, the radio was wrecked, and the bridge badly knocked about.

Receiving *Halcyon*'s radio message, the destroyer HMS *Success* (1901, 'B' class) set a course to join them, while three more destroyers of the Yarmouth Patrol in harbour began raising steam. The submarines *E-10*, *D-5* and *D-3*, lying at Gorleston, moved out to join the chase, but tragically *D-5* struck a mine and sank.* A fishing drifter, *Faithful*, rushed to the spot to provide assistance and picked up four survivors, regardless of the danger that other mines might cause. Later, another drifter, *Homeland*, rescued one other. Twenty-one men died, but *D-5*'s CO, Lieutenant Commander Godfrey Herbert, was one of those rescued. The crew of *Faithful* were awarded £75 for their lifesaving efforts in dangerous waters.

Another vessel operating near the harbour entrance was the armed yacht *Zaza*.† She had been requisitioned as a patrol vessel in September 1914 and fitted with a 12pdr and two 6pdr guns. A naval reservist observed her from his hotel window as she tried to dispose of a mine by gunfire. Suddenly, he saw *Halcyon* take off seawards and then quickly return seeking shelter from the hail of gunfire which pursued her. *Zaza* was witnessed to calmly carry on her mine disposal work while hell broke out around her.[4]

At 0740, Hipper ceased firing at the RN ships and instead now directed a bombardment at Yarmouth and Gorleston, the shells falling harmlessly on the beach. When *Stralsund* had finishing minelaying,‡ Hipper withdrew his ships and headed for home.

Later, at around 0830, *Halcyon* limped into harbour at Lowestoft. As she entered into the anchorage to moor alongside the quay, 'throngs of people cheered'. Able Seaman Spiers was relieved. 'Well, I don't want to go through that again, especially in *Halcyon*',[5] he wrote to his mother. Ballard was able to report to the SNO in person. His ship had sustained only one casualty, Able Seaman Harry Scotney, who later died of his wounds, with another three men injured. But the presence of the freshly-laid minefield went unreported until 1100, when a fisherman coming into Lowestoft told that he had seen the Germans laying mines.

On shore, the bombardment had caused panic. Was this the invasion?

---

* The mine was probably a drifting British one.
† *Zaza* was the twin-masted, 423grt personal yacht of William Beardmore of Tullicheun Castle, sole proprietor of the William Beardmore shipyard at Govan since 1886. She was unsurprisingly built by his yard and launched in 1905 with a single screw engine of Beardmore's own manufacture.
‡ She laid 120 mines in total.

Should everybody flee? The local volunteers gathered, but by the time they had assembled, the Germans were long gone. But the first German shells had fallen on British soil.

The navy tried to rally forces to intercept the raiders but was hampered by the fact that Jellicoe was incommunicado, in transit on a train. At Harwich, Commodore Tyrwhitt was surprised by the signal from *Halcyon* stating that she was engaged with a superior force. He ordered the light cruisers *Aurora* and *Undaunted* to make for Smith's Knoll with all speed, and then further directed them to Terschelling, one of the West Frisian Islands. He decided himself to set out for Terschelling with his flagship and a division of destroyers to try to cut off the enemy's retreat. But *Aurora* didn't take in his signal and thus *Undaunted*, with her destroyers, was making for Terschelling alone. When she had reached a position near the mid-sea rendezvous, she sighted to the southward four German cruisers. These now gave chase and her captain, William Blunt, took his forces northward; but then began to turn to the west to try to lead the enemy vessels south towards Tyrwhitt. Sensing a trap, the Germans gave up the chase of *Undaunted* and made off easterly towards Terschelling Light. Blunt then resumed his course and followed them, doing his best to keep touch. Tyrwhitt decided that he must come to *Undaunted*'s assistance and steered to join with Blunt's flotilla. But the Admiralty, having realised that Tyrwhitt's forces were considerably overmatched, recommended by wireless that he concentrate. *Undaunted* was accordingly recalled and by 1500 the Harwich Force had assembled three light cruisers and thirteen destroyers in the middle of the North Sea and began to sweep past Terschelling to the Bight. But the enemy was nowhere to be seen. At 0955, Beatty and a battlecruiser squadron had been ordered south and the squadrons of the Grand Fleet set out from Ireland. But by then Hipper was 50 miles away.

But the High Seas Fleet didn't escape entirely unharmed. The armoured cruiser SMS *Yorck* (1904) had been part of the screening forces which backed

Reginald Tyrwhitt as a Rear Admiral.
(Author's collection)

SMS *Yorck*, sunk by mines in the Jade with the loss of half her crew, seen here in 1910. She is passing under the Levensau Bridge over the Kiel Canal.
(US Naval History and Heritage Command NH 45198)

up Hipper's raid. On the return of the fleet to Wilhelmshaven, they encountered heavy fog and anchored in the Schillig Roads to await better visibility. Believing the fog to have cleared sufficiently, the ship's commander ordered *Yorck* to get underway in the early hours of 4 November. Owing to a navigational error, she entered a German defensive minefield in the haze, struck two mines, and sank with heavy loss of life, perhaps 336 men in total. Her captain, Pieper, was convicted by a court martial of disobeying orders and negligent homicide, and was sentenced to two years in prison.

The Germans announced a victory and the Kaiser was delighted with the perceived success of his navy, coming after the losses at Heligoland Bight. Admiral Hipper was awarded the Iron Cross for his part in the raid but he refused to wear it, feeling that little had been accomplished. The *New York Times* quoted an official British communique, which ridiculed the German's claims. 'There is no truth whatsoever in the German report that their ships bombarded Yarmouth. The German reports speak of Yarmouth "forts" but nothing of the kind exists.'[6]

But what if it had been an invasion? Certainly, the navy was slow to react. And at the Admiralty there was a sense that the Yarmouth venture was aimed at distracting from some other, larger, attack. With the Grand Fleet at Lough

Swilly, it would have taken a very long time to get to the scene and the pre-dreadnoughts at Sheerness would have been outclassed if they had tried to take on the High Seas Fleet unsupported, and the Germans took heart from the fact that they had crossed the North Sea there and back without interception and were encouraged that their tactics would pay dividends.

The Admiralty took some lessons from the raid too. After a conference in London, it was decided to restore the original dispositions as designed by Rear Admiral de Robeck in April 1914 when he was Admiral of Patrols. Rear Admiral G A Ballard, who now held the post, was instructed that he was to reconcentrate the destroyers in divisions as laid down in the War Orders (they had become dispersed hunting minelayers), and leave the prevention of minelaying to the trawlers of the Auxiliary Patrol. In accordance with these orders Rear Admiral Ballard's two flotillas, the 7th and 9th, were each organised in four divisions, one division of each flotilla to be always in reserve cleaning boilers. Of the active divisions, two of the 7th Flotilla were kept at Yarmouth ready for immediate action night and day, and one in the Humber. In the Humber also was one division of the 9th Flotilla; another division lay in the Tyne and the third patrolled between Flamborough Head and Hartlepool.

The 3rd Battle Squadron, consisting of all eight *King Edward VII*-class battleships, the penultimate British pre-dreadnought class, was moved from Portland to Rosyth in order to be better positioned to counter future raids. Vice Admiral Sir Cecil Burney, commanding the Channel Fleet with its 5th Battle Squadron of old pre-dreadnought battleships at Sheerness, was ordered that at the first intimation of a hostile expedition he was instantly to attack it, regardless of its strength, and call up the 6th Battle Squadron (equally obsolescent ships, at Portland) to his flag. 'In this way it was thought fairly certain that with the assistance of the Harwich and Nore flotillas he could prevent any landing in force, while ample provision was made with submarines and minelayers to render the enemy's retreat disastrous.'[7]

Questions about the navy's losses and the raid were raised in the House of Commons. Dr Thomas Macnamara, Parliamentary and Financial Secretary to the Admiralty, was on the receiving end of a diatribe from William Joynson-Hicks, MP for Brentford, who seemed preoccupied with spying as the cause of all Britain's ills, and was troubled by the prospect of invasion.

> There is one other question with regard to the East Coast. There is widespread anxiety with regard to spying on the East Coast. There is widespread anxiety with regard to the naval disasters we have had on the East Coast. There is a widespread feeling that signals have been

given from the East Coast to the German Navy by which disasters have taken place. How about the loss of those three cruisers? There is a widespread belief that there were signals either by wireless or somehow that enabled the submarine to get in, and that there were also some means by which the mine chart off the East Coast was known to the German flotilla that came over to Yarmouth ten days ago. How was it they could get over so easily? The right hon gentleman will not believe anything of the kind. He may say that I am spy mad, but he is spy mad in the other direction. He will not believe that what has been done in every village in Belgium and France may be done in this country.[8]

The spectre of invasion hung over the country.

Shells from the Sea

The raid on Great Yarmouth achieved little but had convinced Hipper of the potential for such speedy, hit-and-run raids entrapping a section of the Grand Fleet and causing issues of civilian morale. He persuaded Ingenohl to ask the Kaiser for permission to conduct another mission, and when it was granted sent out the submarine *U-17* to reconnoitre his chosen targets. Her commander reported that he could not see any mines or significant sea defences, and there was a steady flow of shipping passing by.

The German battlecruiser SMS *Von der Tann* (1909), eight 11in guns, pictured in 1911. In 1914 she participated in the Battle of Heligoland Bight and the coastal raids.
(US Library of Congress LC-DIG-ggbain-16927)

The light cruiser SMS *Strassburg* (1911). She carried twelve 10.5cm (4.1in) guns and 120 mines. The ship went to the Italian navy in 1919 as part of war reparations. (Author's collections)

The German battlecruiser SMS *Seydlitz* (1912), mounting ten 11in guns. She was Hipper's flagship for the coastal raids of 1914. (US Naval History and Heritage Command NH 46838)

The light cruiser SMS *Stralsund*. (US Naval History and Heritage Command NH 92631)

For the attack, Hipper's force comprised the battlecruisers SMS *Seydlitz*, *Von der Tann*, *Moltke* and *Derfflinger*, together with the armoured cruiser *Blücher*, light cruisers *Strassburg, Graudenz, Kolberg* and *Stralsund* and eighteen destroyers. Ingenohl decided to bring out a significant part of the High Seas Fleet, some eighty-five ships, to support and reinforce Hipper. He did not ask the kaiser's permission for this, as his standing orders required him to. Their target – the Yorkshire coast around Scarborough, Whitby and up to Hartlepool.

Of the three towns, only one might be described as a site of military value. Scarborough Spa became one of Britain's first seaside resort in the eighteenth century and boomed again when the railways came in 1845. Its skyline was dominated by the Grand Hotel on St Nicholas Cliff. Designed by the well-known northern architect Cuthbert Brodrick, it was completed in 1867 and at the time of its opening was the largest hotel, and the largest brick structure, in Europe. When war came, observation posts, in the form of trenches, were dug along the cliff tops and manned by Territorials and other volunteers. The route up from South Bay via Eastborough was sandbagged and all steps ascending from the foreshore were blocked with barbed wire. Between Scarborough and Seaton Delaval, a TF unit, the 7th (Cyclists) Battalion of the Devonshire Regiment was deployed along the cliff tops. Whitby had been a Georgian spa, then a whaling town and finally another tourist destination, aesthetically enhanced by the ruined abbey on the cliffs above the town. Only Hartlepool was a full-time port. The area had become heavily industrialised with an ironworks (established 1838), and shipyards and docks (established in the 1870s), all benefitting from the proximity of the Durham coalfields. By 1913, there were 43 ship-owning companies located in the town, with responsibility for 236 ships. The largest of these, Ropner's, operated fifty-seven tramp steamers in 1914. The harbour was defended by an RGA volunteer detachment on the Heugh, overlooking the port, and another at the lighthouse, both originally fortified in 1860.

On 14 November 1914, in the wake of the attack on Great Yarmouth eleven days previously, Chief of Admiralty War Staff Vice Admiral Henry Oliver sent a telegram at 1915 to the CinC Nore (Admiral Sir Richard Poore) and the Admiral of Patrols (Ballard) 'send *Rinaldo* to Hartlepool to act under orders of AOP for protection against invasion. Acknowledge.'[9]

HMS *Rinaldo* was a *Condor*-class sloop, laid down in 1898 and launched in 1900. Originally fitted with a full set of barque-rigged sails, she was designed to carry four 4in guns and four 3pdrs and serve overseas, showing the flag. Recalled to Britain as part of Fisher's reforms, she had first been laid up and put into service as a tender to HMS *Vivid*, a stone frigate naval barracks and training establishment at Devonport.

When war came she was hastily pressed into action as a makeshift monitor with Admiral Horace Hood's Dover Patrol, and spent October bombarding the Belgian coast in the course of which she suffered eight wounded and one fatality. It demonstrates the level of concern regarding an invasion that an obsolete sloop would be considered an appropriate protector for a valuable port. Her four 4in guns were an asset, even if she was no longer thought one. In any case, she wasn't at Hartlepool on the day the war came there.

In the battle to prevent the Germans dominating in the North Sea, the Royal Navy had a hidden advantage over the *Kaiserliche Marine*, one which it was anxious to keep extremely secret. The German navy had started the war with three principal codes, and 'within four months the Admiralty had acquired copies of all of them'.[10] These were processed by a secret signals intelligence group, housed in Room 40 of the Old Admiralty building, and from which the organisation took its name, 'Room 40'. They could read the HVB general code from September 1914, used by the High Seas Fleet. It was able to decipher SKM, the most widely used in the German navy, in October, and the final VB code, used by flag officers and for communicating with warships overseas, was acquired in November. Thus Jellicoe could be given warning of when a signal traffic increase and/or decrypts indicated that something was afoot across the North Sea, even if it could not always tell him what was actually about to take place. And on 14 December 1914, such a warning was given.

The Admiralty and the Grand Fleet immediately began their dispositions. They did not, of course, know where the Germans would strike; possibly it would be East Anglia again. But they could position themselves across the most likely route they would take for home after the attack. This is an important point for later consideration – the navy did not set up to prevent the raid, but to bring the German fleet to battle.

Additionally, the Admiralty were unaware that Ingenohl was to sally out with the High Seas Fleet. Instructions flowed from the London to Jellicoe. The 1st Battlecruiser Squadron (Beatty), with HMS *Lion Queen Mary*, *Tiger* and *New Zealand*, together with the 2nd Battle Squadron (Vice Admiral Sir George Warrender) comprising the dreadnoughts HMS *King George V*, *Ajax*, *Centurion*, *Orion*, *Monarch* and *Conqueror*, and the 1st Light Cruiser Squadron (Commodore William Goodenough) consisting of HMS *Southampton*, *Birmingham*, *Falmouth* and *Nottingham* were all ordered out. Warrender as senior admiral present was in command. This was perhaps an unfortunate choice, for Warrender was someone whose mind worked gradually and his growing deafness exacerbated his slowness of response.

Commodore Tyrwhitt at Harwich was sent to sea with his light cruisers,

HMS *Aurora* and *Undaunted*, and all forty-two of his destroyers. Commodore Roger Keyes, also Harwich based, was instructed to send eight submarines and his two command destroyers, HMS *Lurcher* and *Firedrake*, to take station off the island of Terschelling, positioned to catch the German ships should they turn west into the English Channel. But Jellicoe protested to the Admiralty that although such dispositions should be sufficient to deal with Hipper, they would not be able to match the High Seas Fleet, should they be in company. He wanted to sally out with three battle squadrons. This request was denied but the 3rd Cruiser Squadron (Rear-Admiral William Pakenham) from Rosyth, with the armoured cruisers HMS *Devonshire*, *Antrim*, *Argyll* and *Roxburgh*, was added. Jellicoe chose the point for this disparate gathering to assemble – 25 miles south-east of Dogger Bank.

Hipper left the Jade at 0300 on the 15th. Ingenohl followed him 12 hours later with most of the High Seas Fleet; fourteen dreadnoughts, eight pre-dreadnoughts, nine cruisers and fifty-four destroyers. The weather deteriorated markedly; at 0635 on 16 December, Hipper ordered his destroyers and three light cruisers back to the main fleet, the conditions being too bad to risk them. Only *Kolberg* of his light cruisers remained as she was carrying 100 mines to lay off the British coast.

Now he divided his squadron; *Seydlitz*, *Blücher* and *Moltke* proceeded towards Hartlepool, while *Derfflinger*, *Von der Tann* and *Kolberg* approached Scarborough. *Kolberg* began to lay mines off Flamborough Head, and at 0800, the two battlecruisers opened fire with a total of eight 12in and eight 11in guns between them, some 2,000–3,000 yards from the shore.

Death rained down on Scarborough. The town was undefended and there were no RN ships in the vicinity. It was shooting practice for the German gunners. The inhabitants had received no warning. The first people knew of the attack was when shells started exploding around them. There was panic. Was this the much-feared invasion?

People started to run for the railway station* and the roads leading out of town. Shells hit the coastguard station, the cavalry barracks, the disused castle and the suburb of Falsgrave. The barracks held men of the Yorkshire Hussars, a TF regiment formed with the Haldane reforms. They turned out, were issued with rifles and told to prepare for an invasion. They manned the trenches and waited. The Scarborough War Signal Station on Castle Hill was destroyed and a wireless station further inland was the probable target of the shells that fell on Falsgrave.

---

* The *Scarborough Mercury* of the following day reported that 'no one was allowed into the station without a ticket' and the clerks had a busy trade selling tickets to Leeds and York.

Damage to Scarborough lighthouse, caused by a shell which struck it a glancing blow before ricocheting into the Grand Hotel. (Author's collection)

Three churches were hit, the Grand Hotel badly damaged, the Royal Hotel, Scarborough, was hit by four shells, one of which destroyed room 112, and the gable end of the town hall was shot away. At the steps of the Granville Hotel on the Esplanade, Alice Duffield was one of the first to be killed when a shell exploded almost on top of her. A shell struck the lighthouse but failed to explode and ricocheted into the Grand Hotel. The boarding houses on St Nicholas Cliff collapsed and a row of cottages in Stalby Road became brick and rubble.

The Grand Hotel, Scarborough, made a good target for German gunnery. The photograph shows the damage to the saloon, December 1914. (Author's collection)

Two pictures of shellfire damage at Scarborough. Left a house on the Esplanade, and right the Grand Picture Palace. (Author's collection)

The wreckage of a room in a house in Scarborough. (Author's collection)

One shell damaged three houses. It went straight through a house on the Esplanade, made a hole in the garden wall and struck No 1 Belvedere Road across the road, killing a servant girl, Emily Crosby, and then hit No 2, finally embedding itself in the garden – all of this without exploding. The architect of the renovated Royal Hotel, Whitby, Louis Norman Sanderson, was living on the Esplanade at the time. Possibly as a result of this strike from the sea, he joined the RNVR as a sub lieutenant on 28 December. Another architect was killed; 'Mr John Hall JP was dressing for the day, when a shell howled through his walls and blew him, and his bedroom, into limbo.'[11] Having suffered multiple wounds, he died as he arrived at hospital. The two children of a Mrs Bennett, of 2 Wykeham Street, were found in the wreckage of their home. One of the children had his head blown off and the other was disembowelled. Postman Alfred Beal was killed as he delivered letters, and 15-year-old Boy Scout George Taylor died on his way to purchase a newspaper.

Five-year-old George B Halliday was staying at his grandmother's house at Scalby, a village on the northern edge of Scarborough, three to four miles to the north-west of Scarborough beach. Writing 68 years later, he remembered 'people making for the moors with bundles on their backs, some with wheelbarrows and prams'. Even at this distance from the action, Scalby was not safe. 'Grandmother, myself and her family were watching outside when a large bomb [shell] passed over, just cleared the church tower and buried without exploding, just by the road leading to Hackness.'[12]

After 30 minutes of bombardment, the battlecruisers moved on to target Whitby. One shell fell into a field behind the abbey, possibly aimed at the railway station; another demolished the abbey's west end. The local coastguard station was again targeted. A great smoking gap appeared in the houses of Esk Terrace.

Five hundred shells had been fired at the towns; seventeen civilian inhabitants were killed and many more injured.

What of Hartlepool? A naval patrol had sailed from Hartlepool at 0500 that morning, comprising 3rd Division of the 9th Destroyer Flotilla (9DF), *Doon*, *Test*, *Waveney* and *Moy*. Part of the Admiral of Patrols' flotillas, 9DF's duty was the protection of the north-east coastline between the Firth of Forth and the Tyne. These were small 'River'-class vessels, launched between 1903 and 1905, displacing 535 tons. The largest gun they carried was a 12pdr, a pop gun against the big German ships. One hit from even the secondary armament of the battlecruisers would have finished such little craft. *Doon*, under Lieutenant Commander Harry MacLeod Fraser, observed three large vessels approaching at 0745; he immediately closed to investigate, opening up a gap between his vessel and the other three. When the Germans opened fire he and the other three destroyers turned away. The third salvo from the enemy hit *Doon* and shot her wireless away. *Test* signalled 'enemy in sight'.

There were also three RN ships in Hartlepool harbour itself. The scout cruiser *Patrol* (1904), leader of 9DF, under the command of Captain (D) Alan Cameron Bruce and a second scout cruiser, *Forward* (1904), which had no steam up. They were both in Victoria Dock, more of a tidal basin than a dock and small for the 370ft long scout cruisers. Generally, a tug was necessary to help them out. There was also the submarine *C-9*. When Bruce received *Test*'s signal he replied 'What enemy?' The reply came from the Port War Signal Station; 'three ships in sights, not answering challenge, apparently firing to seaward'. Bruce ordered *Patrol* to leave harbour, commanding a tug to assist.

Meanwhile the destroyers were running for their lives. *Test* was hit by a 5.9in shell and only saved from destruction by her coal bunkers. *Doon* had her searchlight destroyed. Men died on her decks. Fortunately, after ten minutes, the Germans turned all their attention on the town.

It might be questioned as to why the British ships did not attempt a torpedo attack, part of their *raison d'etre*. According to the gunnery officer in *Patrol*, Lieutenant E C Brent, 'it seems a pity that it was not attempted (except in the case of *Test* which had shorter range torpedoes), as there was probably a sporting chance of its success, while the enemy were engaged in shelling the town and firing at *Patrol*'. But they apparently 'thought it would be no use making a torpedo attack'.[13]

Meantime *Patrol* had managed to leave her moorings and was running for the exit channel as fast as she could, through a hail of shot and shell.

The scout cruiser HMS *Patrol* (1904), damaged at Hartlepool. (Author's collection)

'During the whole of the time that *Patrol* was steaming down the fairway channel, she was passing through a zone of very heavy and rapid fire,' Brent later reported. And when at 0828, *Waveney* signalled 'two battleships, dreadnought-class', Brent noted laconically that 'there was nothing for *Patrol* to do but go on!'[14] Both her captain and navigator were knocked flat on the bridge by the wind of a passing shell, and at 0838 she managed to signal 'heavily engaged with battlecruisers'. Just then *Patrol* was hit by two 11.2in shells simultaneously. One went straight through the ship on the fore lower mess deck. Then she was hit by a 5.9in shell. The ship rapidly filled with water and Bruce grounded her whilst they tried to repair the damage. This probably saved her, for the German gunners did not realise she had stopped and fired ahead of *Patrol*'s position.

At 0850, the bombardment ceased and the German ships sailed away. *Forward* had continued to try to raise steam and leave the dock, but the tug refused to assist because of all the shells falling into the area. When she finally emerged, the enemy had departed. She asked Bruce if he wanted her to stand by him, but he ordered; 'no, scout towards enemy, keeping out of range'.[15] *Patrol* finally made it to the Tees and anchored with 3ft of water in her messdecks.

The submarine *C-9* had followed *Patrol* out of the dock but was hit on the conning tower by shell fragments, which caused her to dive for protection. She bounced off the bottom, lost control and by the time her commander felt able to surface, the German ships had gone.

What about the town and the battery? The three ships targeting the port boasted twenty 11in and twelve 8.3in guns between them. At 0810 they opened fire on the town. Hartlepool was a defended site with a volunteer RGA battery, the Durham Volunteers. Allocated three guns in the Owen report, there were now two 6in guns at the Heugh Battery and one at the Lighthouse Battery.

The commander of the RGA TF detachment was Lieutenant Colonel Lancelot Robson, a doctor and former mayor of Hartlepool. Under him were eleven officers and 155 local volunteers. At midnight on the 15/16th, Robson received a message saying that a German squadron was in the North Sea and expected to attack Hartlepool.* This did not seem to greatly trouble him and he went to bed. He later stated that the guns were always manned one hour before dawn, so there was no need for panic. At 0805 he received a message 'three warships coming at great speed . . . they are our ships flying the Royal Navy ensign'.[16] All three German ships were using British flags as a disguise. As they opened fire, they hauled them down and raised the insignia of the *Kaiserliche Marine*.

Lieutenant Colonel Lancelot Robson, who commanded the RGA battery at Hartlepool. (Author's collection)

Robson left his breakfast half eaten and ran to the Heugh to be greeted by the barking of the battery dog. The false flags had confused the gunners as to the identity of the approaching ships, but when shells began to fall around them, they returned the fire. The first shots from the sea severed the telephone cable connecting Robson to the rest of his command and fire control was then out of the question. Each gun was fought separately using autosights. Heugh Battery engaged first SMS *Seydlitz* and then *Moltke* until these warships passed out of its arc of fire. The German strategy was initially to fire at the batteries, and then leave that task to *Blücher* while the others fired at the town and harbour. Hence the RGA gunners concentrated on the static *Blücher* which was firing at Lighthouse Battery. They found their shells had no effect on the armoured sides of the ships, so instead aimed at masts

---

* No such warning was sent to the port SNO, nor did Robson share it with him.

and rigging. The accuracy of the gunnery was sufficient to cause *Blücher* to move behind the lighthouse to avoid further hits. Two of her 5.9in guns were disabled and the bridge and an 8.3in gun were damaged. Seven hits were claimed by the RGA men in total.

The Germans used armour-piercing (AP) shells with delayed action fuses, which proved to be an error as many failed to explode or ricocheted around the town, because they were travelling horizontally, rather than plunging. Nonetheless, their gunfire caused considerable damage and slaughter and, as at Scarborough, the roads and the railway station were jammed with fleeing civilians, anticipating an invasion. Hits were obtained on the Heugh battery apron and the position would surely have been destroyed if common shell had been used.

The Baptist Chapel in Hartlepool, showing the shellfire damage. (Author's collection)

Houses in Carlton Terrace, Hartlepool, after they had been struck by German shells. (Author's collection)

St Barnabas church. (Author's collection)

In an action lasting some 42 minutes, the two batteries fired 112 rounds between them, although the Lighthouse Battery managed only fifteen of these due to persistent misfire problems. The three German ships fired 1,150 shells into Hartlepool. They damaged 300 houses, hit seven churches, the public library, two schools, an engineering works, cement factory, tram station and Irvine's shipyard. A shell passed right through Lloyd's Bank and the gasworks was hit, which with one explosion deprived the town of artificial light.

At the railway station a shell came through the wall and onto the platform, making a huge breach. A train was standing in the station at the time, and the badly shocked passengers jumped out and refused to continue the journey. A porter was seriously injured in the leg by bits of flying brick, The offices of the *Northern Daily Mail* were hit and partially wrecked. In front of the building a telegraph pole was carried away and a round entered the concrete shell of the readers room and exploded. Yet another projectile struck the side of the Mill House Inn, not far away. It took the corner of the building off, crashed through an adjoining wall, and finally cleared away the two ground floor rooms of a house in Poplar Grove.

The havoc in Moor Terrace and Victoria Terrace was terrific. The rectory was damaged by exploding shells and its roof blown off. It became known to the locals as 'hellfire corner'. In front of the Scandinavian church,* a 12in shell made a huge hole 'big enough to hold a horse and cart'.[17] And on the headland, one shell fell in the courtyard of Ambleside,† killing the cook. Salvation Army Adjutant William Avery lived with his six children in a Salvation Army house at 7 Victoria Place; he died working upstairs, while his family sheltered below. In William Street, a shell hit the Dixon household. Mr Dixon was away with the army, but his wife was maimed and three of their six children – George aged 14, Margaret aged 8, and Albert aged 7 – were killed.

John O'Heugh was a bonus clerk at Ricardson's, Westgarth and Co, Marine Engineers. He was having breakfast with two colleagues when the newsboy brought the morning papers and told them that 'the Germans are here. I just said "hop it" but before he was down the stairs a shell dropped into the generating station putting all the machinery out of action.'[18] They ran for home, dodging shells as they went and at the railway workshop stopped and sheltered behind a wall. From there they saw the shell that hit the gasometer 'which exploded' and noted shells falling into the coal dock.

Trying a route across the West Harbour footbridge, O'Heugh

---

* The Swedish or Scandinavian church was on the corner of Middleton Road and Clarence Road and opened in 1885.
† Ableside was a large house in Elwick Road overlooking the Burn Valley Gardens, built around 1900. It was the home of William Ropner who was son of renowned shipowner Sir Robert Ropner.

remembered 'opposite the dockmaster's house a man lay dead. In Harbour Terrace a shell passed through an upper bedroom, blowing out an iron bedstead: feathers were flying all over. At the entrance to Irvine's Yard, a newsboy lay dead. Ironically, a German collier in dock was struck by a shell.'[19] O'Heugh saw the fleeing crowds first hand. 'Proceeding towards Greenland, we met crowds of people leaving the town, making for the country. Some were in their nightclothes and dressing gowns. One lady was carrying her Christmas cake.'[20]

George Jobling's house was hit, knocking him across the room. When he recovered, 'I went round to the door and found three children among a lot of bricks, two of them being my son's children. They had been killed by a shell which struck my house', he told the subsequent inquest.[21] His son was a stoker in the Royal Navy, away on duty.

In 1970, the *Northern Daily Mail* carried a piece of doggerel written by an anonymous lady who had seen the bombardment as a child. Some passages pay testament to the invasion panic which effected the populace.

'. . . Run for your lives, the Germans are here . . .'
'. . . .Heading for the country other families we met
How we got there I'll never know
The railway station was full as we passed
Of people trying to get out of town fast'.
And most piteously;
'Reaching our home again in despair
On finding the roof was no longer there'.[22]

In the harbour, merchant ships were hit; *City of Newcastle*, SS *Firfield*, SS *Sagama River* (on which two men were killed), the troopship *Munificent* (where a steward lost his life), *Phoebe* (whose 2nd mate died) and *Ingrid II*.

Three RGA volunteers died, William Stephen Houston, Robert Spence and Edward George Hopgood, while the raid also resulted in the first death of a British soldier from enemy action on British soil for 200 years, when Private Theophilus Jones, of the Durham Light Infantry, aged 29, was killed. He was one of six DLI men to lose their lives in the attack.

In Hartlepool, nine soldiers and sixty-four civilians were killed, including six aged 8 or under. In West Hartlepool, fifty-five were killed, fourteen of whom were aged 8 or less. Among the dead was John Shields Ryalls, just four months- old.

All day people queued at the Post Office, lit by oil lamps, to cable relations of their survival. They thought themselves lucky that it hadn't been the invasion they so feared.

Where Was the Navy?

The Admiralty, as noted above, had not intended to stop the German bombardment, even if it could locate the enemy fleet. But it did mean to catch them on the return. At Harwich, Tyrwhitt received conflicting commands. Jellicoe suggested that he rendezvous with the heavy ships headed down the coast. But Tyrwhitt had already been instructed to try to get in touch with the enemy off the east coast and shadow them if he could. Accordingly, he made towards Yarmouth, arriving at 0630 on the 16th. The weather was filthy and he sheltered his force behind the shoal banks,* awaiting developments.

When he received a signal with news of the attack, Tyrwhitt took his light cruisers and all his destroyers and tried to get out of the sheltering shoals through the Haisborough Gap. But the seas were too steep. He sent the destroyers back to Yarmouth and proceeded with the cruisers; and found nothing. In bad weather he was too far away for making contact and was never less than about 600 miles away from the enemy.

Beatty and Warrender were heading for the rendezvous point when the destroyers escorting the 2nd Battle Squadron (2BS) made contact with some German destroyers and light cruisers, beginning a close-range action. This first contact led to misunderstanding on both sides. Ingenohl believed that the whole Grand Fleet was out and in close proximity. Without telling Hipper, he turned tail and made for home at the fleet's best speed. Warrender, however, thought he was in the vicinity of only light German forces and set off in pursuit. His six battleships and Beatty's four battlecruisers were thus pursuing virtually the entire High Seas Fleet. If Ingenohl reversed his course again, within 20 minutes and in daylight he would have the tactical situation that he had planned for – ten prized British capital ships at his mercy.

Meanwhile, Hipper was blithely returning to the Jade, in blissful ignorance of his superior's desertion. When Warrender received news of the raid and confirmation of the place and time, he immediately reversed course and it seemed that now the boot would be on the other foot, and Hipper's ships would be the ones to meet a larger force.

At 1125, Goodenough's light cruisers sighted Hipper's advanced look out and engaged, *Birmingham* and *Southampton* exchanging fire with the enemy. At this point the German battlecruisers were only 50 miles distant. But now Beatty made the first of what would be three catastrophic signalling errors which would cost him three battles over the next two years. Believing that

---

* There are extensive shoals off the Norfolk coast running from Caister south to Great Yarmouth, including Caister Shoals, Cockle Shoals, Cross Sands, Corton, Holm Sands and Scroby Sands.

HMS *Orion* (1910), five turrets each with two 13.5in guns. Famously she was ordered not to fire on the German ships in sight. (US Naval History and Heritage Command NH 57802

two light cruisers were sufficient to deal with the enemy forces in sight, he ordered Goodenough's other two, *Nottingham* and *Falmouth*, to resume their lookout position and take station five miles ahead of him. Goodenough, taking the signal to refer to all his ships, broke off contact. Hipper altered course at the same time. The opportunity was gone. There was another brief contact between Warrender's escorts, but Hipper was safe and in dreadful weather slipped the trap. At one point the battleship HMS *Orion* (1910, ten 13.5in guns) sighted and trained her guns on German ships and her captain, Frederic Dryer, requested permission to fire from his division commander, Rear Admiral Robert Arbuthnot. Arbuthnot refused, stating that they must wait for an order from Warrender, an order which never came.

Beatty blamed Goodenough and tried to have him replaced. But in fact, the fault was his, or rather that of his signals officer, Lieutenant Commander Ralph Seymour. If it was anybody's fault that Hipper escaped, it was Seymour's.

'All concerned' wrote a furious Fisher 'made a hash of it'. The enemy escaped from the very jaws of death. Jellicoe too was 'intensely unhappy; we had', he said, 'the opportunity of our lives'.[23]

Aftermath

The day after the attack, George Halliday went to Scarborough with his aunts and 'all along the sea front was shattered'.[24] At Hartlepool, the afternoon was bright and sunny. It brought thousands of rather ghoulish visitors to see the damage, amongst them Lord and Lady Londonderry.*

The field of some 100 mines laid off the Yorkshire coast was troublesome because the minesweeping trawlers had thus far only to keep clear a swept channel from the Downs to Flamborough Head, that is, inside the minefields which the Germans had laid off the eastern counties and the Humber, and which had been purposely left intact. Now the channel had to be continued northwards past Scarborough, and until it was swept all navigation between the Tyne and Flamborough Head had to be stopped. Much of this new field was incorporated into an extended East Coast War Channel.

The bravery and good showing made by the RGA volunteer detachment at Hartlepool was recognised when Lancelot Robson was granted the Distinguished Service Order. Sergeant T Douthwaite was awarded a Distinguished Conduct Medal for extracting a live cartridge from the breech of the Lighthouse Battery gun after a misfire, and Acting Bombardier J J Hope and Bombardier F W Mallin each received the Military Medal for their actions.

Vice Admiral Franz von Hipper who commanded the German battlecruisers forces (1st Scouting Group) from 1914 until August 1918. His bombardment of English coastal towns in 1914 earned him the soubriquet of 'the baby killer' in Britain. (Author's collection)

The SNO Hartlepool was sent a letter from the Hartlepool and District Traders Defence Association which reported a resolution adopted at their last meeting, in which they 'expressed their admiration of the gallant conduct of the officers and men of His Majesty's ships stationed at Hartlepool in so bravely going out to engage the enemy who were in such outstanding force on the occasion of the attack on the Hartlepools'.[25]

But the general population felt a considerable uncertainty. 'The bombardment of a civil town was a conception, absolutely new, not to be grasped or understood in a long half hour of bewildering shock.'[26] Churchill

---

* Charles Vane-Tempest-Stewart, 6th Marquess of Londonderry, former Conservative politician and owner of many coalmines in County Durham. The family seat was Wynyard Hall near Stockton-on-Tees.

An enlistment poster, playing on the Scarborough/Hartlepool raids. (Library of Congress LC-USZC4-10890)

Another Scarborough-derived enlistment poster, using the image of a little girl to tug at the emotions.
(Library of Congress LC-USZC4-11297)

wrote to the mayor of Scarborough of 'the stigma of the baby killers of Scarborough'.[27] Lieutenant Stephen King-Hall of HMS *Southampton* noted in his diary that 'as an exhibition of Teutonic frightfulness, it may be held to have succeeded. Its most permanent result was the stimulus it gave to recruiting.'[28] Locally-born artist James Clark painted *The Bombardment of the Hartlepools, 16 December 1914* for the Royal Academy's Summer Exhibition.

The Admiralty did not help the matter with a series of communiques which were glib to say the least. 'The Admiralty take this opportunity of pointing out that demonstrations of this character against unfortified towns, though not difficult to accomplish provided that a certain risk is accepted, are devoid of military significance.'[29] This rather avoided the fact that people had died. A subsequent notice tried recognise this; 'We share your disappointment that the miscreants escaped unpunished . . . the stigma of the baby killers of Scarborough will brand its officers and men while sailors sail the sea.'[30]

In Chelsea, Georgina Lee reflected that 'it is mortifying that the German cruisers were able to come 400 miles to bombard three cities [*sic*] and return

'Feed the Guns', a photograph of a money-raising campaign which references the bombardment of 1914. The speakers are standing outside the Pavilion Hotel, Scarborough. The hotel was designed by architect William Baldwin Stewart, built in 1870 and demolished in 1973. (Author's collection)

to Kiel, without any of our fleet being able to stop them. How did they get through? On the way back they sowed mines in the North Sea which have already sunk three of our merchant steamers.'[31] *The Times* thundered 'the Royal Navy says it wishes the Germans would come out and fight. They have come out, and fired on our defenceless towns with impunity. What then does the navy want?'[32]

As for the Admiralty, Admiral Sir Henry Oliver, Chief of the War Staff, placed the blame for the raid on the Admiral of Patrols, George Ballard.

> We had a useless R A [rear admiral] on the East Coast of England and I could not get him shifted. When the Germans bombarded Scarborough and Hartlepool, we knew from Room 40 the afternoon before that something was intended but not enough to know what. He had definite orders to send out two submarines from Hartlepool to be at gun range, according to visibility, off the harbour at dawn. He failed to send them out the night before and they did not start out till after the bombardment began; one was crossing the bar while the shells were falling. We lost a fine chance of laming a battlecruiser and

perhaps bringing on an engagement if her consorts delayed retiring to help her.[33]

'The Scarborough raid made Britain momentarily more ill at ease than anything since the great retreat of the early days.'[34] It was 'as if an attempt had been made to violate Britannia in her own drawing room'.[35]

With the fear that the next raid could be the invasion, it was suggested that Beatty's battlecruisers be sent from Scapa to Sheerness. But Jellicoe saw this as too great a risk to the concentration of the Grand Fleet that would be necessary if the High Seas Fleet came out. Instead 'something was done to bring the battlecruisers more closely into the anti-invasion system. On December 20 Admiral Beatty was ordered to move down from Cromarty and join the 3rd Battle Squadron [eight *King Edward VII*-class pre-dreadnoughts] and the 3rd Cruiser Squadron [four armoured cruisers] at Rosyth.'[36] Later, in the spring of 1915, the monitor *Prince Rupert* (1915) was moored in the Tees, where her two 12in guns, taken from decommissioned *Majestic*-class pre-dreadnoughts, would act as a floating fortress.

Scandal

The raids on Scarborough and Hartlepool were seen as a brutal attack on civilians, an example of Hunnish violence such as had already been reported in Belgium. Much was made of the fact that the attacks contravened the Hague Convention (see Appendix 13).

A painting by William Wylie of HMS *Prince Rupert*, showing her twin 12in gun turret trained around to starboard. She is depicted as in 1916, when her rig had been reduced and an additional 6in and 12pdr gun fitted. (National Maritime Museum PAE2668)

As the navy's Official History put it:

> it was over two centuries since anything like it had occurred upon our shores, and not since De Ruyter's raid on Sheerness had a foreign enemy killed British troops on English soil. ... With the nation at large the prevailing note was one of stern resentment at the shameless breach of the laws of civilised warfare. An open seaside resort had been ruthlessly shelled, a crowded seaport with slender defence had been bombarded without the notice which the Hague Convention prescribed, and the effect was rather to intensify the popular conviction that a people capable of such barbarity could not be permitted to escape chastisement.[37]

At the Admiralty, Captain Herbert Richmond was enraged by the attack.

> This 'insulting the enemy's coast' is quite out of date, apart from any questions of the Hague Convention ... we now know from a letter of an officer of the *Moltke* that they intended to bombard Yarmouth in their last silly raid ... The whole thing is supremely childish and evil-minded ... Of course the German press will represent this as a glorious feat of their navy, proving that they command the North Sea and can move where they desire at will.[38]

War Illustrated further opined 'whatever may be the outcome of this raid, this country's foretaste of the horrors of war as waged by the Kaiser's uniformed serfs in bombarding open towns is very timely. It should be the greatest stimulus to recruiting.'[39]

As became normal for every significant event of the war, both sides struck medals to be sold to raise funds for good causes or the war effort generally. In Scarborough a local newspaper, the *Scarborough Mercury*, commissioned sixpence and half-crown sized medals in aluminium, bronze, silver and gold, the latter two being hallmarked in Birmingham. The medal depicted:

> Obverse. In a circle the arms of Scarborough (centre), a ribbon below; above, a distant view of the sea and three ships bombarding the town (left), shells bursting overhead; below, two separate views (left and right) of the town and beach. Inscription (around arms): 'SIGILLUM COMUNE BURGENSIN DE SCARDEBURG.'* On the ribbon, the legend 'SCARBOROUGH STILL UNDISMAYED.' And on the reverse

---

* 'The common seal of Scarborough'.

was inscribed 'BOMBARDMENT OF SCARBOROUGH & NONCOMBATANTS BY THE GERMAN FLEET DEC. 16TH 1914.'

These sold for prices between three pence (sixpenny aluminium) to seven shillings and sixpence (silver half-crown) and were available from the paper's offices or jewellers' and stationers' shops in the town.

The Germans did likewise, with a medal which commemorated the raids on Scarborough <u>and</u> Hartlepool. It pictured;

> Obverse: Winged Victory carrying a flaming sword in her right hand and a wreath in her left. Legend: 'GOTT SEGNETE DE VEREINIGTEN HEERE.'* Reverse: Inscription, 'BESCHIESS VON SCARBOROUGH U. HARTLEPOOL DURCH DEUTSCHE SCHIFFE 16 DEZ. 1914.'†

'Remember Scarborough' became a British recruitment trope, used on posters and advertisements urging men to enlist. Hipper was branded 'The Baby Killer' and this disparaging soubriquet was used in newspaper and propaganda articles wherever his name was cited.

But the fact remained that the *Kaiserliche Marine* had breached Britain's defences without riposte. Could an invasion fleet, was the question on many lips.

---

* 'God bless the united army'.
† 'Bombardment of Scarborough and Hartlepool by German ships 16 Dec. 1914'.

8

A Troubled Island, 1915

The year 1915 did not start well for the Royal Navy

On 20 December 1914, command of the Channel Fleet (effectively 5BS at Sheerness and 6BS at Portland) passed from Admiral Burney to Vice Admiral Lewis Bayly. Bayly was taciturn, hard driving and considered something of a martinet. Believing his new command in need of gunnery practice, a reasonable worry as the pre-dreadnoughts of 5BS and 6BS were supposed to be the initial bulwark against invasion, at the end of the year he took the 5th Battle Squadron to Portland to exercise both of his new commands.

On 31 December 1914, with the gunnery practice over, Bayly refused to put into port for the New Year celebrations. Instead, both Battle Squadrons were at 10 knots, cruising around in the dark, with no escort. All ships had been darkened at nightfall and at 1900 the fleet turned through sixteen points in accordance with an Admiralty Fleet order requiring an alteration of course soon after dark in areas where a submarine attack was possible. At 0200 on the first day of 1915, the fleet was again turned through sixteen points, in succession, which meant that they all executed their turn in the same place.

Unbeknown to Bayly or anybody else, the formation had a stalker. The German submarine *U-24* had been built in 1912 and armed with four torpedo tubes firing 50cm (20in) torpedoes (which could carry a 362lb charge of TNT for up to 3,500 yards) and an 8.8cm (3.4in) gun. One of the first class of German submarines to be powered by a diesel engine, her gun was of larger calibre than her predecessors to allow her to attack merchant ships on the surface and thus save on expenditure of torpedoes. Capable of 17 knots on the surface and 9–10 when dived, she carried a complement of thirty-five under 32-year-old *Kapitänleutnant* Rudolph Schneider.

That last day of December, lurking off Portland Harbour and waiting for prey, Schneider had spotted the 6th Battle Squadron sailing away from him. Later he sighted three large warships steaming down channel and decided to shadow them. There was a very heavy sea running but visibility was good throughout the day and into the evening and he found trailing them easy, particularly so as they were cruising at modest speed and were not zig-zagging. Just after midnight on 1 January 1915, aided by a full moon,

Schneider was able to identify the three vessels he had been shadowing as battleships. Manoeuvring *U-24* towards them undetected, he selected his target and fired one torpedo at HMS *Queen* (1902), which missed.

As 5BS completed its 0200 sixteen-point turn, which placed it some 20 miles off Start Point, the rearmost ship was HMS *Formidable*. Launched at Portsmouth in 1898, she was not completed until 1901, due to problems with the contractors building her machinery (who went into liquidation) and engines (strikes at the engineering shops). Displacing over 15,000 tons and armed with four 40-calibre 12in guns and twelve 6in BL, she was considered to be under-gunned for her size and by the time she was ready for service she would be soon overtaken by the more heavily armed and faster *King Edward VII*-class of battleships. Home to 780 crew, she was considered a good steamer. Now she swam into Schneider's sights, and he fired a single torpedo. At 0220 it hit home, blowing a huge hole in *Formidable*'s side and disabling the ship's dynamo room, robbing her of lighting and power for the wireless and other electrical apparatus.

The ship swiftly assumed a 20-degree list, which meant the lifeboats on one side were unusable. Moreover, the weather was terrible, with a storm-force wind. As men battled to save themselves and the ship, at 0305 *U-24* launched another torpedo, hitting home again on the starboard side close to her bow. *Formidable* sank by the bow at 0445; 583 officers and men died, including her captain, Arthur Loxley.

A painting of HMS *Formidable* by Charles L Dixon, depicting her in Plymouth Sound. (Author's collection)

HMS *Formidable* and her captain (inset) Arthur Loxley. (Author's collection)

Bayly was relieved of command of the Channel Fleet* and the Admiralty issued instructions that there should be no training exercises conducted in the Channel without destroyer escort. It was a shocking way to start the year, and the loss of so many sailors and a battleship, sunk so close to the shores they were protecting, did nothing to improve the mood of the nation.

A Victory of a Sort

In his raids of November and December 1914, Hipper had been unpleasantly surprised that the Royal Navy seemed to know he was out. He convinced himself that this must be because British or neutral fishing vessels in the Dogger Bank area were reporting his movements to the British. He decided to put an end to it.

His plan was to send the battlecruisers of the 1st Scouting Group to clear the area of fishing vessels and dubious neutrals and to attack any small Royal Navy warships that they came across, with the High Seas Fleet covering the withdrawal. This limited operation conformed to the ban by the Kaiser on aggressive moves by the High Seas Fleet, which had been reiterated on 10 January. But as Hipper prepared for this new mission, Room 40 was once again able to issue an alert.

The 1st Scouting Group and their support sailed on 23 January and comprised three battlecruisers, *Seydlitz*, *Moltke* and *Derfflinger*; together with the slower and less well armed armoured cruiser *Blücher*. There were also four light cruisers and a strong destroyer flotilla. Beatty, with his battlecruisers and Goodenough's 1 LCS, together with Tyrwhitt and the Harwich Flotilla were ordered to a rendezvous on the north-east part of the Dogger Bank and the Grand Fleet was directed to a holding position further north.

---

* He was soon reinstated in a high position, being placed in charge of the Coast of Ireland Command in July 1915.

On 24 January, just after 0700, two of the Harwich cruisers, *Aurora* and *Undaunted*, sighted SMS *Kolberg* (1908), twelve 10.5cm (4.1in) guns, with four destroyers in company. HMS *Aurora* challenged by searchlight which brought the response of a single letter flashed from the German light cruiser and a burst of gunfire, which was immediately returned. The German fire was accurate but fell off as *Kolberg* sustained hits. Nonetheless, *Aurora* was struck three times. The German received a hit below the waterline and after a shell exploded under her forebridge, *Kolberg* turned away and headed east. *Aurora* with *Undaunted* then resumed their course.

However, they next observed enemy forces far off their starboard quarter and turned to keep them in sight. This brought them in touch with *Southampton* and 1 LCS to whom they reported the presence of the German ships they had seen. A few minutes later, Goodenough spotted the German main body, which, having spread out for a sweep of the area, had hastily concentrated on receiving the alarm from *Kolberg*.

Meanwhile, having seen the gun flashes, Beatty worked up speed to give chase, with Tyrwhitt and his 'M'-class destroyers in company, and by 0750 he could see the smoke of the German battlecruisers. Hipper had turned away and was making all steam to escape to the south-east. Tyrwhitt was

Beatty's flagship at Heligoland, Dogger Bank and Jutland, HMS *Lion* (1910) as pictured in 1919. She mounted eight 13.5in guns with a top speed of 28 knots. (US Naval History and Heritage Command NH 77291)

An iconic picture of SMS *Blücher* sinking. Until the Second World War, the original hung in the Naval Secretary's office at the Admiralty. (photo; private collection)

ordered to take his destroyers and get ahead of Beatty's force to scout the ships he was opposing. The 'M' class were the fastest destroyers in the fleet and were unleashed as they worked up to their full speed of 35 knots. They closed the range to 9,000 yards before the rearmost enemy ship, *Blücher*, altered course to open fire and forced them to turn away.

The running fight which now developed has been described many times and it seems redundant to cover it in detail here. Sufficient to say that in a stern chase of British pursuing German battlecruisers, which lasted several hours, *Lion* received a hit which crippled her, causing Beatty to lose control of the tactical situation. Moreover, an emergency turn-away from a non-existent submarine and a second signalling gaff by Beatty's flag lieutenant, Seymour, caused the British force to focus on *Blücher*, which was set ablaze and wrecked, whilst allowing the remainder of Hipper's ships to escape.

Blücher capsized and sank shortly after 1145. The media made much of this success and with *Blücher* sunk, 'technically, the Dogger Bank was a British victory. The enemy had fled the field, *Seydlitz* had been damaged, over 1,000 German seamen had been lost (killed or taken prisoner). British casualties were less than fifty . . . the *Lion*'s injuries were not vital.'[1] But despite press adulation, the Royal Navy had lost the chance for an annihilating battle, and for Beatty, 'the disappointment is more than I can bear to think of. Everybody thinks it was a great success when in reality it was a terrible failure.'[2] It was a mutilated victory, but one which at least gave the country some cheer.

On 2 February 'the Dogger Bank action cost von Ingenohl his command'.[3]

> The *Admiralstab* reviewed the whole conduct of the war since the High Sea Fleet had been in Admiral von Ingenohl's hands, and came to the conclusion that he had not realised the truth that dissipation of forces is always disastrous, particularly for the weaker side. The only possibility of guarding against further disasters appeared to be a change of command. Moreover, the confidence of officers in their leader had been shaken, and this mistrust might spread to the nation, with serious results. In view of these opinions, it was decided to relieve both Admiral von Ingenohl and also his Chief of Staff.[4]

He was replaced by Admiral Hugo von Pohl, who cautiously followed the Kaiser's dictates not to risk his big ships. Had they but known it, the citizens of Britain were saved from coastal attack by surface ships, by direction of German's 'Supreme Highest'. Perhaps more by luck than judgement, the navy had succeeded, for now, in seeing off the coastal raiders.

Two days after this change of German naval command, Germany declared unrestricted submarine warfare. This meant that any ship, naval or civilian, would be torpedoed and sunk on sight and without warning; the announcement stated that 'Germany now declares all waters surrounding Great Britain and Ireland . . . as an area of war . . . beginning 18 February 1915 it will endeavour to destroy every merchant ship found in this area without it always being possible to avert the peril that threatens persons and cargos'.[5] This was a direct attempt to disrupt the Allied supply chain and in part retaliation for the increasingly successful Royal Navy blockade of Germany. In particular, it was timed to strike in the spring in order to disrupt Argentinian and Australian wheat shipments to Britain in the hope of causing a shortage before the British harvest was taken in.

The RGA Strike Back

Despite the considerable sums of money invested in them, Britain's coastal artillery defences rarely got to grips with the enemy. An exception came on 29 January 1915.

Walney Island is a 14-mile-long stretch of land, connected to the mainland by a bridge built in 1908, off the north-west coast at Barrow-in-

Furness. The sheltered strait between Barrow and Walney proved ideal for shipbuilding and from the middle of the nineteenth century the great armaments and shipbuilding concern of Vickers grew up there, producing everything from guns and submarines to airships. In 1911, a fort was constructed on the island, to give protection to the Vickers complex, armed with two 6in guns. When war came, this fortress was manned by the volunteers of Number 7 Company, Lancashire and Cheshire Royal Garrison Artillery, a TF unit formed in the Haldane reforms of 1908.

At around 1430 on Friday 29 January, a submarine was observed to surface some 7,000 yards off the fortification. The *Barrow News* reported the following day that 'the coastguards signalled to the vessel, but received no reply. It soon became evident that the vessel belonged to the German navy, and the guns were trained on her, and the men awaited orders to fire. The first shots, however, came from the submarine. There were two shots, and both fell some distance short. That, if nothing else, settled the nationality of this impudent intruder.'[6]

The U-boat fired just two rounds, thought to be aimed at the airship sheds on the island, to which the RGA gunners replied with eleven 6in shells from their battery. With excessive enthusiasm, an eyewitness stated that the shots went

> dead into the submarine. 'It was really magnificent practice,' he remarked, with evident satisfaction. Asked if he had any doubt that it was a submarine, the gentleman interviewed was quite emphatic on the point that it was one. 'There is no doubt about it,' he said, and he was equally convinced that the craft was sunk by the firing from the forts, and did not submerge of her own account. 'She went down too rapidly for that,' he added. After the vessel disappeared the guns fired several further rounds right on the spot where she had been.

The battery commander was more reticent, replying to a reporter that 'I would rather say nothing about it'.[7]

Nonetheless, the gunners were jubilant; 'needless to say, the men of the RGA were overjoyed at the thought of having engaged in actual warfare, with such, presumably, notable success', reported the *Barrow News*.

That night, a search was made at sea for wreckage or bodies, but none was found. This was unsurprising, for the offending U-boat, *U-21* commanded by *Kapitänleutnant* Otto Hersing,* had left the scene and the

---

* Hersing in *U-21* had torpedoed the scout cruiser HMS *Pathfinder* on 5 September 1914, the first British warship to be sunk by a U-boat

The sinking of the *Linda Blanche* (*Kaperung und Versenkung des englischen Handelsdampfer Linda Blanche*) by Willy Stöwer. She was sunk by *U-21* the day after the submarine had bombarded Walney Island. SS *Linda Blanche* (1914, 530grt) was built by Scott & Sons and owned by the Anglesey Shipping Co, Bangor. (Author's collection)

following day would sink three steamers – *Ben Cruachan*, *Kilcoan* and *Linda Blanche* – in the same sea area. *U-21* carried a 10.5cm (4.1in) deck gun and 300 rounds of ammunition, so it is entirely possible that the prompt intervention of the RGA battery saved the airship sheds and other facilities from a more sustained bombardment. But Hersing had sent a message that it wasn't just the east coast that was endangered.

Invasion Response Planning

There may have been no invasion in 1914, but 1915 saw a flurry of response plans being developed, largely using powers granted under the Defence of the Realm Act.

The process was led by the county lord lieutenants, the chief constable and local army officers. Essex was near to France and here the recommendations generated by the Samuel committee showed up in a document created in January 1915. The population of Essex, all 1.4 million of them, were to be evacuated, *en masse*, to Hertfordshire and Oxfordshire, should the Germans invade. Under the evacuation plan, Essex residents were told they could only take jewellery and money and food for up to three days. Crops and livestock were to be destroyed, along with firearms, petrol, tyres and vessels. Alcohol would also be destroyed, following rumours of drunken Germans behaving barbarically in Belgium and France.

Censuses of horses, animals, grain stores etc were carried out, but practical problems immediately emerged. Who would provide compensation for lost beasts or property? How would their values be proved. The chief constable apparently said the police would issue vouchers but surely they would have other things to do. And the army representatives averred this would mean too much compensation and was unnecessary. And anyway, what would people eat and drink?

By February, local directives had been developed – but how to communicate them? Youths were enlisted to paint arrows on walls indicting the routes evacuees should take when leaving,* to keep other roads free for military use. Organisers would wear armbands, ringing of church bells would be the signal the invasion had happened, and residents were advised not to lock their doors when deserting their property. By May, public warning posters had been prepared and distributed, even though the Home Office stressed that there was no immediate threat.

In Norfolk, Local Emergency Committees were formed under the direction of the lord lieutenant of the county, the Earl of Leicester, and a Central Organising Committee for Norfolk was created, for which, for example, the Norwich representatives were the lord mayor and the town clerk. And a Civilians' Emergency Corps was established, whose purpose was, in the event of invasion, to destroy horses to prevent the animals falling into enemy hands.

Further from the sea, a similar debate was taking place in Surrey. There the primary concern was how the county would cope with the impact of the fighting on the south coast and the potential movement of thousands of fleeing people. On 20 January, the *Surrey Comet* published a long feature detailing how Surrey would be effected by invasion. It noted that there would be an important role for the police: 'Should it be necessary at any time to clear any portion of the county for military operations, notices will be sent through the police to individual owners in regard to various types of vehicles

---

* According to Historic England, some of these direction arrows can still be faintly seen. A plaque at Orford House in Ugley, Essex, reads 'this and many similar arrows were painted to direct non-combatants inlands across country, avoiding main roads to facilitate the movement of troops in the event of a successful landing by the Germans on the East Coast'.

or livestock, etc, giving them orders for removal or destruction.' Readers were also notified that 'special routes' had been laid out in these plans, 'avoiding main roads for the removal of cattle', and arrangements had been made for 'local guides', with 'billeting stations fixed, and areas into which live stock will be removed selected'. Owners of animals, it added, 'would furnish their own herdsmen'. Reflecting the legal points regarding armed civilians noted in Chapter 5, the *Comet* also warned that the actual defence of the county was to be in the hands of authorised forces only: 'The civil population will not be allowed to bear arms unless duly enlisted in a Volunteer Corps which has been recognised by the War Office. A register of affiliated Volunteer Corps is being made.'[8]

Spy mania continued to flourish and 1915 saw the publication of *My Adventures as a Spy* by Lieutenant General Sir Robert Baden-Powell. This stirring tome included chapters on such topics as 'different degrees of spies', 'German plans for invading England', 'secret messages and how carried', and 'exploring a foreign dockyard'.

By posing as an American, Baden-Powell was informed of the German plan

> by which they proposed to invade our country . . . The German idea then – some six years ago – was that they could, by means of mines and submarines, at any time block the traffic in the British Channel in the space of a few hours, thus holding our home fleets in their stations at Spithead and Portland.
>
> With the Straits of Dover so blocked, they could then rush a fleet of transports across the North Sea from Germany, to the East Coast of England, either East Anglia or, as in this plan, in Yorkshire. They had in Germany nine embarking stations, with piers and platforms, all ready made, and steel lighters for disembarkation purposes or for actual traversing of the ocean in case of fine weather.[9]

William Le Queux further added to the paranoia with the publication in February of yet another sensationalist book, *German Spies in England: An Exposure*. Received with favourable reviews, it fabricated a system of German espionage that ranged from German prostitutes around Piccadilly Circus to 'naturalised' businessmen of the highest social standing. Hairdressers and waiters were also picked out as particularly suspicious. The Home Secretary wrote to chiefs of police warning them to be on their guard against enemy agents posing as circus performers or commercial travellers to gain intelligence information. On 1 February, photographs were required for British passports for the first time, and in May, the Asquith government decided to intern all enemy aliens resident in Britain.* Unfortunately there was nowhere immediately available to put them, so the Admiralty chartered nine transatlantic liners for the purpose.

Following the events of the previous year at Yarmouth, Scarborough and Hartlepool, and aside from invasion, bombardments from the sea also worried coastal dwellers. In Suffolk, the 'Emergency Committee of the Halesworth† Police Division' saw fit in January 1915 to issue a warning notice entitled 'Instructions for the Guidance of the Civil Population in the Event of Bombardment from the Sea'. Signed by G Bence-Lambert,‡ the committee's chairman, it enjoined the populace to follow the instructions agreed by the War Office and the Admiralty in the event of attack, viz:

> 1. Inhabitants of houses should go into the cellars or lower rooms. If the houses are on a sea front, where they are exposed to direct fire from the sea, the inhabitants should leave by the back door and seek shelter elsewhere.
> 2. Gathering into crowds or watching the bombardment from an exposed position may lead to unnecessary loss of life.
> 3. If an aircraft is seen or heard overhead, crowds should disperse and all persons should if possible take shelter.
> 4. Unexploded bombs should not be touched, as they may burst if moved: the local military authorities should be informed where they are as soon as this can be done safely.

People remained afraid. Of course, there may also have been some devious logic in continuing to promulgate invasion fears through such planning documents as noted above. For a cowed nation is much easier to direct and govern. Thus, two purposes were served. Contingencies were in place; and the nation largely did as DORA told it.

The USA

Invasion fears were not confined to Britain; during 1915, they were rife in America too.§ As Professor Patrick Weil has noted, 'until 1914, the United

---

* The act, dated 13 May, effected all adult male enemy aliens between the ages of 17 and 55 and remained in force until 1919.
† Fifteen miles south-west of Lowestoft.
‡ Who was Colonel Guy Lenox Bence-Lambert of Thorington Hall, and once of the Connaught Rangers.
§ During the 1890s Germany had identified the USA as its future main global rival. From 1890 to 1901 the German Naval High Command, especially Rear Admiral Ernst Otto von Diederichs, laid a number of far-fetched plans for landing an army on American soil. Boston, New York and Washington were identified as targets. Full confidence was expressed that the small American fleet could be dealt with easily, as could the small US army. Indeed, the American naval theorist Alfred Thayer Mahan had envisaged just such a German attack on the US east coast, precipitated by economic rivalry and implicitly supported by a neutral Britain.

States had been protected by 3,000 miles of water off its east coast and 5,000 miles off its west coast. These oceans were mainly controlled by Britain, so that the United States could afford to be ignorant and inactive on the global stage without great consequence.'[10] War changed that. Under the headline 'The United States – An Undefended Treasure Land', *Scientific American* magazine editorialised:

> Today war falls like a thunderbolt from heaven, and the first is often the decisive blow . . . The days of small standing armies, of slow preparation, and of still slower transportation have passed. The possible enemies of today are fully prepared. They control almost unlimited transport, and once in possession of sea control can land when and where they wish, certain that no well-organised or thoroughly equipped force will be ready to oppose them. The weakness of our military establishment, our total lack of reserves, or trained men, or of adequate reserves of material, are known to the last detail by all our possible antagonist.[11]

Early in 1916 a group of suffragists in Maine, led by one Lurana Sheldon Ferris, formed a 'Woman's Defence Club' to instruct women to shoot and defend themselves and their families from German attack. The *New York Times* reported that they 'would not be as helpless as Belgian women' and rather than wait to be raped or killed by 'madmen' she and her colleagues were 'prepared to kill' if necessary.[12] Meanwhile, in 1915 the US War Department had estimated that 'Germany, if not interfered with, could land 337,000 men in America in sixteen days and 440,000 men in thirty-one days'.[13]

There was clearly vested interest in these claims, for a standing army had never been popular in the USA, but a 'Preparedness Movement' was afoot, led by ex-president Theodore Roosevelt and former Chief of Staff of the US Army Leonard Wood, and many in the USA were concerned that their boundaries were both long and open.

May Mayhem

The month of May brought with it two events which had a profound effect on the war. In the early afternoon of 7 May, the Cunard liner *Lusitania*, 30,396 tons, on passage from New York to Liverpool with 1,959 passengers and crew aboard, arrived off the coast of Ireland, the so-called Western Approaches. Here German submarines lurked to intercept vessels headed for British ports.

She had left the USA on 1 May, the warnings placed in newspapers by the German embassy of the possibility of attack on British and neutral ships by U-boats ringing in her passengers' ears. Since her departure, the six days following had resulted in twenty-six ships sunk in the war zone around the coast of Britain. The previous day the Admiralty had sent a message to the *Lusitania*'s master, William Turner, that there were submarines active in the area he was now entering (three had indeed been sent to the Irish Sea and Bristol Channel). Turner was a careful man. He had the lifeboats swung out, the watertight doors closed and the number of lookouts doubled.

Sometime before 1100, the liner had run into fog and Turner slowed his speed to 15 knots. He also wanted to take a sight using the lighthouse on the tip of the Old Head of Kinsale; and he may have hoped to delay his arrival at Liverpool so as to cross the harbour bar at high tide.

U-20 had three torpedoes left, having already sunk three merchant vessels in the last three days. She sighted the big ship at 1320, when the U-boat was on the surface; given that standing orders required her to keep two torpedoes for her return journey, she could only fire once. *Kapitānleutnant* Walther Schweiger ordered a dive and began to manoeuvre for a firing position. A chance starboard turn by the *Lusitania* helped him and at 1410 he fired a single G-type torpedo at a range of only 700m; he couldn't really miss.

On the bridge, Captain Turner suddenly saw the torpedo. 'I immediately tried to change course but was unable to manoeuvre out of the way of it,' he told the *World* newspaper.[14] The explosion in her side mortally wounded the big Cunarder. Her radio operators sent out an SOS 'Come at once. Big list.

RMS *Lusitania* in 1907. (Author's collection)

A trot of German submarines in harbour at Kiel, including *U-20* (second from left), the U-boat which sunk the *Lusitania*, and *U-21* (extreme right foreground) which shelled Walney Island. (Library of Congress LC-DIG-ggbain-17782)

Ten miles south of Old Kinsale Head'[15] and the crew endeavoured to launch the lifeboats; but the conditions of the sinking made doing so extremely difficult, and in some cases impossible, due to the ship's severe list. All of the lifeboats on the port side were incapable of launch and those on the starboard side were now very high above the water because of the 30-degree list the ship had quickly taken. In all, only six out of twenty-two regular lifeboats, together with a number of her twenty-six collapsible rafts were launched successfully. Eighteen minutes after the torpedo struck, she sank.

When the final reckoning was made, 1,198 men women and children had died in the sinking, mainly civilians, going about their quotidian lives. Ninety-four of the victims were children; thirty-five out of thirty-nine babies on board drowned. Also among the dead were 128 American citizens. Whether they liked it or not, the USA was effected by the war, and the nation's slow walk to joining the conflict began with the *Lusitania* tragedy.

Meanwhile, relations between the two mercurial men at the top of the Admiralty, Churchill and Fisher, came to a head in May over the ill-starred Dardanelles campaign, an initiative forced through by Churchill and now clearly a disaster. The failure of the attempt to force the Dardanelles by naval power alone had meant the landing of a large force of soldiery, which immediately incurred heavy losses. It seemed to many people that Britain was engaged in a war in Anatolia which it could not win.

But Churchill kept on pushing, sending more and more ships and equipment there. Additionally, Churchill's arrogation to himself of the powers which had traditionally belonged to the First Sea Lord and the Board of Admiralty had become a matter of great contention between the Sea Lords, Churchill and Jacky Fisher himself. Churchill increasingly issued orders for ships and equipment to be sent without Fisher's prior consent. At 0500 in the morning of 15 May, Fisher received four minutes from Churchill calling for yet more reinforcements to the Dardanelles. It was the straw that broke the camel's back. Before he ate his breakfast, Fisher sent his resignation to both Churchill and Prime Minister Herbert Asquith.

Fisher's resignation set in train events that Churchill and Asquith found themselves powerless to resist. His departure, coupled with the breaking news concerning a shortage of high explosive shell on the Western Front, threatened to topple the Liberal government. To stave off opposition attacks on his ministry and the progress of the war, Asquith was forced to agree to a coalition, and the Conservative Party's price for coalition included the sacking of Churchill. On the 20th Asquith wrote to Churchill asking him to leave the Admiralty, a departure which Churchill reluctantly accepted the following day. The coalition government was formed on the 25th, with Conservative ex-prime minister A J Balfour as First Lord of the Admiralty. As his First Sea Lord he had a compromise candidate, Admiral Sir Henry Jackson – a good administrator and a fine technician but lacking much verve.

Many people were pleased to see Churchill go. Others regretted the loss of his drive and passion. One of the latter was Georgina Lee, who noted that she had always admired him for those qualities 'of courage, originality and extraordinary energy'. She also credited him with saving the country from invasion; 'the public lose sight of his splendid feat in mobilising the navy before war was declared. He thereby saved the country from the surprise *coup de main* which the Germans had hoped to achieve.'[16] For her, Churchill had forestalled an invasion.

The Raid on Cumberland

The area of Britain's west coast around Whitehaven, Cumberland, seems an unlikely spot for a German naval attack. True, Churchill had nominated Barrow-in-Furness, to the south, as a potential landing place for a German invasion (see Chapter 4). But none had come and Cumberland was little disturbed by the war, save for the loss of men to the Western Front. Indeed, the last time anybody troubled to invade the area was in 1778, when on 22 April American naval Commander John Paul Jones led a small detachment of two boats from his ship, the USS *Ranger*, to raid the shallow port at Whitehaven, England, where, by his own account, 400 British merchant ships were anchored (they weren't).

Jones and his thirty volunteers rowed into the harbour by cover of night, unnoticed by the two sentinel forts which guarded the entrance. Arriving at dawn. Jones' boat successfully took the southern fort, disabling its cannon, but the other boat returned without attempting an attack on the northern bastion, after the sailors claimed to have been frightened away by a noise. To compensate, Jones set fire to the southern fort, a blaze which subsequently engulfed the entire town. From then on, lead, coal and iron ore mining, together with fishing, were the main occupations of the region. At Lowca, just to the south on Parton Bay, a small community had grown up around a locomotive engineering works, established in 1843. Lowca also had large reserves of coal, which had been mined for centuries.

In the early 1900s, the German firm of Carl Still of Reckinghausen was offered a contract to build a coke oven and chemical plant at Lowca, which would utilise the local coalfields to make metallurgical coke for the nearby blast furnaces and to maximise the products from the coke oven gas. Specifically, they would extract benzene and toluene, the latter a key component in the manufacture of explosives. It became known as the Harrington coke works.

The German company brought its own workforce and many of the Germans spent their weekends touring all over the county, usually in pairs on bicycles with large plate cameras on their backs. They were often observed taking photographs and camping near the top of Honister Pass. By the time the plant was complete in 1913, and the Germans had left for home, they knew West Cumberland well.

However, before the Germans departed, a Canadian engineer came to Lowca with a plan to use a new process for turning benzene into toluene and staked out the outlines of a plant for construction. However, trials were a failure and the idea was dropped; but this was after the Germans had departed. Of Harrington's, the navy's Official History states that 'the plant had been installed by two German firms, whose agents had been careful to carry away complete plans of the works, including photographs taken from the sea'.[17]

On 3–5 August, three submarines, *U-38*, *U-27* and *U-24*, had left Germany to operate between Ushant and St George's Channel. One of them, *U-24* under Rudolf Schneider, was the boat which on New Year's morning had sunk *Formidable*. Her top-secret orders were to begin by going up the Irish Sea to attack the works of the Harrington Coke Oven Co on the

Cumberland coast of the Solway Firth.

At 0430 on 16 August, Schneider surfaced in full view of the surprised harbourmaster Captain Crowley and his assistant, who were out in a fishing boat. Ignoring them, Schneider manned his 8.8cm (3.5in) deck gun and launched an attack on the plant. There were no coast defences of any sort, and he was able to conduct a sustained bombardment lasting nearly an hour, during which over fifty shells were fired.

Early in the attack, a drum of benzol had exploded and, separately, a valve operator, Oscar Ohlson, released some flaming gas. The two together produced a thick smokescreen which impeded the gunlayers. *U-24* then sailed away, 'believing the destruction to be complete, whereas in truth only £800 worth of damage was done, and in four days the works were going again'.[18]

There was slight collateral damage. A dog was killed at the factory; one shell went through a benzene tank, and another landed in the garden of a house at Howgate. A few shells hit the railway embankment north of Parton, without causing anything other than an annoying delay to the running of the day's trains.

The Parton stationmaster, one William Twentyman, found a red-hot nose cap from a shell which was claimed by the government but later returned to him with a £5 reward, and Joseph Holmes, another stationmaster on the line, wrote a poem which was sold on handbills for one penny, 'proceeds of the sale will be given to the Soldiers' Tobacco Fund'. The doggerel ran as follows:

> The Bombardment of the Cumberland Coast
> On August Sixteenth, old Kaiser Bill
> Said to his men, "Now prove your skill,
> And try and reach the Cumberland coast,
> The feat of which I'd like to boast."
>
> The Kaiser's word they did obey,
> And fired away in Parton Bay,
> With shot and shell they did their best
> To put the Lowca works to rest.
>
> The damage done was not so much,
> The Benzol plant they did not touch,
> One shell fell here, another there
> Which gave the workmen quite a scare.

> The inhabitants too grew quite alarmed,
> Because this port is still unarmed,
> This opportunity the enemy seized,
> And rained the shells just where he pleased.
>
> Two shells went through a cottage home,
> The father shouts "A German Bomb,"
> The children then ran out like bees,
> And joined the Lowca refugees.
>
> The submarine then made its way
> Across the dub from Parton Bay,
> To find some other defenceless port
> Where German fiends could have their sport.[19]

Verses four and five attest to the terror that the coastal attacks wrought, irrespective of the outcome.

In its gleeful coverage of the raid, a Hamburg newspaper reported that 'Parton and Harrington have signal stations and coastguards'.[20] This was palpably untrue. They also noted that 'the extreme importance of this bombardment lies in the fact that it proves that the British fleet is not able even to protect the coasts of the Irish Sea from attack by German warships'.[21]

There was a strange predella to the story. It was reported that, around the time of the U-boat bombardment, strange bright lights had been seen on the coast near Whitehaven. The finger of suspicion pointed to Mrs Hildegarde Burnyeat (née Retzlaff) the German wife of one-time Whitehaven Liberal MP* William John Dalzell Burnyeat KC, JP, who lived at nearby Moresby House, and where he still managed to keep a household staff of three, despite the war. Mrs Burnyeat was unashamedly pro-German and in the wake of the submarine raid was arrested by the authorities under DORA and interned at Aylesbury Prison in Buckinghamshire. She was still there when her husband died a year later, aged just 42; she was allowed out to visit him during his last days.

Fortress Britain

While the Germans hurled high explosive at a remote part of the west coast, the eastern littoral now resembled a fortress. A long wall of mines, pierced by occasional swept passages to sea, guarded the coastline. Inside them, the War Channel allowed vessels to sail between ports.

---

* Burnyeat sat from 1906 to 1910 and did not seek re-election.

In Norfolk, Sheringham Golf Links were dug up and entrenched, and six 4.7in guns were mounted on carriages at Weybourne, with two more at Cromer. An armoured train was brought to the county, known as *Alice*, and more officially as 'Number 2'. It ran on fixed tracks along the beachside from North Walsham on the Mundesley line as far as Great Yarmouth and was made up from four carriages (previously Caledonian Railway wagons dating from 1895) sheathed in half-inch thick steel. At either end of each coach was a Maxim machine gun and a 12pdr. From 1915 until the war's end it thundered up and down the railway without firing a shot in anger. In Essex, Harwich received two 9.2in Mark X guns which, for some reason known only to the military mind, were sent from Ireland. With a maximum range of 29,200 yards, they could keep any threatening ship at arm's length. Spy fever continued unabated. *The Times* commented that 'in their eager absorption of the baser side of militarism, the Germans seem to have almost converted themselves into a race of spies'.[22]

All along the coast, watchmen – volunteers, local defence groups, special constables, boy scouts – wandered up and down the headlands and beaches of the east coast looking out to sea for an enemy which, in 1915, did not come. A good example was at Porthcawl in south Wales; here '120 coast and [Bristol] channel watchers were enrolled. These men patrolled the coast from the mouth of the Ogmore River in the east, to Kenfig in the west, and were known as the Porthcawl Volunteer Coast Intelligence. This group, supported by the local Boy Scouts operated day and night and were stationed in the pilot watchtower, which was adapted for the purpose at a cost of £12.' They also produced their own lapel badge, to be worn when on duty.[23]

DORA controlled people's lives; where they could go, what they could do, when they could do it. It determined what you were able eat and drink, who one might associate with, what one could say out loud or

The cover artwork of *The Scouts Active Service Book* edited by Morley Adams and published in January 1916 by Henry Frowde/Hodder and Stoughton. It depicts boy scouts on coast-watching duty. (Author's collection)

read in the papers. Britain had become a huge fortress. Early signs of industrial and civil unrest showed that some chafed against the enforced restrictions. Compulsory registration of all adult males and females aged 15 to 65 was introduced by an Act of Parliament in June, which called for the register to be conducted on 15 August. This was seen by many (correctly) as the precursor to compulsory conscription. The Prussian philosopher of Absolute Idealism, Georg Hegel (1770–1831), posited that the state had the right to demand that its citizens lay down their lives for its survival; this was the founding principle of the Prussian polity. Britain was becoming such a country too.

But the war news was not encouraging. The Royal Navy lost 40 warships during 1915 and a further 127 auxiliaries, of which 65 were trawlers and drifters and five were yachts.[24] As for the army, the Western Front had turned into a war of attrition. In 1914 the British had suffered 90,000 casualties of which 50,000 were killed. That effectively wiped out the pre-war British regular army. Then 1915 brought a litany of failures. In March, Neuve Chapelle cost 11,200 British casualties; April and the Second Battle of Ypres 59,275; May saw 11,619 casualties at Aubers Ridge and 16,648 at Festubert, where CinC of the British Expeditionary Force Sir John French withdrew on the 25th, citing shortage of ammunition, and with no gains to set against his not inconsiderable losses. Coupled with the later Battle of Loos (59,247), these encounters caused the loss of most of the pre-war reservists and Territorials. Secretary of State for War Lord Kitchener's recruitment drive had produced millions of men, but many were not yet ready for combat. And the scale of losses, and dissatisfaction with the prosecution of the war, together with inveigling by his eventually replacement, Douglas Haig, caused the government to ask for the resignation of French on 6 December.

French was given the consolation prize of command of all Home Forces, the bulwark against invasion. Despite the latest revised estimates that the Germans could land up to 160,000 men, or a raid conducted by up to 20,000 troops, French thought an invasion unlikely unless the Germans had first won on the Western Front, and favoured fighting on the coast rather than holding a strong central reserve. Nearly 500,000 men were still held in Britain against the threat of a landing. And so too were naval forces in harbours all along the coast.

The disastrous Gallipoli campaign was ended in December with a successful evacuation, a joint army-navy triumph in retreat. But there had been perhaps 213,000 casualties amongst British and Empire troops. The total Allied dead numbered 28,000 Britons, 10,000 Frenchmen, 7,595 Australians, 2,431 New Zealanders and 1,500 Indians.[25]

Not only were soldiers and naval vessels being lost, but the German unrestricted U-boat campaign had also inflicted increasing damage, at least until it was halted in March 1916, when the sinking of the cross-Channel ferry *Sussex* led to a strongly-worded protest from US President Woodrow Wilson, which caused the Berlin hierarchy to order a stop. The submarines re-joined the High Seas Fleet or transferred their attention to the Mediterranean, where liners carrying Americans were less likely to be found. Britain lost 855,721grt of merchant shipping in the year, 88 per cent of it due to U-boats.[26] Fisher's statement regarding starvation vs invasion looked a little more likely.

9

A Concerted Plan: The Attacks on Lowestoft and Great Yarmouth, 1916

The need to keep watch on the coast for an invading fleet was one of the reasons for a major reorganisation of the home-based National Reserve in early 1916. The so-called Supernumerary Companies, comprising 39,000 men of the National Reserve, were in constant demand to provide guards for munitions works, prisoner of war and internment camps, railways, coastal observation and local defence. Managed by individual County Territorial Associations, they were proving difficult to co-ordinate, and their fluctuating strengths often rendered them of doubtful reliability.

As one of his first actions as CinC Home Forces, Sir John French formed the Royal Defence Corps (by a Royal Warrant of 17 March) by abolishing both the National Reserve and the eighteen Home Service Garrison Battalions (composed of soldiers either too old or medically unfit for active front-line service; the Home Service status indicated they were unable to be transferred overseas) and merging their manpower and responsibilities. The Royal Defence Corps was organised into independent companies of men aged between 41 and 60 with two distinct divisions of role; Protection Companies guarded infrastructure, while Observation Companies kept watch for enemy activity off the coast.*

As noted in Chapter 8, French, the Admiralty and the War Office continued to rely on the revised 1914 estimate that an invasion by up to 160,000 men was possible and that half a million troops must always be stationed in the UK to counter the threat. The attack was deemed most likely between the Wash and Dover. Sir John French favoured defence at the coast and so the plan was to hold the coastline as long as possible. If German troops landed, they were to be attacked by mobile units of cyclists and infantry. The assumption was the invaders would make for London, and were to be assailed and harassed along the way.

Public vigilance was demanded. The *Eastern Daily Press* of 18 July wrote, 'the War Office request that the public will render assistance . . . by notifying

---

* The relevant Army Council instruction noted that the Royal Defence Corps had been created 'to carry out duties connected with the local defence of the United Kingdom, including those hitherto performed by the Supernumerary Territorial Force Companies, as well as those allotted to the Observer Companies now in process of formation' (Army Council Instruction 841 of 19 April 1916).

'... of any bomb or projectile or fragments thereof or any other article discharged, dropped or lost from any enemy aircraft or vessel'.

Eastern coastal defences were strengthened with trenches dug at Weybourne and Sheringham, Sea Palling and Great Yarmouth. South of Lowestoft, the littoral was further reinforced by guns and men. Some forty-eight pillboxes were constructed along the Norfolk coast. Mobile artillery included six 60pdrs* at Weybourne, Mundesley (both in Norfolk) and Pakefield (Suffolk). Cromer also had two 60pdrs on a permanent mount.

There was a further change in 1916 of more far-reaching consequence; conscription. The Conservative/Unionist Party had been calling for conscription since before the start of the war. In the Cabinet, Lloyd George, who in 1915 had taken control of the newly created Ministry of Munitions, also began arguing for the introduction of military conscription in order to sustain the large army that would be needed to inflict a 'knock-out blow' on the Central Powers. The army brass supported conscription as a matter of course, as did the National Service League, Northcliffe *et al*. These forces were opposed by most of the Liberal leadership and MPs. Nevertheless, Asquith eventually buckled.

In January 1916 the Military Service Act was passed. This imposed conscription on all single men aged between 18 and 41, but exempted the medically unfit, clergymen, teachers and certain classes of industrial worker. Conscientious objectors were also exempted, and were in most cases given civilian jobs or non-fighting roles at the front. Conscription began in March and a second act passed in May 1916 extended conscription to married men.

Conscription was far from popular in some quarters and in April 1916 over 200,000 people demonstrated against it in Trafalgar Square. But many saw it as the only equitable solution to the manpower issue. As *The Spectator* put it, 'it is the only fair system, the only system under which the willing horse is not flogged at the expense of the unwilling, and which does not require the good patriot to shoulder not only his own burden but the burden of a selfish fellow citizen. It spreads the sacrifices evenly, as they ought to be spread, and therefore makes the weight on the individual distinctly less.'[1] Although many men failed to answer to the call-up (between March and July 93,000 men did not respond), in the first year 1.1 million were enlisted. By the end of the war 2.5 million men had been called up. Britain was a nation in arms.

Ireland

The island of Ireland has been the subject of invasions, and for some of Britain's enemies, it seemed a likely back door into Britain itself. Lambert

---

* British 5in heavy field guns, designed in 1903–05 and intended for both horse draught and mechanical traction.

Simnel and his supporters sailed from Ireland to land on the Furness peninsula in 1487. Spanish Armada survivors landed in Ireland in 1588; the Spanish came again in October 1601, in a landing by Habsburg Spain during the Nine Years' War; there was the *Expédition d'Irlande* by the French First Republic of December 1796; and the French invasion of Ireland during the Irish Rebellion of 1798. And in the early years of the twentieth century, invasion speculation was almost as rampant in Ireland as it was in England.

In a survey of 12 Irish newspapers between 1890 and 1914, the term 'German invasion' was found 96 times in the *Irish Times*, 61 times in the *Irish Independent*, 33 times in the *Freeman's Journal*, 12 times in the *Southern Star*, 10 times in the *Leitrim Observer* and 9 times in the *Anglo-Celt*. The expression 'German spy' was reported 105 times in the *Irish Times*, 34 times in the *Irish Independent*, 14 times in the *Freeman's Journal* and 6 times in the *Southern Star*, 5 times in the *Leitrim Observer* and 3 times in the *Connacht Tribune*.[2]

There was some basis in fact underlying the scare stories. Irish republican movements, viscerally opposed to British rule, were certainly involved in conversations with German representatives. George Freeman, working for Clan na Gael* (an Irish-American republican organisation), and Theodor Schiemann, a German professor and private adviser to Kaiser Wilhelm II, held a secret correspondence. Freeman was sending information about Irish nationalists in Ireland and in the United States. In 1907, Schiemann enquired into the number of Irishmen serving in the Royal Navy, clearly considering subversion. The British did not seem to be aware of this dialogue. However, they knew of other contacts between the Germans and Irish republicans. In 1912, the Dublin Metropolitan Police (DMP) learnt that the Irish Republican Brotherhood (IRB) had sent an emissary to meet the German ambassador in London. A short time later, the DMP learnt that Clan na Gael was sending one of their men to Berlin.

Republicans sometimes lent their support to Germany; In 1905, the *United Irishman* declared: 'It has been English policy to represent the German Emperor – in Ireland – as a shouting idiot – a policy helped by our imitative and slavish press. The German Emperor is an astute monarch, who has trumped every card which England has played against Germany in Africa, in South America, and in Europe.' And in 1908, Arthur Griffith, the founder of Sinn Féin, praised the Kaiser's foreign policy and approved of Berlin's decision to increase naval expenditure.[3] At the outbreak of war the Irish writer and republican activist Frances Sheehy-Skeffington wrote 'the Germans have no hostility to Ireland; if they land here (as I hope they will)

---
* Which translates as Family of the Gaels.

they will land as the enemies of England, and as such ought to be welcomed as the French were welcomed in [17]98'.[4]

Ireland was a hot potato for the British government. In London, H H Asquith's Liberal government had only held onto power after the General Election of 1910 by relying on the support of the Irish Nationalist MPs under the leadership of John Redmond, who had led the Irish Parliamentary Party since 1900. Their agenda was an independent Ireland and Redmond used his leverage to persuade Asquith to introduce a third Home Rule Bill in April 1912, which would grant Ireland national self-government. But Home Rule was vehemently opposed by many Irish Protestants, the Irish Unionist Party and Ulster's Orange Order, who feared domination in an overwhelmingly Catholic state. It was also opposed by many in the House of Commons, especially the Unionists, who were concerned both by the likely economic impact from an independent Ireland but also resented the break-up of Empire by a government which was only kept in power by the support of the Irish Nationalists (the Unionists had a larger number of seats than the Liberals, some thirty by May 1915).

John Redmond, leader of the Irish party in the British Parliament. (Author's collection)

Many saw real danger in any change in Ireland's relationship with England. Admiral Lord Charles Beresford, himself a member of Ireland's Protestant Ascendancy, wrote of 'an Ireland ruled by a disloyal faction [which] would easily afford shelter to the warships of the enemy in her ports ... thus lodged a fleet or squadron would command the main trade routes to England and might inflict immense damage in a short time'.[5]

When war came, the republicans stepped up their attempts to involve Germany in their fight. Despite the Home Rule bill passing Parliament and receiving royal assent, on 7 September it was suspended for the duration of the war (with Redmond's consent). But the Irish revolutionaries collaborated with their Indian independence-seeking counterparts and mutually sought help from Germany during the war. They also called on their compatriots in America for arms and money. In order not to inflame republican discontent, Ireland was exempted from the Military Service Act and from compulsory conscription.

If they were to stage a revolution, help from Germany would be necessary and – so they reasoned – forthcoming. Certainly, Germany saw subversion as one way of destabilising its enemies. Professor Christopher Andrew has written that 'at the outbreak of war, Berlin believed that the most effective way to subvert the United Kingdom was by assisting Irish republican attempts to end British rule'.[6]

A necessary precursor to a revolt was to obtain armaments and, even better, military support. The Irish patriot and former British consular official, Sir Roger Casement, who had become treasurer of the Irish Volunteers in 1913, had travelled first to America where he had met Count Bernstorff, the German ambassador to the United States, in New York, to propose a mutually beneficial plan: if Germany would sell guns to the Irish revolutionaries and provide military leaders, the Irish would revolt against England, diverting troops and attention from the war on Germany. Bernstorff appeared generally sympathetic and paved the way for Casement to visit Germany itself.

Accordingly, in October 1915 Casement travelled to Germany, via neutral Norway, and met with Arthur Zimmermann, then Under Secretary of State in the Foreign Office, his boss Gottlieb von Jagow, and with the Imperial Chancellor, Theobald von Bethmann Hollweg. But von Jagow was less enthusiastic about helping the revolutionary cause. On 7 November 1915 he noted that 'the military results would be small, possibly even negative, and it would be said that we had violated international law'. Casement persisted but all von Jagow would do was to issue a statement to the effect that should Germany invade Ireland, it would do so with 'goodwill towards a people to which Germany wished only national welfare and national liberty'.[7]

Casement gained permission that he could attempt to recruit an Irish Brigade from POWs held in German camps; this was a failure, with only fifty-five men enlisted. And amongst other things, Casement also asked for a U-boat to sail up the Liffey and a blockship to be sunk at the entrance to Dublin Port. But he did obtain a declaration that Germany would assist any planned insurrection, and in March 1916, Germany offered the Irish nationalists 20,000 Mosin-Nagant M1891 Russian rifles, recovered from the Eastern Front, ten machine guns and accompanying ammunition, and explosives; but definitely no German military advisers. It was much less than Casement had wanted or expected, but he made arrangements for the weaponry to be shipped to Ireland. (They were destined not to reach their destination. The ship carrying them to Ireland was intercepted by the Royal

Navy and the weapons lost to the Irish Republican cause.) It was also agreed that the High Seas Fleet would provide a distraction in support of the revolution planned for Easter, and which eventually took place on Easter Monday, 24 March 1916.

The Lowestoft and Great Yarmouth Raids

Vice Admiral Reinhard Scheer had become Commander-in-Chief of the High Seas Fleet on 18 January 1916, when Pohl became too ill to continue in post. On 1 February 1916, Scheer attended a naval conference in Berlin in which he persuaded the kaiser that the High Seas Fleet must be used aggressively and the power of deciding whether and when it should put to sea must rest with the CinC, not the kaiser. It was also decided to start unrestricted submarine warfare again on 1 March. Scheer was of a more aggressive disposition than his predecessors, and welcomed the chance to support the Irish rising* with a coastal raid designed to attract part of the Grand Fleet onto his entire battlefleet.

Vice Admiral Carl Friedrich Heinrich Reinhard Scheer, commander of the High Seas Fleet from January 1916 to August 1918. (Author's collection)

On 24 April, Admiral Scheer took his ships out. On the basis of faulty intelligence, he believed that the British had two strong forces at sea, to the north off Norway and off the south-east coast of England.† He intended to sail between them, attack the coast and then engage whichever portion of the British ships were attracted to him. His bombardment targets were Lowestoft and Great Yarmouth. Lowestoft was a base of operations for minelaying and sweeping, while Yarmouth was a harbour for some of the Harwich Force submarines.

---

* Professor Holger Herwig states 'the raid was designed to coincide with a planned uprising in Ireland on Easter Sunday [the original timing planned by the rebels]' (Herwig, *Luxury Fleet*, p 174).
† Scheer may have been misled by historical intelligence; it had been a feature of British war planning in 1908 (plans W1 and W2) that there should be a northern and southern fleet. This was also the case in the War Game Manoeuvres of 1912.

The German ships involved included the 1st Scouting Group, comprising of the battlecruisers SMS *Seydlitz*, *Lützow*, *Derfflinger*, *Moltke* and *Von der Tann* under the orders of Rear Admiral Friedrich Boedicker, 'baby killer' Hipper being indisposed through illness. They were supported by the four light cruisers of the 2nd Scouting Group and the fast torpedo boat flotillas VI and IX, with their two command vessels. The main fleet, consisting of Squadrons I, II and III, Scouting Division IV and the remainder of the torpedo flotillas, was to stand off in reserve, ready to come into action if the bombardment group ran into superior forces.

The raiders were accompanied by six airships which would add to the confusion and distraction by bombing Norwich, Lincoln, Harwich and Ipswich. After dropping their bombs, they were to provide reconnaissance for the battlecruisers, which would form the bombardment group. Two U-boats were sent ahead to Lowestoft, while others were stationed off, or laid mines in, the Firth of Forth. Additionally, seven U-boats had been despatched to lay mines off Harwich in the hope of catching the Harwich Force as it sortied.

By noon, all the German resources were in place and they began to pick a route through the British minefields. But at 1600, *Seydlitz* struck a mine and was forced to turn back, escorted by two destroyers and a Zeppelin; Boedicker transferred his flag to *Lützow*.

The German battlecruiser *Moltke* (1910), armed with ten 11in and twelve 5.9in guns. She took part in all the coastal bombardments. (US Library of Congress LC-DIG-hec-01140)

A CONCERTED PLAN: THE ATTACKS ON LOWESTOFT AND GREAT YARMOUTH, 1916

The German light cruiser *Rostock* (1912), ten 4.1in guns, which took part in the Lowestoft raid. She was the first German ship to sight the Harwich Force destroyers' approach. Here she is pictured in the *Illustrated London News* of 10 June 1916. (US Naval History and Heritage Command NH 43041)

Through Room 40, the Admiralty knew that the German ships were at sea at midday. At 2015 an intercepted wireless message gave the information that the enemy was aiming for Great Yarmouth. At 1550, the Grand Fleet was placed at two hours' readiness and at 1905 was ordered to sail south from Scapa Flow while the battlecruisers were likewise instructed to depart from Rosyth. Nobody gave Commodore Tyrwhitt at Harwich any instructions at all.

That night the Zeppelins bombed their targets. The Harwich Force was finally called out at 2300. But it was a much-reduced group due to other commitments, including the support of the Dover Patrol and Vice Admiral Reginald Bacon, who was laying a mine and net barrage off the Belgian coast. Flying his pennant in the light cruiser *Conquest*, Tyrwhitt led out the light cruisers *Cleopatra*, *Penelope* and *Lightfoot* (a *Marksman*-class flotilla leader) with the seven destroyers that were immediately ready to sail. *Nimrod* (another *Marksman*-class flotilla leader) followed later with a further eight destroyers.

Tyrwhitt's instructions from London had been to make for a point between Southwold and the Hook of Holland but as the commodore left port, he received another message saying that the German battlecruisers would pass this position within two hours; if he followed orders then at best he would only be able to intercept them on their return. On his own initiative and following Fisher's dictum that 'any fool can obey orders',[8] he

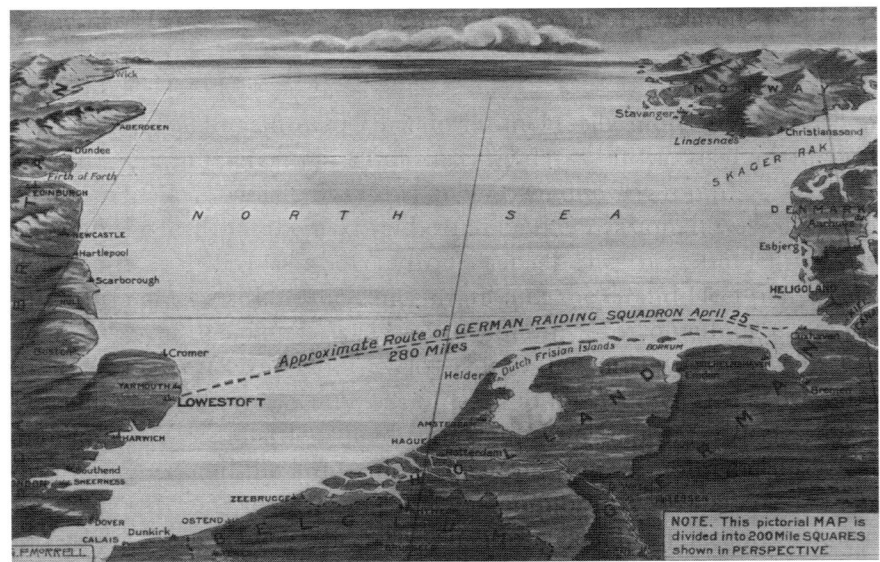

The route to Lowestoft taken by the bombarding squadron, as depicted in
The Graphic of 6 May 1916. (Author's collection)

decided to sail straight up the coast to the point of the German attack. It was a bright moonlit night and the odds were clearly not in Tyrwhitt's favour. But he thought that if he could attract the Germans' attention, he would be able to draw them away from Lowestoft and Yarmouth and save the towns from much damage.

At about 0350 on the 25th, the light cruiser SMS *Rostock*, one of Boedicker's screening ships, sighted British ships in a west-south-westerly direction. Simultaneously, Tyrwhitt reported the sighting of four battlecruisers and six cruisers to Jellicoe and Beatty. He stood on towards Lowestoft to give Boedicker a good sight of him, but the German admiral was not to be drawn, merely detaching light forces to chase Tyrwhitt away. The battlecruisers opened fire on the town at 0410.

Death and destruction came to Lowestoft. Alfred Turner was a fish merchant and fishing vessel owner, living with his family in London Road South. He had gone to bed at 2300 on the 24th only to be woken by the noise of anti-aircraft guns firing at a Zeppelin an hour later. Then at 0415 he heard sudden gunfire, realised it was more than anti-aircraft action, and shouted 'bombardment, all downstairs now as you are'. He was pleased that his kinfolk remained calm and collected. The sound was deafening; it 'continued nearly half an hour as near as I can guess but did not time it. The crash of our falling glass was terrific and the house filled with smoke till we wondered

The bombardment of Lowestoft on 25 April 1916 as imagined in a painting for *Illustirte Zeitung* by Hans Bohrdt. He was art tutor to Kaiser Wilhelm II, who funded many of the painter's projects. (Author's collection)

Shattered houses and a convalescent home in Lowestoft after the raid of 25 April 1916. (Author's collection)

Damaged houses post the Lowestoft/Yarmouth attacks. (Author's collection)

London Road in Lowestoft at the junction with Freemantle Road, damaged in the 25 April 1916 raid. (Author's collection)

if we were afire.' His neighbour's residence suffered a direct hit which ricocheted into his own home. 'Shell struck house next door but one and fell in our back garden, blew up greenhouse, bicycle shed, all back windows blown in and all party walls blown down.'[9]

The German ships then moved off to Great Yarmouth where fog made it difficult to see the target. Realising that the Germans were now headed for Yarmouth, Tyrwhitt turned his force back to the north, sighted Boedicker's light forces and opened fire on them. Hearing the sound of the engagement, the battlecruisers broke off from bombardment of the town and turned towards the sound of the guns.

They opened a heavy fire from a range of 16,000–18,000 yards, at which it was impossible for the British ships to reply. Tyrwhitt immediately turned his ships through sixteen points together, reversing his course, a manoeuvre which put his flagship at the rear of the line. For 13 minutes, *Conquest* was subjected to heavy gunfire and was struck by five heavy shells.

It was a dangerous period. Boy Seaman William Campbell, acting as captain's messenger, recalled that 'we soon found out what we were up against when we started getting the stuff thrown at us that the town had been getting. Battlecruisers of the *Derfflinger* and *Lützow* class turned their 12in guns on our little fleet and as soon as our 6in guns came into range we let then have something back.'[10]

One shell passed through the funnel; then 'a salvo hit her [*Conquest*] on the aft deck and knocked the after-superstructure gun over the side ... I was appalled at the damage'.[11] The explosion also set ablaze some cordite, stored next to the gun. Without thought for his own safety, Ordinary Seaman William David Williams, known to his mates as Taffy, barehandedly threw the burning charges overboard and saved *Conquest* from a possible disaster. Aged just 18, Swansea-born Williams had joined the navy as a boy in January 1915. After less than a year in *Conquest*, he would be awarded the DSM for his actions.[12] But it came at a price. His hands were severely injured and just eight months later, on 23 August, he was invalided out of the navy, owing to 'burns both hands in action'.[13]

Conquest took a severe battering; twenty-three men were killed, including Tyrwhitt's personal servant. The destroyers received a pounding too. HMS *Laertes* was hit by a shell which penetrated the boiler room, putting one boiler out of action and wounding five men. She would most likely have blown up and sunk except for the swift response of Stoker 1st Class Ernest John William Clarke. He unhesitatingly went to release the steam pressure valves and in so doing was very badly scalded, which left him with 'extensive burns to the face, arms and hands'.[14] Thirty-eight-year-old Clarke, who had been in the navy since 1898, received the DSM[15] for saving his ship; but he did not live to enjoy it, dying from his injuries on 10 May.

Alfred Turner observed Tyrwhitt's ships take on the Germans and paid tribute to the courage they showed.

> Very heavy firing recommenced at sea and we knew there was a fight, so we all went up and saw our little torpedo boat destroyers steaming north to meet the Hun dreadnoughts. They passed in front of our house and a very few minutes afterwards the leader stopped and the whole line steamed round him, each boat firing a broadside (as she turned) at the Germans. It was magnificent but was not war. It was a case of a wasp stinging a tiger.
>
> It was suicide to attack the enemy but in doing so they drew the fire from the town and the Huns fired their 12-inch guns at them but failed to hit them except once that I saw.
>
> The columns of water were going up where the shells went into the sea exactly like very high church steeples all round our boats. There were nineteen of our little things and it all happened about four to five miles from the beach. I would not have missed seeing it for £50.[16]

The Harwich Force had at least spared Great Yarmouth from much damage and possibly ameliorated the attack on Lowestoft. Boedicker turned away and started to withdraw, perhaps fearful that Tyrwhitt was drawing him onto a larger British force. Lieutenant Brian Schofield in *Manley* noted that 'for a difficult half an hour the Germans gave us everything they had got but Com (T) withdrew in a leisurely manner until, suspecting that they were being lured into a trap, the German ships turned and ran for home'.[17] Tyrwhitt was having none of that. As soon as he realised that his opponent was no longer pursuing him, he reversed course again and in the damaged *Conquest*, still capable of 20 knots, he led his forces back towards the enemy. He regained visual contact at 0830, about the same time as the Admiralty ordered him to return to base.

As Tyrwhitt headed for Harwich, *Penelope* was torpedoed by *UB-29*. The explosion carried away her stern post and rudder; the whole after part of her had practically been blown off. But she managed to steam back to Harwich at 22 knots steering with her engines. *Conquest* made it to Chatham, carrying in her an unexploded 8.3in German shell.

During the engagement, the Germans had attacked two armed fishing boats. *King Stephen* had been converted to the Q-ship *Ledger* but in a previous life as a fishing vessel had gained German opprobrium when the

The torpedo gunboat turned minesweeper HMS *Dryad* (1893) in wartime grey. As built, she was armed with two 4.7in QF, four 6pdrs, a Nordenfelt machine gun and five 18in torpedo tubes, of which two were removed on her conversion to 'sweeper. (Author's collection)

skipper refused to rescue the crew of the Zeppelin L-19, which had crashed into the sea near Dogger Bank. *Ledger/King Stephen* was sunk by a destroyer, *G-41*, and the crew taken prisoner. The second was the drifter *Moss*, once of Yarmouth, armed with a solitary 3pdr gun, which was damaged in the shelling of Lowestoft with six men killed including Skipper Percy Shreeve.*

In the harbour, the merchant ship SS *FD Lambert* (1892) was hit by shellfire and her crew took to their boats. They were picked up by HMS *Dryad* (1893), originally a torpedo gunboat, converted to a minesweeper just before the war. Her crew took the freighter under control and saved her.† Meanwhile Beatty, and far behind him Jellicoe, had been struggling through heavy seas in the hope of cutting off the German retreat. But by noon it was clear that such pursuit was hopeless. As this realisation dawned, the Harwich submarine HMS *E-22* was torpedoed just before 1200 by *UB-18*. She had been part of a patrol line established to intercept the German raiders. Thirty-one of her thirty-three crew died when *E-22* was sunk, including her captain, on his first mission in her, 30-year-old Lieutenant Reginald Thomas Dimsdale. He was the younger son of Charles Robert Southwell Dimsdale, 7th Baron Dimsdale, a title awarded in the Russian peerage to his ancestor Thomas by Catherine the Great in 1762. His older boy had already been killed at Ypres; now he had lost both his sons. The two survivors had been on the bridge and got clear; they were picked up by the attacker and made prisoners of war.

The Germans claimed a victory.

> At daybreak on April 25 a section of our high sea forces bombarded with good success the fortifications and important military buildings at Great Yarmouth and Lowestoft, and afterwards opened fire on a detachment of enemy airmen, small cruisers, and torpedo boat destroyers. A big fire was observed on one cruiser. One destroyer and two enemy patrol boats were sunk. One of the latter was the trawler *King Stephen* which refused some time ago to save the crew of the German Airship L-19 when in distress. The crew‡ of the trawler were taken prisoner.[18]

---

* The drifter lived to fight another day, serving in the Second World War as the anti-submarine vessel *Guiding Light*.
† This action led in May 1919 to a court claim for salvage. The officers and men of *Dryad* stated that the *F D Lambert* had been abandoned and, in saving her, they were entitled to salvage money. The master of the salved vessel, Captain Lamb, denied abandonment, stating that he and his men were simply trying to get out of the way of the firing. The judge, Sir Samuel Evans, gave judgment, saying that the patrol boat had rendered services of this kind as part of its duty, not for salvage. But nonetheless he awarded Dryad £380 for their work.
‡ It was a different crew to that of the airship incident, although the Germans took some convincing of the fact.

The *Cologne Gazette* also claimed that HMS *Galatea* had been torpedoed, which would have been difficult as she wasn't there.[19] The British press communication on the other hand praised Tyrwhitt and his ships, which 'although outmatched in point of size and numbers ... held on tenaciously ... time and again the British hit the German monsters'.[20]

Aftermath

As the German ships headed for home, they avoided the patrol lines of submarines sent to intercept them, encountering only two neutral steamers and some fishing vessels.

Arthur Marder thought that 'the raid was hardly a brilliant exploit, whether from the point of view of strategy, tactics or results'.[21] The Germans had sunk one patrol vessel and damaged another, and badly smashed up two light cruisers and a destroyer; they had also sunk a submarine. In exchange they had a major unit, the battlecruiser *Seydlitz*, laid up after mining.

The harm done to the naval establishments at Yarmouth and Lowestoft was light. However, some 240 houses had been destroyed or damaged and between the two towns four civilians were killed and twelve injured. But the German battlecruiser squadron had failed to take advantage of its superior numbers to engage the Harwich Force and inflict greater suffering.

The German U-boats sent out to intercept British ships leaving harbour had not found any targets. Nor had six British submarines stationed off Yarmouth and six more off Harwich. However, Germany did suffer U-boat losses; *UB-13* was lost on a mine net with no survivors and on the 27th one of the German patrol submarines, *UC-5*, was captured when it grounded on the Shipwash Shoal, off Harwich. The crew attempted to sink her but the scuttling charges failed to explode. She was later salvaged and used to raise war bonds in the UK and USA. *Firedrake* claimed prize money for her capture, which was not in fact paid until 1920.[22]

At least the town of Lowestoft was grateful for the intervention of the Harwich Force. On 3 May, the town mayor wrote to Their Lordships at the Admiralty from his town hall;

> My Lords
> I am desired by the Town Council to express to the Lords of the Admiralty the high appreciation of the inhabitants of this borough of the splendid way in which, during the bombardment of the town on the morning of April 25th, the enemy ships, though greatly superior force, were engaged by the British squadron. The council is convinced that, but for this plucky intervention at a critical moment, the town would have suffered much greater destruction of property

and loss of life. It is also desired, if it meets with Their Lordships' approval, that an expression of appreciation may be conveyed to the gallant officer in command and the officers and men under him.
I have the honour to be, your Lordships Obedient Servant
J W Brooke*, Mayor.[23]

The Admiralty copied the letter to Tyrwhitt and he circulated it to all commanders and ships who took part.

The general public were shocked at this sudden return of coastal raids and potential invasion of the eastern littoral. It showed that the country was still vulnerable to such attacks and that invasion or landings were possible. As a result, new anti-invasion trenches were dug at Pakefield, two miles to the south of Lowestoft town centre, which were inspected by King George V.

First Lord of the Admiralty A J Balfour wrote to the mayors of Lowestoft and Yarmouth reassuring them that the fleet could protect them and that dispositions would be made to ensure they would. The recipients were probably not entirely confident in this promise. Later in the year, RN monitors were sent to be guard ships at the two towns.

The Times headlined the assault as 'all apparently part of a concerted German plan',[24] while *The Spectator* raised the invasion bogey; 'we have little doubt that the attack upon Lowestoft and the Zeppelin raids of the past week were intended to have an auxiliary effect. It is also quite possible that there may have been thoughts of playing Germany's trump card of a military raid on our coasts.' The same publication also pleaded for a calm response after the events in Ireland. 'If we are to do what will most disappoint the Germans, and that surely is a thing worth doing, we must pick up the pieces in Ireland with as little fuss as possible, and show the minimum of annoyance and disturbance.'[25]

In fact, the rebellion was rapidly suppressed, and its leaders executed. After the outbreak of the Easter Rising, the army ordered the 59th Division (2nd North Midland, a Territorial unit formed in 1915 and held in readiness to combat an invasion of the east coast) to Ireland to put down the revolt and garrison the country. In September 1916, the 59th participated in military manoeuvres, designed to replicate an invasion by German forces. Amongst the orders for the division was 'any German troops south of the Liffey [river] are to be vigorously attacked'.[26] The spectre of invasion now stalked in Ireland too.

---

* John Walter Brooke (d 1924) was the owner of J W Brooke and Co, an engineering company in Lowestoft which latterly specialised in the application of the internal combustion engine to marine propulsion. He was mayor from 1914 to 1917.

O'Connell St, Dublin, after the Easter Rising. The GPO, which became the centre of the revolution, is at left, and Nelson's Pillar at right.
(National Library of Ireland on the Commons)

A Lack of Cohesion

Beatty and Tyrwhitt were both enraged by the missed opportunity to catch the High Seas Fleet and by what they saw as a lack of coordination at the Admiralty. On 18 May Beatty wrote to Jellicoe on their joint behalf attacking the Admiralty War Staff for its lack 'of cohesion and combination between the various units ... the system of water tight compartments [in Whitehall] has reached its climax'. He accused the Chief of the War Staff, Vice Admiral Henry Oliver, of having 'priceless information given to him [from Room 40] which he sits on until it is too late for the sea forces to take action'.[27]

Beatty continued in the same vein, the anger steaming off the page. 'There was absolutely no reason why every unit should not have been on the move three and a half hours before it actually was. Commodore (T) did not actually leave Harwich until 2300. He received many contradictory orders ... he had no idea where I was or where I was going. I had no idea of anything appertaining to the Harwich Force ... [there was] no plan, no combination and no decision.'[28] It was a damning indictment.

Beatty and Tyrwhitt met and the former tried to put together a more constructive memorandum based on their discussions, that nonetheless made telling points. On 26 May, he wrote to 'The Commander in Chief' (Jellicoe) but meant for Admiralty consumption;

> I have the honour to report that my conference with Commodore (T) was of the utmost value in so much that we were enlightened considerably on points which effected our respective commands in the event of having to cooperate.
>
> I would submit ... that it would be most advantageous and in the best interests of the Service if a further conference could take place, at which those who construct and devise plans and operations and those who have to carry them out should meet and gain that communion of thought without which successful accomplishment is doubtful. To this end I submit the following points on which it is desirable the commanders of such as the Harwich Force and the Battle Cruiser Fleet should be enlightened and receive guidance as to how the Admiralty intends them to act under certain circumstances.[29]

He went on to suggest that the Harwich Force should be kept at a certain minima of ships, such that he knew they could support his battlecruisers if necessary; that neither of them knew if the Force would be used to attack an enemy fleet; what positions should the Harwich Force and the Battlecruiser Fleet take up if the enemy came out; that they should be informed of any orders given to the Dover Patrol in the light of the enemy coming out; they should be told if any new minefields had been laid which were not in the Secret Fleet Orders; that they were unaware of any Admiralty plans for dealing with all enemy offensive operations, other than invasion; and that positions should be defined which they could take up without waiting for further instruction when an alarm was given. There was soon to be cause to confirm the need for such change.

10
But What If They Come? 1916

The raid on Lowestoft and Great Yarmouth again brought home the vulnerability of the east coast of Britain. Once more, raiders had come, made gunnery practice, and disappeared into the North Sea. Only Tyrwhitt's Harwich Force, outnumbered and overmatched, had arrived in time to prevent further destruction than was inflicted. What if there had been troopships too?

The Spectator magazine imagined how Britain would respond to such an invasion.

> We know that if the Germans somehow managed to land, we should have settled down to trench fighting within the first forty-eight hours, and that the Germans would be in the hopeless position of fighting with their backs to the sea, not to a vast stretch of German territory; and, further, that behind them would be, not the huge pieces of artillery upon which they relied in Flanders, but only field-pieces of moderate size. The notion of rushing across giant howitzers or huge naval guns is a dream, unless of course they achieved, not merely a surprise raid, but also the complete command of the sea.[1]

Command of the sea was still viewed as vital to protect Britain from subjugation. However, 'at the beginning of 1916, information came to hand that the Germans were collecting large numbers of lighters and barges at bases in Flanders'.[2] Invasion danger could not be overlooked.

It will be recalled that the 5th and 6th Battle Squadrons of pre-dreadnought battleships had been stationed at Sheerness and Portland at the beginning of the war, both to protect the coasts and to take on any invading force. But these formations had been broken up during 1915 (5 BS in April, 6 BS in June), some sent to Gallipoli as bombardment vessels, some to be laid up or used as guard ships. There were no large naval units on the east coast south of Rosyth.

Hence, as a sop to public opinion, and to ease the fears of the politicians, the Admiralty sanctioned the move of the 3rd Battle Squadron of pre-dreadnought battleships from Rosyth to Sheerness. Commanded by Vice

HMS *King Edward VII* (1903), the name ship of the *King Edward VII* class. (Author's collection)

Admiral Edward Eden Bradford,* 3 BS comprised seven *King Edward VII*-class† together with HMS *Dreadnought* herself from June. They departed Scotland on 29 April.

The *King Edwards*, dating from 1902–05 and armed with four 12in, four 9.2in and ten 6in guns, the latter in a central battery, were known as the 'Wobbly Eight'. In a fight with the German all-big-gun battleships or battlecruisers they were likely to come off worst, not least because 'these ships were quite useless owing to their roll and the proximity of their guns to the waterline. They were useful only in reasonably calm weather or against shore targets.'[3]

Herbert Richmond, now captain of HMS *Commonwealth* in 3BS, recorded that there was 'great sadness on the part of some captains, who look upon us as a sacrifice if the battlecruisers come over . . . possibly the invasion fears have also have a connection which our presence here . . . we are made into coast defence battleships'.[4]

Tyrwhitt was less than pleased for he had to detach eight destroyers to keep watch over them. And to make things worse, Jellicoe, who never felt that he had enough destroyers for the Grand Fleet, now believed he had insufficient to provide a full screen for the battle fleet and so two divisions

---

* Who was replaced by Acting Vice Admiral John de Robeck from 19 July.
† The seven ships, which excluded the name ship of the class, were *Britannia* (flag), *Africa*, *Commonwealth*, *Dominion*, *Hindustan*, *Hibernia* and *Zealandia*.

And one of the 3rd Battle Squadron *King Edward*s, HMS *Commonwealth* (1903).
(Author's collection)

(eight ships) were sent from Harwich to join him at Scapa, further denuding the forces available to the east coast, especially as two light cruisers of the Harwich force had been forced into the dockyard for repairs after the encounter off Lowestoft.

Sunderland Saved

Admiral Scheer felt the pressure for increased naval action building around him, at a time when the German armies were dying in their thousands at Verdun. Historian and retired naval officer Baron Curt von Maltzahn summed up the prevailing German mood; 'even if today large parts of our fleet [were lying] at the bottom of the sea, our fleet would have accomplished more that it does now by lying well preserved in our ports'.[5]

In response to such views, Scheer planned a follow-up raid to the one on Lowestoft, this time on Sunderland, a clear military target with docks, shipbuilding and other important war industries. Submarines, recalled from unrestricted warfare on 25 April owing to the fallout from the *Sussex* affair (see Chapter 8), were once again available to him. He decided to send them and his battlecruisers to raid on 17 May. The U-boats would lie off the Firth of Forth to catch Beatty's ships as they came out to meet Hipper's force, while the High Seas Fleet would linger off Scarborough wating to for Hipper to lead Beatty into his arms.

But *Seydlitz*, damaged in the previous foray, was still under repair and so the sortie was postponed until 23 May. Further delays in getting the ship ready caused a another pause until the 29th. The U-boats had sailed on the 17th and were now approaching the end of their endurance. Scheer had to act now, or not at all. *Seydlitz* was finally ready but high winds meant that his airships could not scout ahead. As this was key to his operational design, Scheer came up with an alternative scheme. He would send Hipper's scouting forces (the battlecruisers) up the Danish coast into the Skagerrak as bait. This would certainly bring out the Grand Fleet, which would have to pass over his U-boat trap and Scheer would be somewhat protected by being closer to his own bases and minefields. At 0200 on 31 May Hipper's ships put to sea. Scheer and the German fleet followed at 0330. Sunderland was saved; but what would be the cost?

The Battle of Jutland

The story of the Battle of Jutland has been told many times; too many indeed to need repetition here. The course of the battle was characterised by misleading Admiralty communications to Jellicoe, poor signalling by Beatty, and missed opportunities due in part to overcaution. As a result, the contest was inconclusive, although there were heavy British loses, it remained a tactical victory for the Royal Navy. But Commodore Tyrwhitt and his Harwich Force were never allowed to join the fight.

The Force had been in continuous action since the beginning of the war and were experienced and battle hardened. And Jutland was the sort of fight that they should have been involved in, acting as the southern wing of the

Grand Fleet, as originally planned in 1914. But they were confined to port by the Admiralty. The best destroyer commander and the most experienced destroyer skippers were kept chained to Harwich, attack dogs curbed on a leash.

Signals intercepted by Room 40 on 30 May indicated that the High Seas Fleet was coming out. Jellicoe and Beatty were alerted and were at sea by 2230. Tyrwhitt was told to stand by for action with all available ships and be ready to sail at daylight. If he had been released at that point, Tyrwhitt's force would have reached Jellicoe by nightfall and could have participated in the night actions of the 31st which, without him, allowed Scheer and his fleet to escape.

Did concern regarding invasion prevent a British victory at the Battle of Jutland on 31 May 1916? Instead of sending Tyrwhitt into the fray, the Admiralty held him back, fearful of a detached German squadron, under cover of the main fleet action, falling on Dover or Dunkirk and shipping in the Downs, in a raid similar to the previous east coast attacks; or worse, an invasion in force.

Tyrwhitt fretted all through 31 May as the battle unwound far to his north. As early as 0450 he sent a telegram to the Admiralty pointing out that he had received no orders. He was told that he was to remain at one hour's notice. To ease his tension, he went to his nearby home to do some gardening but returned when his flagship picked up Beatty's transmission that he was in action with the enemy battlecruisers.

At 1715, he could take no more and gave the command to put out to sea, informing the Admiralty what he was doing at the same time. As he did so he received a message from Whitehall telling him to complete with fuel and be ready to relieve the light cruisers and destroyers with the battlecruiser squadrons. He ignored it and held on to his course northwards. The Force had got as far as the Cork Light Vessel when Tyrwhitt received a peremptory signal instructing him to return to Harwich immediately and await orders.

Eventually, at 0330 on 1 June, the Harwich Force was ordered to sea to escort the damaged battleship *Marlborough* to the Humber. A little later Com (T) was told there was no need of him, and he could return to base.

The failure to utilise the Harwich Force and the question of coordinating its movements with the Grand Fleet were discussed at a meeting at the Admiralty on 25 June but no definite solution was arrived at. The Admiralty staff held to the position that, as they could not know Admiral Scheer's objectives whenever he put to sea, they could not order the Harwich Force north until the enemy's intentions in all directions, including that of an invasion fleet, became clear.

But keeping Tyrwhitt and his ships at Harwich made little sense. 'The precise reasons for retaining the Harwich Force remain obscure',[6] noted the authors of the Naval Staff Appreciation of 1921. They hypothesised three potential explanations. Firstly, that the High Seas Fleet might come south. But if it did how could Tyrwhitt with five light cruisers and twenty destroyers oppose it? Secondly, the Admiralty might have been expecting a repeat of Lowestoft. However, what could the Harwich Force do which was over and above what it had done on 25 April, namely retire. In both these instances, the Force was not a fit instrument for the tune the Admiralty wanted to play. The only other conjecture was defence against invasion but given the warnings the Room 40 could provide, this would not be a secret. As the Naval Staff Appreciation notes 'one of the previously recognised duties of the Harwich Flotillas was to assist the Commander in Chief [Jellicoe] in a fleet action, and this important function seems to have been to a large extent forgotten or overlooked'. 'His [Tyrwhitt's] retention there [at Harwich] must be regarded as a grave mistake'[7] was the overall view of the Naval Staff Appreciation. Reginald Tyrwhitt and his captains would have agreed.

Five weeks later, Tyrwhitt was still fuming, writing to his friend Roger Keyes that 'I'll never forgive that old figurehead Oliver, who was at the bottom of it all . . . I got snubbed for going to sea on my own account . . . I know I was right and anyone in my place would have done the same.'[8] Invasion phobia had struck again.

* * * * *

Over 6,000 British sailors died at Jutland and fourteen ships were sunk. As historian Correlli Barnett put it, 'the navy, as shield of empire, was never again accorded quite the same religious faith'.[9] Five days later, on 5 June, another significant loss occurred at sea when the armoured cruiser HMS *Hampshire* hit a mine west of the Orkney Islands and sank in a Force 9 gale. Amongst the 737 dead was Lord Kitchener, Secretary of State for War, who was on passage for Russia. David Lloyd George took over the responsibility for the War Office.

New Orders, Old Caution
The problems of coordination between the Grand Fleet, Admiralty and Harwich, noted above and in Chapter 9, brought forth the issue of new instructions for the Harwich Force. After Jutland, both Jellicoe and the Admiralty had set up various working groups to distil what learning could be gained from the battle and make any necessary changes to orders and to tactics or *matériel*.

Among the outputs from this process were new Grand Fleet Battle Orders. As part of these Jellicoe, who was convinced the object of Scheer's sorties was to lure the fleet over submarines, specified that the fleet would not go further south than a line drawn roughly from the Farne Islands to Horns Reef, except if there was a good possibility of bringing the High Seas Fleet to action in daylight. Effectively this meant that the whole of the east coast south of the Tyne was to be defended by the local port flotillas, the Harwich Force and the 3rd Battle Squadron at Sheerness.

New orders were also created for the flotillas at Harwich. These instructions, issued in August, specifically enjoined the Admiralty to send the Harwich Force out to one of five named rendezvous points in the southern North Sea 'until sufficient information is available'. This positive intent no doubt pleased Tyrwhitt. But the fear and caution within the Admiralty regarding any potential secondary attack on Dover/Dunkirk placed a caveat on this, one insisted upon by the Admiralty in a letter of 19 August; paragraph five of the battle orders states that 'in the event of the enemy having stronger flotillas than the Dover Patrol can account for, based on the Belgian Ports, it may be necessary to retain some part of the Commodore (T)'s force in southern waters'.[10] Invasion caution once more.

Seaham

The quiet harbour town of Seaham, some six miles south of Sunderland, had seen little of the war. It was not defended and had no permanent Royal Navy presence. Seaham Colliery employed 3,000 men and produced 6,000 tons of coal a day, vital for the war effort. There was an ironworks nearby, and a bottle works in the town itself. Men had marched off to war, but Seaham carried on as before.

On Tuesday 11 July 1916, two women were walking home from an evening at Dawdon, a mining village south of Seaham. They were Jennie Brown and her cousin Mary Slaughter. Mary, 35 years old, actually lived in Hebburn but recent Zeppelin attacks against Tyneside had frightened her and she left her blacksmith husband John behind to go and stay with her relatives in Seaham, which she thought would be safer. She was wrong. At 2220, *UB-39* rose up from the North Sea, only 400 yards off shore, and opened fire on Seaham with her 8.8cm (3.5in) deck gun. She fired thirty-nine shells and then departed into the night as she had come.

Chaos reigned. Although many shells fell harmlessly in the fields behind, some did explode in the town. Miner Carl Mortinson and his family at 14 Doctor Street had a lucky escape. A shell demolished their back yard wall, crashed into the house, flew across the kitchen, missing Mrs Mortinson, and landed at the front door. The rest of the family upstairs in bed were safe. Another struck a wagon load of timber. A pit chimney was damaged, and many windows shattered from the blasts.

Mary and Jennie had been taking a short cut through Seaham Colliery yard when a shell exploded there. 'They heard a noise like an explosion, and saw a bright flash in the distance'.[11] Jennie stumbled and fell prone; when she got up, Mary was lying on the ground apparently injured. She had been hit in the arm, foot and head by shrapnel and died a few hours later in Sunderland Infirmary. Mary Slaughter was buried four days later in Hebburn Cemetery, in an unmarked grave. At the inquest into her death, the coroner summed up by stating 'the jury would have no difficulty in coming to the conclusion that death was due to the explosion of a shell fired by a German submarine. They need not enter into any other question, nor did he think they should make any comment on the extraordinary mode of warfare. He thought, in view of everything, they could safely leave vessels of the class of the German submarine to his majesty's navy.'[12]

UB-39 was commanded by Werner 'Fips' Fürbringer, who would become a legend among submariners for his exploits in the war, which included sinking 101 ships. In 1933 he published his memoirs, in which he revealed that his brother had been killed on the Western Front six weeks beforehand and claimed that his real target at Seaham was the ironworks – although he spectacularly missed both that and the colliery, the only damage to which was caused by a shell which hit a chimney and the one which killed Mary. In the foreword, he dedicated the volume to his brother, killed at Verdun, and to 'Mrs Mary Slaughter of Hebburn, a young lady visitor to the town of Seaham'.[13] Fürbringer seems to imply that lobbing a few shells at an undefended coal port was some sort of catharsis for the loss of his sibling. If so, it would seem a poor show. His brother died fighting the French, not the British, and surely torpedoing a warship would have been a better retribution.

Sunderland Saved Again

After Jutland, Scheer had only two battlecruisers available in the 1st Scouting Group, *Moltke* and *Seydlitz*. But he was determined to demonstrate that there was still fight in the fleet and to show the world his unbroken strength. For his next sally he attached three of his dreadnoughts to Hipper's force, including the brand-new *Bayern* (1915, eight 38cm/15in guns). Scheer also insisted that he would only sail with scouting Zeppelins ahead and would never go out without them again.

At 2100 on 18 August he took the High Sea Feet out with the target again Sunderland. The operational plan was as originally conceived. Ten airships would act as forward scouts, and twenty-four U-boats would lie in wait for the Grand Fleet to emerge.

Once again, Room 40 alerted the Admiralty that the German fleet was preparing to leave harbour and the Grand Fleet put to sea, temporarily under the command of Admiral Burney, as Jellicoe was having a break (he joined his flagship by light cruiser from Dundee). They were at sea before their enemy.

Tyrwhitt was ordered to sail for Brown Ridge and to be on the lookout for the German fleet by early dawn on the 19th; with his broad pennant in *Carysfort* he took all of the 5th Light Cruiser Squadron, *Lightfoot* and his remaining eighteen 'L-' and 'M'-class destroyers. By 0300 Tyrwhitt was in

HMS *Carysfort* (1914) which became Commodore Tyrwhitt's flagship in May 1916. Armed with two 6in and eight 4in guns, she could achieve over 28 knots. (US Naval History and Heritage Command NH 61308)

position and patrolling at 20 knots. Around 1000 a message from a submarine indicated that the High Seas Fleet was to his north and, having relayed the message to Jellicoe, the commodore steamed northwards, hoping to get in touch with the enemy or get behind their line of retreat.

Jellicoe was heading south-east until the light cruiser HMS *Nottingham* was torpedoed at 0600 and again at 0710, sinking her. Unable to tell if it was a torpedo or a new minefield, Jellicoe assumed the latter and turned north, away from German ships.

Meanwhile Scheer had received a Zeppelin sighting report which indicated that a number of battleships and light cruisers were to his south. Believing this to be the detached portion of the British fleet which he had so set his heart on finding, he turned towards it and abandoned the

bombardment planned for Sunderland. But he had been misled – it was the Harwich Force that the airship had spotted.

At 1254, Tyrwhitt had not seen the enemy, or received any fresh orders, and so decided to return to his assigned station, setting course away from the High Seas Fleet as he did so. Scheer then learned from a U-boat that Jellicoe and the Grand Fleet were coming down on him some 65 miles distant and at 1435 gave up his chase of the Harwich ships and headed for home.

Despite receiving, later than intended, a confusing series of signals from Jellicoe, Tyrwhitt divined what Scheer was doing and turned again on a course which would give him a chance of intercepting the enemy. And at 1730, *Lightfoot* reported that she had sighted a large number of vessels steering east; the commodore first turned south to give himself some sea room and then settled onto a course to shadow the German Fleet.

Realising that he was being tailed, Scheer made dispositions for a night attack by stationing a powerful force of destroyers to his rear. Tyrwhitt would surely have made such an attack under cover of darkness but two things now deterred him. Firstly, at 1832, Jellicoe signalled that he was too far away to support him (in fact he was already retiring); and secondly, the Harwich Force would not be able to make contact with the German ships until after the moon had risen. At 1932 the commodore signalled that he had called off the chase. To have taken the offensive, unsupported and in bright moonlight, would surely have resulted in failure and ill-affordable losses to his ships. 'I retired gracefully as I did not feel inclined to take them on alone', he wrote later.[14]

The battleship SMS *Westfalen* (1908), torpedoed by *E-23* during the action of 19 August 1916. She mounted twelve 11in and twelve 5.9in guns. The torpedo put her out of action for two months. (US Library of Congress LC-DIG-ggbain-25466)

There was, however, one success for the Harwich Force to enjoy. The 8th Flotilla submarine HMS *E-23*, under Lieutenant Commander Robert Ross Turner, had managed to torpedo the battleship SMS *Westfalen* north of Terschelling at 0505 on 19 August; but the German ship was able to return to port, with an escort of destroyers.

Tyrwhitt's turning away drew criticism in some quarters, even from the Germans. Their official history of the naval war remarked that 'the reasons which caused him and Admiral Jellicoe not to attack the heavy German forces . . . and leave them entirely unmolested stand in basic opposition to the German conception of the use and independent attack of torpedo boat forces'.[15]

But there was never any official criticism of Tyrwhitt's actions, at the time or later. Tyrwhitt berated himself for not standing on longer when he had turned back at 1254, writing to Jellicoe 'I am afraid we failed you . . . and I am kicking myself'. And with regard to the night attack, he added 'I could have made one but I don't think I would have succeeded in doing any harm and should most certainly been cut up as the night was not very dark'.[16]

Sunderland was again saved, and the High Seas Fleet left the field once again. On 6 October, Germany resumed her submarine campaign in the North Sea and Western Approaches. The Ems and the Flanders U-boat flotillas were no longer at the service of Admiral Scheer as watching outposts for the fleet during a sortie and without them he was reluctant to come out. 'A deadlock had thus been reached, and it seemed that for the future the two great battle fleets could but lie inactive, watching one another across a kind of "No Man's Sea," where attack and defence were concerned only with transport and commerce.'[17]

Jellicoe Decides to Stay Away

After the abortive Sunderland raid of 19 August, Admiral Jellicoe reasoned that Scheer's operations were intended to draw him over German submarines or mines; and that this constant 'coat-dragging' was the High Seas Fleet's only operational strategy. Moreover, he thought that 'unless we could protect our light cruisers with destroyer screens we should suffer heavy losses by striving to bring the enemy to action whenever he left harbour'.[18]

Up until now, the Grand Fleet and the battlecruisers at Rosyth had always put to sea when a German raid was identified. Jellicoe now judged this too risky. 'He could no longer undertake, without an adequate destroyer screen, to guarantee coastal towns against bombardment, or to interfere with the early stages of a landing, and he strongly urged that the plan of disregarding the submarine and mine menace and "seeking the enemy in any locality, whenever he was known to be at sea" was no longer tenable.'[19]

Jellicoe now extended the area of the North Sea that the Grand Fleet would not seek to enter, stating that, in his opinion, 'the fleet ought not to operate in the area to the south of Lat 55 degrees 30' N. and the east of Long 4 degrees E. Experience had shown that waters so far to the eastward could not be properly watched by our cruisers'.[20] There was an important corollary to this change, which was accepted by the Admiralty. These plans meant that the duty of defending the North Sea and the British coasts south of Sunderland was to devolve upon the local defence flotillas, the Humber and the Harwich Forces, and the 3rd Battle Squadron. 'Admiral Jellicoe made it quite clear that his proposals were independent of whether the fleet was based at Rosyth or Scapa; and that only if he could be given more destroyers would he be willing to reconsider his decision.'[21]

Had the German high command and Admiral Scheer but known it, the way was clear for raids, invasion, or any other harassment of the east coast. A small number of older destroyers, the Harwich Force and seven outdated battleships were all that stood in their way.

* * * * *

Towards the end of 1916, David Lloyd George led a putsch which finally ousted Prime Minister Asquith, taking up the position himself on 6 December. On the 11th Lloyd George appointed Sir Edward Carson as First Lord of the Admiralty, replacing Balfour; a week earlier Admiral Jellicoe had been offered and had accepted (not without reservations) the post of First Sea Lord in succession to Jackson.

Jellicoe had commanded the Grand Fleet since the outbreak of war, groomed for the role by Fisher over many years. He had been appointed by Churchill as war was declared, replacing the incumbent CinC, Admiral Sir George Callaghan. Jellicoe protested so much against taking the role in this

Admiral Sir John Jellicoe in the unform of Admiral of the Fleet, who became CinC Grand Fleet on the outbreak of war and First Sea Lord on 30 November 1916. (Author's collection)

manner that it almost verged on insubordination. Now he had another position that he appeared not to relish, telling a small group of officers that he expected to last only six months in the post. That he 'was a very tired man when he came to Whitehall . . . after twenty-seven months in the most exacting and responsible of sea going commands' and the fact that he 'had always shown a reluctance to delegate'[22] would tell against him.

Carson was the leader of the Unionist cause, a strong advocate for Ulster and Northern Ireland. He had made his reputation as a formidable barrister, not least when he represented the Marquess of Queensbury in the case that destroyed Oscar Wilde, and had served as Attorney General when the coalition government was formed in May 1915. Jellicoe's replacement as CinC Grand Fleet at Scapa was David Beatty, with command of the battlecruisers going to Vice Admiral William Pakenham. What would 1917 bring to the British coasts?

11
'Shoot and Scoot', 1917

A previously unknown mechanical invention found itself in use to guard the British littoral, especially in East Anglia – the armoured car.

Armoured cars had probably been first conceived by the Royal Naval Air Service (RNAS), itself only in existence since July 1914. Some squadrons of RNAS aircraft had been sent to Dunkirk and Antwerp at the beginning of the German offensive. Naval aviation pioneer Commander Charles Samson came up with the idea of using touring cars to scout ahead for potential airfields and rescue downed pilots. Samson saw further opportunities when he armed one vehicle with a Maxim gun and ambushed a German car near Cassel on 4 September. At his request, shipbuilders in Dunkirk added boilerplate to his existing Rolls-Royce and Mercedes vehicles and the new armoured car squadrons were soon used to great effect forming part of RNAS mechanised raiding columns, as well as fulfilling the roles initially

A squadron of RNAS Lanchester armoured cars. They were built on the chassis of the Lanchester Sporting Forty, which had a side-valve, 5.5-litre, six-cylinder engine. These vehicles saw wide usage with the RNAS and the army. The Lanchester was the second most numerous armoured car in British 1914–18 service after the Rolls-Royce.
(Author's collection)

envisaged for them. By November 1914 they had become the Royal Naval Armoured Car Division (RNACD), eventually expanding to twenty squadrons, with a depot in Wormwood Scrubs and a headquarters at 48 Dover Street in London.

But the big and powerful cars necessary were expensive to procure, and the Admiralty had no qualms about accepting offers from wealthy individuals to pay for their acquisition and conversion. One such was Oliver Stillingfleet Locker-Lampson, a British politician and Conservative MP. In December 1914 Locker-Lampson received a commission in the Royal Navy Volunteer Reserve with the rank of Lieutenant Commander. This was largely on the basis of an understanding with the First Lord of the Admiralty, Winston Churchill, that Locker-Lampson would personally fund the establishment of an armoured car squadron for the RNACD. Locker-Lampson recruited men from his family area of Cromer and from elsewhere in Norfolk, Huntingdon and from among his London acquaintances. It cost him £30,000* to acquire and equip the cars, which became Number 15 Squadron, RNACD, some of which funding came secretly from the Ulster Volunteer Force with which he had strong links. Number 15 Squadron and Locker-Lampson served on attachment to the Belgian army in 1915 before both were sent to Russia.

Another armoured car pioneer was Hugh Richard Arthur Grosvenor, 2nd Duke of Westminster, known to his friends as 'Bendor'. He was a major landowner and one of the wealthiest men in the world. Amongst his possessions were seventeen Rolls-Royce cars which became the basis of Number 2 Squadron.

The establishment of trench warfare meant there was less scope for such vehicles in France, and they were in part utilised in other theatres of war. Some RNAS and army-operated cars came to East Anglia and were deployed as part of the anti-invasion forces. Amongst the places they were sent to was the sleepy fishing and tourist town of Southwold in Suffolk.

Southwold

Southwold, at the mouth of the River Blyth and facing east into Sole Bay, was no stranger to the threat of raids or invasion. The Battle of Sole Bay in 1672, the first engagement of what became the third Anglo-Dutch war, was fought within sight of the town and its residents at the time were armed and prepared to repel an invading enemy.

The long, wide, gently sloping and sandy beaches were tailor-made for a landing in force and when war came in 1914, Southwold's citizens lived in

---

* Perhaps £2.8 million today, according to the Bank of England.

permanent fear of invasion from an enemy whose naval bases were just 250 miles away and whose battle front was a mere 80 miles distant.

The proximity to Belgium meant that the town was soon receiving hundreds of refugees who were accommodated at the Constitutional Hall. The tower of the church of St Edmund King and Martyr became an observation point and under DORA rules was used at night to spot those who were breaking regulations regarding the showing of lights. Barbed wire was placed across the beaches.

A troop of the TF Lincolnshire Yeomanry arrived and set up camp on the Common. They were replaced in January 1915 by fifteen armoured cars from the RNACD, who in turn were supplanted by 670 men of the Royal Sussex Cyclists (a bicycle-mounted TF unit) in March. The cyclists departed for France and in their place came the Bedfordshire Regiment and then the Montgomery Yeomanry (TF) with 500 horses, stabled on the Common. These dispositions reflected the coastal defence plan: Territorial units* for home defence coupled with cyclists and armoured cars to provide mobility and a reaction force.

Despite this activity, Southwold was not a defended port. There was (and is) a feature known as Gun Hill and it boasted six old 18pdr muzzle-loaders, presented to the corporation in 1745 by the Royal Ordnance for defensive purposes and last fired in 1842. These could not, under any circumstances, be considered viable in 1914. It had a lighthouse, curiously sited within the town, and built by Trinity House in 1887 as a coastal mark for passing shipping and as a guide for vessels sailing into Southwold Harbour. Otherwise, it was unremarkable from a martial perspective.

That did not mean that the population was unafraid of invasion or attack. Town Clerk Ernest Read Cooper (who was also Captain of the Fire Brigade, Master of the Harbour and adjutant of the local volunteer force) was worried about the likelihood of the Germans arriving on his doorstep. 'As things were looking lively in the North Sea,' he confided to his diary on 25 November, 'and we were promised more raids, I packed up all my silver in a box and my sister, Clara Stanford, took it one day in her car to Halesworth.'[1] Two weeks later, perhaps encouraged by what had happened at Great Yarmouth, he packed up his house, sent his wife and baby to stay with 'Grannie' in Sutton, Surrey, discharged the maids, and moved in to a boarding house next door. Cooper noted that 'people began to get nervous and visitors who were coming for Christmas cancelled their arrangements. The large St Felix school for girls broke up hurriedly.'

---

* All of the TF units referenced above eventually made their way to France. Their sojourn on the east coast served both as defence but also for training.

When on the night of 15/16 April 1915, a Zeppelin bombed the town, he again sent his wife and baby to Sutton and placed all his life insurance and other investment policies in the care of the London and Westminster Bank in that town.

The Lion of Flanders

Sixty-year-old German Admiral Ludwig von Schröder was recalled from retirement on the outbreak of war and named as commanding admiral in Flanders, in charge of both seagoing forces and the 1st Marine Division. This formation was boosted in mid-November 1914 when additional naval infantry formations were raised and added to his command to form *Marinekorps Flandern*.

Schröder felt that there were many opportunities for interference with British shipping if he had sufficient naval resources. Eventually

The German regional commander of naval forces and marines in Flanders, Admiral Ludwig von Schröder, in front of the City Hall in Bruges. (US National Archives and Administration NAID 17391048)

A German 'A'-class torpedo boat, similar to *A-2* and *A-6* which were sunk by Harwich Force destroyers on 1 May 1915. The photograph is of *A-68*. (Author's collection)

A typical German 'V'-class destroyer.
(US Naval History and Heritage Command NH 111338)

the authorities in Berlin agreed and he was sent a force of small torpedo boats and submarines. He formed these into the Flanders Torpedo Boat Flotilla made up of fifteen 'A'-class torpedo boats under the command of *Korvettenkapitän* Hermann Schoemann. The 'A' class were designed as coastal torpedo boats, displacing 107 tons, 134ft long, lightly armed with a single 5cm (2in) deck gun (later versions mounted two 8.8cm [3.5in] guns) and two torpedo tubes; they could also carry four mines. Built in 1914, their top speed was 20 knots.

On 1 May 1915, two units, *A-2* and *A-6*, were sent on a rescue mission to pick up a downed seaplane's crew. Instead, they became involved with four armed trawlers and three Harwich Force destroyers, an action in which both German ships were sunk and Schoemann killed. The encounter demonstrated to Admiral Schröder that the 'A' class were simply not good enough ships to use for raiding; and the defeat enhanced Schröder's pleas for reinforcements and heavier vessels, a request which was eventually satisfied.

On 3 March 1916 he received three larger torpedo boats, *V-47*, *V-67* and *V-68*, equipped with three 8.8cm (3.5in) guns, six torpedo tubes and twenty-four mines. Capable of 33.5 knots these vessels formed the Flanders Destroyer Half Flotilla and gave Schröder the chance to launch surface operations once more. In October, having received further temporary reinforcements, the so-called Battle of the Dover Straits saw a German attack on the Dover Barrage sink three British armed drifters, a transport and an old destroyer, with another drifter and a destroyer damaged. The German press lauded this as a great success and Schröder gained the nickname 'The Lion of Flanders'.

January 1917

In January 1917, Admiral Schröder decided to resume his raiding. At 2300 on 25 January, German light forces appeared off Southwold and bombarded the town for nearly 10 minutes. Ernest Cooper had just gone to bed when 'there was a double explosion followed almost directly by another, very loud and close, like the lifeboat gun'.[3] He hurriedly made up a shelter downstairs with a 'bomb proof table'.

Two parachute star-shells and some sixty-eight rounds were fired, most of which were 'overs' falling in the marshes. The starshells come down at Easton and Chilvers Farm; only five projectiles landed in the town itself. Two shells hit the police station, destroying the chimney and causing bricks to fall into the room where two girls were sleeping. 'Iona Cottage', a pretty gabled white house half way up Constitution Hill, was hit and suffered from shrapnel or shell fragments, with six pieces penetrating the ceiling of a bedroom, two of which exited through the bed into the room below. The owners, Mr and Mrs Prestwidge, were sleeping in another room; fortunately, they survived. Also, 'Balmore', a large house on the seafront just 30 yards from the lighthouse, was hit in the first-floor bay window; a shell passed through the room in which the householder, Mr Webb, was hurriedly dressing. Miraculously he escaped injury. Shell fragments fell all over the town.

The Special Constables turned out, but most of the townsfolk went back to bed again and Ernest Cooper averred that 'there was no panic'. There was no retaliation from the town; 'as far as I know there was no reply from the shore, and I don't know that we have any guns which would have been of use if there had been time'.[4]

There was confusion as to the forces involved. Reporting to the War Cabinet the following day, Jellicoe stated that 'Southwold was bombarded last night probably by a submarine, as only small shells were fired. Most of the shells fell in fields; two houses were damaged, but there were no casualties.'[5] In 1933, the Royal Navy's Training Department noted only that 'German destroyers had appeared off Southwold on January 25 at 2300, and after firing some three score shells, which fell behind the town, made off to the north-east',[6] and today, the Southwold Museum website claims 'four German destroyers and one submarine'.

British sources at the time put a brave face on it. The official communiqué stated that only one enemy unit was involved;

> It was officially reported in London early on Friday afternoon that a small German vessel which had not been identified had approached the Suffolk coast of England on Thursday night, and had fired shells

without causing any casualties and making only slight damage. From unofficial reports it is learned that the raider appeared off the east coast of England on Thursday at 11 o'clock at night. It commenced firing star shells, and a sharp bombardment lasting for three minutes followed. No one was injured. There was no panic, and the damage done was slight.[7]

The Germans meanwhile put a different spin on matters, claiming they had been looking for RN ships and that Southwold was a place of military interest. A Berlin official message through Reuters announced that the raid on the Suffolk coast was 'made by our light forces, which penetrated the English coastal waters south of Lowestoft, in order to attack hostile guardships: but despite a search, we could not find the enemy. Thereupon our torpedo boats shelled the fortified place of Southwold. Full [sic] hits were observed. We returned safely without observing the enemy.'[8]

For a town already traumatised through three years of daily expectation of a German landing, the impact was significant. At Reydon School, to the north-west, the headmistress reported that only 107 children out of a roll of 160 attended on the 26th. Shells had fallen around Reydon, and several pieces of shrapnel were picked up in the school's playground.

There were no British naval units in the harbour. Ernest Cooper thought that this was probably a good thing. 'Most nights we have patrol boats or minesweepers [these would in both cases been auxiliary patrol armed trawlers or drifters] in the harbour but the sea was so heavy so they were spared as they would have been bound to do something and were not strong enough to tackle destroyers, as we seldom see anything of the navy now.' He was also less than pleased with the response of the land forces. 'I saw no concentration of troops, so far as I know none came into the town and if it had been possible to land in force, I don't think our small garrison would have made much of a show.' Cooper was also annoyed that some newspapers apparently called it a 'comic bombardment' and a 'silly raid'. 'To those in it, there was nothing comic or silly but a very present danger.'[9]

Southwold was in no way a defended place; but just to make sure the Germans didn't take Gun Hill literally, the old guns there were buried after the raid in case the enemy thought they represented a fort. Frightened, but not yet cowed, Southwold resumed its wartime life.

Germany Takes a Risk

The attack on Southwold may not have been very significant in the great scheme of things. But there was another German initiative in January that was.

Merchant-ship sinkings, primarily by U-boats, were causing great concern in Britain. In 1916, 1.2 million gross tons of British shipping, or 2.3 million tons including other Allied and neutral nations, had been lost to enemy action. Sinkings by U-boats accounted for some 73 per cent of this total. In January 1917, the month's totals were 153,666 tons and 368,521 tons respectively.[10] Apart from the obvious loss of cargos, the shipyards could not replace the tonnage fast enough and hence the available shipping lift was decreasing every month.

However, Germany was suffering badly from the Royal Navy's blockade of foodstuffs and war necessities. The morale of the German nation on the home front was at rock bottom. The harsh 'Turnip Winter' of 1916/17 had devastated Germany's food crops and the blockade of her trade was reducing supplies still further. Everything was in short supply and food rationing was severe, leading to public unrest and rioting. The Royal Navy had brought hunger and misery to the home front and many in Germany cried out to inflict similar pain on Britain and her allies*

On 1 February 1917, Germany declared unrestricted submarine warfare. In doing so the Imperial government knew that there was a very strong risk that America would be tipped into the war by such an action. But the German command group had been convinced by some clever calculations from Department B-1 (the Economic Warfare Plans group) that within five months Britain could be brought to her knees through lack of food, primarily wheat, as a result of such a campaign.

The German Ambassador to the United States of America, Count von Bernstorff, had written an exculpatory letter to US Secretary of State Lansing on 31 January justifying this new campaign of unrestricted warfare, in which he blamed Germany's decision on the British and called their blockade illegal under international law.

His note averred that,

a new situation has thus been created which forces Germany to new decisions. Since two years and a half England is using her naval power for a criminal attempt to force Germany into submission by starvation. In brutal contempt of International Law, the group of powers led by England not only curtail the legitimate trade of their opponents, but they also, by ruthless pressure, compel neutral countries either to altogether forego every trade not agreeable to the Entente Powers, or to limit it according to their arbitrary decree ... the English Government, however, insists upon continuing its war of

---

* Germany had introduced food rationing in January 1915. Imports fell by 55 per cent over the course of 1915–16 and food shortages were widespread. By 1917 the official ration gave just 1,000 calories.

starvation, which does not at all affect the military power of its opponents, but compels women and children, the sick and the aged, to suffer for their country pains and privations which endanger the vitality of the nation.[11]

Germany also stated that hospital ships would now be regarded as legitimate targets. Thus any final regard for the rules of the sea, the Treaty of London or Prize Rules went out of the window. All neutral and Allied ships at sea were at risk of being sunk without warning or aid. Lieutenant Commander Charles Poignand, captain of the destroyer HMS *Menace* (1915), was less than impressed. '[It is] reported today that the Huns propose to sink all ships on sight, hospital ships included. I wonder why they took the trouble to make the announcement as that is what they have been doing already for some time period.'[12] Nonetheless, it did not take long for the results of this new campaign to be seen. In February 540,006grt of Allied and neutral shipping was sunk by U-boats. Food supply began to dominate the public debate on both sides of the North Sea.

'Don't Waste Bread', an exhortatory poster issued by the Ministry of Food at the height of the U-boat crisis in 1917. Before the war, four out of every five slices of bread consumed in Britian came from imported wheat. (Author's collection)

There was no food rationing in Britain* at this time. Whilst food shortages did occur every now and again, the government first attempted to control the matter through the encouragement of voluntary restraint. Articles appeared in newspapers during February 1917 indicating that the government's food controller, Lord Devonport,† wanted to avoid compulsory rationing but that there was a need to economise. People were requested to restrict their eating to no more than 4lb of bread or food made

---

* Rationing of sugar would be introduced on 31 December 1917.
† Hudson Ewbanke Kearley, 1st Viscount Devonport, a British grocer and politician. He founded the International Tea Company's Stores, and became the first chairman of the Port of London Authority.

from 3lb flour; 2lb 8 oz of meat (including bacon and sausages); and 12 oz of sugar a week. Fish or eggs, however, were said to be freely available (such quantities would have seemed bounteous to the enemy).

This is not to suggest that there was no rationing 'pain' in Britain. Under the DORA regulations it was legislated in April 1917 that the 'manufacture and sale of light pastries muffins, crumpets, and teacakes is prohibited. Scones must contain no sugar.' Furthermore 'the use of wheat, rice, and rye for other purposes than seed and flour for human consumption is prohibited'. Both of these measures were clearly targeted at preserving flour for the manufacture of bread. Tea shops were also targeted; 'no individual customer shall be served at any meal whatsoever which begins between the hours of 3 pm and 6 pm with more than 2oz in the whole of bread, cake, bun, scone, and biscuit'.

However, the government was concerned that rationing might become necessary and hence kept the facts of the number of merchant ships sunk out of the public eye to avoid panic. At the War Cabinet (a new body introduced by Lloyd George to manage the war) of 13 February, it was decided that 'the Admiralty should stop at once the publication of losses of Allied and neutral merchant ships'. With regard to U-boats, 'a statement might be made in the sense that the Admiralty are not dissatisfied with the number of enemy submarines they have reason to believe never returned home'.[13] This was sophistry of the highest order.

In London, Georgina Lee confided to her diary that 'the whole of civilised Europe depends for its salvation on our English ships and our sailors, God bless them'.[14] Fisher's dictum regarding starvation versus invasion crept a little closer to reality.

Invasion Impossible?

The invasion debate rolled on in 1917 and the Admiralty continued to assert the view that no invasion was possible, despite its failure to prevent a number of raids. On 16 March 1917, a meeting was held at the War Office between senior army and navy personnel. Roger Keyes, soon to be a rear admiral, prepared a memorandum of the points discussed, although in what official capacity is not now known.

From this note, it can be seen that the Imperial General Staff estimated that Germany could spare 160,000 men for the invasion of Britain, and that this force could be disembarked in 32 hours. In turn, the Admiralty calculated that Germany was possessed of sufficient shipping lift to convey them. However, First Sea Lord John Jellicoe gave as his opinion that such a beach landing was a remote possibility, given the difficulties entailed. Keyes enthusiastically agreed with this view. Moreover, in the First Sea Lord's judgement a raid of this type would suffer very considerable losses and would be likely to be repulsed. They would need to secure one or more ports to ensure even modest success.

When the issue of the success of the mock invasion at the 1913 manoeuvres (see Chapter 4) was brought up, Jellicoe dismissed them, as the conclusions drawn from the exercise were erroneous (in his view) and that the Germans would never attempt to rush transports into a port, as had been done in 1913 at the Humber, without a preliminary bombardment, and probably an invasion via beaches near to the target. The Admiralty further illustrated their position by the difficulties that the Allies had had with beach landings at Gallipoli, this despite a very considerable preliminary bombardment – a sort of 'if we can't they can't' argument.

Keyes concluded his note with what appears to be his personal opinion. 'It is inconceivable that any landing on a large scale will be attempted while the Grand Fleet is in being, or even in the absence of the Grand Fleet in the face of the great risks the transports will run from mines and attack by submarines and the [light forces] in the southern area.' He went on to posit that as there were Germans at Gallipoli, they would have learned the same lessons re the difficulties of beach landings and that 'I cannot believe that they are so mad as to undertake such a forlorn, hopeless exercise'.[15] Clearly the views of the sailors were deeply held. But they do smack of a 'proof by induction'.

Kent in the Firing Line, February–April 1917

The county of Kent juts out into the North Sea, closing it against the coast of Europe to create the English Channel and the Straits of Dover. The Kentish village of St Margaret's-at-Cliffe is reckoned to be the nearest village in England to the coast of France, standing half a mile inland from the steep chalk cliffs of St Margaret's Bay, a mere 21 miles from the French coast. Towns such as Margate, Ramsgate and Broadstairs were Edwardian holiday resorts but now, along with Dover, home to the Dover Patrol, were fully in the firing line of war.

Coastal defence guns were situated all along the Kent coast. At Margate, 6in naval guns were positioned along the seafront at Palm Bay and more guns were sited at Foreness, between Cliftonville and Broadstairs. The Royal Naval Air Station at St Mildred's Bay, Westgate-on-Sea, to the west of Margate, was established in June 1914 and continued to operate throughout the war. An airfield adjacent to the seaplane base was opened in 1915 and, the following year, an airfield was established at Manston, three miles behind Margate.

These precautions failed to prevent Margate being the victim of an attack from the sea. On the night of 25/26 February 1917, the German Flanders

Flotilla sortied to make an assault on the Dover Barrage, which used nets, mines and attendant drifters to try to close the Dover Strait. But this time the navy was able to ameliorate the severity of the attempted raid. The German plan was for one flotilla to attack the Barrage while a half flotilla of torpedo boats sought targets of opportunity off the Kent coast. In total eleven vessels sortied from Zeebrugge and having evaded British patrols, six of them were accidentally intercepted by the destroyer HMS *Laverock* (1913), armed with three 4in and one 3pdr guns and two sets of twin 21in torpedo tubes. She was commanded by 28-year-old Lieutenant Henry Armstrong Binmore RN, who did not hesitate to engage and fought his ship with such vigour that the Germans thought they were fighting at least three enemy destroyers. Nor did *Laverock* lose a man. The German force withdrew and instead bombarded Margate, Broadstairs, Westgate-on-Sea and North Foreland wireless station before retiring. No significant damage occurred, but in Reading Street, Broadstairs, shells killed a Mrs Morgan and her two daughters, a baby and a girl of 9. Her other four children survived.

Three miles from Broadstairs was 'Elmwood', the country home of the newspaper proprietor Alfred Harmsworth, Lord Northcliffe. A self-made man who worshipped his creator, Northcliffe had helped drive Britain into the war. Now the war came to him. At 2330 on 25 February, 'Elmwood' was hit; shrapnel rained down on its roof and a shell made a hole in the gardener's cottage. With surpassing arrogance and self-importance, 'Northcliffe was convinced that the attack was a deliberate assassination attempt', telling his staff that his house had been lit up 'by twenty star-shells from the sea . . . the authorities have no doubt that my house was aimed at'.[16] But he did set up a relief fund for the motherless Morgan children

The German press predictability made a better story out of the raid than the reality. The Reuters correspondent in Amsterdam filed a story which was widely carried. He noted that,

> a Berlin official report gives a fantastic account of the recent bombardment of the British coast. It says: 'German torpedo boats reached the Channel beyond the Dover-Calais line and entered the mouth of the Thames. The British scattered after a fierce artillery fight, and avoided further action by a hasty retreat. We did not suffer loss or damage. The enemy was not further observed here. Another section raided without finding any guard as far as North Foreland, and bombarded the coast defence works at Margate. Our vessels were quite near the coast but no commercial traffic was observed.' It is hardly necessary to state that the German account is a travesty of the facts.[17]

* * * * *

The coastal towns were once more a target the following month. The Flanders Flotilla devised a two-part raid in which one section would attack destroyers and armed trawlers patrolling near the Dogger Bank while another section carried out a bombardment of the coast.

On the night of 16/17 March the two groups of vessels left Zeebrugge and split into two parts. The destroyers HMS *Paragon* and HMS *Llewellyn* engaged eight German torpedo boats of the first grouping and *Paragon* was sunk by a torpedo. Her captain, Lieutenant John Francis Bowyer, survived but seventy-five of her crew were lost, including Bowyer's elder brother, Richard Grenville Bowyer, also a lieutenant and serving alongside his sibling. *Llewellyn* rammed a ship, 'probably a German destroyer'. Immediately Vice Admiral Bacon, commanding the Dover Patrol, ordered his forces out and Signalman G E Haigh, on board the destroyer HMS *Swift* at Dover, saw fire and rockets at 2300 and all the available warships in Dover harbour put to sea.

HMS *Laforey* had joined the Dover Patrol less than a fortnight previously, on 5 March, having served with the Harwich Force. Attracted by the sight of an explosion, she moved in to investigate and, finding a field of debris, started to search for survivors, signalling *Llewellyn* to join her. Neither ship noticed that the German vessels were still in attendance and two German ships, SMS *G-87* and SMS *S-49*, launched torpedoes against the British ships, one hitting and damaging *Llewellyn*, and then escaped unseen in the dark. But the overall result was inconclusive for both sides. As Haigh's diary entry recorded, 'no definite results'.[18]

The coastline was not undefended, for five armed drifters were on the lookout that night between Broadstairs Knoll and North Sand Head. One, *Paramount*, was to the eastward. At 0030 *Paramount* sighted three destroyers coming from the north-east and at once fired her green rocket, the signal for 'enemy in sight'. They passed her close astern and opened a heavy fire. But she had extinguished every light and escaped unhurt. The destroyers sank a small steamer, SS *Greypoint*, which had broken down and anchored off Broadstairs, and the armed drifter *Redwald* received five hits. Two boxes of 3pdr ammunition blew up, wounding the skipper and a trimmer seriously and six other ratings slightly. She was beached and subsequently brought into harbour. The German force then opened fire on the coastal towns. Meanwhile, at 0045 on the 17th, HMS *TB-4* (one of Fisher's *Cricket*-class coastal destroyers of 1906) reported to Admiral Bacon that Margate and Ramsgate were under attack. She tried to follow the enemy as they made off but could not keep up. Margate, Ramsgate and Broadstairs had all received fire, but the damage was slight; only three houses were hit and there were no casualties.

In his report to the Admiralty of the incident, Admiral Bacon pointed out the difficulties inherent in defending against this sort of raid. 'The enemy had only to keep a rigid lookout for one hour and fire a torpedo at anything seen and run away, while the British boats had night after night to keep a lookout the whole night through. The enemy could decide whether he should "shoot and scoot" or carry out a more or less prolonged attack.'

Interestingly, at least from the point of view of the inhabitants of the Kent coast, he went on to add that 'as regards the raid on the coast, the attacks against the shore were comparatively harmless and his main preoccupation was to cover and protect the shipping in the Downs'.[19]

The Second Battle of the Dover Strait

Dover was the next target of the Flanders raiders, although not the original intention when they had left harbour. On the evening of 20 April 1917, twelve German torpedo boats set out from Zeebrugge with the aim of attacking the Dover net barrage and associated drifters and support vessels. Defensive minefields prevented them reaching their objectives so instead they contented themselves with a bombardment of Dover and Calais, six vessels to each port.

The six ships operating against Dover were the 5th Torpedo-Boat Half Flotilla under the command of *Korvettenkapitän* Gautier, each armed with three 10.5cm (4.1in) guns and six torpedo tubes. Gautier found his target and made an attack around midnight, firing 350 rounds at Dover, and then withdrew heading for home. He had, in fact, done little damage as most of the shells fell either on the cliffs or inland above the town.

Two Royal Navy flotilla leaders, HMS *Swift* and HMS *Broke*, had been assigned patrol duty off Dover. The captain of *Swift* was Commander Ambrose Maynard Peck, while *Broke* was led by Commander Edward Ratcliffe Garth Russell Evans, known to his friends as Teddy and a famous polar explorer. He had been seconded from the navy to the *Discovery* Expedition to the Antarctic in 1901–04, when he served as second officer on the relief ship, and afterwards planned his own Antarctic expedition. However, he suspended this intention when offered the post of second-in-command on Captain Robert Falcon Scott's ultimately fatal expedition to the South Pole of 1910–13. Specifically, he was to be the captain of the expedition ship *Terra Nova*. He accompanied Scott to within 150 miles of the Pole on foot, but became seriously ill with scurvy and only narrowly survived the return journey. In one way he was lucky, for although he nearly died, he at least eventually survived, unlike the entire group which had

HMS *Broke* (1914), Teddy Evans' ship at the Second Battle of the Dover Strait. (Author's collection)

continued towards the Pole, including Scott himself. Called back to active service in 1914 from the lecture circuit, he always sailed with a stuffed penguin mascot strapped to the mast of his vessel, in recognition of his exploits. A national hero once already, he was about to gain renewed fame.

The *Broke* had been built for the Chilean Navy and was purchased by the Admiralty at the outbreak of war. Armed with two 4.7in guns, two 4in, two 2pdrs and two torpedo tubes, she had already had an interesting war, being involved in the night action at Jutland, losing her bow in a collision with HMS *Sparrowhawk*. *Broke* (and her sister *Botha*) was a much-prized berth because the Chileans, unlike their Royal Navy brethren, had spared no expense on the officers' accommodation which included silver-plated chandeliers in the captain's cabin!

Swift, built in 1905 and unique in design, was at that time armed with one 6in gun which had been fitted in 1916 at the expense of two forward 4in, two 4in, and two torpedo tubes. The 6in proved to be a disaster as it was impossible to train and needed two men on the muzzle to help move it.

The 'Tribal'-class destroyer HMS *Amazon*, meanwhile, had been ordered to Calais to collect a VIP (who later turned out to be none other than Lloyd George) but when the gun flashes of the German bombardment were spotted the transport duty was cancelled. *Swift* and *Broke* were ordered to intercept the German vessels and *Amazon* to patrol to prevent the enemy approaching Dover again, saving the town from further woes.

It was a calm, intensely dark night and visibility was poor; but at 0145 and about 600 yards range the two British intercepting ships sighted the six

Germans near the Goodwin Sands, trying to hurry home unseen in the gloom. Confusion reigned as the usual problems of identification were considered but this was resolved when in answer to Commander Peck's recognition signal, the British vessels heard fire gongs and the German ships opened fire with every available gun. Fortunately, every shot was an 'over'.

Commander Peck, leading the British line, immediately swung his ship and attempted to ram the foremost German vessel, missed, and spun round to launch a torpedo, which found its mark in SMS *G-85*, and then essayed another ramming attempt, causing his intended victim to cease fire and rush off into the darkness. *Swift* had been hit portside below the bridge in the stokers' mess deck and another shell had carried away her wireless aerial without exploding. In return, she had achieved one hit with her temperamental 6in which had struck the second ship of the German line in the engine room 'cutting her practically in half'.[20] Peck continued the chase until his ship lost speed due to her injuries and made his task futile.

Meanwhile, the *Broke* was caught up in the sort of engagement which was as old as naval warfare. Evans had opened fire on the German line, which was now at full speed and belching smoke and flame from their funnels. They returned the fire, wounding Evans' helmsman, Able Seaman Rawles, four times in the legs. Despite his wounds he was able to follow orders to port the helm and at 27 knots the *Broke* squarely rammed the enemy third in line, the *G-42*, commanded by *Kapitänleutnant* Bernd von Arnim. *Broke*'s bows embedded themselves in the German ship's hull and the two vessels found themselves locked in a deadly embrace. The crash as the *Broke* 'buried her bow into the enemy . . . reverberated around the hills and cliffs, followed by firing in the night, was something I will never forget', noted an eyewitness.[21]

Commander Evans ordered a rapid cannonade, sweeping the German's decks with gunfire, whilst his enemy did the same. Men were mown down on both sides, including von Arnim himself. Of the eighteen men working *Broke*'s forward guns, soon only five were left standing. But Midshipman Donald A Gyles, RNR, a 19-year-old merchant apprentice co-opted into the Royal Navy, kept one gun in action, despite a severe shrapnel wound to his eye and wounds to his leg and arm.

The Germans now tried to board the *Broke* to end the carnage and swarmed over her forecastle. Gyles, armed only with a pistol, stood tall and fired at them; one German sailor, 'a regular giant', flung himself onto Gyles from behind and tried to take the pistol off him but was in turn run through with a cutlass by a British rating. To the call of 'repel boarders' a pitched battle of pistols, rifles, sailors with cutlasses and marines with bayonets raged on *Broke*'s decks, which ended with Evans' men proving triumphant and sweeping the German attackers into the sea, except for two who lay down and feigned death. Throughout the action Evans bellowed to his crew 'remember the *Lusitania*, men'.[22]

Finally Evans managed to extract his ship from his victim, leaving it sinking, to seek new prey. He fired a torpedo at one German vessel and engaged another before attacking the only two remaining torpedo boats he could see. This proved an overweening ambition for *Broke* took a shell in her boiler, which significantly reduced her speed and left her powerless to sustain a chase. Even now *Broke*'s troubles were not over, for Evans saw an enemy vessel on fire in the distance and the crew calling for help. Evans ordered his ship to limp towards them, only for the Germans to re-open fire on him. He returned fire and pulled back into the night whereupon his boilers finally gave out.

In the darkness *Swift* had stumbled on a sinking German vessel, her crew mustered on deck and crying out for assistance. Peck approached with caution, for two of the enemy's crew were closed up by a torpedo tube, when suddenly the enemy vessel heeled over and sank. *Swift* lowered her boats and began to pick up survivors. The German vessel turned out to be the one rammed by the *Broke*. *Swift* then had to wait for daylight as she had lost her bearings; additionally Peck had to flood the starboard side to keep the hole in her port side above the water. But on the 22nd she was out on patrol again.

The *Broke* was eventually found by British destroyers sent from Dover and taken under tow to the Eastern Arm of Dover harbour. As she entered port, all the drifters, with whom Evans was something of a cult hero, began sounding their sirens and hooters. Amid the cacophony, an officer ran along the harbour wall calling for the row to stop. 'Go to 'ell', was the reply, 'it's Teddy.'[23] Her crew was given a huge welcome in the grateful town and many received a free drink in the pubs that night to thank them for sparing the citizens from further shelling.

Two British ships had attacked six German vessels and sunk two of them, despite suffering some damage themselves. In the dark days of early 1917 it was a welcome victory and riposte. Both Evans and Peck were speedily awarded the Distinguished Service Order and advanced to the rank of captain; and Evans was feted by the press and the propaganda machine as 'Evans of the *Broke*'. Gyles too became an instant hero. On his release from hospital in Deal he went home to Hornsey where newspapers made much of his ordeal. His quondam headmaster at Stroud Green Elementary school, H W Christmas, described him, with no doubt some vested interest and pride, as 'a typical product of the modern elementary school'.[24] Gyles was also featured, in an etching of his personal battle, on the front cover of *War Illustrated* in May. Midshipman Gyles was awarded the Distinguished Service

Cross, and Able Seaman Ernest Ramsden Ingleson, who had saved Gyles' life, received the Distinguished Service Medal. *Broke*'s helmsman Able Seaman William George Rawles was awarded the Conspicuous Gallantry Medal.

Broke lost twenty-one men killed and had another thirty-six wounded. *Swift* had one fatality and four wounded. But the German appetite for such encounters was clearly reduced – there were no more German surface raids in the Strait for 10 months.

The action became known as the Second Battle of the Dover Strait* and national newspapers published long articles about the bravery of the men of the *Broke* and the *Swift*. The *Daily Sketch* front-page headline was 'They Died Defending Our Shores', with pictures of the funeral procession for the British dead through the Market Square in Dover. One hundred and forty German officers and men were rescued from the sea by *Swift* and other ships of the Patrol, and they suffered the indignity of being jeered at by the good citizens of Dover, so recently the target of their shells, as they watched them being marched off to prisoner-of-war camps. It was probably better than drowning though.

Ramsgate

The harbour at Ramsgate was an important base for the Dover Patrol, being home to some thirty armed drifters. From this base they served four days at sea and two in harbour, turn and turnabout, patrolling and serving the Dover barrage. A frequent target for air attack and constantly at risk from the sea, at the end of March 1917 Ramsgate gained a guard ship in the shape of the monitor *Marshal Ney*.

The product of Fisher's secret plan to land troops on Germany's Baltic coast, she had been designed to carry twin 15in guns with a shallow draft to enable her to come close to shore for bombardment purposes. She and her sister *Marshal Soult* were diesel powered, which meant that they had no need of boiler rooms which suited their low draught, nor did they require large funnels, which reduced the amount of superstructure. The engines provided were originally designed for much smaller freighters and proved particularly troublesome; *Soult*'s Vickers-built engines never achieved her design speed of 9 knots, finding 6 knots difficult enough, which meant that in any sort of seaway she had to be towed into position, and *Marshal Ney* was fitted with very unreliable German-manufactured MAN engines, which unsurprisingly became harder and harder to maintain and find parts for. Launched in June 1915, she was dubbed 'practically a failure' by *Jane's Fighting Ships*.

---

* The first had occurred in October 1916.

In January 1917, *Ney* was sent to be refitted and her twin 15in guns were removed (to be given to the rather more successful monitor *Erebus*). Instead, she was equipped with a single 9.2in gun and four 6in, and on completion in March despatched to Ramsgate as guard ship under the command of Commander Reginald James Newall Watson, something of a gunnery expert and a former instructor at HMS *Excellent*, the navy's gunnery school. When first arriving at her new station, *Marshal Ney* met an easterly gale off Dungeness and signalled that she was helpless and in danger of grounding. Admiral Bacon recognised that the tide would take her clear and signalled her new captain that 'the *Marshal Ney* usually navigated the waters of the Patrol sideways!'[25]

Her gunnery officer probably did not suit her new captain. He was Lieutenant Commander Francis Charles Cadogan, who had joined the ship the month beforehand. Cadogan was the grandson of the 4th Earl Cadogan and the son of Captain the Hon Charles George Henry Cadogan, but seemed ill-equipped to be an officer on board a fighting ship. His captains certainly thought so. Captain Loder-Symonds, writing in December 1916, noted that 'he is well read and has some literary attainments, but his qualities fit him more for clerical work than as executive officer of a sea-going ship'. A subsequent captain of *Ney*, Henry Luxmoore, clearly found him unhelpful, writing he 'would be better at office work than an executive officer, as he has not very good manners with junior officers and men'.[26]

However, he would have his moment of fame. On 27 April, several German destroyers opened fire on Ramsgate with high explosive and star shell. Some sixty rounds were fired, most of which landed in open country, but two citizens were killed with three more injured, and twenty-one houses together with two stables were hit with £6,000 of property damage caused. Manston airfield also came under fire. Further destruction was avoided because *Marshal Ney* opened fire from her anchorage. The sudden appearance of 9.2in and 6in shells exploding amongst the enemy destroyers – any one hit from which would invariably be fatal – persuaded the Germans to call off the attack and they ran for home.

The two fatalities in Ramsgate covered the age spectrum. One was 61-year-old John William Hobday. The other was an attractive 22-year-old girl, Ivy Edith Thorncroft. She was the daughter of a respected Ramsgate tradesman and Wesleyan lay preacher, Norton Thorncroft, and a popular member of the local ladies' rink hockey team. Cut down in the young bloom of life, the town turned out to pay their respects as her coffin was carried to rest, escorted by three naval officers. One wonders if there was a would-be suitor amongst those close attendants.

* * * * *

While Kent was under attack, there were important developments elsewhere. The United States of America finally declared war on Germany on 6 April 1917. But it would take until 1918 before their massive financial and industrial strength could begin to make itself felt on the battle front.*

However, there were two instant benefits; firstly, America's entry made the Royal Navy's blockade of Germany even tighter, as the USA was the source of many contraband products. And secondly, America immediately sent much-needed destroyers to British waters.

This latter, coupled with American arguments, political pressure, and the realisation that the Admiralty's belief that they could not deploy enough escorts to institute convoying of merchant ships was based on erroneous data, led to the introduction of convoy for all merchant shipping from late May. The impact was to significantly reduce the sinking of cargo vessels by U-boats and afford some relief to the food and materials shortages that Britain and her allies had begun to experience.

Scarborough Once More

On Tuesday 4 September 1917, the war must have seemed far from Scarborough. Admittedly there were some minesweepers, trawlers armed with little 3pdr or 6pdr guns, moored in the bay. But the attack of 1914 was three years past, and the much-feared invasion had not yet come. 'The day had been beautifully fine and there were many merry picnic parties on the coast and moors. Thousands of holidaymakers thronged the north and south beaches and promenades. At a few minutes to seven in the evening, when many people were on their way to the Spa, a loud explosion was heard, followed by others in quick succession.'[7] Scarborough was under attack again.

Four miles to the south-east, the panic-stricken spectators could see the outline of a submarine. It was *UB-21*, a UB-II type vessel, armed with six torpedoes and an 8.8cm (3.5in) deck gun with 120 rounds. For ten minutes her commander, Franz Walther, rained shells into the town. His gunlayers' aim seemed erratic and shells fell in the sea and various parts of the town. 'Many people were boating, fishing and bathing when the submarine opened

---

* It is interesting to note that when the United States entered the war, it immediately introduced conscription. On registration day, 5 June 1917, nearly ten million US males between the ages of 21 and 31 were required to sign up for the draft. America too introduced draconian restriction of civil liberties. For example, the Espionage Act of 1917 punished 'false statements with intent to interfere with the operations of military forces' and empowered the Postmaster General to censor material 'advocating or urging treason, insurrection or forcible resistance to any law of the United States' (Weil, *Madman*, p 105). If found guilty, offenders faced a maximum fine of $10,000, or imprisonment for not more than 20 years, or both. Criticism of the government was banned in the 1918 Sedition Act which prohibited many forms of speech, including any disloyal, profane, scurrilous, or abusive language about the form of government of the United States . . . or the flag of the United States, or the uniform of the Army or Navy.

fire. Bathers made a dash for shelter, but the boating parties had to remain afloat, and as it turned out they were in perfect safety.'[28]

Hastily, the armed trawlers raised anchor and began to head towards the attacker, which caused Walther to dive the boat and slip away, having fired off some thirty projectiles. 'A shell which struck the house occupied by Mr William Jackson, at 107 Hoxton Road, smashed the brickwork and not a single article of furniture remained whole in the sitting-room. Women's jackets and hats were torn to shreds.'[29] There was also damage to the railway station and nearby Pavilion Hotel, and in Queens Street, St Thomas Street, James Street, Victoria Road, Cambridge Street, Somerset Terrace and St Nicholas Cliff. Some shells had been directed at the minesweepers, but none hit.

Three people had been killed; Mrs Elizabeth Scott was the wife of a local police constable. A resident of Hoxton Road, she was struck by fragments from the shell which hit number 107 as she stood in the doorway of her house and died at 2230. Lance Corporal J W Parry of Manchester was injured in the South Bay and died in hospital. And Thomas Temple Pickup, a 64-year-old cabinet maker, was injured near the Rose and Crown public house and expired on the way to hospital.

Six people were injured, some badly. Particularly sad was 17-year-old Alice Appleby who lived on Whitehead Hill. She was wounded in the leg whilst walking on Longwestgate and subsequently had to have the leg amputated, In his excitement a boy also fell over on the pier and broke his collarbone.

But the raid was virtually ignored by a public and media now almost inured to German 'atrocities' and numbed by the mass slaughter on the Western Front. The official communiqué put out by the government simply stated that 'a German submarine appeared off Scarborough yesterday evening and fired 30 rounds, half of which fell on land. Three persons were killed and five [*sic*] injured, but the damage done to property was only slight.'[30] The *Daily Telegraph* headlined a short piece 'an exciting ten minutes for Scarborough as a U-boat comes calling'.[31] At least the local coroner, Mr Pickup, manged to raise some bluster, opining at the inquest into the dead that 'the Germans had the absurd idea that the murder of children, women and old men would cause such terror in England that we would desire a disgraceful peace. It was an utterly foolish dream; the effect would be just the opposite.'[2]

The war continued. And so did the fear of invasion. For on 17 September, the Operation Division of the Admiralty Naval Staff issued a statement of naval policy. It read:

> The ultimate objects of British Naval Policy are defined as;
> Firstly to bring pressure to bear on the enemy people so as to compel their government to come to terms and secondly to resist the pressure

applied by them so that we may carry on the war undisturbed. In order to achieve these objects British naval power must be directed into the following channels:

a. The protection of the Sea Communications of the Allied armies more particularly in France where the main offensive lies

b. Prevention of enemy trade as a means of handicapping his military operation and exerting pressure on the mass of his people

c. Protection of British and Allied trade on which depends the supply of munitions and food to the allied armies and people

d. Resistance to Invasion and Raids.[33]

Prevention of invasion and raids was still a top-four priority.

* * * * *

Prime Minister Lloyd George was increasingly dissatisfied with the performance of the Admiralty under First Sea Lord Jellicoe. In July he appointed one of his own men, Eric Campbell Geddes, as First Lord of the Admiralty. He was neither a politician or a sailor but a hard headed businessman and previously deputy general manager of the North-eastern Railway, one of several 'men of push and go' who the prime minster drafted into government to get things done.

Geddes and Jellicoe had difficulty seeing eye to eye. The workaholic Jellicoe, a poor delegator who tried to involve himself in all decisions, was gumming up the works and making it difficult for the Admiralty to get things done. Geddes saw one of his roles as ungumming things. So on Christmas Eve 1917, Admiral Sir John Jellicoe received a letter from Geddes asking for his resignation. Jellicoe himself believed that it was his determination not to 'acquiesce in his [Geddes] high handed treatment of senior flag officers' coupled with the issues around convoys. Writing on Christmas Day to his friend Vice Admiral Reginald Bacon, he noted that 'I have had many disputes of late with the First Lord on this subject. The latest was the convoy enquiry.'[34]

Jellicoe was replaced by Admiral Rosslyn Erskine Wemyss, 'Rosy' to his friends, an emollient monocle-wearing scion of minor aristocracy, good friends with King George V, and well connected in society. He would also do Geddes' bidding rather more willingly than his predecessor.* It was Wemyss who would lead the navy into 1918.

---

* Writing to Rear Admiral de Chair on 29 December, Jellicoe stated that 'I fear Wemyss will not stick up to him. I have often told Wemyss that he must realise that he is a colleague and not the First Lord's servant' (de Chair, *The Sea is Strong*, p 236).

12

Last Knockings, 1918

At the beginning of 1918, the collapse of the Russian Front due to the Bolshevik takeover of the Russian state, the subsequent civil war, and the Treaty of Brest-Litovsk (signed 3 March 1918) meant that Germany suddenly had a large number of men and machines which could be deployed to the Western Front or, as some believed, to form an invasion force against Britain.

This process had actually started even before the Russo-German Armistice had been signed. On 14 December 1917, the British War Cabinet heard from Major General Sir George Macdonogh, Director of Military Intelligence, that the Military Attaché in Petrograd, General Alfred Knox, had 'reported that the Germans were moving the greater part of their heavy artillery from the Eastern Front to the West'.[1]

So yet more Allied soldiers were required for the trenches of France and Belgium. But politicians, especially Lloyd George, were reluctant to supply them (in part, perhaps, because he thought that the army would use them wastefully in ill-conceived assaults): a further 175,000 trained soldiers were kept back in Britain, when they had been requested for the Western Front in Spring 1918,* 'as a precaution against attempted invasion and internal unrest'.[2] In total, in January 1918 there were 1.5 million soldiers in Britain, included those wounded or in training.[3]†

Invasion fears were thus clearly still current.‡ But what about 'internal unrest'. Many people chafed against conscription, DORA regulations, and specifically in the area of industrial relations. The British workers of the First World War were and are often portrayed as patriotic and stoic, but this was far from the case. Between 1915 and 1918, 16,921,000 days' work were lost to industrial action (see Appendix 14), with 1918 the worst year.

---

* This led to the so-called 'Maurice debate' in the House of Commons where it was suggested that Lloyd George had deliberately denied men requested by Haig, after Major General Sir Frederick Maurice had written to the press challenging the veracity of Lloyd George's statement to the House regarding the numbers of men sent to the Western Front.
† It should also be noted that there were competing demands for manpower. In December 1917, a Cabinet committee on manpower concluded that labour priority for food production, shipbuilding, forestry, the navy, and the air force restricted the supply of so-called Category A men to the army to 100,000 rather than the 615,000 sought by the War Office (Strachan, *The British Home Front*, p 217).
‡ Despite the views expressed by the Admiralty at the 16 March 1917 meeting discussed in the previous chapter.

Royal Naval officers devised their own methods to deal with strikes or stoppages. Rear Admiral Dudley de Chair commanded the 10th Cruiser Squadron, which in December 1914 was converting to use armed merchant ships as cruisers. The work was being carried out at Liverpool and he was anxious that it should be completed, and he could get back on blockade patrol. However, not everyone in Liverpool shared de Chair's sense of urgency to get the merchant ships converted and on duty. Trouble was experienced with the trade union which ordered a strike because 'a man who was using his acetylene blow lamp on one of the gun mountings did not have the authorised number of men sitting down watching him work'. The Admiral was incensed. 'I was full of fury that . . . these pro-enemy loafers who stayed on shore should batten on the seamen who were protecting their homes.' De Chair sent for the head of the union; in fact he sent an armed guard to fetch him. When the hapless official arrived de Chair told him that 'if the men working on board the ships of the 10th Cruiser Squadron were not at work within the hour he would be put in prison'.[4] This had the desired effect.

There were multiple causes of strikes, not least 'dilution' – the replacement of skilled workers by those less trained or by women – and inflation reducing real incomes. But there were also significant elements of Bolshevik, Socialist and Syndicalist revolutionary philosophy in the actions taken by firebrand trades unionists. The government had powers under the Defence of the Realm Act to deal with labour unrest, and was initially keen to negotiate and prevent delays to the production of products vital to the war effort. But it was also willing to deploy the big stick. The Munitions of War Act, passed in 1915, gave the newly-created Ministry of Munitions power to declare factories 'controlled establishments' and restrict the freedom of workers to leave, through a system of certificates and of tribunals. And the Ministry was given the authority to regulate wages in the industry in 1916. Strikes in war industries were made illegal and labour disputes went to compulsory tribunals. But in reality, strikes continued in the UK throughout the war.

This was particularly true on 'Red Clydeside' where repeated strikes by engineering workers in munitions factories and shipyards led the government to internally deport or imprison the leaders. At the Vickers gun factory in Cumbria in March 1917, engineers protested against changes to their wages that they considered would leave them out of pocket. By April, the strike had not been resolved and government was ready to arrest the shop stewards. Though the strike was eventually settled, its consequences were serious for the war effort; it had caused a three-week delay in guns being sent out from Barrow, holding up the delivery of fifteen howitzers and some forty-two other pieces of artillery.

Other strikes were for seemingly trivial reasons. At a factory in Newcastle, two female workers were dismissed for wearing trousers outside the factory gates, prompting the seventeen other women working at the firm to go on strike and subsequently be dismissed. And workers at Roway Iron and Steel Works in West Bromwich went on strike in protest against a tax levied on ginger beer, which they considered essential to their work.

In January 1918, a new comb-out to bring more men into conscription led to strikes in Clydeside and the Welsh Valleys. The Clyde Workers Committee called for the declaration of an immediate armistice, while on 30 August 1918, 10,000 of the 19,000 London police failed to report for duty, calling for a rise in pay and recognition of their union. Lloyd George stated that Britain 'was nearer Bolshevism that day than any other day since'.

Uncertain of workers' loyalty, various government bodies outside of the Secret Service set up their own intelligence operation, targeting organised labour. These included the Board of Trade, the Admiralty Shipyard Labour Department, the Army Contracts Department and GHQ Home Forces. The government wanted to ensure it could protect against both invasion and internal revolt, such as had crippled Russia and was a growing threat in both Germany and France. And so the soldiers were retained at home, not to deal with Germans 'but with domestic dissent, labour unrest, or renewed Irish insurrection'.[5]

Great Yarmouth, January 1918

The night of Monday 14 January 1918 was one of gale-force winds and torrential rain on Britain's East Anglian coast. Wisely, most of the inhabitants of Great Yarmouth were tucked up in bed, trying to keep warm. However, their rest was rudely interrupted when at 2255 a star shell suddenly burst above the town. It was followed by a hail of fifty shells from four German destroyers which appeared from the murk. The bombardment lasted only five minutes and then stopped as suddenly as it had started, leaving only the keening of the wind.

Groggily, the inhabitants stepped out of their houses to see what had happened; and then retired once more, for the full impact could not be assessed until daylight. A number of houses had suffered damage to their roofs and many windows had been blown in. In a small, terraced house in St Peter's Road, two civilians, 53-year-old Mary Ann Sparks and her husband Arthur, were in bed when a shell hit the roof of their house and bricks and rafters crashed down on them. Mary was killed outright and Arthur died later in hospital. Two sailors on a ship from Hull, which was in the harbour, were also killed. They had only arrived that morning.

The monitor HMS *Roberts* (1915) with her 14in gun turret prominent Although heavily armed, she was a terrible sea boat, unable to achieve even 6 knots. (US National Archives at College Park NARA-45513189)

Many people had lucky escapes as roofs and ceilings fell on them. One large house on the seafront was hit by two shells, one through the roof and another on the first floor. Three or four shells fell on Gorleston, one of these failing to detonate despite striking the corner of a dwelling, lifting the roof off another, passing through a brick wall and then through another property. The Edward Worlledge school recorded the next day that many boys were late because they were searching for shell fragments. Sixteen rounds had fallen within a 400-yard radius of the school.

Great Yarmouth was a port for naval forces and a guard ship had been stationed there immediately after the last raid from the sea, specifically against such an eventuality as had now occurred. This was HMS *Roberts* (1915),* named for the recently deceased Field Marshal Earl Roberts, the staunch supporter of the National Service League. She was a monitor, armed with two massive 14in guns and two 12pdrs, with two 5in added in 1917. On the one occasion that she had fired her big guns in practice, windows in Gorleston had shattered from the blast. But her guns were silent on the night

---

* In November 1914, Charles M Schwab of the US company Bethlehem Steel offered First Lord of the Admiralty Winston Churchill, the use of four 14in/45cal BL MK II twin gun turrets, originally destined for the Greek battleship *Salamis*. These turrets could not be delivered to the German builders of *Salamis*, due to the British naval blockade. The Royal Navy immediately created a four-ship class of monitors to utilise them. The associated 6in guns were used for coastal defence at Scapa Flow and on Defensively Armed Merchant Ships. It was not an entirely altruistic gesture by Schwab, as his company had just been given an order for twenty 'H'-class submarines for the RN.

of the attack.* The local RNAS station could not get aircraft into the air because of the weather, and none of the coastal submarines based on the port were sallied as the assailants were thought to be too far away.

It was not until 90 minutes after the first shells had fallen on the town that the Harwich Force was called out by the Admiralty. By then, the Germans had long retired and although Tyrwhitt's ships manfully battled into the gale, they saw nothing and returned to Harwich at noon on the 15th.

There was confusion as to the numbers and types of the attackers. The first press announcement on 15 January blamed a single submarine; 'an official report states that Yarmouth was bombarded from the sea on Monday. It is believed that the bombardment was carried out by a submarine. Fire was opened at 2255 and lasted five minutes. Twenty shells fell in the town.'[6] A later report stated the raid was by three destroyers.

The Germans claimed great success; according to the *Sydney Morning Herald*, 'a German official report states: Light forces raided the southern part of the North Sea on the night of 14 January. They advanced northward of the Thames' mouth, and bombarded port establishments, firing over 300 shots. The British Admiralty's comment on the German story points out that the bombardment of Yarmouth lasted five minutes, and only fifty shells were fired. No other port was bombarded.'[7]

But whatever the truth, the raid caused outrage in the House of Commons on 23 January. It was the third time that Great Yarmouth had come under attack from the sea (the town had also been bombed twice from the air). Responding to questions from both Sir Robert Houston, Liverpool West Toxteth (Conservative), and George Lambert, South Moulton (Liberal), Dr Macnamara (Parliamentary Secretary for the Admiralty) stated: 'A report received from one of our patrol vessels off Yarmouth indicates that the vessels which attacked that town were torpedo boat destroyers. The number of vessels is unknown.' Houston challenged this response. 'Is not the right hon gentleman aware that it is reported that the enemy destroyers numbered four; and, seeing the repeated attacks on the east coast and north-east coast by enemy raiders, who invariably escape, will he say, who is in command of the east and north-east coast, and who is responsible'? This drove Macnamara to mount his high horse. 'I am not aware of the statement that the enemy destroyers numbered four. I have not seen that statement. I have given the statement from the responsible officer, of whom I inquired. With regard to the latter part of the hon member's question, if the suggestion that I should give the name of the responsible

---

* Her captain, Commander Frederick Vere Williamson, was relieved six days after the raid and did not serve at sea again for the rest of the war.

officer implies a dereliction of duty on his part, I think that is particularly ungracious and ungrateful of the hon member.'[8] But public anger was clear.

The Western Front

The Germans launched a major offensive on the Western Front, starting with Operation 'Michael' on 21 March 1918. Bolstered by fifty-two divisions released from the Eastern Front, they overran the Allied forces and succeeded in making a deep advance and inflicting heavy losses. However, the second phase, Operation 'Mars', at Arras on 28 March, was held. In the midst of this crisis, the Allies decided to appoint French General Ferdinand Foch as co-ordinator, and soon after as Generalissimo, of Allied armies. Germany then launched Operation 'George' on 9 April; it was during this crisis that Field Marshal Douglas Haig issued on 11 April his famous order of the day; 'there is no other course open to us but to fight it out. Every position must be held to the last man: there must be no retirement. With our backs to the wall and believing in the justice of our cause each one of us must fight on to the end. The safety of our homes and the freedom of mankind alike depend upon the conduct of each one of us at this critical moment.'

Britain was finally denuded of troops as reinforcements were rushed to repel the German attacks. It was necessary to take men from the east coast defences and send them to France and the Volunteers were asked to find 15,000 men to replace them until the Americans arrived in force. Ernest Cooper was one of those who responded to the call and by 29 June he was in command of a special service company of eighty-four men at Bawdsey Manor in Felixstowe. In France the German breakthrough was defeated, and Germans were pushed back and retreating. Cooper was back in Southwold by late August and in his diary entry for the 30th remarked that he found the town full of visitors again.[9]

An Island Problem

Britain has many, many islands, especially in the far north and, as was seen in Chapter 4, there had been concern before the war that these could be used by an invading force. Protecting all these islands was impossible with the forces available.

Lerwick

Rear Admiral Clement Greatorex, SNO Shetland Islands, became concerned as to his ability to defend his command. On 13 January 1918 he wrote to his superior, Admiral F W Brock, asking him to bring to Their Lordships attention that he had just one old destroyer (which was under repair), with which to defend the whole of Lerwick and Shetland. Apart from the destroyer, he had only five whalers, eight minesweeping trawlers, five hydrophone trawlers and seven drifters with a few 3pdr and 6pdr guns and two static 4.7in guns on the Nabb, which had a very limited arc of fire.

With this small force, he stated that he had to defend the seaplane and kite balloon stations now under construction, the hydrophone station, W/T, coal depot, salvage plant, Lerwick itself and the fishing fleet. With the nearest support at Scapa, he felt vulnerable. '[There is] ample time for an enemy force of no more than two destroyers, by a suitable choice of time during the dark period of the year, to effect a raid with impunity'– and destroy the lot. 'I request,' he added portentously, 'that I be informed when other defences will be sent.'[10]

Brock was unsympathetic.

> The question of providing further protection at Lerwick depends on the extent the base will be used in the future, both from a strategic point of view and as a port of call. The arguments put forward by the Senior Naval Officer, Shetlands, can be advanced to some extent as regards the majority of towns on the east coast of Great Britain and, under present conditions, I do not consider Lerwick is sufficiently important to be granted preferential treatment.[11]

Beatty concurred. On 23 January he wrote 'Lerwick . . . is defended by the Grand Fleet . . . You should take every step to hasten the placing two 6in guns on Bressay, which should not be beyond the capabilities of local resources'.[12] There simply were not enough ships to go round.

One of the two 6in guns installed by Rear Admiral Greatorex on Bressay in 1918. (Shetland Museum and Archives)

The Back of Beyond: St Kilda, May 1918

Later in the year, the vulnerability felt by Greatorex was made real elsewhere.

There can hardly be a more isolated or inhospitable part of the British Isles than Hirta, then the only inhabited island[6] of the St Kilda archipelago, some 40 miles west of North Uist in the Outer Hebrides. Here, around eighty men, women and children, battered and bullied by storms, snow, rain, wind and very occasional sun, scratched out an existence on the granite rocks from a few cattle and sheep and the meat and eggs of seabirds. There was no regular contact with the mainland and although a trickle of tourist started to arrive towards the end of the nineteenth century, the islanders were basically left to their subsistence living.

War changed that, for the Royal Navy decided to install a wireless telegraph station on Hirta, part of a chain of such equipment to carry the words of the Admiralty to its minions, and two radio masts were erected, followed by ten more-or-less willing sailors to maintain and operate them. They had only revolvers and rifles for armament and no vessel was retained on the station. When the armed merchant cruiser HMS *Calyx* was ordered to St Kilda to inquire how things were with the wireless station, her captain, Commander Thomas Wardle, was greeted with the worrying statement that 'a terrible thing has happened'. Fearing the worst, he enquired of the islander what disaster had befallen them. 'The minister's cow has had a dead calf', was the grief-stricken reply.[15] And so things remained. War passed Hirta by, and Hirta did its best to ignore the war. Until May 1918.

On Wednesday the 15th, *Kapitänleutnant* Walter Remy had taken *U-90* around Scotland to go on patrol in the Atlantic. The area of St Kilda and its environs was not unknown to him, for he had previously stopped at the equally remote island of North Rona to 'requisition' provisions such as fresh mutton. At 0900 U-boat time, he decided to see if the St Kildan islands were being used for military purposes. He sailed into the channel between St Kilda and Boreray, which allowed him to note that the latter seemed uninhabited whilst he could see at least two men on the former, and the wireless masts. Sticking to periscope depth, Remy headed into Village Bay and then surfaced at 1055, ordering the gun to be manned. Showing a humanity lacking in some of his colleagues, Remy issued a warning for people to leave the area of the buildings, before opening fire from his 10.5cm (4.1in) gun at 1138 his time. The range was initially 3,000m, which, in the absence of any return fire, Remy reduced to 1,700m. In total, *U-90* discharged seventy-four shells and hit the manse, church, and jetty storehouse. But he failed to topple the latticework masts. By now an hour had passed and he could see some armed

---

* Hirta is now uninhabited, the last residents leaving in 1930.

Pictured in 2007, the 4in QF gun mounted on Hirta in 1918, looking towards Dùn. (Creative Commons)

sailors on the shore. Discretion being the better part of valour, Remy resolved not to land and check on the damage he had caused, but instead dived his boat to resume his voyage. No person was injured, one lamb was killed by shell fragments and all the cattle stampeded to the other side of the island.

Stable doors now swung firmly shut. Two armed trawlers were stationed in Village Bay for the remainder of the war and a 4in QF gun was mounted on a promontory above the bay. But it was not complete until October and was never fired in anger.

The Last Act

On 12 April 1918, Admiral Beatty moved the Grand Fleet to Rosyth, leaving only the 2nd Cruiser Squadron and some destroyers behind. His reasoning was that it placed the fleet closer to the German bases. It also fitted with his desire to take a more offensive stance if he could.

This new disposition was soon to be tested. On 23 April 1918, the High Seas Fleet made its final sortie into the North Sea in an attempt to attack the Scandinavian convoys. Faulty intelligence and engine failure in SMS *Moltke* caused the aborting of the foray and, although the Grand Fleet was sent out, no battle or contact ensued. There were no further High Seas Fleet sailings and St Kilda was the last attack from the sea on the British coast of the war.

After the failure of the final German effort on the Western Front, and with revolution and demoralisation rife at home, in large part fuelled by hunger caused by the Royal Navy's blockade, Germany began to seek an armistice. On 5 October, a new government under Prince Max of Baden asked President Woodrow Wilson of the USA to mediate between all parties. One of Wilson's preconditions for so doing was that Germany should end its submarine war. Riding over the objections of Admiral Scheer, now Chief of the Imperial Navy Staff, the German Government made this concession on 20 October. The following day all U-boats at sea were recalled home. The seas became largely free of submarine predators for the first time in over four years.

An enraged Scheer ordered Admiral Hipper, commanding the German High Seas Fleet, to prepare for an attack on Britain and its naval forces, utilising the main battle fleet, reinforced by the newly-available U-boats released from Flanders. According to orders cut on 24 October this was to include an attack against the Flanders coast by the 2nd Torpedo Boat Flotilla, supported by three light cruisers, and against the Thames estuary by the 2nd Scouting Group of light cruisers, accompanied the 2nd Torpedo Boat Half-Flotilla. The raid on the Thames and the Flanders coast were scheduled for dawn on 31 October. It was expected that these raids would draw out the British Grand Fleet from Scapa and the encounter between that force and the High Seas Fleet was planned for the afternoon and evening of the same day. This battle was therefore one that would be fought only for the honour and pride of the *Kaiserliche Marine* when the war was effectively over. U-boat concentrations and wireless traffic all alerted the Admiralty to the possibility of major action and the Grand Fleet and the Harwich Force were put on alert.

Fortunately, Scheer's plan did not come to pass. Revolution was in the air within the German fleet. Years of inactivity and poor officer-men relationships had allowed the disease of Bolshevism to infect the crews. The evening of 29 October was marked by unrest and serious acts of indiscipline aboard the German ships, with the men convinced their commanders were intent on sacrificing them in a deliberate attempt to sabotage the Armistice negotiations. Open revolt broke out in many of the battleships and the men refused to follow orders.

Hipper saw no alternative to cancelling the operation, which he did on 30 October and ordered the fleet dispersed in the hope of quelling the insurrection. It was a narrow escape for all concerned from what would have been a needless and bloody fight, and a relief for those who lived by the Thames estuary and the Flanders coast who would have been at risk from a bombardment.

13

The Invasion of the Air

There had never been a war in the air. But fiction writers such as H G Wells (see Chapter 2) speculated what it might be like. Bombardment from above and invasion from the skies were common themes. Perhaps because of this, the Hague Conference of 1899 banned combatants from delivering projectiles or explosives from balloons or other aerial vessels ('The Contracting Powers agree to prohibit, for a term of five years, the launching of projectiles and explosives from balloons, or by other new methods of a similar nature'). And a further Hague meeting in 1907 reinforced this prohibition.

However, in 1908, the British government felt sufficiently concerned to require a subcommittee of the CID to examine the threat posed by airships and aeroplanes. It reported that airships might transport small raiding parties to attack special objectives and also bomb ships and dockyards. Additionally, the report recommended building a British airship as a naval scout, HM Airship no 1, which became known as *Mayfly* (and which never flew).

German airship development was significantly more advanced than its British counterpart, largely due to the pioneering work of Graf Ferdinand von Zeppelin. In 1912, the German navy ordered its first airship, L-1, 518ft long and powered by three 170hp engines which could drive it at 47mph. This craft caused a wave of Zeppelin panic in Britain during the winter of 1912–13, when it was reported that a German airship had flown over Sheerness on 13 October; this was L-1 on an endurance trial.

It is difficult today to imagine the perturbation caused by the realisation that an aerial machine could fly over Britain. At no time in world history had there been an airborne military threat. Now suddenly everyone felt vulnerable, not just from the danger of land invasion but by attack from the heavens too.

In 1912 the Committee of Imperial Defence recommended that military aviation be formalised. This led to the founding of the Royal Flying Corps (RFC) with a naval and a military wing. That same year, it was decided that the War Office was responsible for defending Britain against air attack; but they failed to produce any plans. The Admiralty was rather more proactive and commenced the construction of a chain of coastal aerodromes for heavier-than-air craft working with ships at sea. This same CID committee also foresaw that aircraft would be unable to shoot down Zeppelins and found that the surest way of attacking them would be by a superior force of armed airships.

In 1913, the agreement regarding air defence was amended; now the naval wing of the combined air service would defend naval targets close to their aerodromes, while the War Office protected Britain. But when in June 1914, the CID asked the War Office for its plans for defence, it was revealed that they had none. In any case, all their available squadrons were assigned to the BEF, to operate in France. Finally, in July 1914, the naval wing became the Royal Naval Air Service (RNAS), reporting to the Admiralty directly. When war came, the RNAS boasted ninety-three aircraft, six airships and two balloons.

On 8 August, the Admiralty ordered air coastal patrols from the Moray Firth to Dungeness, seeking an invasion force, and RNAS aircraft flew above the transport ships as the BEF sailed for France. Then it transpired that the War Office had no plans to defend London from air attack, as they didn't believe it could happen. Churchill hurriedly arranged for three naval anti-aircraft guns to be installed to protect Whitehall and the government buildings there. Persistent rumours circulated of a Zeppelin base at Grasmere, in the Lake District; these were only disproved when a Blériot monoplane was sent to fly over the area, piloted by Bentfield Charles Hucks, an aviation pioneer, the first Briton to perform the loop and now a captain in the RFC.

Then on 3 September, Secretary of State for War Lord Kitchener had asked Churchill if the navy, via the RNAS, could take over the responsibility for Britain's aerial defence, as the RFC was fully committed in France. Churchill consented. The navy was now responsible for sea _and_ air defence against invasion.

The Bombing of Britain

The first German bombs to fall on British soil were dropped on Dover on Christmas Eve 1914. It was a clear, cold, bright day when at 1045 a Friedrichshafen FF 29 German floatplane flew over the town. Pilot Lieutenant von Prondzynski leaned over the side of his plane and saw Dover Castle and the naval harbour below him. He lifted his bomb in both hands, controlling the plane with his knees and heaved the weapon over the side of the plane. It missed any target of military significance; but the explosion broke some windows in St James' rectory, made a crater 10ft across in the garden of auctioneer Thomas Terson, knocked the gardener, James Banks, out of a tree he was pruning, and caused £40 worth of damage.

An RNAS Wright seaplane took off from its East Promenade base but was a poor climber and never got remotely near to the intruder. Perversely,

A Friedrichshafen FF 29 floatplane, such as dropped the first bombs on British soil in December 1914. The type was unarmed and when carried, bombs were often stored in the observer's seat. (Author's collection)

the Admiralty had sent two additional aircraft, Bristol TB8s, from Eastchurch to shore up Dover's defences; but they were still *en route*.

This was the second air raid to have targeted Dover; three days beforehand, on 21 December, another Friedrichshafen had dropped two bombs harmlessly into the sea near Admiralty Pier. It was the first of a total of 370 bombs which fell on the town during the war, adding to the discomforts and terrors suffered by its citizens.

But it wasn't pinprick raids by flimsy aircraft that worried the British population. It was the threat of attack by Germany's massive Zeppelins. They comprised a fabric-covered rigid metal framework made up of transverse rings and longitudinal girders, containing a number of individual gasbags. Gondolas slung below the body held engines and crewmen. Various defensive machine guns were carried along with a payload of bombs. Zeppelins could turn off their engines, and drift in silence to carry out surprise attacks, all the more worrying when executed in darkness with the first sign of the intruders being the explosion of their bombs.

Many expected the airships to be deployed immediately. But in fact, the Germans considered that they did not have enough to both act as reconnaissance scouts and undertake bombing missions. The latter role would have to wait while numbers built up. It was not until 9 January 1915 that permission was given for attacks on Britain, from which the capital was to be excluded by express order of the Kaiser. Raids would be 'expressly restricted to military shipyards, arsenals, and in general military establishments and that London itself was not to be bombed'.[1] Maybe Wilhelm was worried about hitting his relatives? In fact, targeting military installations only was a promise that couldn't be kept. Difficulty in navigation, the susceptibility of airships to the winds, against which they could often make no headway, and the primitive means of bomb aiming, all meant that accuracy was a chimera. To use a term from the next global war, the best that could be hoped for was area, rather than precision, bombing.

At the War Council meeting of 1 January 1915, Churchill presented a paper on the airship menace. He noted that 'information from a trustworthy source has been received that the Germans intend to make an attack on London by airships on a great scale at an early opportunity'. Worryingly, he went on to add (perhaps with a view to avoiding later blame) that 'I must make it quite plain that the Air Department of the Admiralty are quite powerless to prevent an attack if it is launched with good fortune and in favourable weather conditions'.[2] The meeting also received a submission, via Churchill, from Captain Murray Sueter of the Air Department which listed the defences available to London (minimal), searchlights (four) and the meetings with police and fire brigades as to the effect of bombing on buildings and personnel.

Sueter pointed out that the Zeppelins would probably come at night and would be assisted by an easterly wind. He noted that the German navy possibly had twenty airships available for the mission and that, as it was impossible to monitor the whole of the coast for their landfall, it was better to 'arrange for dealings with them on arrival near London'.[3] Nonetheless, the Admiralty was organising special lookout stations at Southend, Deal and Folkstone and new aeroplane and seaplane stations were in the process of being established at Ramsgate, Maidstone, Erith, Chingford and Chelmsford. It might be noted that all of these dispositions were concerned with the protection of London – no account seems to have been taken of any other town or city; then as now, Britain was London-centric.

Churchill and Sueter's warnings were echoed by Fisher at the next War Council meeting on 7 January. Fisher added that an attack would soon be made on an east-coast town, information presumably obtained by Room 40. This forecast does not seem to have produced any effect.

On 10 January, the London Hospital received an alert from the War Office to expect air raid casualties. Some people sent their children away to the country. But, as Fisher had predicted, it was not in London but on the east coast that the first blow fell.

A Night to Remember

A trio of Zeppelins had left for Britain on 13 January but had been forced by the weather to abort their mission. They tried again six days later.

On 19 January 1915 three Zeppelins, L-3, L-4 and L-6, took off from their bases in Germany, each with sixteen crew on board, together with eight 110Ib high explosive and eleven 25Ib incendiary bombs. The first two departed from Fuhlsbuttel (Hamburg) and L-6 from Nordholtz (near Cuxhaven).

All of the airships were new M-class Zeppelins, fitted with Maybach engines giving them a top speed of 50mph. L-3 was under the command of *Kapitänleutnant* Hans Fritz; L-4 was commanded by *Kapitänleutnant* Count von Platen-Hallermund; and L-6, *Oberleutnant* Baron von Buttlar, with *Korvettenkapitän* Peter Strasser, who was the head of the Imperial German Navy's Zeppelin Fleet, as a passenger.

Their intention was to navigate for the Humber and bomb positions on the north-east coast. But L-6 soon developed engine problems and began to ice up badly; she turned around and limped back to her base. The other two continued on and made landfall at 1940 – in East Anglia, some 70 miles south of their target, their navigation possibly impeded perhaps by the squally and persistent rain and fog. It is not clear that they knew where they were, but some lights in the distance attracted L-3 and at 2030 she dropped a parachute flare and then began to unload her bombs on Great Yarmouth.

The first bomb,* an incendiary, landed in a waterlogged field at Little Ormesby, causing no damage. The next bomb, another incendiary, fell to the rear of a house on Albermarle Road, resulting in a crater two feet wide but with no casualties. The first high explosive bomb to land hit the pavement at the back of 78 Crown Road and failed to explode. But the fourth bomb fell on St Peter's Plain and killed 72-year-old spinster Martha Mary Taylor and 53-year-old shoemaker Samuel Alfred Smith, injuring two others. The blast also blew out the front of St Peter's Villa and seriously damaged Pestell's Buildings. The fifth bomb failed to explode and was recovered from a stable owned by butcher William Mays in Garden Lane, near South Quay. Bomb number six landed outside the First and Last Tavern on Southgates Road; and the third incendiary to be dropped fell between two vessels in Beeching's South Dock, causing slight harm. None of these produced any

---

* The ordering of the bombs is based on the forensic work of R J Wyatt, and noted in his book *Death from the Skies*.

further casualties. An eighth bomb bounced off the Stone Quay at Trinity Wharf, narrowly missing a sentry and a crane turntable, before falling into the river. Bomb nine fell behind the Fish Wharf, causing extensive damage to the rear as well as destroying the Fish Wharf Restaurant Rooms and fracturing a water main, with one person hurt by flying glass. The last two

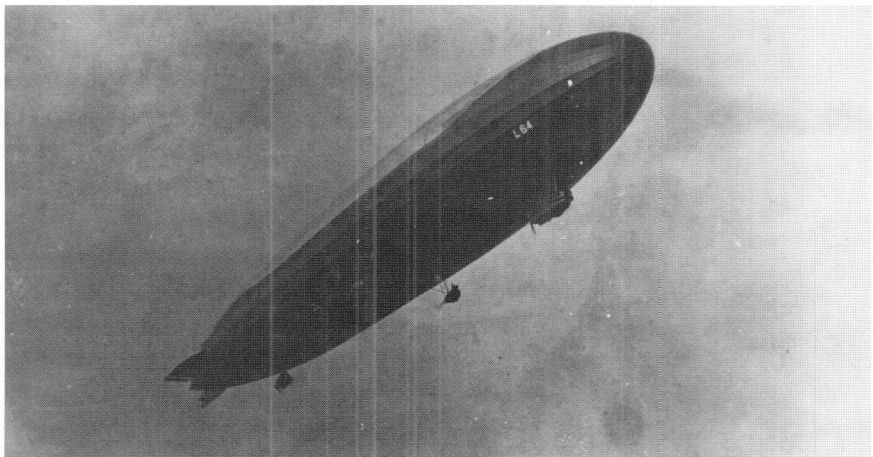

A Zeppelin in flight. This is L-64, built in 1918 with its first flight on 11 March and commissioned two days later. The ship was quickly in service and was involved in a raid on the North of England on the evening of the 12 April. At the end of the war she was taken over by Britain. (US Naval History and Heritage Command NH 60773)

After the bombing; St Peter's Plain in Great Yarmouth, where Martha Taylor died. (Author's collection)

St Peter's Villa, Great Yarmouth, showing the damage caused by a bomb.
The owner, Mr Ellis, was injured in the blast. (Author's collection)

bombs dropped by L-3 hit the steam drifter *Piscatorial* and also the road running along the back of the old racecourse grandstand on South Denes; the only fatality was a large black dog. Martha Taylor and Samuel Smith thus earned the unenviable distinction of becoming the first people in Britain to be killed by enemy bombing.

L-4 was well and truly lost. Von Platen-Hallermund opened his account by dropping a flare and two incendiary bombs on Sheringham, which caused damage but no casualties. L-4 then disappeared out to sea before making landfall again to release another incendiary in a field between Brancaster Staithe and Hunstanton. A fourth incendiary was dropped near to Brancaster church, and landed close to the Red Cross hospital. The fifth bomb was aimed at the wireless station at Hunstanton, although there is some uncertainty about this. Two more fell at Heacham, one of which exploded in Lord's Lane where a number of people were fortunate to escape injury. The seventh bomb failed to explode and was later discovered in a field.

Bomb number nine landed at Snettisham, near the church, blowing out twenty-two of the windows. L-4 then flew between Wolferton and Sandringham* before flying over Dersingham. Navigating by means of following the railway line, L-4 reached the Gaywood District in King's Lynn, dropping a bomb which fell in a field to the rear of Tennyson Avenue. Von

---

* Bringing about the propaganda that the Royal Family had been a target of the raid.

Platen-Hallermund apparently believed he was over Scarborough at this point. The next landed on allotments, and another brought about King's Lynn's first fatalities when it fell on houses on Bentinck Street, killing Percy Goate, aged 14, and Alice Maud Gazely, aged 26. Alice was a war widow, her husband already dead on the Western Front. Percy had been in bed when the bomb landed on his pillow and the house then collapsed around him. Both were later reported to have died from shock. L-4 dropped another bomb on some terraced houses, where it made a large hole and wrecked a blacksmith's premises but caused no deaths. The fifth bomb to descend on King's Lynn fell in a garden by the docks and failed to explode, and the sixth destroyed an engine house and boilers at Alexandra Dock.

L-4's last two bombs landed around Cresswell Street, where the family at Number 63 had a lucky escape when an incendiary hit the house, setting off a fire which was extinguished by neighbours. This final bomb was placed in water by the police to await disposal. In total the raid on King's Lynn led to two fatalities with thirteen people injured. L-4 now headed east and flew past Norwich, which was shrouded in fog and had its lights out, and out to sea to the north of Great Yarmouth.

There was no military response from the ground. Information about the raid only reached the RNAS base at Great Yarmouth after L-3 had turned for home, despite the RNAS headquarters at Lowestoft learning of the airships' landfall when it occurred. The station commander held his three aircraft back to await L-4, but received no further news of her and in the pitch black with his low performance machines, decided that they would have scant chance of stumbling upon the Zeppelin if they were even able to get airborne. Two RFC Vickers Gunbus aircraft from Joyce Green, Kent, took off to patrol south of London, believing the Zeppelins were heading for the city (London-centricity again). As it happened, both of these craft suffered engine problems and made forced landings.

In total, four people had been killed and sixteen injured. Some £7,740 worth of damage was reported to have been sustained. Death and destruction in France and Belgium were now an accepted fact. But this was the first time that ordinary civilians had been killed from the air. Now from both sea and land, Germany had meted out death to the ordinary British citizen, peaceably going about their lives. If they could do that, many speculated, they could invade as well. *The War Illustrated* of 30 January headlined 'the coming of the Aerial Baby Killers', borrowing from Hipper's soubriquet of the previous year. And the official German announcement concerning the raid stated that 'naval airships attacked some fortified places on the English east coast; the weather was foggy and rainy; several bombs were successfully dropped; the airships were shot at, but returned unhurt'.[4]

The raid was followed by the inevitable accusations of the involvement of spies. One or more cars with bright headlights leading the airships on was reported, as was a beam of light from the ground. Holcombe Ingleby, owner of Sedgeford Hall and Conservative MP for King's Lynn, took them very seriously and challenged the views expressed by the Home Office that his suspicions were groundless. One example of his questioning came on 8 February when he asked the Under Secretary for War, Harold Tennant, 'if he can state how many Zeppelins raided the east coast on 19th January; whether the Zeppelins were accompanied by motor cars; if so, whether he can give the number of such cars; and whether any of them have been identified or any of their occupants arrested?'[5] His question was brushed off. A frustrated Ingleby collected the 'evidence' and even published a pamphlet, *The Zeppelin Raid in West Norfolk*, price three pence, putting forward his case. He wrote to *The Times* as well, in the best traditions of English crankery, telling the world that he was right and the authorities wrong.

Much was made of the fact that L-4 passed near Sandringham House, although the king was in London at the time. Two 3in high-angle AA guns were sited at Sandringham as a result. Additionally, Yarmouth was allocated two old 18pdrs, in response to a plea to Prime Minister Asquith from the mayor. But Great Yarmouth would suffer again when L-11 dropped thirteen bombs on the town on 3 April 1916, without causing much damage.

From the air and from the sea, Britain seemed to be vulnerable. But every cloud has a silver lining. In Newtownards, County Down, the Palace Cinema, Great Frances Street, advertised that, although it was unlikely that Zeppelins would travel so far, citizens should seek safety in the evenings by leaving their homes ('no dwelling is bomb proof') and going instead to the Palace 'the only bomb proof building in town' where they could be entertained by three 'sterling programmes, including the "Keystone Comics"'. This boast proved unfortunate, for the building burned to the ground on 2 November 1918.

THE DEFENCE OF LONDON

By spring 1915, London had still not been attacked. But May brought a change with it. On the nights of 10 and 17 May, Zeppelins bombed Southend and other Thames estuary locations. LZ-38 attacked Dover and Ramsgate on 16/17 May and then Southend* again on 26/27 May at about 2300. RNAS aircraft tried to intercept but could not outclimb the airship.

---

* The seaside town of Southend had the great disadvantage of being on the Zeppelins' direct route to London and became something of a dumping ground for German craft unloading surplus bombs before their return home. As a consequence it suffered some 1,236 air-raid warnings during the course of the war.

Finally, war reached the capital. On the last day of the month, a single Zeppelin loitered over the inner north-east suburbs of London for 45 minutes and dropped eighty-nine incendiary bombs and thirty grenades. Seven civilians were killed. It was the first of many assaults; protecting the capital now became an even greater priority.

Harwich Force resources were deployed to defend London. At this time, only the cruisers had anti-aircraft guns, the destroyers possessing solely Maxim machine guns on improvised mountings. The former were sent to patrol the coast from Lowestoft to Orford Ness and report to Tyrwhitt and the Admiralty of any Zeppelins sighted; given the opportunity, they were encouraged to attempt to engage them. But in fact, few Zeppelins were observed in this way and no successes against them recorded.

The navy, it will be recalled, was still responsible for the aerial defence of Britain. Or as Admiral Sir Percy Moreton Scott put it 'By some strange anomaly, the Lords Commissioners for "executing the office of High Admiral of the United Kingdom and of the territories thereto belonging and of the Colonies and other Dominions whatsoever" had become responsible for protecting London against air raids'.[6] Now this doughty old stager, a gunnery expert, opinionated, retired and 62 years old, was once again summoned to service by First Lord Arthur Balfour, who asked him,

> if I would take over the gunnery defence of London, as a temporary measure, since in due course the War Office would assume control of the work, which, as he pointed out, was really theirs and not the Admiralty's. Mr. Balfour suggested that the task would prove interesting, and reminded me that it was certainly important; but at the same time he warned me, with characteristic kindness, that the means of defence at that time were very inadequate.[7]

The resources Scott took over were minimal. The entire anti-aircraft defence of the city was vested in eight 3in high-angle guns, four 6pdrs, with bad gun sights, six pom-poms and some Maxims, which would not fire up as high as a Zeppelin, and were consequently only a danger to the population as the rounds descended to earth. Moreover, they had been issued with ammunition which was less than useful against Zeppelins; what was needed was

> a shell with a large bursting charge of a highly explosive nature was required so that it would damage a Zeppelin if it exploded near it; second, that all that went up in the air had to come down again, and that, in order to minimise the danger to the public from falling pieces,

an explosive should be used in the shell which would break it up into small fragments. The ammunition supplied was exactly the opposite to what we wanted. The shells had so small a bursting charge that they could do no harm to a Zeppelin, and they returned to earth almost as intact as when they were put into the guns.[8]

The old warrior set about rectifying the situation. He obtained explosive bullets (the Pomeroy bullet, see below), persuaded the authorities to train pilots in night flying and to illuminate their aerodromes, designed a new type of shell and arranged for it to be manufactured (in France!). Additionally, Scott devised a mobile platform by mounting a French '75' on a motor vehicle, created a new mounting to allow a 3in gun to be towed behind a lorry, begged and stole artillery from the navy, the War Office and the French, and by sheer force of will created an organisation to operate all these weapons effectively. By the end of the year, this organisation boasted ten 4.7in guns, seven 4in, thirty-five French 75mm, four 4in Greek guns, twenty 15pdrs, twelve 2.95in Russian guns, thirty-four 6pdrs, nineteen 3in and eleven 3pdr guns – 152 in total. It was a remarkable achievement. When on 16 February 1916 the War Office finally took the responsibility that many thought should have been theirs all the time, London had a credible air defence system, and Percy Scott had created it.

Admiral Sir Percy Scott, who took command of London's anti-aircraft defence in 1915. (Author's collection)

The navy played additional roles in the defence of London. One of the more curious of these operations was when, in December 1915 and January 1916, the Dover Patrol was ordered to send all its monitors to the Thames estuary to shoot at Zeppelins. The smaller vessels used their searchlights to illuminate the airborne intruders and the larger ships fired shrapnel from their big guns at maximum elevation, hoping that the falling fragments might puncture the dirigibles' skin. The tactic was not a success as when the anticipated attack came on 31 January, the attacking airships were too far to the north.

At the same time, the Harwich Force was ordered out to intercept them, taking with them two trawlers, *Kingfisher* and *Cantatrice*, both specifically equipped with seaplanes for anti-Zeppelin operations. However, the Force was unable to locate the approaching Zeppelin formation due to thick fog. *Kingfisher* and *Cantatrice* were two of four trawlers purchased by the Admiralty in May 1915; they were equipped for carrying a seaplane by fitting a platform aft. (The other ships were *Jericho* and *Sir John French*. The *Christopher* was added slightly later.) Based at Great Yarmouth, they carried either a Sopwith Schneider or a Sopwith Baby and generally launched in the evening, from around the Haaks Light Vessel. But although seaplanes were flown off on many calm nights in 1915 and 1916 no German airships were ever spotted.

SCOTLAND

The first bombs to fall on Scotland were delivered by the naval airships L-14 and L-22. On 2 April 1916, both reached St Abb's head by dead reckoning. L-14 proceeded up the Firth of Forth and struck at Leith and Edinburgh around midnight. L-22 first bombed Lamberton and Chirnside in the Borders before finding the Forth and then flew around Edinburgh dropping explosives at random.

Warning of the impending air raid was received at 1900 and the police in Leith and the City of Edinburgh instituted air raid precautions: the Electric Light Department lowered all lights, traffic was stopped and lights on vehicles were extinguished. The Central Fire Station and the Red Cross were notified and all policemen, regular and specials, were called up.

In total twenty-four bombs were dropped on the city of Edinburgh. Thirteen people died and another twenty-four were injured in the attack. One bomb fell on a bonded warehouse at Leith, lighting up the whole city. Several others fell along the shore at Leith, one hitting St Thomas's Parish Manse in Sheriff Brae and another falling on a railway siding at Bonnington, where a child was killed. A bomb hit the road by the Mound, Edinburgh, and another ploughed through the home of Dr John McLaren at 39 Lauriston Place. The bomb hit the roof of the building and went through four storeys of ceilings and floors without injuring anyone. Eight-year-old Hamish McClaren was in the house at the time. Years later, he recalled that:

> I don't know whether they were actually trying to bomb the castle and missed it, or whether they were jettisoning the bombs to get away. In the house there was my grandfather and my grandmother, their

three children, of which my father was one, and two maids. The damage was very extensive. The bomb exploded on the roof, blew the roof off, and then the nose of the bomb came down through the four floors of the house and ended up in the pantry.[9]

It was mounted and became a family heirloom.

Private Thomas Donoghue of the 3/4th Battalion Royal Scots was visiting his family at 27 Marshall Street in Newington on the that night. He received severe injuries to his abdomen from a bomb fragment and died eight days later from peritonitis and heart failure. Five men were killed in another house on the same street, and a baby girl born during the bombing was christened Catherine O'May Campbell Raida Smith; Raida was not a family name! Neither Zeppelin reached what was probably their primary target, the naval dockyard and ships at Rosyth.

The RNAS attempted to put up aircraft in response. Two Wright seaplanes at Dundee tried and failed to get airborne, a BE 2c took off from Rochford, and Flight Sub Lieutenant G A Cox took off from East Fortune in an Avro 504C but did not make contact with the intruders, crashed on landing and was injured.

Following the raid, the Chief Constable of Leith not unnaturally queried the large number of vessels lying in Leith Roads every night which

> are fully lighted and the glare in the sky on a dark night can be seen at a long distance. A better guide for a Zeppelin could not be got. On the night of the Raid the Zeppelin came to Leith across the line of the shipping and not till the bombs were falling on Leith were the lights on the ships extinguished. It seems so ridiculous to have the town of Leith in darkness while the sea in front is illuminated.[10]

The Admiralty agreed. A reply dated 10 April 1916 confirmed that the Admiralty 'orders that no lights of any description visible from outboard will be permitted in mercantile shipping anchored in the Leith and Granton roadsteads.'[11]

How to Kill a Zeppelin

At the beginning of the war, there was no clear view of how to bring down a Zeppelin. They could fly higher than most aircraft could reach, being able to climb up to as much as 20,000ft in a matter of minutes at a time when a good aeroplane could struggle up to 10,000 to 14,000ft inside an hour.* Thus

---

* A B.E. 2 aircraft took about 50 minutes to climb to 10,000ft.

airships were largely invulnerable to aircraft. They carried defensive machine guns below and atop, and although an airship represented a huge target, were difficult to seriously damage. Ordinary bullets might penetrate the gas envelope, but hydrogen leakage was very slow as the pressure differential between the gas in the bags and the air outside was minimal. Additionally, there was so much hydrogen and so little oxygen inside the hull that ignition of the gas was unlikely without outside agency.

As a consequence, various methods of downing Zeppelins were developed, of differing utility and, indeed, practicality. Gunfire from an aircraft was an obvious anti-airship ploy; the .303in Lewis gun, originally an infantry weapon, became the standard fit on fighter planes sent to attack the German gas bags. Unfortunately, while a 50- to 100-round burst of machine-gun fire would cause major structural failure in a contemporary aeroplane, it had little effect on an airship. Zeppelins were large enough to soak up enormous quantities of the standard .303in ball ammunition without serious damage.

Woolwich Arsenal developed an exploding bullet but it needed to be so large that it could only be fired from a single shot Martini-Henry carbine; trying to aim and fire this whilst flying a flimsy aircraft was hardly likely to succeed, or enthuse the unfortunate pilot.

Given these limitations, air-to-air bombing was advanced as a method of attack. Hales bombs (a sort of rifle-grenade where a rod was attached to a modified grenade, inserted into the barrel of a standard service rifle and launched using a blank cartridge) and incendiary bombs were both utilised. Then there was the Ranken dart. These were slender, drogue-stabilised 1pdr bombs with sharp steel noses and four pivoting vanes at the tail. When the dart hit the airship's skin, the head would punch through while the vanes caught on the envelope and fired a detonator. The darts were dropped from a 24-round box angled 45º to the rear of the aeroplane. The attacking pilot had ideally to be 300ft above the target and about 20 degrees off the fore and aft axis of the airship, and could drop the darts singly or in one lot. They were probably no less dangerous to those on the ground below than to the Zeppelins themselves.

Even more unlikely was the Fiery Grapnel. This comprised of a pair of four-fluked, anchor-shaped grappling hooks packed with an incendiary mixture and fixed to a length of cable. The fighter was supposed to 'fish' with it until it snagged on a Zeppelin. Then the grapnel would rip the airship open and set it alight. Of course all of the above inventions required the attacking aircraft to get above the intruder; this was a tall order in the aircraft available in 1914 and 1915.

Occasionally, a pilot could get lucky. On 7 June 1915, Sub Lieutenant Reginald 'Rex' Warneford RNAS had the good fortune to spot LZ-37 while *en route* to a bombing raid on the Zeppelin sheds at Berchem St Agathe. He was already airborne and at a considerable height when he began his action. The Zeppelin, on the other hand, was still climbing away from its shed. Had Warneford taken off from an English airfield in response to a Zeppelin warning, the results would have been rather less satisfactory, as the Zeppelin would have easily outclimbed him. As it turned out, Warneford chased the airship from the coast near Ostend and, despite its defensive machine-gun fire, succeeded in releasing six Hales bombs at it, the last of which set the airship on fire. It crashed and blew up, an explosion which also overturned Warneford's aircraft and stopped its engine. Having no alternative, Warneford had to land behind enemy lines and spend 35 minutes repairing his craft, taking off just in time to avoid curious Germans. For his deeds, he was awarded the Victoria Cross but died ten days after the action in an air accident. Nonetheless, his had been the first aerial victory over a German airship.

The solution to the firepower issue eventually came in 1916 and 1917. Technical advances led to gun magazines for anti-Zeppelin missions which were loaded with a mix of Pomeroy bullets – standard .303 British cartridges packed with a 155-grain cupronickel-jacketed lead bullet inside which was a hollow copper tube filled with 15 grains of 73 per cent dynamite – together with Brock bullets containing potassium chlorate, and incendiary Buckingham bullets enclosing pyrophoric yellow phosphorus, which ignited on firing and left a tracer trail of blue smoke. These would all explode on contact and set afire the hydrogen gas. If the fighter pilot could get near to the airship, he now stood a good chance of bringing it down.

The Invasion of the Goths

Towards the end of 1916, the Zeppelin raiders began to suffer disproportionate losses. Better fighter interception and a ring of anti-aircraft guns around key targets had made life precarious for these slow-moving monsters. This caused the Germans to increase the ceiling of their airships, which was achieved by lightening the existing craft through removing one of the engines. The resulting weight saving gave them a ceiling to over 16,000ft.

At the same time, the German planners developed a daylight bombing offensive against London designed to cow the population and enhance their feelings of vulnerability. This campaign was codenamed Operation '*Türkenkreuz*' ('Turk's Cross'). To execute the plan, a new formation – *Kampfgeschwader der Obersten Heeresleitung 3* (*Kagohl 3*), nicknamed the *England Geschwader* – was formed, consisting of six *Kampfstaffel (Kastas)* under the command of *Hauptmann* Ernst Brandenburg. *Kagohl 3* initially operated from Sint-Denijs-Westrem and Gontrode in the eastern Flanders area of German-occupied Belgium, around Ghent.

A Gotha bomber, in this case the G-V, successor to the G-IV. (US Naval History and Heritage Command NH 112945)

The first raids in March 1917 were unproductive but in the same month the Zeppelin force was supplemented by the arrival of Gotha G.IV aircraft, large twin-engined biplane bombers. Armed with up to three machine guns, they could fly at 83mph, climb to over 16,000ft and carry 1,100lbs of bombs.

Subsequently, *Kagohl 3* operated both airships and Gothas. Twenty-three of the latter set off to bomb London on 25 May but ended up attacking targets around Folkestone, killing ninety-five people. They were intercepted by RNAS Sopwith Pups, losing one Gotha in the process. But then on 13 June, in the deadliest raid of the war, Gothas dropped over 100 bombs in daylight, focused on Liverpool Street Station and the East End. They caused 162 deaths, including 18 infants, an entire class of five- to six-year-olds at the Upper North Street School in Poplar,* and 432 injuries.

---

* After a joint funeral in which the East End came to a halt, and with the coffins smothered under eiderdowns of white flowers, the children were buried together in a mass grave.

Next it was the airships' turn. During the night of 16-17 June an attempted raid by six Zeppelins met with little success. Only two reached England and one, L-48, was intercepted near Harwich and shot down by three British fighter planes, an FE 2b, a BE 2 and a DH 2. It eventually crashed just north of Felixstowe.

On 4 July, the Gothas came for Harwich and Felixstowe. At 0655 observers at Orford Ness heard the sound of aircraft. Five minutes later a formation of eighteen Gothas* came into view flying at about 14,000ft. They were engaged by a single DH 4 without success and then split into two groups, one targeting Felixstowe and one heading for Harwich.

The Harwich-bound section dropped six bombs over Shotley, two of which exploded close to the RNAS Balloon Station, killing two men and fatally injuring another. As they passed over Harwich harbour, thirteen bombs were unloaded at the ships below, all of which missed and detonated in the water. Three of the light cruisers, *Canterbury*, *Concord* and *Conquest*, returned fire. Several bombs aimed at Harwich and Dovercourt landed but failed to explode.

Reaching Felixstowe, the Gothas released two bombs on Trimley Marshes. This provided a fortunate increase in naval rations by killing twenty-one sheep. Seven other bombs fell on the marshes without damage. In Felixstowe town, two bombs exploded in Mill Lane, killing five soldiers and injuring ten others. Three bombs exploded near the main railway station but caused only limited damage. Now over the docks, the Germans dropped another eleven weapons, which fell on waste ground, while four exploded near to the Beach Railway Station and two fell to the north of Felixstowe docks. But now they were over the RNAS base and here more significant effects were felt. Two bombs destroyed a Curtiss H-12 Large America flying boat and badly damaged another. Three workmen and five RNAS balloon station personnel were killed. The matter was considered serious enough to be reported to the War Cabinet on 5 July, where it was stated that 'we had lost an America machine which was burnt and another America had been damaged by a shrapnel bomb'.[12] One bomb landed close to St Nicolas' church† and fortunately failed to explode; but in all the raid caused over £2,000 of damage and injured twenty-nine souls. Another seventeen were killed and one fatally injured.

There was a further Gotha assault on Harwich and its surroundings on 22 July. *Kagohl 3* was intending to attack London, but inclement weather meant that an easier raid against Felixstowe and Harwich was substituted

---

* Out of twenty-five which had been despatched.
† The bomb was preserved and is on display in the church.

instead. Sixteen bombers crossed the coast at 0805 and were engaged by the anti-aircraft guns ringed around the two ports two minutes later. Defensive aircraft were immediately put up as well. This time the defence was such that the Gothas turned for home after only 12 minutes over the target. At Felixstowe a RNAS kite balloon air mechanic was fatally injured and in Harwich harbour the minesweeping trawler *Touchstone*, once of Hull, was knocked about with two of her crew wounded. But in all the raid achieved little and was beaten off by a determined defence; nonetheless, thirteen people died and twenty-six were injured. The War Cabinet of the following day was told 'that an approximate estimate of the damage done was £3,000' and that 'one German aeroplane had been brought down over the sea'.[13]

The Gothas came to Dover by night at 2300 on 2 September 1917. They released fourteen bombs of which two were 'crashing Christophers', 200lb trench mortar shells. One officer was killed and six people injured. The following night the giant bombers targeted Chatham, Margate and Sheerness. At Chatham two 112lb bombs fell on the drill hall of the *Pembroke* naval barracks where several hundred men were sleeping. One hundred and thirty-one naval ratings were killed and ninety wounded. They were a mixture of regulars, RNR, RFR and RNVR, all experienced seamen awaiting reassignment to new ships. Three had come from far-off Newfoundland to die. Two ships were also hit; the 'River'-class destroyer *Ettrick* (1902), hulked since the July when her bows had been blown off by a U-boat's torpedo, and HMS *Patrol* (last noted at Hartlepool). Each ship lost a man killed.

The navy gained some measure of revenge before the month was out. On 28 September, twenty-five Gothas came together with two new bombers, the multi-engined Giants (officially, Zeppelin-Staaken R.VIs).* It was meant to have been the heaviest raid on London yet, but the weather frustrated it. Most of the attackers dropped their bombs somewhat randomly on Essex and Kent. Three were lost, one of which was claimed by the monitor guard ship HMS *Marshal Ney* off Ramsgate in a rare (if true, for no wreckage was ever found) triumph for ships against bombers. The monitor had already distinguished herself in April, as narrated in Chapter 11.

Back in London, on Sunday 17 February 1918, the Royal Hospital at Chelsea was hit. Georgina Lee visited the scene two days later and was appalled. 'The devastation is terrible. One of the lovely old residences in the grounds of the Royal Hospital Chelsea was sliced in half by a bomb of terrific force, and literally crumbled to dust . . . two of the five children were found impaled on the railings, dead. The bodies of father, mother and a lady guest were also found in the wreckage.'[14]

---

* These had four Maybach engines and could carry 4,400lbs of bombs.

The above is a sample of the many Gotha raids on the capital and east of England. But slowly an improvised system of barrage balloons, searchlights, anti-aircraft guns, observation posts and fighters repatriated from France, helped ward off the German bombers, which turned to night raids until they were forced by losses to call of the missions in May 1918.

London suffered badly in these attacks. Over the year May 1917 to May 1918, more than 800 civilians were killed in German air raids on London and some 1,500 injured. During September 1917, a week of continuous attacks reduced many in the East End to panic. Over 300,000 people took shelter in the Underground and the government instructed newspapers to cease publication of pictures and limit accounts of destruction. But the defenders had destroyed 24 Gothas and another 37 were lost to accidents over a total of 397 sorties.

Results

According to the official history of the war in the air, airships made 51 bombing raids on Britain during the war in which 557 people were killed and 1,358 injured. The airships dropped 5,806 bombs, causing damage worth £1,527,585. Eighty-four airships took part, of which 30 were either shot down or lost in accidents. Aeroplanes carried out 52 raids, dropping 2,772 bombs of 73.5 long tons weight for the loss of 62 aircraft, killing 857 people, injuring 2,058 and causing £1,434,526 of damage.[15]

14

Defending the Shores

This book is primarily about the Royal Navy and its part in protecting the country from invasion and incursion. But it was not, of course, alone in this mission, as has been narrated. In this section the experiences of some of the men who manned the coastal defences are related. The chapter also considers the role of women volunteers in defending Britain's shores and examines the overall reasons for, and psychology of, volunteerism

Lieutenant Arthur Maitland was a regular army officer in the 2nd Battalion of the Essex Regiment. As the world ticked down to war, he and his fellow officers were enjoying dinner in their mess when fear of German sabotage rudely interrupted their repast. 'One of our companies was sent off to a place called Chattenden [see also Chapter 4] to guard the naval powder magazine, the place is the biggest in England and should it be blown up would paralyse the whole fleet.'[1] A couple of days later, he was playing cricket against a team of mixed naval and Royal Marine backgrounds when, having made 120 all out and reduced their naval opponents to 30 for 2, they were suddenly summoned back to barracks and told that they must immediately entrain for Sheerness. A surprise German attack, even before the outbreak of war, was occupying minds. As Maitland informed his mother, 'this is known as the precautionary period and we are part of the Eastern Coast Defence Force . . . we have to protect our portion of the coast against possible invaders, Sheerness being a particular point'.[2] The regiment's role in this activity did not last long, as TF units replaced regulars; the Essexes were sent to France as part of the BEF and Maitland served there throughout the war, winning the Military Cross.

Hugh Chance was an Eton schoolboy. When war broke out, he was actually on annual camp with the Eton Officer Training Corps (OTC) at Aldershot. Determined to play his part Chance, the son of the owner of Chance Brothers of Smethwick, manufacturers of glass and lighthouses and whose family home was at Blackmore Park, near Malvern,* cast around for an army formation that would take him in. Eventually he joined the 8th Battalion of the Worcestershire Regiment as a subaltern. This was a TF battalion, with its headquarters in Silver Street, Worcester.

---

* Demolished in 1925.

As part of the 61st Division they were sent to Essex 'to guard the coast against a possible German invasion and to dig trenches'.[3] After a short stay in the Billericay area, he was moved to Maldon. Here in 1915, Chance experienced his first Zeppelin attack.

> One night, when we were watching a film in the local cinema, we heard a great roaring and rushing out into the street we found a huge Zeppelin airship flying overhead. Some bombs and incendiaries were dropped round the ironworks near the harbour and a light left burning in Battalion HQ brought another shower, which fortunately did no damage apart from destroying a wooden carpenter's shop and killing a blackbird.

This first encounter was quickly followed by another when their tented camp was bombed. They were frustratingly unable to retaliate for 'we had only a few Lee-Metford rifles and no ammunition' and the gunners 'were equipped with Crimean muzzle-loading guns'. Furthermore, with possible exaggeration, Chance claimed that 'at this point in the war, the East Coast anti-aircraft defence consisted of two Rolls-Royce [armoured] cars each carrying a small pom-pom'.[4] Spy mania contributed to his next move. 'Mersea Island lies at the mouth of the Blackwater and was reputed to be a place where German spies were landed from submarines. So a detachment of the 2/8th was sent to guard and patrol the coast.'[5] Tiring of such duty, Hugh Chance eventually joined the RFC and became a prisoner of war when shot down.

Another who found himself digging trenches was Captain John Burdon Sanderson Haldane, later a world-famous geneticist and biologist. Writing to his sister Naomi Mitchison, herself a well-known author and socialist, in 1914 while serving with the 3rd Battalion, The Black Watch, he described their life in Scotland. 'We are defending Nigg, which is the key to Invergordon and the north . . . we spend one night a week in trenches, another as a flying picket (in camp but sleep in our own clothes).'[6] He assures her of his safety; 'we aren't likely to be reached', he averred and then, showing a naive belief in Jellicoe's bellicosity, added 'unless Jellicoe allows the Germans to attack in the hope of bottling then up in the Moray Firth, which he quite possibly might. Normally, we are quite safe . . . cruisers, torpedo boats and searchlights are always going, the mouth of the Firth is fortified.'[7] Anticipating Fisher, he expected the navy to stage an invasion of Schleswig-Holstein in December 1914.

One more who found himself involved in coastal trenches, but coming from a very different social position, was George Smith. From a working-class background, he seems to have volunteered and enlisted in either the 3rd (Reserve) or 4th (Extra Reserve) Battalion of the East Surrey Regiment, which remained in England with the dual role of home defence and of training and preparing reinforcement drafts of reservists, special reservists, recruits and returning wounded for the regular battalions.

Smith's letters home indicate a touching concern for his wife, Lily, and his young family. He tells her to assure them he is well and will return home safely and consistently checks that Lily is receiving the financial allowances that are due to her.

He was based in Dover, at a training camp. Food was good; bacon, bread and good butter for breakfast, beef, tomatoes and haricot beans for 'dinner' (the mid-day meal) and tinned herrings for tea. However, 'I am not drinking any beer, it is like weak tea'.[8] They paraded every day from 0630 for five hours and by 1 October 1914, Smith wrote that he was 'quite a soldier now'. Zeppelins troubled him; 'we shall be safe where we are but we never know when they are coming here with those airships'. By November, George told his wife that 'we have got barbed wire and entrenchment all over the county, it is hard work digging the trenches, some days we have to walk sixteen miles before we start digging'.[9] And later that month, 'I have been digging trenches all this week, we do six hours digging per day'. Not so much soldiering as navvying! But he was proud of his handiwork. 'If the Germans do get here, they won't get any further.'[10] Eventually, George Smith was sent to France. He was killed there on 31 May 1915.

Women at War

So far in this book, we have considered the role of volunteerism solely in a male context. But increasingly, women took part in coastal and national defence as well. Women started to enter the workforce in traditionally male jobs from the beginning of the war and, as has been noted, this became a cause of industrial unrest in some industries. But progress was inexorable and in April 1915 even the army issued an instruction authorising the employment of women as cooks and waitresses. By March 1917, the first female cooks had arrived in France, as members of the Women's Auxiliary Army Corps (WAAC). This body, formed in 1916, restricted women to 'feminine', auxiliary roles, such as store work, administration, and catering. There were no military ranks in the WAAC; instead, officers were named 'controllers' and 'administrators' – it was believed that only men could hold the king's commission!

Josephine Tennent became an ambulance driver with the Women's Army Auxiliary Corps on the Western Front. 'The idea was that the women were to take over and free men for other jobs,' she related in later life.

> They had done all the driving up until then and they had always been two to an ambulance. Now, we were one to an ambulance, so there were times when we did the work of two men. At one time, when there was a German advance, things were so bad that we drove day and night for 48 hours and only stopped for two hours on our beds during that time.

Before the war, it had been unthinkable that a women would be able to act as a driver and a car mechanic. But now, as Josephine explained,

> you had to keep your car in running order, you had to do all the daily jobs, you see, filling up and oiling and greasing and this and that. To swing those cars – there were no self-starters – was extremely hard work. And it took a bit of getting used to, to give it the right sort of flick you see. The tyres were the great trouble because, in those days, tyres went down at the drop of a hat, you know. And I've known as many as – I think I'm not exaggerating – if I say I've had at least three punctures in a day.[11]

In April 1918, the WAAC was renamed Queen Mary's Army Auxiliary Corps (QMAAC) in honour of its achievements. Over 57,000 women served with the WAAC, at home and abroad, before it was disbanded on 27 September 1921.

Then there was the Women's Legion, begun in 1915 by Edith Vane-Tempest-Stewart, Marchioness of Londonderry. It was comprised of volunteers who wore military-style uniforms and took on various duties within Agricultural, Canteen, Cookery and Motor Transport sections. Estimates vary but it seems some 6,000 volunteers had joined its ranks by 1918.

The navy too established a women's arm, the Women's Royal Naval Service (WRNS), popularly known as the 'Wrens', which was formed in November 1917. By the end of the war the service had 4,821 members (Statement of the First Lord of the Admiralty, Explanatory of the navy estimates, 1919-1920), not counting the 2,867 Wrens who had joined the Women's Royal Air Force when the RNAS was merged with the RFC on 1 April 1918 to form the Royal Air Force.

Alice Russell and her sister drove a baker's delivery van up until 1917 when the work dried up. Alice left and

> I joined the WRNS and that was the start of it. I'd always been interested. Mother made us sailor suits when we were kiddies, you know, skirts. A cousin lived with me who was the same age and we

were both dressed in these sailor outfits. I've always loved the Navy ... I don't know why, having been born and brought up in Birmingham, you see. Then of course nothing would satisfy me but ... well, I went to a place in Birmingham and joined.[12]

Alice served as a driver with the WRNS and the Women's Royal Air Force, both located at the RNAS Training Establishment, Cranwell, later RAF Cranwell.

WRNS lived a somewhat closeted existence. Eighteen-year-old Mary Battersby joined the WRNS at Queenstown in the Coast of Ireland Command. 'They wanted an English girl for decoding,' she remembered.

My mother thought girls should only work in canteens so she wouldn't sign my application form for the Wrens but my brother, an assistant paymaster at Queenstown, invited me over for a month's holiday and signed my form. I had a small room to myself under constant guard. The harbour was heavily mined and my work was connected with guiding our ships in and out – sloops, Q-ships, destroyers and minesweepers. I lived with my brother and I remember that [once] when we left the flat together and walked about fifty yards before going our separate ways to work, ten shillings was deducted from my pay as a fine for walking in public with an officer.[13]

Then there were the Voluntary Aid Detachments (VADs),* volunteer nurses, unqualified and often upper or middle class, who worked without pay in hospitals at home and abroad undertaking basic nursing duties. VAD nurses received basic first aid training and were often mentored by the more experienced professional nurses. At least 800 VADs served on the Western Front, and during the four years of war some 38,000 VADs worked in hospitals or as ambulance drivers and cooks. Vera Brittain, of *Testament of Youth* fame, was a VAD nurse.

The first women police officers were enrolled during the war. One of the main responsibilities of the so-called 'Women's Patrols' was to maintain discipline and monitor working women's behaviour around factories or female workers' hostels. They also carried out inspections of women ammunition operatives to ensure that they did not take anything into, or out of, factories which might cause explosions.

Even the Girl Guide movement, formed in 1910 as the girls' equivalent of the Boy Scouts, joined the war effort. They packaged up clothing to send

---

* Originally founded in 1909 under the auspices of the St John's Ambulance organisation.

to British soldiers at the front, prepared hostels and first-aid dressing stations for use by those injured in air raids or accidents, tended allotments to help cope with food shortages, and provided assistance at hospitals, government offices and munitions factories.

Finally, many women worked for Britain informally and often out of sight. Georgina Lee made waterproof bags for gasmasks in her spare time and then became involved in 1915 with the Belgian relief efforts, finding clothing, food and accommodation for Belgian refugees who had fled the war. She proved so successful in this that the Belgian Government in Exile awarded her the Queen Elisabeth Medal.*

The war became the catalyst of a process of final emancipation for women. Beatrice Browne served as a typist with the Women's Royal Naval Service. She felt that the war proved an important time for women.

> I think that the service people, not only WRNS, but the other two services, also, pioneered the beginning of votes for women and freedom for women more. Because up until then, we were brought up in a very, very strict Victorian stilted youth. It gradually got that you were free, and when the war was over, that first war, you got more freedom. I know I had, I was allowed out later at home when I got back. And you got ideas, you know. I remember starting hockey and cricket and tennis at my office and more or less it taught you to be a leader, which I think we were.[14]

As can be seen, volunteerism was by no means solely a man's preserve, it was a virus which infected male and female alike.

The Psychology of Volunteering

The VTCs at their peak boasted some 500,000 men. From a force of just 250,000 regulars in 1914, the army had absorbed nearly five million men by the end of the war (of which 2.7 million were voluntary enlistments to December 1915). The Territorial Force, volunteers to a man, suffered 577,016 casualties in all theatres and its officers and men won seventy-one Victoria Crosses.[15] The Royal Navy had a strength at the Armistice of 407,316† officers and men. Of these, 50,218 were RNVR, 37,145 RNR(T) and 23,453 RNR – all volunteers. Additionally, the coast watchers under Royal Navy aegis numbered 2,400 civilians and 1,700 boy scouts.[16]

---

* The Queen Elisabeth Medal was awarded to Belgian and foreign women who had personally dedicated themselves to the relief of Belgian civilians and soldiers in connection with the war by providing financial, material or medical assistance.
† This total excludes the 55,066 men of the RNAS who transferred to the RAF on 1 April 1918.

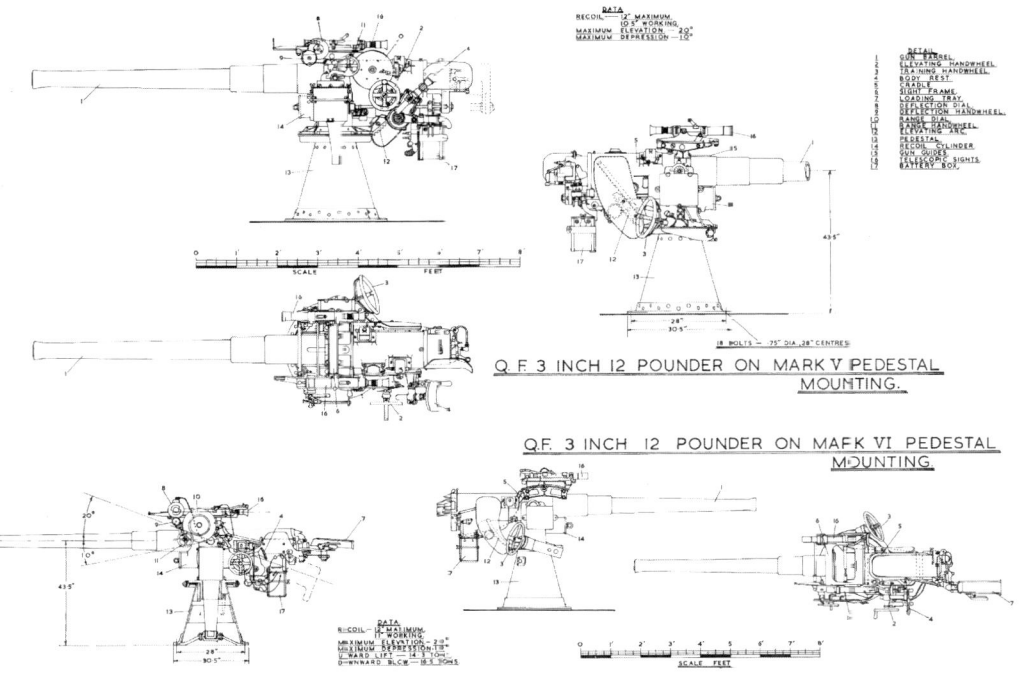

A detailed line drawing of a 12pdr gun, as intended in coastal defence for close-in engagement of torpedo boats etc. One hundred and three of these weapons had been deployed around British coastal defences by April 1918.
(© Seaforth Publishing, John Lambert Collection)

All classes of men, women and boys volunteered in droves. All of which begs the question 'Why did the people of Britain respond so quickly and in such numbers to the call to defend their shores'?

One reason was surely pure patriotism, and another an awareness among the educated classes of economic rivalry with Germany. Additionally, the war had brought some industries to a near standstill, making the army a welcome change from unemployment, short-time working and pecuniary pressure. For some it was the chance for adventure; for others revulsion at the reported German atrocities in Belgium. But there were psychological reasons too.

The American philosopher and psychologist William James gave a speech in 1906, turned into an essay in 1910, entitled *The Moral Equivalent of War*.*
To paraphrase, he suggested that warfare was so common because of its

---

* William James. *The Moral Equivalent of War*. Lecture 11 in Memories and Studies, Longman Green and Co (New York, 1911), pp 267–96. Posthumously published.

positive psychological effects, both on the individual and on society *in toto*.

Britain before the war was a divided country with very considerable class-based issues, a continuous wave of worker strikes and stoppages, a very unequal distribution of wealth and a growing sense of dissatisfaction with life among the general population. When war came, it delivered a social sense of unity in the face of a collective threat. It brought all types of people together and the whole community suffered or was cheered together. It produced a sense of cohesion, with goals that could be shared. The 'war effort' inspired citizens to behave in an honourable and unselfish fashion in service of a higher, national good. It brought a fractured society together.

James also proposed that conflict supplied meaning and purpose to otherwise dull or empty lives, contrasting with the monotony of everyday life. Warfare also enabled the expression of higher human qualities, such as discipline, courage, unselfishness, and self-sacrifice. These qualities were deeply engrained in the pre-1914 British self-image and ethos, based as it was on a reverence for the Greek and Roman legends and the cult of chivalry. As one historian has written, 'every public schoolboy was familiar with the Iliad and the Odyssey and the poetry – with its emphasis on honour, discipline, athleticism and courage in the face of death – spoke across the ages about what it meant to be a gentleman and a scholar at the height of empire'.[17]

And so the zeitgeist of the age and the exigencies of the time came together and the volunteers flowed.

A BL 6in Mk VII coast defence gun, photographed at the Royal Artillery Museum, Woolwich, London in 2011. (Creative Commons)

15

Science Ashore and Defence Afloat

The pre-war Royal Navy is sometimes depicted as being slow to utilise the advances in science that became open to it. It might be fairer to say that the navy trusted tradition and proven merit and did not want to be on the 'bleeding edge' of technological advance. Fisher's regime as First Sea Lord produced significant innovation, as has been noted in Chapter 3, and when war came, certain sections of the Admiralty moved quickly to use technology to help protect Britain's shores. The clearest example is that of 'sigint', information derived from the interception and decoding of the enemy's signals traffic.

The First World Wide Web

By 1914, the world was girdled by a web of submarine cables which carried communications from country to country in the form of telegrams or 'cables' (so named for their method of transmission). The traffic conveyed by this communications web was difficult to intercept and allowed for privacy between sender and receiver. For Germany, five cables linked her directly to France, Spain and the Azores and from thence to the rest of the world, especially the USA.

Wireless telegraphy had also been developed, especially by Guglielmo Marconi. In 1899 his equipment sent the first radio signal from Britain to France and in 1901 from Britain to the USA. By 1908 most RN ships had Marconi-based wireless telegraphy (the Germans had a similar system using Telefunken equipment), and by 1909, Marconi had been awarded the Nobel Prize for his work, at the early age of just 36. But the technology was still in its infancy and amongst the issues that it produced was that wireless signals could be intercepted and read by those for whom they were not intended.

A few hours after Britain and Germany went to war, the paddle steamer HMTS* *Alert* (1890), owned by the General Post Office (GPO) and used as a cable repair and maintenance vessel, departed Dover on a secret mission, a task known only to the man in charge of the operation, Superintendent Bourdeaux. She had no Royal Navy escort and was therefore in danger of interception by German patrols. Her objective was to find, drag up, and cut

---

* His Majesty's Telegraph Ship.

The cable ship *Alert*, which cut Germany's cable communications with the outside world on 5 August 1914. (Author's collection)

the German cable network. Four cables were cut overnight, starting with the one to Spain. In worsening weather, *Alert* struggled with the fifth cable, losing many of her grapples in the process. The work was threatened by the arrival of a flotilla of unidentified destroyers, but *Alert*'s crew continued their efforts and succeeded in cutting the cable just as the warships drew near. The unwelcome visitors turned out to be French, and after questioning Bourdeaux and discovering the cutting of the German cables, the French crew raised a cheer.

Alert returned home unnoticed; but she had produced a significant coup.* For now, German communication would perforce be by radio, where it could be intercepted more easily. Germany could no longer send private telegrams or cables to its colonies or to America. This little-known success was to make a major contribution to the defence of Britain.

Room 40

It has already been noted how the intelligence provided by Room 40 allowed Jellicoe to know some of his enemy's intentions in advance. Room 40 had been established in the early days of the war. Rear Admiral Henry Oliver,† at that time Director of Naval Intelligence, was receiving wireless intercepts

---

* The cutting of the cables had been advocated by a subcommittee of the CID in December 1911. Paragraph 55-4 recommended that the Admiralty should 'instruct the General Post Office as to the cutting of the four German cables to Vigo, Tenerife and the Azores in the English Channel' (CAB 38/19/56, TNA). The remaining German-controlled cables, running from Monrovia (Liberia) to Brazil and from the Azores to New York were severed in 1915.

† Succeeded by Captain Reginald 'Blinker' Hall in October 1914. It was Hall who made Room 40 the potent force it became.

which were clearly in code. Meeting the Director of Naval Education, Sir Alfred Ewing, for lunch, he persuaded Ewing to join his department and set up a codebreaking team. This group was placed in Room 40, Admiralty Old Building, hence its name. They operated in complete secrecy, with very few people 'in' on the knowledge, and produced some stunning wins, including the famous 'Zimmerman Telegram'.

But first they had to receive the German radio intercepts. Some were collected by mobile operators. On one occasion the authorities despatched to the eastern counties a car equipped with Marconi apparatus and two skilled technicians. They were promptly arrested as spies by the spy-mad Essex police. After an exchange of telegrams they were freed but at 1900 called in again to say they had been arrested in another part of the county. When liberated once more, they refused to move without an escort of a TF officer. One was provided and the following morning, in another county, they were once more detained. This time the triumphant plod telegraphed to London 'three German spies arrested with car and complete wireless installation, one in the uniform of a British officer'.[1] Other messages were collected by the navy's sole radio interception post at Stockton-on-Tees.

But both of these methods were a drop in the ocean. The solution was provided by two gifted amateurs, Richard John Bayntun Hippersley, a wealthy country squire, and Edward Russell Clarke, a barrister. Both were what would later be called 'radio hams'; and they each had amused themselves pre-war by listening to German naval signals traffic. DORA had

A view of Hunstanton coastguard lookout, Marconi station and lighthouse around 1908. This became the first site of a Y-station in late 1914. (Author's collection)

made all amateur radio equipment illegal. So now they came to see Ewing and informed him that Germany was transmitting many more signals than realised, and at shorter wavelengths than the navy was monitoring. Russell Clarke said he would be prepared to intercept these signals if granted official facilities.

Ewing obtained the necessary permissions and Hippersley and Russell Clarke set up at Hunstanton coastguard station (and site of an old Marconi transmitter), ideally situated to pick up signals from the German transmitters at Norddeich and Neumunster. When they arrived there they found a wooden mast with no aerial, but they were soon intercepting wireless traffic. The station was very successful, intercepting German naval and airship signals, and was the first of fourteen wireless intercept (known as 'Y-stations') which were established along the British coast as well as three at Otranto, Ancona and Malta.

They were of two types, one for intercepting the signals and one for identifying where they were coming from. Sometimes both functions were operated at the same site, with the direction finding (D/F) hut being a few hundred metres from the main interception building, because of the need to minimise interference. The sites collected radio traffic, which was then either analysed locally or if encrypted, passed for processing by Room 40 in London. The stations were manned by GPO operators, and each had a dedicated land telephone line in order to send information directly to the Admiralty. For centuries, frigates and lookout vessels had patrolled off foreign harbours to bring back information as soon as the enemy fleets put to sea, and of their dispositions. By 1914, the minefield and the submarine had made such Nelsonian methods of intelligence-gathering impossible. Room 40 and the Y-stations won the information war for Britain.

Inventions

The Admiralty received many suggestions, well intentioned if not altogether well thought out, as to how it might win the war. What was needed, however, was a more rigorous and scientific method of advancing research into new and better weapons or technology. This led to the formation of the Admiralty Board of Invention and Research (BIR). It was established in 1915 by the then First Lord of the Admiralty, Arthur Balfour, and its mission was to develop and test new designs of weapons and equipment and get them to be mass produced quickly, without burdening the regular military command structure. Striving to keep ex-First Sea Lord Jacky Fisher engaged in the war effort after his resignation, Balfour asked him to chair the organisation.

Convening for the first time on 19 July, the BIR mainly concerned itself with naval warfare inventions, especially air power and, importantly, anti-submarine weapons, which was the focus of one of the BIR's six divisions. This body examined some rather *outré* suggestions, including training seagulls to obfuscate submarine periscopes with their excreta, arming cormorants with bombs and teaching sea lions to carry depth charges. Unsurprisingly these projects were not progressed. But the real thrust of the work was on the key issue of detecting submarines when they were underwater and therefore, to all intents and purposes at that time, invisible.

This became the particular focus of Professor Sir William Henry Bragg who, together with his son William Lawrence, had been jointly awarded the 1915 Nobel Prize for Physics in connection with their investigations of crystal structure using X-ray spectrometry. Bragg's primary effort for the BIR was directed at perfecting a hydrophone, a device for detecting underwater sound and thus pinpointing the location of a submarine. Bragg, working for the Board of Invention and Research, became resident director of the navy's own Hawkcraig experimental research station at Aberdour (Fife), HMS *Tarlair*, which was under the control of Commander (later Captain) Cyril Ryan RN and a staff of RNVR officers.

By late 1916, it was obvious that premises larger than Hawkcraig were required, and some naval officers and W H Bragg, together with thirty-six civilian scientific staff, relocated to start a new base in Harwich, at Parkeston Quay.* By 26 December, the organisation was in place and known as Admiralty Experimental Station (AES), Parkeston.

In fact, both Hawkcraig and Harwich produced viable and eventually successful devices. After the war, Jellicoe credited AES Harwich with the development of the Mark I directional hydrophone in 1917 'and other exceedingly valuable work was carried out there connected with the detection of submarines'.[2]

Bragg's work on underwater detection systems was important in the anti-U-boat war. But he also helped develop a system which directly protected harbour entrances and the coast of Britain.

INDICATOR LOOPS
Large metal objects have an inherent magnetic effect. This can be used to create an electric current in a conductor in certain circumstances. An induced current in a stationary loop of wire can be produced when a magnet (for example a submarine) moves overhead. Even if wiped or degaussed, submarines still have sufficient magnetism to produce a small current in a loop.

---

* The move was also political, as Ryan and Bragg had fallen out.

It was this insight which persuaded a Scottish physicist, Alexander Crichton Mitchell, to place a cable on the seabed of the Firth of Forth as part of work at HMS *Tarlair*. He demonstrated that the passage of a submarine induced a current of about a millivolt which could be detected on a galvanometer. A rheostat was used to give the two loops identical resistances, so that no current flowed until a vessel approached. However, whilst it could detect passing ships, all sorts of land-based objects affected the cable too and, as his report to the BIR did not make clear that this issue could be overcome (by the use of a figure-of-eight loop), the project was shelved. But in 1917, William Henry Bragg took the concept up again, working at AES Harwich. He called them 'indicator loops' and by mid-1917 had reasonable models working.

If an indicator loop indicated the presence of a vessel, and if no surface ship could be seen, then U-boat was the default assumption because British submarines would come into harbour surfaced. Depth charge bearing A/S vessels could be sent to attack the intruder.

In some cases, the loops were positioned beside controlled minefields in which the mines were connected by electrical cable back to a control hut on shore and the mines could be detonated manually by an operator there (these were 'observation mines', see Chapter 2).

The first recorded use of indicator loops was at Dumpton Gap, Broadstairs, near Margate. These operated from 27 April 1918 until the armistice. A refinement of the system was installed at Scapa Flow, as part of the harbour defences. A loop of cable was placed in a rectangle several hundred yards long by perhaps 60 yards wide around the line of observation mines. When a ship passed over the loop a shore-based galvanometer would indicate its presence by the movement to the left or right of a centred needle. When the needle crossed the centre position on its way back from its maximum deviation the enemy vessel was over the centre of the loop, and hence over the mines. The explosives were then fired electrically by the shore-based operator in the mine control hut. On 28 October 1918, this was how *UB-116* was destroyed in the controlled minefield at Hoxa Gate, with the loss of thirty-four crew, so near to the end of the war. (Appendix 15 shows the other locations where indicator loops were installed.)

A drawing of a 'model' harbour defence system displays a number of indicator loops covering all of the entrances to a theoretical harbour in a 'Manual of Coast Fortresses' held at The National Archives.[3] It demonstrates that by the war's end, the induction loop system was seen as the most seaward part of the layered defence of a port or harbour against a raid or invasion.

Acoustic Mirrors

One of the problems with fighting off Zeppelin and (later) Gotha/Giant raids was that they could appear quite suddenly. By the time they had been sighted (it was usually dark as well) and RNAS or RFC fighter aerodromes notified, the damage had often already been done and the aerial invaders were on their way home. How could some prior notice of the bombers' arrival be gained?

The answer came in a spin-off of work being undertaken on using sound to range on enemy guns, conducted on the Western Front by W Lawrence Bragg. One of the technologies developed by his team was the Tucker microphone, named for its inventor, William Sansome Tucker,* a very sensitive device which used the vibration of platinum metal filament to detect and locate sound.

The remains of Kilnsea Acoustic Mirror, a concrete dish about 15ft in diameter. The metal post that held the microphone can also be seen. It is sited at the landward end of Spurn Head.
(James M Towill via Creative Commons)

Tucker's work eventually led to vast parabolic 'sound mirrors' being constructed from concrete. These reflected incoming sound to a microphone or trumpet at the parabola's focal point. These were connected to a stethoscope used by the listener operator, usually from one of the National Volunteer units, who could issue a warning by telephone of incoming traffic. Aircraft would not normally be detected until they were around 25 miles away, which gave a warning period of 10 to 12 minutes. In this time, it was hoped that AA batteries and fighter aircraft could be readied.

Many such installations were built in 1917 and 1918, mostly by the Royal Engineers, along Britain's eastern coast. They were not an Admiralty responsibility, but played their part in helping naval aircraft and guns in deterring or preventing aerial raids.

The M-N Scheme

One of the largest defensive engineering projects attempted by the Admiralty was 'Admiralty Scheme M-N'. This was a plan for eight towers to be built

---

* Tucker was a physics lecturer who volunteered as a private soldier as part of the London Electrical Engineers, TF. He finished the war as Director of Acoustical Research in the RAF and with the rank of major.

and positioned in the Dover Straits, roughly along the line of the existing Dover Barrage, to form an anti-U-boat and invasion barrier. M-N was the brain child of Civil Engineer in Chief to the Admiralty, Sir Alexander Gibb, who had previously delivered the Rosyth Dockyard project in timely fashion. He was assisted in part by engineer Guy Maunsell, who would gain his own fame in the next global conflict.

Each tower was intended to have two 4in guns, searchlights and other defensive paraphernalia. A/S nets were to be stretched between them, and an induction loop system, with an operator in each tower, would also form part of the plan.

In June 1918, a party of Royal Engineers arrived at Southwick Green in Sussex where they established a camp. Construction of the first two towers was soon underway on the south side of nearby Shoreham harbour. But by the end of the war, only one was approaching completion, a 92ft tall metal cylinder sitting on a raft of concrete. It was never deployed as intended, but in 1920 the completed tower was towed by two paddle-wheel tugs to Nab Rock, in the deep-water approach to the eastern Solent, to serve as a lighthouse. Its honeycomb base was flooded, and the structure sank to the seabed where it has remained ever since.

The Nab tower, seen in 2012 after it had been refurbished. It is the only survivor of the 1918 project M-N cross-Channel barrier scheme. (Creative Commons)

At sea, on land and in the air, war again proved to be the locomotive of scientific development and the navy was a beneficiary, as was the nation.

* * * * *

Defence Afloat

In several countries, coastal defence was effected in whole or part by a particularly designed type of vessel, intended only for operations close to the littoral. These were coastal defence battleships or cruisers and were developed especially in France and Scandinavia, and countries such as Thailand with many coastal islands to defend.

They were in operation mostly during the period from 1860 to 1920. In form, such ships were smaller warships which sacrificed speed and range for armour and armament. They were attractive to nations that could not afford full-sized battleships and/or wished only to defend their shores. Some vessels had limited blue-water capabilities; others operated in rivers. They represented, to a greater or lesser extent, mobile artillery which could be moved from location to location by sea and with reasonable celerity. The coastal defence ships differed from, for example, monitors by having a higher freeboard and usually possessing both greater speed and a secondary armament. They varied in size from around 1,500 tons to 8,000 tons.

The Royal Navy was not immune from such thinking but largely eschewed the concept. However, it did briefly essay an attempt at such craft.

Rendel Gunboats

Also known as 'flat-iron' gunboats, from their shape, Rendels were a development of the vessels originally developed for coastal bombardment (not defence) in the Crimean War. These were the *Aetna*-class ironclad floating batteries, wrought iron-armoured floating steam and sail-powered platforms carrying fourteen 68pdr smoothbore guns at a maximum speed of 5 knots. In 1856, these were on display at a royal review of the returning fleet at Spithead. It was the first time that such vessels had been seen at a royal review. *The Times* noted that the floating batteries were,

> four low, flat, squat, black, unwieldy constructions, the *Trusty*, the *Glatton*, the *Thunder*, and the *Meteor*, remained motionless at anchor. Their appearance inspires a doubt whether they are capable of motion; they were, however, a feature of the scene, for to compensate for their shapelessness they had put on the gayest of toilettes; they were more brilliantly 'dressed' than any other vessels in the harbour. It was in vain; beauty of form – the one thing needful for the eye of

the amateur – was not there; their ugliness is irredeemable; garlands of roses would not give grace to these hippopotami.[4]

These brutes sparked an idea for a smaller vessel in the mind of George Rendel, a naval architect. In 1859 Sir William Armstrong had formed the Elswick Ordnance Company in order to supply guns for the British army. Rendel was one of three partners in the business. In 1864 the Elswick Ordnance Company was merged with Armstrong's original company to form Sir W G Armstrong and Company. George Rendel was one of seven partners in the new company, and was in joint charge of the ordnance departments.

In 1867 Armstrong signed an agreement with a local shipbuilder, Dr Charles Mitchell, whereby Mitchell's shipyard would build warships and Armstrong's company would provide the armaments. George Rendel was put in charge of the new enterprise, and he designed the early ships produced by it. These became the Rendel gunboats (aka flat-iron gunboats). With the assistance of the leading gunnery expert Admiral Sir Astley Cooper-Key, Rendel developed a class of craft designed for defensive coastal operations. Around 100ft long with only a 6ft draught, the gunboats mounted a single heavy gun, which was held in a fixed position on the vessel and aimed by pointing the entire craft, in the manner of a punt gun.

Many navies adopted the design, and in Britain, the *Ant*-class ships represented the acme of the type. This was a group of twenty-four Royal Navy iron-hulled flat-iron gunboats mounting a single 10in (18-ton) muzzle-loading gun, and built between 1870 and 1880. They carried no masts or sails, being among the first Royal Navy vessels so equipped. Power came from two screws and a two-cylinder steam engine which could take the 250-ton ship to 8.5 knots.

A model of the flat-iron gunboat HMS *Arrow*. The method of storing and loading the muzzle-loading gun can be clearly seen. (Creative Commons)

According to the Admiralty 'Pink List' the function of the Rendels was 'Gunboats for the Attack and Defence of Coasts'.[5] However, they were not to be used in the defence role and were soon seen as obsolete, being decommissioned, sold off, converted to other uses, or operated as tenders. At the outbreak of war, six remained in service* as tenders or harbour service vessels and were swiftly recommissioned and re-armed for service as quasi-monitors off the Belgian coast, as part of the Dover Patrol.

Bustard in particular had a late flowering, being prominent in several bombardments of the littoral, before becoming the last of the flat-irons to be retired, in 1916.†

COAST DEFENCE SHIPS

The invasion fears of the mid to late nineteenth century (noted in Chapter 1) called forth a number of Royal Navy ships which were purposely intended for coastal defence. The first of these might be said to be HMS *Prince Albert*, ready for service by 1866. She was an iron-built, shallow draught, low freeboard, turret ship armed with four 9in muzzle-loading rifles, one per turret, and displacing 3,880 tons. *Prince Albert* was specifically designated as for 'coast defence',[6] conceivably because of her extremely limited range, for she carried only sufficient coal for around 100 hours steaming in calm weather. For most of her life she was kept in reserve and was sold for breaking in 1899, long after she had ceased to be of any military value.

The Naval Estimates for the five years following *Prince Albert* all included monies for the construction of ten armoured vessels, all classified as only suitable for coastal defence. Seven of these became the *Cyclops*-class of coast defence monitors. These were breastwork monitors (i.e they had a raised armoured citadel above the hull) named *Cyclops*, *Gorgon*, *Hecate* and *Hydra*, all launched in 1871, together with *Magdala*, *Abyssinia* and *Cerberus*.

These craft mounted a pair of 10in rifled muzzle-loading guns in each of two turrets. Each shell weighed 407lbs while the gun itself weighed 18 long tons, and was credited with the ability to penetrate a nominal 12.9in of wrought iron armour at 100 yards range, formidable for the time. They were heavily armoured but two steam engines drove them at just 11 knots.

By the time they were completed (some five years after launch on average), however, the perceived need for them had passed and *Gorgon*, *Cyclops*, *Hecate* and *Hydra* were immediately placed in reserve, never leaving the Home station, while *Magdala* and *Abyssinia* went to India and *Cerberus* to the State Government of Victoria.

---

* These were *Ant, Blazer, Bloodhound, Bustard, Kite* and *Mastiff* (renamed *Snapper* in 1914).
† Other countries adopted the Rendel design in quantity, particularly the Netherlands and China.

HMS *Cyclops* (1871). (Author's collection)

The four English-based vessels were briefly reactivated during the Russo-Turkish War of 1878, but they were placed on the non-effective list in 1901 and sold for scrap in 1903.

Admiral George A Ballard, already met in this book, described them as 'full-armoured knights riding on donkeys'.[7] Their crews hated them, as their decks were frequently awash in even a moderate sea, and the accommodations were rated the worst in the fleet, referred to by ordinary seamen as 'ratholes with tinned air'.[8]

The coast defence turret ship HMS *Glatton* (1871), in a painting by William Frederick Mitchell (who usually signed his works as W Fred Mitchell). Her low freeboard is evident, and the single turret can be seen forward. (Author's collection)

The *Cyclops* class were followed by three ships which had no sisters nor shared any detail of design, except insomuch as they all had a single turret. These were *Glatton* (1871), with two 12in muzzle-loading rifled guns; *Hotspur* (1871) built as an armoured ram with a single 12in 25-ton muzzle-loading rifle and two 64pdr muzzle-loading rifles; and *Rupert* (1872), another armoured ram mounting two 10in 18-ton rifled muzzle-loading guns and two 64pdr smoothbores.

Again, these vessels spent little time in commission; *Rupert* served as guardship at Berehaven in 1888; *Hotspur* likewise at Holyhead in 1893. By 1907, all had been scrapped, the last being *Rupert*, which had latterly had been a guardship at the Royal Naval Dockyard in Bermuda, where she was sold. With her passing, the period in which a vessel suitable only for a passive war effort was regarded as being valuable to Britain ended.

However, it transpired that this was not quite the end of the use of coastal defence vessels in the Royal Navy. HMS *Glatton* and her sister ship *Gorgon* (both launched in 1914) were originally ordered as coastal defence ships for the Royal Norwegian Navy, as *Bjørgvin* and *Nidaros* respectively. Both were, however, requisitioned before being handed over to the Norwegians at the beginning of the war, but were not completed until 1918.

They displaced 5,746 tons at deep load, with a length of 310ft and a draught of 16ft 4in, and were powered by two vertical triple expansion steam engines, which developed a total of 4,000 ihp from four Yarrow water tube boilers, giving a maximum speed of 12 knots. Armament was two 9.2in guns arranged in two single gun turrets, one each fore and aft with a secondary battery of four six-inch guns, also in single-gun turrets, two of which superfired over the 9.2in turrets.

It was intended to use the vessels as monitors, but *Glatton* blew up at Dover on 16 September 1918, two weeks after she had been commissioned and before she could be put to use. *Gorgon*, commissioned in May 1918, survived the war, and to this strange Norwegian hybrid ship and her captain Commander Charles A Robertson-Scott, younger son of a major general, went the honour of firing the Dover Patrol's last shots of the war against the Germans on the occupied coast of Belgium in October 1918.

COASTAL DEFENCE IN OTHER REALMS

The Imperial German Navy also commissioned a number of coast defence vessels. The *Siegfried* class, launched between 1889 and 1893, comprised six ships armed with three 24cm (9.4in) and eight 8.8cm (3.5in) quick-firing guns together with four 35cm torpedo tubes. Their defined purpose was to protect the German coastline from naval attacks. They were obsolete by the outbreak of war, and saw only limited service in their intended role before

The German coast defence ship *Odin*, seen in a lithograph by Hugo Graf. (Creative Commons)

they were withdrawn from active duty. The ships then served in a variety of secondary duties, including barracks ships, target ships, and in the case of *Beowulf*, an icebreaker in the Baltic Sea. Nonetheless, all survived the war, to be sold or broken up in 1919 and 1920.

This class was followed by the *Odin*s, two ships *Odin* and *Ägir*, launched in 1894 and 1895. They had the same gunnery fit out as the preceding class, but only three torpedo tubes. The specific thinking behind their inception was that of guarding the entrances to the newly-opened Kiel canal. Again, they survived the war, and on 17 June 1919, both ships were struck from the naval register. They were sold to the A Bernstein Company in Hamburg who eventually had the ships rebuilt as freighters, but not before an attempt was made to sell them to the newly formed Polish Republic, which was guaranteed access to the sea at Puck (Putzig). If you have sea, you need a navy, and the firm of Leszczynski offered Poland two of the *Odin* and *Siegfried*-class vessels, an offer wisely rejected as being far too costly to maintain.

The k u k Kriegsmarine of the Austro-Hungarian Empire was largely concerned with defending the empire's 1,130 nautical miles of coastline in the Adriatic Sea. Austria had also dabbled in coastal defence ships. SMS *Kronprinz Erzherzog Rudolf* had been launched in 1887 as a local defence ship of 6,830 tons, armed with three 30.5cm (12in) and six 12cm (4.7in) guns. In 1914, she was based at Cattaro (now Kotor) Bay. And in 1895,

Austria launched the *Monarch* class of three coast defence ships, *Budapest*, *Monarch* and *Wein*, which when war came formed the 5th Battle Division but initially remained in reserve. They were of 5,785 tons displacement, with four 24cm (9.4in) in two pairs and six 15cm (5.9in) guns, with an assortment of smaller weapons.

Budapest and *Wien* were sent to Trieste in August 1917 to bombard Italian fortifications in the Gulf of Trieste. There were still there during the night of 9/10 December, at anchor in Trieste's harbour, and protected by heavy hawsers positioned as a boom across the mooring's entrance. Here they were subjected to a daring attack under cover of darkness by Italian MAS craft, small, wooden, torpedo-armed motor boats. Towed to their start line by two torpedo vessels, *MAS-9* and *MAS-13* crept up to the barrier and used hydraulic shears to cut the protective cables. Suddenly going to full power, *MAS-9* fired two torpedoes at *Wien*, hitting her amidships. *MAS-13* launched at *Budapest* but missed; nonetheless, both little craft were able to escape without harm. The attack blew a hole some 34ft wide abreast the boiler rooms. All of the watertight doors had been left open in *Wien* and the ship capsized in five minutes despite an attempt to counter her list by flooding the trim tanks on the opposite side. Forty-six crewmen died. As for the bold Italian commander, Luigi Rizzo, he was awarded the Gold Medal of Military Valour.

SMS *Wien* (1895), one of three Austrian *Monarch*-class coastal defence ships. She was sunk by *MAS-9* on 9 December 1917. (US Naval History and Heritage Command NH 88936)

France enjoyed a 40-year flirtation with coastal defence battleships, starting with *Taureau*, a 60m long ram with two 24cm (9.4in) 16-ton guns designed in 1865 and with a wooden hull. She was followed by four more armoured rams of the *Cerbere*-class, each displacing 2,720 tons and mounted the same weapons fit out. The 1870s saw two classes of two ships each, the *Tonnerre*s and the *Tempête*s. These were single turret vessels with a mostly steel hull and featuring a single turret forward of a tall narrow (2.4m wide) superstructure which theoretically allowed the guns to fire down the length of the ship to the stern. Reportedly, when attempted in *Tonnerre*, the shot blew away part of the forward superstructure.

In 1884, *Tonnant*, an essay at a larger ship, of 5,010 tons, was finally completed with a low freeboard tumblehome hull, and one barbette mounted 34cm (13.3in) gun in a barbette fore and aft. *Furieux* was laid down in 1878 and not completed until 1887. She displaced 5,925 tons, could manage 13 knots and had the same armament as her predecessor.

The French coastal defence battleship *Bouvines*, pictured in 1895, shortly after commissioning. (US Naval History and Heritage Command NH 88828)

The *Terrible* class of four was completed in the late 1880s. Of 7,530 tons and with two 42cm guns each in a single turret, they were followed by two more classes of two. *Jemappes* and *Valmy* mounted two 34cm guns and were laid down in 1890, while *Amiral Tréhouart* and *Bouvines* followed, mounting two 30.5cm (12in) and eight 10.2cm (4in) guns. Finally, there was *Henri IV*, with the innovation of a superfiring turret, a 13.8cm (5.4in) gun which fired above the aft 27.4cm (10.7in) single gun. Another 27.4cm weapon was fitted in the bow.

When war came only three of the coastal defence ships remained in service. *Henri IV* acted as a guard ship at Bizerte until early 1915 when she was sent to the Dardanelles and finally to Taranto as a depot ship. She was stricken in 1921. *Amiral Tréhouart* spent the war as a submarine depot ship and was sold for scrap in 1920. And *Bouvines*, already stricken in July 1913, was then utilised by the Inspection Service at Cherbourg between 1914 and 1917. She was condemned in 1918 and sold for scrap in 1920. Only *Henri IV* fired her guns in anger. And so ended France's line of coastal defence vessels.

Finally, in the early years of the submarine, all navies regarded them as primarily coast defence vessels. Fisher ordered more of the 'C' class when becoming First Sea Lord for exactly that purpose (see Chapter 3). When war came, the Royal Navy used the 'A' class (1902–05) for harbour defence duty, the 'B' class (1904–06) for local defence and in the Dardanelles (before paying all but one off in 1918), and the 'C' class for coastal defence at Leith, Harwich, Hartlepool, Grimsby and Dover. And when the US Navy entered the war in 1917, the US Naval Directory listed thirty-nine submarines of various types allocated to 'Coast Defence' on both Atlantic and Pacific seaboards.

16

In Conclusion

The war ended with an armistice, at 1100 on 11 November 1918. For Ernest Cooper 'flags soon came out, the bells began to ring and a few of us adjourned to the mayor's house and cracked some bottles of fizz'.[1] Georgina Lee and her husband went for dinner with friends; the men wore morning dress. At Harwich, Reginald Tyrwhitt, now a rear admiral, held a celebratory dinner for his ships' captains. Freed at last from their collegiate vow of abstinence, taken in sympathy with George V, they drank wine described as 'Kaiser, 1918 (bottled in Holland)'.

Britain's coasts were once more relieved from the threat of invasion, raid or attack. But that fear had certainly been real and drove policy decisions at many levels. As historian Correlli Barnett has written, 'throughout the war, British military deployment abroad was affected by the presumed danger of invasion at home'.[2] Men and equipment were kept in Britain when desperately needed on the Western Front and elsewhere.

Lloyd George, who as prime minister had tried to restrict the flow of men to the Western Front at the beginning of 1918 (see Chapter 12), claimed in his very self-serving memoir that he had not been to blame for retaining men to guard against invasion. 'It had been said that I was responsible for keeping masses of men at home because of my "obsession" as to the danger of a German invasion. I have never entertained such a fear. In fact, I always regarded it as a bogey, invented by those who wanted to establish permanent conscription.'[3] This is patent nonsense. Conscription came in spring 1916; he was not war minister until July that year, and became prime minister in December. In both those positions, conscription was an established fact when he took the post. And in 1910, Lloyd George had offered the Unionists conscription as a sop in his stillborn plan for a coalition after the 1910 general election.

The invasion concern didn't end with the war. Anti-invasion batteries were still being built in 1921, when the Tyne Turrets were commissioned. These were two 12in Mk VIII guns taken from the pre-dreadnought battleship HMS *Illustrious* (1896) and installed in Roberts Battery at Hartley, near Seaton Sluice north of the Tyne, and Kitchener Battery in Marsden, near Lizard Point south of the river. The positions had been planned during the war but were not completed until three years after its conclusion, only

The *Majestic*-class battleship HMS *Illustrious* (1896) photographed before 1902. Armed with four 12in and twelve 6in guns, she was paid off at the end of 1915 and two of her 12in guns were used in the Tyne Turrets.
(US Naval History and Heritage Command NH 60117)

to be scrapped in 1925 as a cost-saving measure. When built they were rivalled in power only by the Dover harbour Admiralty Pier Turret (see Chapter 1).

So what, if any, were the German intentions at the beginning of the war?

German Invasion Planning

In February 1896, Captain Baron von Lüttwitz of the General Staff published an article wherein he claimed that 'the unassailableness of England is legend',[4] by which he meant that England's coasts were capable of being invaded. This may be taken as the start point of German military thinking about the possibilities of invasion.

The first formal plan was conceived in 1897 by Admiral Eduard von Knorr, commander of the Imperial German Navy, against a background of increasing Anglo-German rivalry and German naval expansion, which was amplified by the passage of the First Naval Law of 1898. Recognising the inferiority of the small German fleet, his concept called for a pre-emptive strike against the Royal Navy to establish temporary naval supremacy. This would be followed by an immediate landing before British naval reinforcements could be rushed from the Mediterranean and elsewhere.

In refining the proposals, his staff decided that the shortest possible sea-crossing would be necessary for success, which would entail the seizure of port facilities in Belgium and the Netherlands to embark the expeditionary force. Reconnaissance of the English east coast was completed and potential landing sites were selected. These avoided the heavily-defended area south of Dover, and included Flamborough Head, the Humber estuary below Grimsby, Lincolnshire, the East Anglian coast from Great Yarmouth, Norfolk, to Southwold and the Suffolk coast from Southwold to Orford Ness. (And so the good burghers of Southwold were right to be apprehensive when war came!)

On 31 May, the operation was presented to the Kaiser. It called for a sudden strike against the Thames to disrupt England's coastal trade and destroy her reserve fleet, and then the rapid transportation of an invasion force across the Channel. Comments were invited from Alfred von Schlieffen, Chief of the German General Staff, who stated that an invasion was impractical. His staff suggested that it would require up to 320,000 troops to defeat the British home defences and capture London, and that a quick victory would be necessary if the expeditionary force was not to be cut off and forced to surrender. Nor did Admiral Alfred von Tirpitz, State Secretary of the German Imperial Naval Office, support the proposal. He thought the fleet and the German merchant marine were both too small to carry out such a plan. As a result, the planning was paused and finally shelved in 1899.

However, Britain's travails in the Boer War produced a window of opportunity with most of the army committed to winning the conflict in South Africa, leaving only four battalions of the regular army at home by March 1900. Lieutenant General Colmar Baron von der Goltz, commander of the Engineer Corps of the army, saw in this an opportunity to gain temporary naval superiority and launch an invasion. His stratagem, submitted at the end of March, involved the use of a fleet of barges towed by tugs to convey an invasion force. However, this was not considered feasible by the Great General Staff and was not pursued.

Nonetheless, such ideas coincided with the expansion of the docks at Emden which would allow for the embarkation of some 300,000 men, if required. And as a form of practice, Germany ran several amphibious landing exercises in 1901, the largest of which involved disembarking 1,700 marines. That same year, a German staff officer produced a paper detailing how an expeditionary force of one cavalry and four infantry divisions might live off the land, destroy the British defensive army and capture London. It was not taken forwards.

But invasion planning was resumed during the Balkan conflict of 1912–13. Kaiser Wilhelm 'ordered the General Staff and the Admiralty Staff to work out an invasion of England in a grand style',[5] and as late as 1914, 'the German Navy was approached by the former director of the Treptow Observatory* with a scheme to transport troops to Britain with underwater wagons across the seabed'.[6] But the fact remains, Germany had no formal strategies for an invasion of Britain when war came.

British fears were, however, very real, and fanned by parliamentarians, books, newspapers, *et al.* DORA prohibited any informed debate and so fear and rumour did their work. Moreover, until late in 1914 the government allowed no reporting of the progress of the war, neither were journalists permitted in the war zone. The people were fed a diet of propaganda and half-truths. William Pead was a wealthy brewer in Litchfield. In early August he observed that 'everyone is eager to buy papers in which we find little war news and what there is is mostly unreliable'. Four days into the war, Pead noted that the 'usual foolish rumours were rife [of] great naval victories and a German invasion of Scotland'.[7]

It was not until May 1915 that accredited reporters were allowed at the Front. Once terror has been inculcated, it is hard to overcome it. And so, the population believed invasion was imminent right up to the end of the war. And a subjugated nation is a compliant one.

Espionage

Spy mania was both the cause of and the product of fearfulness. As a result, many innocent people were traumatised through false arrest or accusation, and internment was the fate of people who came from German or Austrian backgrounds. But German espionage, despite all the furore, made little headway in Britain.

At the beginning of the war, police and the SSB rounded up all the agents they were aware of. As a result, no German agent was able to, for example, send information about the timing of the departure of the BEF. This irritated the Kaiser beyond measure, as Gustav Steinhauer, the head of the British section of German Naval Intelligence, later acknowledged. 'Apparently unable to believe his ears, [he] raved and stormed for the better part of two hours about the incompetence of his so-called intelligence officers, bellowing: "Am I surrounded by dolts? Why was I not told? Who is responsible?" And more in the same vein.'[8] German sources demonstrate that at least 120 spies were sent to Britain.[9] SSB/MI5 caught sixty-five of them. Nineteen were sentenced to death.

---

* Now the Archenhold Observatory.

Furthermore, good protective security meant that it was difficult for any espionage agents to act with freedom, unlike in America, where the 'Black Tom' explosion of 30 July 1916 saw German spies blow up $20 million of military supplies. Britain remained thankfully free of such incidents.

Spy fever was real, but espionage was limited.

The Committee for Imperial Defence

The Committee for Imperial Defence played a pivotal role in preparing Britain for war and possible invasion. Indeed, the CID studied the concept of the invasion of Britain on at least five separate occasions between 1902 and 1914, and Balfour, who created it, was pleased with his creation. When he left office at the end of 1905, he felt concern for its future under a Liberal government and travelled to Balmoral specifically to lobby the king, his advisors and Haldane to protect it.

The CID did survive and thrived under the guidance of successive secretaries, Clarke and, especially, Hankey. Even when out of office, Balfour could not resist its lures. In 1912, Haldane asked him to join the CID permanently. Balfour regarded that as politically inexpedient. But he did submit to the blandishments of Secretary for War Colonel John 'Jack' Seeley and join a subcommittee of the CID looking once more at invasion. On 7 October 1914, at the first meeting of the CID in wartime, Balfour was asked to become a permanent member, an invitation that this time he accepted.

When Lloyd George came to power in December 1916, he created a War Cabinet, which mimicked many of the functions of the CID and whose secretary was once again the indefatigable Maurice Hankey.

German Coastal Raids

The Imperial Navy made twenty gunnery attacks on British towns (see Appendix 16). Their initial purpose was to draw a portion of the Grand Fleet out, which could then be defeated in detail. The terror and death inflicted on the citizens of the target communities was a by-product of this stratagem, and for Germany a not unwelcome one. It suited German designs that invasion fear should lead to the retention of soldiers in Britain. The less in the theatres of fighting, the better. If their coastal raids helped spread the contagion it was all to their good. Their tactics failed, however, owing to the appliance of science. The Y-system and Room 40 were always able to alert the Grand Fleet as to German intentions.

Scarborough was considered at the time a most heinous attack, as it was an undefended port and thus protected by the Hague Convention. In 2010, local archaeologist Bob Clarke asserted that the Germans were justified in attacking the town as the castle had long been associated with coastal guns, especially as Burniston Barracks had been constructed specifically with artillery in mind, and that there was a wireless station in the town. It remains a moot point.

As it transpired, it was the invasion of the air by Zeppelins and Gotha bombers which produced the most damage and casualties. Against this Britain had constructed no defences, and anti-air counter mechanisms had to be hastily improvised.

Apart from Hartlepool and Walney Island, coastal artillery fortifications hardly fired their weapons in anger. As this became apparent, men and guns were taken away from them and the soldiers replaced with men unfit for service at the front owing to age or injury. The heavy investment in fortresses proved to be unnecessary, except perhaps to calm pre-war public opinion. It proved a largely fruitless posting for the TF RGA gunners as well. As one fortress commander wrote to his men after the armistice; 'the general officer commanding wishes to convey his thanks to all ranks who . . . who have manned the coast defences of the port for a period of four years and four months. The duty has been hard and monotonous, *and has not been relieved by the interest of repelling a hostile attack*.'*[10]

But it will never be known whether the mere existence of the coastal fortifications helped create an anti-invasion mindset amongst German planners.

Fighting a War in Europe

This book has detailed how British war planning shifted from reliance on naval force and a small armed force, 'a projectile to be fired by the navy', to a Continental commitment, conscription, and a mass army. Around 1900, Prime Minister Lord Salisbury said to those in the War Office who were pushing for a larger army 'our army will not find itself in that condition [fighting a major foe] in a blue moon; what they ought to practise is the rapid expedition of a relatively small force to any point in the empire where it might be wanted. Your business is that of a military fire brigade.'[11] As Professor Ian Beckett has noted, 'pre-war assumptions had dictated that a future war would be short and that Britain would adopt the "business as usual" approach of a limited maritime commitment resting principally on a naval blockade'.[12]

Yet by 1914, Lord Kitchener was calling for a million-man army. It has been argued many times that this European commitment was a mistake and that the slaughter on the Western Front might have been avoided by Fisher's Baltic plans, Churchill's Turkish war, or Lloyd George's preference for attacking through Italy or Salonica.

---

* Author's italics for emphasis.

Many, Fisher included, believed that Germany could be defeated by the use of Britain's maritime power to impose a complete blockade on Germany, physical and economic, which would bring her to her knees without the need for a confrontation on land. But this required an amphibious army to secure choke points and offshore bases and attack maritime targets. The Army General Staff absolutely refused to join in that debate and the civilian leadership did not challenge them. As Professor Andrew Lambert has written, this was in part because 'the Anglo-French staff talks linked to the soldiers' preferred strategy of dispatching a small army to France, helping to sustain the Anglo-French Entente of 1904, which promised in turn to preserve peace'.[13] And after declaring war, four civilian ministers – Asquith, Grey, Haldane and Churchill – together with Kitchener, and with no other Cabinet member present, met with nine army generals and just one admiral, Battenberg, the First Sea Lord, and were unwilling to challenge the soldiers' declarations that Germany could only be beaten on land. Indeed Churchill, who should have argued the navalist case, was gung-ho for the commitment. All, except Kitchener, expected a short war. The result was that the two armed services were separated and left fighting two different wars.

Once involved in a Continental war, Britain had to double-down for if Germany would have triumphed, her borders would be the English Channel and the Atlantic coasts. At that point invasion would have been both possible and likely, and Britain could in turn have been both blockaded and defeated. A land war, however horrible it turned out to be, was unavoidable. The navy's preferred strategy was impossible without army support and required the closure of the Baltic to impose a full blockade on German imports of critical war supplies such as iron ore and ball bearings. Churchill and Asquith would not acquiesce in this, for fear of offending the Scandinavian neutrals and, indeed, Asquith and Churchill prevented Fisher's papers on the subject from being circulated at the War Council.

As a result, Britain threw away her source of advantage and millions of young British men became casualties of war.

Volunteerism

The time immediately before and after the start of the war was the heyday of volunteerism. From the TF and the RNVR to the plethora of volunteer quasi-militias and armed bands, men, boys and women put others before themselves and volunteered for a myriad of duties. There had been other periods of enthusiastic amateurs, such as the Napoleonic wars and the invasion scares of the mid to late nineteenth century, but 1914–18 was surely peak volunteer.

Coastal defence was high on the list of tasks undertaken by these part-time soldiers and sailors. From TF RGA gunners to boy scouts to 'grandfather scouts', patrolling the cliff tops, watching the beaches, and waiting for the enemy invasion to appear filled many a waking hour. The whole country seemed to be in arms against incursion although, as has been seen here, in fact not everyone embraced the selflessness concept. On Red Clydeside, in the docks, in the mines, there was still opposition to the war, to women being employed in 'men's jobs' and an increasingly Bolshevik undertone of discontent. But overall, the nation stepped forwards with an eagerness to serve. It was the age of self-sacrifice.

The Royal Navy

Did the navy fulfil the expectations of it with regard to home defence? If the question is looked at from the point of view of the average citizen of a coastal town, say Scarborough or Hartlepool, the answer must be 'no'. It did not prevent attacks in which innocent members of the public died, nor did it catch and punish the perpetrators. The 'sure shield' proved not so sure. And indeed, the configuration adopted by the Grand Fleet, remaining in the far north at Scapa and then later Rosyth, mitigated against it ever being able to protect the littoral. As has been seen, the plan was more to intercept the German fleet after it had made its attack.

But if we ask a different question, 'did the Royal Navy play a pivotal part in winning the war', the answer must be 'yes'. The day-to-day grind of blockade and interdiction of blockade runners bound for Germany played a key role in breaking German domestic morale. (And this might have happened sooner if Fisher's Baltic plan had been taken up.) Once convoy was adopted, the German U-boat campaign was broken, and U-boats sunk in quantity. The bottling-up of the German fleet meant that it was never able to cut loose amongst Britain's colonial possessions and divert attention from the Western Front. And although it was a close thing for a few months of 1917, Britain always maintained command of the seas, at home and globally. Food, equipment, soldiers from the Empire or the USA were never prevented from reaching Britain or France.

It is also appropriate to note the pre-war role of Jacky Fisher in readying the navy for the coming conflict and in successfully predicting some of the form it would take. As journalist and author Harold Begbie observed 'no man I have ever met gave me so authentic a feeling of originality as this daredevil of genius, this pirate of public life, who more than any other Englishman saved British democracy from a Prussian domination'.[14]

Envoi

No invasion came; and the damage caused by German bombardment of coastal towns, although hurtful to pride, was not significant. It was never the intention of the German General Staff to invade Britain, although the threat of it tied up many forces on the Home Front which might otherwise have been used elsewhere. And, of course, the British anti-invasion measures put in place were probably a deterrent to the concept. The defence of the British coast, although haphazard and somewhat reactive, worked out in the end.

There is, however, a lesson for today to be drawn. Our coasts are once more undefended and our navy tiny. Our vulnerabilities are of a different kind to 1914, however. As journalist and naval expert Ian Ballantyne has written, 'in fact, the biggest damage may come via sabotage attacks on the undersea infrastructure deeply embedded in our everyday lives and fundamental to national security and prosperity. It could be a devastating blow, causing suffering for millions of people.'[15] Coastal defence, and the defence of our connection to the outside world, is still a vital strategic need.

There is a strange circularity of debate, now vs then. In July 2023, the Conservative government announced its latest 'Defence Command Paper'. This reduced the army to its lowest post-war level ever of 73,000 fully trained men by 2025. It also aimed to 'inspire youth' and increase the number of army cadets in schools from 135,000 young people to just under 200,000 amateur, underage potential soldiers. The associated press release claimed that the intention was to create an UK Global Response Force that will enable forces to 'get there first'. So once again, the strategy of government seems to be a small, 'projectable' professional army with a volunteer force for home defence. But this time, we have virtually no navy to defend our shores or, indeed, to guarantee the transfer of this small army to wherever it was intended to go in time of strife.

In the 1914 July Royal Review at Spithead, the Royal Navy fielded over 200 war vessels, including twenty-four dreadnoughts and battlecruisers, twenty-five pre-dreadnoughts and eighteen large cruisers; moreover, this total excluded vessels stationed in far places – and it was nowhere near enough for the war they had to fight. According to the 2021 version of the Defence Command Paper, the navy's Type 23 frigates will be replaced by three new types of frigate – Type 26 anti-submarine ships, general purpose Type 31s, and Type 32s and the aim is for the UK to have more than twenty destroyers and frigates by 2030.

But as the chair of the House of Commons Defence Committee, Tobias Ellwood, told MPs in July 2023, 'at the time of the Gulf War in 1990, the Royal Navy had fifty-one frigates and destroyers and today it has just eighteen'.[16] In any case, these promised frigates are only politicians' promises, and therefore worth little.

Furthermore, on 21 January 2024, the *Sunday Times* reported former

Defence Secretary Penny Mordaunt, herself a naval reservist, as saying that 'the future Royal Navy must be able to continue to secure our interests, which are entirely predicated on being able to thwart efforts to deny us access to the seas in certain parts of the world . . . we must not just ask ourselves by how much Russia and China are increasing their fleets, but why'.

What of the spirit of volunteerism? In early 2024 there was an outcry when General Sir Patrick Sanders, the Chief of the Defence Staff, suggested that people of appropriate age should be prepared to join a citizen army in case of war with Russia. This brought opprobrium, especially from the so-called Generation Z (loosely, those born between 1997 and 2012). According to *The Spectator* of 13 February that year, typical statements made were 'I love not dying' and 'yes, I'd be called a coward if I didn't fight but what use is it being a hero if you are dead'? More justifiably perhaps, others said that 'I'd rather die fighting my own government', and 'I couldn't fight for the people who are currently representing our country', and one MP was quoted as saying that 'when you look at the mess that is modern politicians, why on earth should people want to put their life on the line for the likes of us?' Quite where the country would be had these attitudes been prevalent in 1914 beggars belief.

Finally, there is a resonance today with regard to DORA. The Defence of the Realm Act imposed limits on the nation's freedoms in an unprecedented manner and arrogated to government rights that it had never before held. Fear was deployed to reinforce the limitation of individual freedoms and compulsory removal of property; fear of invasion, fear of Zeppelins, fear in general, and all reinforced by the press. Meanwhile censorship supressed any debate.

Over 100 years on and we saw exactly the same tactics deployed by the government to instil fear in the population, and hence gain compliance, under its draconian and destructive lockdowns of 2020 and 2021. Terror was weaponised, discussion suppressed, the intelligence services used to track dissenters' behaviour, the police turned against the citizenry; even sex was banned (a prohibition which the banners themselves ignored). But unlike in the time of DORA, Britain was not at war. And yet the population largely accepted government lies and half-truths.

What does all this say about Britons now? Are we still willing to defend our shores? And our freedoms?

Author's Notes

This is my fourteenth book of naval history and I hope it has given you, the reader, enjoyment. *Spectre of Invasion* was a pleasure to write and, as always, thanks are due to a select group of people for their assistance and advice in the preparation of it.

Julian Mannering, Managing Editor of Seaforth Publishing, both came up with the proto-concept and commissioned me to write it. I am grateful to him for the opportunity.

I owe thanks to G A Michael Sims for permission to quote from the letters of his great-grandfather, Alfred Turner. Roger J C Thomas of English Heritage pointed me to some useful source material for the book and I appreciate both his time and his advice.

Research was aided by The Special Collections Unit of the Library of Leeds University, who were most helpful, and as usual The National Archives at Kew and the Imperial War Museum in London proved fertile hunting grounds. At the Churchill Archives in Cambridge, I once again received prompt and efficient assistance from Alan Packwood and his team.

American picture archives are more generous than British ones and many images are provided free of charge, a benefit to authors not granted by any British picture repository. I offer my gratitude to the Library of Congress in Washington DC and the US Naval History and Heritage Command at the Washington Navy Yard for their help in this regard.

Peter Wilkinson produced his usual excellent map and Janet Andrew devised the index.

Finally, my thanks go to Vivienne, without whose support my task would be immeasurably more difficult.

Most books contain imperfections of commission or omission. If there are errors or solecisms in this volume the fault is mine alone and I should like to hear of them.

Steve R Dunn, Worcestershire, 2025

Appendix 1

The Major Saxon Shore Forts (late fourth century AD)

Branodunum (Brancaster, Norfolk)
Gariannonum (Burgh Castle, Norfolk)
Othona (Bradwell-on-Sea, Essex)
Regulbium (Reculver, Kent)
Rutupiae (Richborough, Kent)
Dubris (Dover Castle, Kent)
Portus Lemanis (Lympne, Kent)
Anderitum (Pevensey Castle, East Sussex)
Portus Adurni (Portchester Castle, Hampshire)

Appendix 2
Cinque Port Benefits

Exemption from tax and tallage
Rights of sac and soc (jurisdiction over criminal and civil cases within their liberties)
Rights of toll and team (authority over the sale or passage of cattle and other property within their liberties)
Rights of bloodwit and fledwit (authority to punish shedders of blood, and those seized in an attempt to escape justice)
Rights of pillory and tumbril (authority to punish delinquents)
Rights of infangthief and outfangthief (authority to imprison or execute thieves or other felons)
The right of mundbryce (the right to enter private property in order to erect banks or dikes as a defence against the sea)
Rights of waifs and strays (the right to appropriate unclaimed property and stray animals)
Rights of flotsam, jetsam and ligan (the right to appropriate the debris and cargo of wrecked ships)

In summary, they were granted a degree of self-government, legal jurisdiction, and pecuniary advantage.

Appendix 3
The Henrician Castles

Brownsea Castle	Poole Harbour	1545–7
East Cowes Castle	Isle of Wight	1539–42
Sandown Castle	Isle of Wight	1545
Sharpenode Bulwark	Isle of Wight	1545–7
St Helens Bulwark	Isle of Wight	1539–45
West Cowes Castle	Isle of Wight	1539–40
Worsleys Castle	Isle of Wight	1522–5
Yarmouth Castle	Isle of Wight	1545
Calshot Castle	Hampshire	1539–40
Hurst Castle	Hampshire	1541–4
Netley Castle	Hampshire	1542–5
St Andrews Castle	Hampshire	1543–4
Southsea Castle	Hampshire	1538–4
Sandsfoot Castle	Dorset	1541
Portland Castle	Dorset	1539–40
Camber Castle	Sussex	1513–43
Deal Castle	Kent	1539
Sandgate Castle	Kent	1539–40
Sandown Castle	Kent	1539–40
Walmer Castle	Kent	1539
Gravesend Blockhouse	Kent	1539
Higham Blockhouse	Kent	1539
Milton Blockhouse	Kent	1539
East Tilbury Blockhouse	Essex	1539–41
West Tilbury Blockhouse	Essex	1539
Pendennis Castle	Cornwall	1540–5
Little Dennis Blockhouse	Cornwall	1537–40
St Mawes Castle	Cornwall	1540–5
St Catherine's Castle	Cornwall	1538–40
Devils Point Artillery Tower	Devon	1537–9

Appendix 4
Major Unit Distribution by Station c. 1898

Battleships and cruisers combined

Home 15
Mediterranean 38
China 27
East Indies 10
Australia 16
Cape and West Africa 20
South America 4
Pacific 9
North America and West Indies 15

(Source: Ferguson, *Empire*, p 246)

Appendix 5
The Home Defence Squadrons in 1900

Major Vessels
<u>The Channel Squadron:</u> renamed The Channel Fleet in 1901.
5 battleships and The Cruiser Squadron

<u>The Coast Guard</u>; unofficially termed 'The Home Fleet' when mobilised for summer manoeuvres. Renamed The Home Fleet in 1903.
9 battleships, dispersed around the coast and 4 cruisers

Appendix 6
Types of Gun Recommended by the Owen Committee

9.2in BL gun (Early)
: The early 9.2in of 22 tons came in Marks I–VII. Operational from 1881 until 1918. Maximum effective range of 10,000 yards.

9.2in BL gun (Later)
: The later 9.2in of 22 tons came in Marks IX and X. Operational from 1899 until 1957. Maximum effective range of 29,200 yards.

6in BL gun (Early)
: The 6in gun of 5 tons came in Mark II–IV. Operational from 1880 until 1905. Maximum effective range of 10,000 yards.

6in BL gun (Later)
: The 6in BL gun. This gun came in Marks V–VII and became one of the most widely deployed guns of this calibre. Operational from 1899 until 1957. Maximum effective range of 11,600 yards. One hundred and three of the Mk VII type were deployed around the British coast.

4.7-inch QF gun
: The 4.7in Quick Fire (QF) in Marks I–IV. Operational from 1887 until 1920. Maximum effective range of 10,000 yards.

12pdr QF gun
: The 12pdr 12-cwt QF gun was introduced in 1894 and manufactured by Armstrong Whitworth, Elswick. Over 8,000 of the guns were built and remained in service until after 1945. Maximum effective range of 11,750 yards.

Appendix 7
UK Coastal Artillery 1914

Source: Maurice-Jones, *History of Coast Artillery in the British Army*, pp 185ff

Defences	Defended Port	Batteries	Armament
East Coast	Thames Medway	Sheerness	6 9.2in 6 6in 4 4.7in 6 12pdr
		Slough Fort	2 9.2in 2 6in
		Coalhouse Fort	4 6in
Harwich Coast	Harwich	Landguard Fort	2 6in 2 4.7in
		Harwich	2 6in 2 4.7in
South-eastern Coast	Dover Newhaven	Dover	5 9.2in 6 6in 5 12pdr
		Newhaven	2 6in
North-eastern	Tyne Tees Hartlepool Humber	Tyne	2 9.2in 6 6in 3 6in
		Tees	4 6in 4 6in 2 4.7in
		Hartlepool	3 6in
		Humber	4 6in 4 4.7in
Southern Coast	Portsmouth Portland & Gosport	Portsmouth	2 9.2in 2 6in 20 12pdr
		Isle of Wight	12 9.2in 9 6in 3 12pdr
		Spithead Forts	8 6in 2 4.7in
		Hurst & Calshot Castles	2 4.7in 8 12pdr
		Portland	6 9.2in 10 6in 8 12pdr

Defences	Defended Port	Batteries	Armament	
South-western	Plymouth	Plymouth	8	9.2in
	Falmouth		13	6in
			3	4.7in
			15	12pdr
		Falmouth	4	6in
North-western	Mersey	Mersey	6	6in
	Barrow		2	4.7in
		Barrow	2	6in
	Milford Haven	Milford Haven	4	9.2in
	Cardiff		6	6in
	Barry		8	12pdr
	Swansea	Cardiff	4	6in
		Barry	2	6in
		Swansea	2	4.7in
Scottish Coast	Forth	Forth	6	9.2in
	Clyde		12	6in
	Tay		14	4.7in & 4in
	Aberdeen		12	12pdr
	Scapa Flow	Clyde	4	6in
			4	4.7in
		Tay	2	6in
			2	4.7in
		Aberdeen	2	4.7in
		Scapa Flow	None mounted	
North Irish Coast	Lough Swilly	Lough Swilly	2	9.2in
	Belfast		2	6in
		Belfast	4	6in
South Irish Coast	Queenstown	Queenstown	4	9.2in
	Berehaven		6	6in
			8	12pdr
		Berehaven	2	9.2in
			6	6in
			2	4.7in
			8	12pdr
Channel Islands	Jersey	Jersey	6in	
	Guernsey		4.7in	
	Alderney	Guernsey	6in	
		Alderney	6in	
		Jersey	12pdr	

Appendix 8
Comparative Naval Expenditure 1900–1913

In local currencies, indexed 1900 expenditure = 100

Year	Britain	France	Russia	Germany
1900	100	100	100	100
1905	110	85	120	148
1910	135	99	93	260
1913	162	136	235	287

(Derived from data in Stanglini and Cosentino, *The French Fleet*, p 309)

Appendix 9
Fleet Distribution 1907, 1909, 1912; Heavy Ships Only

The journey to concentration.

March 1907–March 1909
The Channel Fleet; the fully-manned battle fleet in home waters, merged in March 1909 with the Home Fleet and became the 2nd Division, Home Fleet.
14 battleships
1st Cruiser Squadron

The Home Fleet; Merged in March 1909 with the Channel Fleet and became the 1st Division, Home Fleet. Dreadnoughts allocated to the Nore as being the nearest base for the North Sea. Ships in the Nore Division had full crews, and the others had $\frac{3}{5}$th crews.
<u>Nore Division</u>
7 battleships plus HMS Dreadnought, to which were added battlecruisers in 1908.
5th Cruiser Squadron
<u>Portsmouth Division</u>; split between 3rd and 4th Divisions.
5 battleships
<u>Devonport Division</u>; split between 3rd and 4th Divisions.
3 battleships
4th Cruiser Squadron undertakes training cruises to West Indies.

The Atlantic Fleet; its role was to act as reinforcement for either the Channel Fleet or the Mediterranean Fleet.
8 battleships
2nd Cruiser Squadron

The Mediterranean Fleet
6 battleships
3rd Cruiser Squadron

March 1909–April 1912

All ships in home waters were grouped into a single fleet – the Home Fleet. Within that fleet there were two levels of availability. The ships of the 1st and 2nd Divisions were fully operational, while those of the 3rd and 4th Divisions were partially manned. The Atlantic Fleet and Mediterranean Fleet continued as separate entities.

The Home Fleet
1st Division; became 1st Battle Squadron in June 1912.
7 dreadnoughts
1st Cruiser Squadron
1st Destroyer Flotilla
2nd Division – became 2nd Battle Squadron in June 1912.
10 pre-dreadnoughts
2nd Cruiser Squadron
2nd Destroyer Flotilla
3rd/4th Divisions; administered by a single flag officer of Vice Admiral rank.
Nore
8 pre-dreadnoughts
Portsmouth
4 pre-dreadnoughts
Devonport
3–7 pre-dreadnoughts
also
4th Cruiser Squadron; continued cruises to West Indies.
The Atlantic Fleet; became 3rd Battle Squadron April 1912.
7 pre-dreadnoughts
5th Cruiser Squadron
The Mediterranean Fleet; became 4th Battle Squadron April 1912.
6 pre-dreadnoughts
6th Cruiser Squadron

Appendix 10
Distribution of Destroyers and Submarines, 1909

Home Fleet
Destroyer Flotillas 1–2 stationed with Home Fleet 1st and 2nd Divisions.
Destroyer Flotillas 4–6 stationed at Nore, Portsmouth, Devonport.
Nore Submarine Flotilla, split into III and VII Submarine Flotillas.
Portsmouth Submarine Flotilla, split into II and IV Submarine Flotillas,
V Submarine Flotilla formed as training unit (1910).
Devonport Submarine Flotilla, split into I Flotilla and VI Flotilla (training unit).

Atlantic Fleet
None assigned

Mediterranean Fleet
Destroyer Flotilla, replaced by 5th Destroyer Flotilla in 1911.

Appendix 11
Guard Ships Deployed as at January 1915

Battleships:
Hannibal (1896), *Illustrious* (1896), *Jupiter* (1895), *Magnificent* (1894), *Majestic* (1895), *Victorious* (1895).

Cruisers:
Brilliant (1891), *Diadem* (1896), *Hermione* (1893, also used simultaneously as a depot ship), *Sirius* (1890), *Wallaroo* (1890).

Appendix 12
The Consolidated DORA Act of November 1914

An Act to consolidate and amend the Defence of the Realm Acts. 27th November 1914.

Be it enacted by the King's most Excellent Majesty, by and with the advice and consent of the Lords Spiritual and Temporal, and Commons, in this present Parliament assembled, and by the authority of the same, as follows:-

1. – (1) His Majesty in Council has power during the continuance of the present war to issue regulations for securing the public safety and defence of the realm, and as to the powers and duties for that purpose of the Admiralty and Army Council and of the members of His Majesty's forces and other persons acting on his behalf; and may by such regulations authorise the trial by courts-martial, or in the case of minor offences by courts of summary jurisdiction, and punishment of persons committing offences against the regulations and in particular against any of the provisions of such regulations designed:-

(a) to prevent persons communicating with the enemy or obtaining information for that purpose or any purpose calculated to jeopardise the success of the operations of any of His Majesty's forces or the forces of his allies or to assist the enemy; or

(b) to secure the safety of His Majesty's forces and ships and the safety of any means of communication and of railways, ports, and harbours; or

(c) to prevent the spread of false reports or reports likely to cause disaffection to His Majesty or to interfere with the success of His Majesty's forces by land or sea or to prejudice His Majesty's relations with foreign powers; or

(d) to secure the navigation of vessels in accordance with directions given by or under the authority of the Admiralty; or

(e) otherwise to prevent assistance being given to the enemy or the successful prosecution of the war being endangered.

(2) Any such regulations may provide for the suspension of any restrictions on the acquisition or user of land, or the exercise of the power of making byelaws, or any other power under the Defence Acts, 1842 to 1875, or the Military Lands Acts, 1891 to 1903, and any such regulations or any orders made thereunder affecting the pilotage of vessels may supersede any enactment, order, charter, byelaw, regulation or provision as to pilotage.

(3) It shall be lawful for the Admiralty or Army Council -

(a) to require that there shall be placed at their disposal the whole or any part of the output of any factory or workshop in which arms, ammunition, or warlike stores or equipment, or any articles required for the production thereof, are manufactured;
(b) to take possession of and use for the purpose of His Majesty's naval or military service any such factory or workshop or any plant thereof;
and regulations und this Act may be made accordingly.
(4) For the purpose of the trial of a person for an offence under the regulations by court-martial and the punishment thereof, the person may be proceeded against and dealt with as if he were a person subject to military law and had on active service committed an offence under section five of the Army Act:
Provided that where it is proved that the offence is committed with the intention of assisting the enemy a person convicted of such an offence by a court-martial shall be liable to suffer death.
(5) For the purpose of the trial of a person for an offence under the regulations by a court of summary jurisdiction and the punishment thereof, the offence shall be deemed to have been committed either at the place in which the same actually was committed or in any place in which the offender may be, and the maximum penalty which may be inflicted shall be imprisonment with or without had labour for a term of six months or a fine of one hundred pounds, or both such imprisonment and fine; section seventeen of the Summary Jurisdiction Act, 1879, shall not apply to charges of offences against the regulations, but any person aggrieved by a conviction of a court of summary jurisdiction may appeal in England to a court of quarter sessions, and in Scotland under and in terms of the Summary Jurisdiction (Scotland) Acts, and in Ireland in manner provided by the Summary Jurisdiction (Ireland) Acts.
(6) The regulations may authorise a court-martial or court of summary jurisdiction, in addition to any other punishment, to order the forfeiture of any goods in respect of which an offence against the regulations has been committed.
2. – (1) This Act may be cited as the Defence of the Realm Consolidation Act, 1914.
(2) The Defence of the Realm Act, 1914, and the Defence of the Realm (No. 2) Act, 1914, are hereby repealed, but nothing in this repeal shall affect any Orders in Council made thereunder, and all such Orders in Council shall, until altered or revoked by an Order in Council under this Act, continue in force and have effect as if made under this Act.

(Source: MUN 5/19/221/8, TNA)

Appendix 13
Chapter I of Convention No 9, Second Hague Conference

I. The bombardment by naval forces of undefended ports, towns, villages, dwellings or buildings is forbidden.

A place may not be bombarded solely on the ground that automatic submarine contact mines are anchored off the harbour.

II. Military works, military or naval establishments, depots of arms or war material, workshops or plant which could be utilised for the needs of the hostile fleet or army, and ships of war in the harbour, are not, however, included in this prohibition. The commander of a naval force may destroy them with artillery, after a summons followed by a reasonable interval of time, if all other means are impossible, and when the local authorities have not themselves destroyed them within the time fixed.

The commander incurs no responsibility for any unavoidable damage which may be caused by a bombardment under such circumstances.

If for military reasons immediate action is necessary and no delay can be allowed to the enemy, it is nevertheless understood that the prohibition to bombard the undefended town holds good, as in the case given in the first paragraph, and that the commander shall take all due measures in order that the town may suffer as little harm as possible.

III. After due notice has been given, the bombardment of undefended ports, towns, villages, dwellings, or buildings may be commenced, if the local authorities, on a formal summons being made to them, decline to comply with requisitions for provisions or supplies necessary for the immediate use of the naval force before the place in question.

Such requisitions shall be proportional to the resources of the place. They shall only be demanded in the name of the commander of the said naval force, and they shall, as far as possible, be paid for in ready money; if not, receipts shall be given.

IV. The bombardment of undefended ports, towns, villages, dwellings, or buildings, on account of failure to pay money contributions, is forbidden.

Appendix 14

Days Lost to Industrial Action in Britain, 1914–1918

'000s
1914: 9,878
1915: 2,953
1916: 2,446
1917: 5,647
1918: 5,875

(Source: UK Office of National Statistics)

Appendix 15
Sites of Indicator Loop Systems

England: Dumpton Gap, Straits of Dover, Portsmouth, Portland, Plymouth, Falmouth.

Scotland: Scapa Flow, Firth of Forth (May Island), Loch Long, Oban Bay, Rosyth and Cumbrae.

Ireland: Berehaven (planned), Queenstown (planned), St George's Channel, North Channel.

Appendix 16

British Communities Attacked from the Sea by German Naval Forces

Place	Date	Year
Great Yarmouth	3 November	1914
Scarborough	16 December	1914
Whitby	16 December	1914
Hartlepool	16 December	1914
Lowca	16 August	1915
Lowestoft	24 April	1916
Great Yarmouth	24 April	1916
Seaham	11 July	1916
Southwold	25 January	1917
Margate	25/26 February	1917
Broadstairs	25/26 February	1917
Dover	20 April	1917
Ramsgate	27 April	1917
Scarborough	4 September	1917
Great Yarmouth	14 January	1918
St Kilda	15 May	1918

Notes

The following abbreviations will be used.

Collections
BL   British Library, London.
CAC   Churchill Archive, Churchill College, Cambridge.
IWM   Imperial War Museum, London.
LC   Liddell Collection, Special Collections Unit, University of Leeds.
NMM   National Maritime Museum, Greenwich.
NMRN   National Museum of the Royal Navy, Portsmouth.
PC   Private Collection.
TNA   The National Archives, Kew.

Books
FTDTSF Marder, *From the Dreadnought to Scapa Flow*, 5 vols
NO   *Naval Operations, The History of the Great War based on Official Documents*, 5 vols.

It is the convention that page numbers be given for citations. This is not always possible in the modern world. Some digitised documents lack page numbering, and some archives hold unnumbered single or multiple sheets in bundles under one reference or none at all. Thus, page numbers will be given where possible, but the reader will understand that they are not always available or, indeed, necessary.

Chapter 1
1. Savage, *Anglo-Saxon Chronicles*, p 288.
2. Morris, *The Norman Conquest*, p 337.
3. Ibid.
4. Morris, *A Great and Terrible King*, p 150.
5. Ibid, p 156.
6. Ibid, p 282.
7. Hansard, H of C Debates 10 August 1870, vol 203, col 1787-8.
8. Hansard, H of C Debates, 1 August 1870, vol 203, col 1289.
9. Wilson, *Empire of the Deep*, p 485.
10. Dixon, *Ships of the Victorian Navy*, p 46.
11. *The Times*, 13 January 1860.
12. *Country Life*, 6 March 1986.
13. Fisher, *Memories*, p 149.
14. Kerr, *RNVR*, p 17.
15. Ibid, p 18.
16. Ibid, p 24.

17. Book title, Margerison, *Our Wonderful Navy; the story of the sure shield in peace and war*.
18. Scott, *50 Years in the Royal Navy*, p 60/61.
19. Ibid, p 198.
20. Marder, *FTDTSF*, vol 1, p 6.
21. *Guide to the Naval Review*, June 1897, p 2/3.
22. Quoted in Darwin, *Unfinished Empire*, p 308.
23. Data from Ferguson, *Empire*, p 247.
24. Maurice-Jones, *History of Coast Artillery*, p 171.
25. Data from Maurice-Jones, *History of Coast Artillery*, p 170.

Chapter 2
1. *The Mercury*, Hobart, 29 July 1902.
2. Davies, *A Supernatural War*, p 16.
3. Andrew, *Defence of the Realm*, p 9.
4. Ibid, p 13.
5. Ibid, p 10.
6. Morgan-Owen, *Fear of Invasion*, p 82/83.
7. Hansard HL Deb 28 April 1902 vol 107 cc5-145.
8. Balfour speech, Hansard 5 March 1903, col 1579.
9. ADM 1/8880, TNA.
10. Ibid.
11. CAB 3/1/3, TNA.
12. CAB 2/1/20, TNA.
13. CAB 38/11/15, TNA.
14. Hansard Volume 138: debated on Thursday 28 July 1904.
15. Hansard HC Deb 13 April 1905 vol 145 cc89-9090.
16. Hansard HL Deb 10 July 1905 vol 149 cc4-494.
17. Hansard HL Deb 14 May 1906 vol 157 cc99-12399.
18. Maurice-Jones, *History of Coastal Artillery*, p 172.
19. Hankey, *Supreme Command*, vol 1, p 31.
20. CAB 38/14/11, 22 October 1908, TNA.
21. Hansard H of C, vol 8, col 1389, 29 July 1909.
22. Otte, *Statesman of Europe*, p 222.
23. Hansard, Volume 169: debated on Monday 18 February 1907.
24. Quoted in Heffer, *The Age of Decadence*, p 436.
25. *The Spectator*, 31 July 1909.
26. Judd, *The Quest for C* p 104/128.
27. Andrew, *Defence of the Realm*, p 30.
28. Judd, *The Quest for C* p 163.
29. Docs 12152, IWM.

Chapter 3
1. Roberts, *Salisbury*, p 539.
2. Ibid.
3. Ibid, p 540.
4. Ibid.
5. Bogdanor, *The Strange Survival of Liberal Britain*, p 316.
6. Ridley, *Bertie*, p 376.

7. Ibid, p 380.
8. Kowner, *Tsushima*, p 15.5
9. 26 Feb 1904 memo to Cabinet, quoted in Burk, *The Lion and the Eagle*, p 363.
10. Otte, *Statesman of Europe*, p 203.
11. Ibid, p 290.
12. Lambert, *Admirals*, p 312.
13. Gough, *Churchill and Fisher*, p 61.
14. Jameson, *The Fleet that Jack Built*, p 109.
15. Marder, *FTDTSF*, vol 1, p 59
16. Rose, *George V*, p 72.
17. Otte, *Statesman of Europe*, p 352.
18. FO 371/670/721, 4 January 1909, TNA.
19. Hansard, H of C, 29 March 1909, cols 52-70.
20. Marder, *FTDTSF*, vol 1, p 332.
21. Lambert, *Sir John Fisher's Naval Revolution*, p 10.
22. Quoted in Lambert, *The British Way of War*, p 193.
23. Lambert, *Sir John Fisher's Naval Revolution*, p 122.
24. Mackay, *Fisher*, p 300.
25. Ibid, p 302.
26. Jameson, *The Fleet that Jack Built*, p 103.
27. Fisher, *Memories*, p 18.
28. Wilson, *Empire of the Deep*, p 503.
29. Fisher, *Memories*, p 54.
30. Mackay, *Fisher*, p 286.
31. Jameson, *The Fleet that Jack Built*, p 108.
32. CAB1/7/740, TNA.
33. Otte, *Statesman of Europe*, p 419.
34. Ibid, p 439.
35. Adams, *Balfour*, p 179.

Chapter 4
1. *The Times*, 22 July 1911.
2. CAB 38/19/48, TNA.
3. Hankey, *Supreme Command*, vol 1, p 81.
4. Lambert, *Sir John Fisher's Naval Revolution*, p 268.
5. Morris, *German Air Raids*, p 5.
6. CHAR 13/22A/56-60, CAC.
7. Ibid.
8. Ibid.
9. Ibid.
10. CHAR 13/6B/359-369, CAC.
11. CHAR 13/6B/417-428, CAC.
12. Judd, *The Quest for C*, p 246.
13. Cowan, *Memoirs*, p 252, COW17, NMM.
14. Lambert, *Sir John Fisher's Naval Revolution*, p 286.
15. Bogdanor, *The Strange Survival of Liberal Britain*, p xxvi.
16. Ferguson, *Empire*, p 299/300.
17. Ibid, p 291.
18. Adams, *Bonar Law*, p 170.

19. Hansard, H of C debates, 1 August 1914, vol 65, col 1823.
20. Ferguson, *Empire*, p 299/300.
21. Stevenson, *Cataclysm*, p 220.
22. Maurice-Jones, *History of Coast Artillery*, p 180.
23. Ibid, p 182.
24. Ibid.
25. Morris, *German Air Raids*, p 6.
26. Vigo, *Naval Strategy*, p 16.
27. Ibid, p 43.
28. Ibid, p 117.
29. Roynon, *Home Fires Burning*, diary 26 August 1914, p 23.

Chapter 5
1. Vigo, *Naval Strategy*, p 65.
2. Hankey, *Supreme Command*, vol 1, p 32.
3. Ibid.
4. Ibid, p 31.
5. Barnett, *The Swordbearers*, p 116.
6. Hankey, *Supreme Command*, vol 1, p 31.
7. Marder, *FTDTSF*, vol 1, p 426.
8. Simpkins, *Kitchener's Army*, p 42.
9. Beckett, Simpson, *A Nation in Arms*, p 131.
10. Cameron, *1914*, p 169.
11. Docs 12152, IWM.
12. Cameron, *1914*, p 170.
13. Docs 12152, IWM.
14. Andrew, *Defence of the Realm*, p 53.
15. Ibid.
16. Bostridge, *The Fateful Year*, p 301.
17. Hankey, *Supreme Command*, vol 1, p 220.
18. For example, *The Times*, 26 October 1914.
19. *Daily Mail*, 13 October 1914.
20. Ibid.
21. Roskill, *Earl Beatty*, p 86.
22. Marder, *Portrait of an Admiral*, p 112.
23. Egremont, *Some Desperate Glory*, p 46.
24. *The Times*, 15 October 1914.
25. Roynon, *Home Fires*, p 49.
26. CAB 38/28/40, TNA.
27. ADM 137/965, TNA.
28. CAB 38/28/48, CAB 38/28/40, TNA.
29. Diary 20 October 1914, docs 11521, IWM.
30. Ibid, 19 October 1914.
31. CHAR 13/43/87-98, CAC.
32. Ibid.
33. Ibid.
34. Ibid.
35. Ibid.
36. *NO*, vol 1, p 39.

37. *The Spectator*, 7 November 1915.
38. All quotes ADM 116/1351, TNA.
39. Noted in Simkins, *Kitchener's Army*, p 43.
40. Roynon, *Home Fires*, p 63.
41. Dittmar and College, *British Warships*, p 290.
42. ADM 137/1971, TNA.
43. *Daily Mail*, 1 December 1914.
44. *Essex at War 1914-1918*, p 6.
45. Diary 25 November 1914, docs 12152, IWM.

Chapter 6
1. ADM 186/604, TNA.
2. DRAX 1/11, CAC.
3. d'Enno, *Fishermen Against the Kaiser*, p 60.
4. Taffrail, *Swept Channels*, p 69.
5. ADM 186/604, TNA.
6. Taffrail, *Swept Channels*, p 242 and data from Dittmar and College, *British Warships*.
7. CHAR 13/43/87-98, CAC.
8. 12 August 1915, MSS 255/6/4, NMRN.
9. MSS 255/6/5, NMRN.
10. DRAX 1/12, CAC.
11. Ibid.
12. Chatterton, *The Auxiliary Patrol*, p 25.
13. Ibid.
14. Kerr, *RNVR*, p 94.
15. Chatterton, *Auxiliary Patrol*, p 26.
16. Ibid, p 44.
17. Ibid, p 23.
18. Fayle, *Seaborne Trade*, vol 3, p 465.
19. Bacon, *Dover Patrol*, vol 1, p 71.
20. Maxwell, *The Motor Boat Patrol*, p 53.
21. CHAR 13/46/77-78, CAC.
22. Chatterton, *The Auxiliary Patrol*, p 24.
23. *Yachting Monthly*, March 1916.
24. *NO*, vol 1, p 17.

Chapter 7
1. Andrew, *Defence of the Realm*, p 55.
2. Docs 24251, IWM.
3. Ibid.
4. Docs 12189, IWM.
5. Docs 24251, IWM.
6. *New York Times*, 9 November 1914.
7. *NO*, vol 2, p 10.
8. Hansard HofC Volume 68: 12 November 1914.
9. CHAR 13/42/96, CAC.
10. Boyd, *British Naval Intelligence*, p 106.
11. Cameron, *1914*, p 178.

12. Halliday letter, 2 Feb 1982, LIDDLE/WW1/DF/148/1/63, LC.
13. Docs 10813, IWM.
14. Ibid.
15. Ibid.
16. Docs 25439, IWM.
17. *Northern Daily Mail*, 15 February 1969, LIDDLE/WW1/DF/148/1/63, LC.
18. Ibid.
19. Ibid.
20. Ibid.
21. Bostridge, *The Fateful Year*, p 325.
22. *Northern Daily Mail*, unknown date 1970, LIDDLE/WW1/DF/148/1/63, LC.
23. Marder, *FTDTSF*, vol II, pp 143–4.
24. Halliday letter, 2 Feb 1982, LIDDLE/WW1/DF/148/1/63, LC.
25. Docs 10813, IWM.
26. Cameron, *1914*, p 179.
27. Marder, *FTDTSF*, vol 2, p 149.
28. SK-H diary, 16 December 1914.
29. Cameron, *1914*, p 180.
30. Ibid, p 181.
31. Roynon, *Home Fires*, p 70.
32. Cameron, *1914*, p 181.
33. Oliver, *Memoirs* II, pp 117–18, NMM.
34. Cameron, *1914*, p 182.
35. Barnett, *The Swordbearers*, p 128.
36. *NO*, vol 2, p 50.
37. Ibid, p 46.
38. Marder, *Portrait of an Admiral*, p 131/132.
39. *War Illustrated*, 26 December 1914.

Chapter 8
1. Marder, *FTDTSF*, vol 2, p 166.
2. Roskill, *Earl Beatty*, p 113/114.
3. Marder, *FTDTSF* vol 2, p 165.
4. Naval Monographs VIII, part IV, p 3.
5. Striner, *Woodrow Wilson*, p 26.
6. *Barrow News*, 30 January 1915.
7. Ibid.
8. *Surrey Comet*, 20 January 1915, via History@Kingston, Dr Steven Woodbridge blog 16 January 2021.
9. Baden-Powell, *My Adventures as a Spy*, p 24.
10. Weil, *Madman*, p 72.
11. *Scientific American*, 27 February 1915.
12. Jeffery, *1916*, p 311.
13. *New York Times*, 18 May 1919.
14. CHAR 13/64/53-54, CAC.
15. Nolan, *Secret Victory*, p 68.
16. Roynon, *Home Fires*, p 114.
17. *NO*, vol 3, p 130.
18. Ibid.

19. Cumbria County Council's Local Studies Library.
20. *Whitehaven News*, 10 July 1998.
21. Ibid, 3 May 2012 on line.
22. *The Times*, 15 October 1915.
23. GGAT 137 Defence of the Realm: Coastal Defence and Port Facilities, p 55.
24. *British Warships Lost at Sea*, pp 7, 28.
25. CAB 19/1/ 28-33, TNA.
26. Fayle, *Seaborne Trade*, vol III, p 465.

Chapter 9
1. *The Spectator*, 22 April 1916.
2. Aan de Wiel, *German Invasion*, p 31.
3. Ibid, p 32.
4. Quoted in Pennel, *A Kingdom United*, p 174.
5. Beresford, *Home Rule and Naval Defence*, p 191.
6. Andrew, *Defence of the Realm*, p 86.
7. Townshend, *The Easter Rising*, p 105.
8. Fisher, *Memories*, p 38.
9. All quotes from letter to brother Francis, Sims PC.
10. LIDDLE/WW1/RNMN/REC/012.
11. Ibid.
12. *London Gazette* 29635, 20 June 1916.
13. ADM 188/715/34318, TNA.
14. ADM 188/463/288420, TNA.
15. *London Gazette* 29635, 20 June 1916.
16. All quotes from letter to brother Francis, Sims PC.
17. Schofield, *The Royal Navy in Peace and War*, p 30.
18. *Aberdeen Daily Journal*, 27 April 1916.
19. *Argus*, Melbourne, 15 May 1916.
20. Ibid.
21. Marder, *FTDTSF*, vol II, p 427.
22. ADM 12/1567A, TNA.
23. Letter 3 May 1916 in Tyrwhitt PC.
24. *The Times*, 25 and 26 April 1916.
25. *The Spectator*, 29 April 1916.
26. Aan de Wiel, *German Invasion*, p 40.
27. Roskill, *Earl Beatty*, p 145.
28. Patterson, *Tyrwhitt*, p 159.
29. Beatty memo 26 May 1916, copy in PC.

Chapter 10
1. *The Spectator*, 19 February 1916.
2. Morris, *German Air Raids*, p 92.
3. Agar, *Footprints in the Sea*, p 46.
4. Marder, *Portrait of an Admiral*, p 208/209.
5. Herwig, *Luxury Fleet*, p 175.
6. Naval Staff Appreciation, p 43.
7. Ibid, p 24.
8. Quoted in Marder, *FTDTSF*, vol III, p 51.

9. Barnett, *The Swordbearers*, p 182.
10. Naval Monographs XVII, p 273.
11. *Northern Echo*, 13 July 1916.
12. Ibid.
13. Ibid, 9 July 1916.
14. 22 August 1916, DRBK 5-10, CAC.
15. Quoted in Marder, *FTDTSF*, vol III p 295/296.
16. Add MS 49032, BL.
17. *NO*, vol IV, p 49.
18. Ibid, p 47.
19. Ibid.
20. Ibid, p 48.
21. Ibid.
22. Roskill, *The Naval Air Service*, p xiv.

Chapter 11
1. Diary 25 November 1914, docs 12152, IWM.
2. Ibid, 11 December 1914.
3. Ibid, 25 January 1917.
4. Ibid.
5. CAB/23/1 26 January 1917, TNA.
6. Naval Staff Monographs, vol XVIII, part VIII, p 104.
7. *The Argus*, Melbourne, 29 January 1917.
8. *Barrier Miner*, Broken Hill, NSW, 29 January 1917.
9. Diary 25 Jan 1917, docs 12152, IWM.
10. Fayle, *Seaborne Trade*, vol III, p 465.
11. von Bernstorff to Robert Lansing, 31 January 1917, www.firstworldwar.com.
12. Diary 1 Feb 1917, docs 4643, IWM.
13. CAB 23/1/64, TNA.
14. Roynon, *Home Fires*, p 203.
15. Add MS 82494, BL.
16. Roberts, *The Chief*, p 310.
17. *The Ballarat Courier*, 2 March 1917.
18. Docs 7431, 17 March 1917, IWM.
19. Naval Staff Monographs, vol XVIII, part VIII, p 277.
20. Docs 7431, 21 April, IWM.
21. Docs 10964, IWM.
22. Ibid.
23. Coxon, *Dover in the Dark Days*, p 74.
24. *Marlborough Express*, 26 July 1917.
25. Bacon, *The Dover Patrol*, vol 1, p 63.
26. ADM 196/143/493, TNA.
27. *Daily Mail* via *Bendigonian*, 6 December 1917.
28. Ibid.
29. Ibid.
30. *Northern Times* (WA), 8 September 1917.
31. *Daily Telegraph*, 6 September 1917.
32. *Daily Mail* via *Bendigonian*, 6 December 1917.

33. Operations Division, Naval Staff, 'Present Naval Policy', 17 September 1917, quoted in Marder, *FTDTSF*, vol V, p 298.
34. Letter 25 December 1917, Jellicoe to Bacon, in Private Collection.

Chapter 12
1. CAB/23/4, TNA.
2. Stevenson, *Cataclysm*, p 331.
3. Strachan, *The British Home Front*, p 22.
4. de Chair, *The Sea is Strong*, p 188.
5. Strachan, *The British Home Front*, p 22.
6. *Sydney Morning Herald*, 17 January 1918.
7. Ibid, 19 January 1918.
8. Hansard HC Deb 23 January 1918 vol 101 cc963-4.
9. Diary, various dates, docs 12152, IWM.
10. ADM 137/1894, 97-99, TNA.
11. ADM 137/1894, 100, TNA.
12. ADM 137/1894, 103, TNA.
13. Chatterton, *The Big Blockade*, p 77.

Chapter 13
1. Morris, *German Air Raids*, p 11.
2. CAB 37/123/1, TNA.
3. Ibid.
4. *Argus*, Melbourne, 3 March 1915.
5. HC Deb 08 February 1915 vol 69 c241.
6. Scott, *50 Years in the Navy*, p 304.
7. Ibid.
8. Ibid, p 305.
9. BBC Scotland news website 24 February 2014.
10. National Records of Scotland, HH31/21/8 fols 23-26.
11. Ibid.
12. CAB 23/3/24, TNA.
13. Ibid.
14. Roynon, *Home Fires*, p 224.
15. Jones, *The War in the Air*, vol VI, p 164.

Chapter 14
1. Letter to mother, 1 August, docs 16585, IWM.
2. Ibid.
3. Docs 6416, IWM.
4. Ibid.
5. Ibid.
6. Docs 681, IWM.
7. Ibid
8. 7 November 1914, docs 2523, IWM.
9. Ibid, 22 November 1914.
10. Ibid, 29 November 1914.
11. Oral History 8558, IWM.
12. Oral History 3161, IWM.

13. Stuart-Mason, *Britannia's Daughters*, p 22.
14. Oral History 3162, IWM.
15. Information, Beckett and Simpson (eds), *A Nation in Arms*, p 152.
16. Statement of the First Lord of the Admiralty, Explanatory of the Navy Estimates, 1919-1920.
17. Crawford, *Fallen Glory*, p 84.

Chapter 15
1. Andrew, *Secret Service*, p 178.
2. Jellicoe, *Crisis of the Naval War*, p 66/67.
3. WO 33/697, TNA.
4. *The Times*, 24 April 1856.
5. Preston, Major, *Send a Gunboat*, p 11.
6. Ballard, *The Black Battlefleet*, p 217.
7. Ibid, p 219.
8. Ibid, p 218.

Chapter 16
1. Diary 11 November 1918, docs 1215, IWM.
2. Barnett, *The Swordbearers*, p 119.
3. Lloyd George, *War Memoires*, vol II, p 1585.
4. Herwig, *Luxury Fleet*, p 50.
5. Ibid, p 81.
6. Ibid, p 149.
7. Docs 14927, IWM.
8. MI5.gov.uk.world-war.
9. Ibid.
10. Maurice-Jones, *History of Coast Artillery*, p 201.
11. Quoted in Darwin, *Unfinished Empire*, p 309.
12. Beckett, Simpson, *A Nation in Arms*, p 12.
13. Lambert, *The British Way of War*, p 433.
14. Mackay, *Fisher*, p 421.
15. *Warships International and Fleet Review*, June 2023.
16. Ibid, August 2023.

Bibliography

The following resources have been cited in the text.

Primary Sources
Various files in the ADM, WO, FO, CAB and MUN series, individually cited, The National Archives, Kew.
Memoirs of Admiral Sir Walter Cowan, COW 17, National Maritime Museum, Greenwich.
Memoirs of Admiral Sir Henry F Oliver, 2 vols, 1946 (unpublished), OLV/12, National Maritime Museum.
Papers of G Halliday, LIDDLE/WW1/DF/148/1/63, Liddle Collection, Special Collections, Leeds University Library.
Papers of W H Campbell, Liddle/WW1/RNMN/REC012, Liddle Collection.
Private Papers of Admiral Henry Jackson, MSS 255, National Museum of the Royal Navy, Portsmouth.
Papers of Sir Winston Churchill in the CHAR 13 series, Churchill Archive Centre, Cambridge.
Private Papers of the Admiral the Hon Sir Reginald Aylmer Ranfurly Plunkett-Ernle-Erle-Drax, DRAX, Churchill Archive Centre.
The Papers of Admiral Sir John de Robeck, DRBK 5/10, Churchill Archive Centre.
Papers of Admiral Sir Reginald Y Tyrwhitt, held in private collection.
Letters of Alfred Turner, held in G A M Sims private collection.
Private Papers of Lieutenant Commander C E Evans, Documents 12189, Imperial War Museum, London.
Private Papers of Captain Charles Poignand, Documents 4643, Imperial War Museum.
Private Papers of G E Haigh, Documents 7431, Imperial War Museum.
Private Papers of W G Evans, Documents 10964, Imperial War Museum.
Diary and Papers of Ernest R Cooper, Documents 12152, Imperial War Museum.
Private Papers of J H Spiers, Documents 24251, Imperial War Museum.
Private Papers of Captain E C Brent, Documents 10813, Imperial War Museum.

Private Papers of Captain C J Wintour, Documents 11521, Imperial War Museum.
Coast Artillery Papers, Documents 25439, Imperial War Museum.
Private Papers of G S Smith, Documents 2523, Imperial War Museum.
Private Papers of Naomi Mitchison, Documents 681, Imperial War Museum.
Private Papers of Colonel A E Maitland, Documents 16535, Imperial War Museum.
Private Papers of Colonel Sir Hugh Chance, Documents 6416, Imperial War Museum.
Private Papers of William Pead, Documents 14927, Imperial War Museum.
Josephine Tennent, Oral History 8558, Imperial War Museum.
Alice Russell, Oral History 3161, Imperial War Museum.
Beatrice Browne, Oral History 3162, Imperial War Museum.
Jellicoe Papers, Add MSS 48990, Add MSS 49032, British Library, London.
Keyes Papers, Add MS 82494, British Library.

Secondary Sources
BOOKS
The place of publication is London, unless otherwise stated.

Adams, R, *Balfour, The Last Grandee* (John Murray, 2007).
_____, *Bonar Law* (John Murray, 1999).
Agar, A, *Footprints in the Sea* (Evans Brothers Ltd, 1959).
Andrew, C, *Defence of the Realm* (Penguin, 2010).
Bacon, R, *The Dover Patrol*, two volumes (New York: George H Doran and Co, 1919).
Baden-Powell, R, *My Adventures as a Spy* (C Arthur Pearson, 1915).
Beckett, I and Simpson, K (eds), *A Nation in Arms* (Barnsley: Pen and Sword Military, 2014).
Barnett, C, *The Swordbearers* (Eyre and Spottiswoode, 1963).
Beresford, C, 'Home Rule and Naval Defence', in *Against Home Rule* (F Warne and Co, 1912).
Bogdanor, V, *The Strange Survival of Liberal Britain* (Biteback Publishing, 2022).
Bostridge, M, *The Fateful Year* (Viking, 2014).
Boyd, A, *British Naval Intelligence Through the Twentieth Century* (Barnsley: Seaforth Publishing, 2020).
Burk, K, *The Lion and The Eagle* (Bloomsbury, 2018).
Cameron, J, *1914* (Cassell and Co, 1959).

Chatterton, E Keble, *The Auxiliary Patrol* (Sidgwick and Jackson, 1923).
_____, *The Big Blockade* (Hurst and Blackett, 1932).
Corbett, J, and Newbolt, H, *Naval Operations, The History of the Great War based on Official Documents*, vols I – V (republished Naval and Military Press and Imperial War Museum, 2014).
Coxon, S ('Dug Out'), *Dover during the Dark Days* (John Lane, The Bodley Head, 1919).
Crawford, J, *Fallen Glory* (Old St Publishing, 2016).
Darwin, J, *Unfinished Empire* (Allen Lane, 2012).
Davies, O, *A Supernatural War* (Oxford: Oxford University Press, 2021).
De Chair, D, *The Sea is Strong* (George G Harrap and Co, 1961).
D'Enno, D, *Fishermen Against the Kaiser* (Barnsley: Pen and Sword Maritime, 2010).
Dittmar, F, and College, J, *British Warships 1914-1919* (Ian Allan, 1972).
Dixon, C, *Ships of the Victorian Navy* (Southampton: Ashford Press Publishing, 1987).
Egremont, M, *Some Desperate Glory* (Pan MacMillan, 2014).
Fayle, C E, *Seaborne Trade* vol III (Sussex: Naval and Military Press, facsimile edition; originally John Murray, 1924).
Ferguson, N, *Empire* (Penguin, 2004).
Fisher, J, *Memories* (Hodder and Stoughton, 1919).
Gough, B, *Churchill and Fisher: the titans at the Admiralty who fought the First World War* (Barnsley: Seaforth Publishing, 2017).
Hankey, M, *The Supreme Command*, vol 1 (George Allen and Unwin, 1961).
Heffer, S, *The Age of Decadence* (Random House, 2017).
Herwig, H, *Luxury Fleet; the Imperial German Navy 1888-1918* (George Allen and Unwin, 1980).
Jameson W, *The Fleet that Jack Built* (Rupert Hart-Davies, 1962).
Jeffery, K, *1916* (Bloomsbury, 2015).
Jellicoe, J, *The Crisis of the Naval War* (New York: George H Doran, 1920).
Jones, H, *The War in the Air; being the story of the part played in the Great War by the Royal Air Force*, vol VI (Oxford: Clarendon Press, 1937).
Judd, A, *The Quest for C* (Harper Press, 2000).
Kerr, J, and Granville, W, *The RNVR* (George G Harrap and Co, 1957).
Kowner, R, *Tsushima* (Oxford: Oxford University Press, 2022).
Lambert, A, *Admirals* (Faber and Faber Ltd, 2009).
_____, *The British Way of War* (Yale University Press, 2021).
Lambert, N, *Sir John Fisher's Naval Revolution* (Columbia SC: University of South Carolina Press, 1999).
Lloyd George, D, *War Memoirs*, vol II (Oldhams Press, 1936).

Longmate N, *Island Fortress* (Hutchinson, 1991).
Mackay, R, *Fisher of Kilverstone* (OUP, 1973).
Marder, A, *From the Dreadnought to Scapa Flow*, vol I, vol II, vol III (Barnsley: Seaforth Publishing, 2013; originally published 1961).
_____ (ed), *Fear God and Dread Nought*, vol 2 (Jonathan Cape, 1952).
_____, *Portrait of an Admiral; the life and papers of Sir Herbert Richmond* (Cambridge, Mass: Harvard University Press, 1952).
Margerison, J, *Our wonderful navy; the story of the sure shield in peace and war* (Cassell and Co, 1919).
Martin, C, and Parker, G, *Armada* (Yale University Press, 2022).
Maurice-Jones, K, *The History of Coast Artillery in the British Army* (Uckfield: Naval and Military Press, undated).
Maxwell, G, *The Motor Launch Patrol* (J M Dent and Sons, 1920).
Morgan-Owen, D, *The Fear of Invasion* (Oxford: Oxford University Press, 2017).
Morris, J, *German Air Raids on Britain 1914-1918* (Sampson, Low, Marston and Co Ltd, 1925).
Morris, M, *A Great and Terrible King* (Penguin, 2021).
_____, *The Norman Conquest* (Penguin, 2022).
Nolan, L, and Nolan, J, *Secret Victory* (Cork: Mercier Press, 2009).
Otte, T, *Statesman of Europe* (Allen Lane, 2020).
Patterson, A, *Tyrwhitt of the Harwich Force* (MacDonald and Jane's, 1973).
Pennell, C, *A Kingdom United* (OUP, 2012).
Ridley, J, *Bertie* (Chatto & Windus, 2012).
Roberts, A, *Salisbury, Victorian Titan* (Weidenfeld and Nicolson, 1999).
_____, *The Chief. The Life of Lord Northcliffe* (Simon and Schuster, 2022).
Rose, K, *King George V* (Macmillan, 1984).
Roskill, S, *Earl Beatty* (Collins, 1980).
_____ (ed), *The Naval Air Service*, volume 1, 1908-1918 (Navy Records Society, 1969).
Roynon, G (ed), *Home Fires Burning: The Great War Diaries of Georgina Lee, 1914-1919* (Stroud: Sutton Publishing, 2006).
Savage, A, *Anglo-Saxon Chronicles* (Papermac, 1988).
Schleihauf, W (ed), *Jutland, The Naval Staff Appreciation* (Barnsley: Seaforth Publishing, 2016).
Schofield, B, *With the Royal Navy in War and Peace* (Barnsley: Pen and Sword Maritime, 2018).
Scott, P, *Fifty Years in the Royal Navy* (John Murray, 1919).
Simpkins, P, *Kitchener's Army* (Barnsley: Pen and Sword Military, 2021).
Stanglini R, and Cosentino, M, *The French Fleet: Ships, Strategy and*

Operations 1870 – 1918 (Barnsley: Seaforth Publishing, 2022).
Stevenson, D, *Cataclysm* (New York: Basic Books, 2004).
Strachan, H (ed), *The British Home Front in the First World War* (Cambridge: Cambridge University Press, 2023).
Striner, R, *Woodrow Wilson and World War 1* (Lanham, Maryland: Rowman and Littlefield, 2016).
Stuart-Mason, U, *Britannia's Daughters* (Barnsley: Pen and Sword, 1992).
'Taffrail', *Swept Channels* (Hodder and Stoughton, 1935).
Townshend, C, *Easter 1916* (Penguin, 2006).
Vigo, M, *Naval Strategy and Operations in Narrow Seas* (Frank Cass, 1999).
Weil, P, *The Madman in the White House* (Cambridge, Mass: Harvard University Press, 2023).
White, J, *Zeppelin Nights* (Vintage, 2015).
Wilson, B, *Empire of the Deep* (W&N, 2014).
Wyatt, R, *Death from the Skies* (Norwich: Gliddon Books, 1990).

NEWSPAPERS AND MAGAZINES
Aberdeen Daily Journal.
Argus (Melbourne).
Ballarat Courier.
Barrier Miner (Broken Hill, NSW).
Barrow News.
Bendigonian (Victoria).
Country Life.
Daily Mail.
Daily Telegraph.
Daily Sketch.
Eastern Daily Press.
London Gazette.
Marlborough Express.
Northern Daily Mail.
Northern Echo.
Scientific American.
Sunday Times.
Surrey Comet.
Sydney Morning Herald.
The Mercury (Hobart).
The Spectator.
The Strand.
The Times.
The War Illustrated.

Warships International and Fleet Review.
Whitehaven News.
Yachting Monthly.

ON LINE RESOURCES
BBC Scotland news website
www.firstworldwar.com.
GGAT 137 Defence of the Realm: Coastal Defence and Port Facilities (March 2018).
History@Kingston, Kingston University, Surrey.
MI5.gov.uk.
National Records of Scotland.
Naval-history.net.
UK Office of National Statistics.

OTHER
Aan de Wiel, J, *German Invasion and Spy Scares in Ireland, 1890s-1914: Between Fiction and Fact* (Presses universitaires de Rennes, 2012).
British Vessels Lost at Sea (Patrick Stephens, 1988).
Cumbria County Council's Local Studies Library, Whitehaven.
Essex Record Office publication *Essex at War 1914-1918*.
Diary of Stephen King-Hall;
https://sites.google.com/site/kinghallconnections/7400-s-hms-southampton—1914.
Guide to the Naval Review, June 1897.
Naval Monographs volume VIII, part IV, Admiralty Training Division.
Naval Monographs volume XVII, Admiralty Training Division.
Naval Staff Monographs, volume XVIII, part VIII, Admiralty Training Division.
Statement of the First Lord of the Admiralty, Explanatory of the Navy Estimates, 1919-1920, HMSO.
The Navy List (various dates as cited).

Index

ill refers to an illustration; *n* to a note; *port* to a portrait

A Bernstein and Company 290
Aberdeen 87, 123
Aboukir (Br) 135
Abyssinia (Br) 287
acoustic mirrors 283, 283*ill*
Admiral of Patrols 10, 89
admirals: status of 28–30
Admiralty, the 23*n*, 46–7, 86, 123, 141, 157, 160, 186, 227–8, 250; 'Pink List' 132, 287; *see also* Room 40
Admiralty Board of Invention and Research (BIR) 280
Admiralty Experimental Station (AES) 281
Admiralty Naval Staff 238–9
Admiralty Pier Fort 24
Admiralty Pier Turret, Dover 24, 24*ill*
Admiralty trawlers 123–4
Admiralty War Staff 85–6, 89, 202
aerial warfare 250–68
Agadir incident 79–80, 125
Agamemnon (Br) 24–5, 25*ill*, 76*ill*
Agincourt (Br) 32
Ägir (Ger) 290
aircraft: BE 2c: 262; Vickers gun bus 257
airships 250–1; *Mayfly* 250
Ajax (Br) 145
alcoholic drinks: DORA legislation against 114, 117
Alert (Br) 277–8, 278*ill*
Alexandra (Br) 29, 32
Alfred the Great 13–14
Alfree, Geoffrey 128
Alice (train) 183
aliens, internment of 175
Aliens Restriction Act (1914) 118
Altham, Colonel Edward A 44
Amazon (Br) 232
Amiral Tréhouart (Fr) 293
Amphion (Br) 105–7
Andrew, Christopher 190
Anglo-Celt, The (newspaper) 188
Anglo-Japanese Treaty (1902) 64

Anglo-Russian Entente (1907) 65
Antrim (Br) 146
Antwerp 19–20, 99–101
Appleby, Alice 238
Arbuthnot, Rear Admiral Robert 158
Argyll (Br) 146
armed merchant cruisers (AMC) 133
Armistice 194
armoured cars 218–19, 218*ill*
Armstrong, Sir William 286
Armstrong Company 23
Arnim, *Kapitänleutnant* Bernd von 233
Arnold-Foster, Hugh Oakeley 52
Arrow (Br) 286*ill*
Asquith, Herbert Henry 54, 91, 96, 179, 187, 216, 258, 300; and Agadir 80–1; and Antwerp 100–1; and Ireland 189; and People's Budget 71; relations with Churchill 100, 179
Atkinson and Son Brewery 114
Aube, Admiral Hyacinthe 9
Aubers Ridge, Battle of (1915) 184
Audacious (Br) 103*ill*, 104
Aurora (Br) 139, 146, 168
Austin, Alfred, *To Arms* 8
Australian Station 32
Austria-Hungary 90
Austro-Hungarian Navy 84, 290–1
Auxiliary Patrols: organisation of 131
Avery, Salvation Army Adjutant William 155

Bacon, Vice Admiral Sir Reginald 76, 128–9, 193, 230–1, 236, 239
Baden-Powell, Lieutenant General Robert 58, 98; *My Adventures as a Spy* 174
Baillie-Grohman, Lieutenant Harold 137
Balfour, Arthur 45–8, 46*port*, 78, 179, 201, 259, 280; and CID 298
Balkan Wars (1912–13) 125, 297
Ballantyne, Ian 302
Ballard, Captain George A 89, 137, 138, 141, 144, 161, 288
Balta Sound 87
Barfleur (Br) 35
Barnett, Corelli 209, 294

340

Barrow News 171
Battersby, Mary 273
Battle of Worthing, The (novel) 38
Bayern (Ger) 211
Bayly, Admiral Lewis 17, 124, 165
Beal, Alfred 149
Beatty, Vice Admiral David 135, 139, 162, 199, 246–7; and Battle of Dogger Bank 167–9; and Battle of Jutland 207–9; and raid on Lerwick 246–7; raid on Great Yarmouth 157–8, 199, 202–3; relations with Churchill 100, 102–4; views on trawlers 124–5
Beauchamp, Lord 92
Beckett, Ian 299
Begbie, Harold 301
Belgian refugees 220, 274
Belgian Revolution (1830) 20
Belgium 9, 19–20, 91–2, 99–100
Ben Cruachan (Br) q172
Bence-Lambert, G 175, 175*n*
Beowulf (Ger) 290
Beresford, Captain Lord Charles 31, 60, 135, 189
Berlin (Ger) 79, 80*ill*, 104
Bernstorff, Count 190, 225–6
Bethmann Hollweg, Gottlieb von 190
Binmore, Lieutenant Henry Armstrong 229
Birmingham (Br) 145, 157
Bjørgvin (Nor) 289
Black Legion 18, 27
Black Prince (Br) 32, 84
Blackwood's Magazine 37
blockades 84–5, 84*n*, 225, 237, 299–301 close blockades 17, 81–5, 73
Blücher (Ger) 137, 144, 146, 152–3, 167, 169, 169*ill*
Blücher, Prince and Princess 98
'Blue Water' school 32
Blunt, Captain William 139
Boedicker, Rear Admiral Friedrich 192, 194, 196–7
Boer War 44, 45*n*, 296
bombs: Fiery Grapnel 263; Hales bombs 263–4; Ranken darts 263
Bonar Law, Andrew 91
Bonaparte, Louis Napoleon 21–2
Boom Defence Vessels (BDV) 110
booms 110
Borkum Island 85
Botha (Br) 232
Boucher, Lieutenant Maitland Walter Sabine 122
Boulogne 84
Bourdeaux, Superintendent 277–8

Bouvines (Fr) 292*ill*, 293
Bowyer, Lieutenant John Francis 230
Bowyer, Richard Grenville 230
Boy Scout movement 93
Boyce, William and David Garrick, *Heart of Oak* 18
Bradford, Vice Admiral Edward Eden 205
Bragg, Sir William Henry 281, 283
Bragg, William Lawrence 11, 281, 283
Brandeburg, *Hauptmann* Ernst 264
bread: DORA regulations on 115, 227
Brennan, Louis 35
Brennan torpedoes 9, 35–6, 51
Brent, Lieutenant E C 150–1
Brest-Litovsk, Treaty of (1918) 240
Brett, Reginald Baliol, Viscount Esher 77
Britain: relations with France 64
British Army 33–4, 77–8; 7th Cyclists Battalion of Devonshire Regiment 144; 25th Royal Fusiliers 58; Essex Infantry Brigade (TF) 112; Lancashire and Cheshire Royal Garrison Artillery (TF) 171; Lincolnshire Yeomanry (TF) 220; manpower (2023) 302; Montgomery Yeomanry (TF) 220; relations with Royal Navy 86, 93; Royal Sussex Cyclists (TF) 220; Worcestershire Regiment (TF) 269; Yorkshire Hussars 146
British Expeditionary Force (BEF) 80–1, 96, 99, 101, 251, 297
British Motor Boat Club (BMBC) 125
British Summer Time 114
Brittain, Vera, *Testament of Youth* 273
Broadstairs: raid on 223–31
Brock, Admiral F W 245–6
Brodrick, Cuthbert 144
Broke (Br) 231–5, 232*ill*
Brooke, John Walter 201*n*
Brooke, Rupert 100
Brown, Jennie 210
Browne, Beatrice 274
Bruce, Captain Alan Cameron 150
Budapest (Austro-Hungary) 291
Burney, Sir Cecil 88, 141, 165, 212
Burniston Barracks 299
Burns, John 92
Burnyeat, Hildegarde and William John Dalzell 182
Bustard (Br) 287
Buttlar, *Oberleutnant* Baron von 254
Buzzard (Br) (ship) 53

Cadogan, Lieutenant Commander Francis Charles 236
Calais 16, 84, 99

Callaghan, Admiral Sir George 84–5, 88, 216
Calyx (Br) 247
Campbell, Boy Seaman William 196
Campbell-Bannerman, Henry 48, 54–5, 55*n*
Cantatrice (Br) 261
Canterbury (Br) 260
Cap Trafalgar (Ger) 133
Cape and West Africa Station 32
Carl Still Company, Reckinghausen 180
Carmania (Br) 133
Carson, Sir Edward 216–7
Carysfort (Br) 212, 212–13*ill*
Casement, Sir Roger 190
Cavendish, Edward, Duke of Devonshire 45*n*
Centurion (Br) 145
Cerberus (Br) 287
Chadwyck-Healy, C E H 52
Chair, Rear Admiral Dudley de 241
Chamberlain, Joseph 12
Chance, Hugh 269–70
Charles I, King 17
Charles II, King 17
Charlton, Rear Admiral Edward Francis Benedict 'Ned' 131
Charteris, Francis Richard, Earl of Wemyss 'Rosy' 44, 48, 239
Chatham 24, 85, 95
Chattenden depot 86, 269
Chatterton, Edward Keble 130
Chesney, George Tomkyns, *The Battle of Dorking* 37–8, 37*ill*
Childers, Erskine 10; *The Riddle of the Sands* 39
Chilean Navy 232
China Station 32, 66
Christmas, H W 234
Christopher (Br) 261
Churchill, Winston 58, 72, 85, 108, 130, 219, 299–300; on air defence 251, 253; and raid on Antwerp 99–101; advisory paper on potential invasion 87; relations with Fisher 78–9; and reorganisation of RN 82–4
Cinque Ports 15, 306
City of Newcastle (Br) 156
Clacton (Br) 117
Clan na Gael (organisation) 188
Clark, James, *The Bombardment of the Hartlepools* (painting) 160
Clarke, Bob 298–9
Clarke, Edward Russell 279–80
Clarke, 1st Class Stoker Ernest John William 197
Clarke, Captain George Sydenham 45, 55
Cleopatra (Br) 193
Cliffe Fort 36

Clyde Workers Committee 242
Clydeside 301; strikes 241
Coast of Ireland Command 124, 273
coastal artillery 11, 93, 311–12
coastal batteries 23–4
coastal defence ships 9, 285–93
coastal raids 11, 323
Cologne Gazette 200
Colomb, Vice-Admiral Philip Howard 32
Colville, Admiral Stanley 102
Committee of Imperial Defence (CID) 10, 45–7, 53–4, 80, 87, 110, 250–1, 298
Commonwealth (Br) 205, 206*ill*
Concert of Europe 20
Concord (Br) 266
Congress of Vienna (1815) 19–20
Connacht Tribune 188
Conqueror (Br) 145
Conquest (Br) 193, 196–8, 260
conscription 57, 184, 187, 237, 242, 294
Conservative and Unionist Party 12, 187
Cooper, Ernest 97, 220, 223–4, 245, 294
Cooper-Key, Admiral Sir Astley 286
Corbett, Julian 73, 134
Coronel, Battle of (1914) 136
Cosens and Company 133
Count of the Saxon Shore 13
County Associations 59
Cowan, Captain Walter 89
Cox, Sub-Lieutenant G A 262
Cradock, Rear Admiral Sir Christopher 'Kit' 135–6
Creagh, General Sir Edward Garrett O'Moore 97–8
Cremer, Sir William 48
Cressy (Br) 135
Crippen, Dr Hawley Harvey: arrested on *Montrose* 110
Cromarty 51, 95–6
Cromer 183, 187
Crosby, Emily 149
Crowley, Captain 181
Cumberland 179–82
Cumming, Mansfield 58, 87–8
Cunard liners 133
Curties, Captain Henry, *When England Slept* 41
Curtis, Albert Charles, *A New Trafalgar* 38
Cyclops (Br) 287, 288*ill*

Daily Mail 10, 39, 43, 99, 107, 113
Daily Sketch 235
Daily Telegraph 238
Dampier, Captain Cecil 104
Dardanelles campaign 178–9, 293

INDEX   343

Dawson, A J, *The Message* 41
Deal, Kent 9
Declaration of London (1909) 107
Defence (Br) 84
Defence Command Paper (2023) 302
defence electric lights (DEL) 51, 93
defence flotillas 132–3
Defence of the Realm Act (DORA, 1914) 10, 18, 113–18, 172, 183–5, 279–80, 303, 318; (1804) 18
Derfflinger (Ger) 144, 146, 167, 196
destroyers
    British 62–3
    German; *G-41*: 199; *G-42*: 233; *G-49*: 230; *G-85*: 233; *G-87*: 230
Devonshire (Br) 146
Device Forts 16, 16*n*
Devonport 132–3
Dimsdale, Charles Robert Southwell, Baron Dimsdale 199
Dimsdale, Lieutenant Reginald Thomas 199
Discovery Expedition (1901–4) 231
Disraeli, Benjamin 20
Dissolution of the Monasteries 16
Dogger Bank, Battle of (1915) 167–70
Donoghue, Private Thomas 252
Doon (Br) 150
Douthwaite, Sergeant T 159
Dover 9, 15, 86, 115*ill*, 228; air raids on 251, 267; impact of DORA on 115–17; passes for residents in 115*ill*; raid on 11, 231–5
Dover Barrage 235, 284; raid on 222–3, 229, 284
Dover Patrol 92, 116, 128–9, 132, 135, 145, 193, 203, 210, 230, 235, 289; and air raid on London 260–1
Dover Straits: raids on 228–35
Doyle, Sir Arthur Conan 40
Drake (Br) 68*ill*, 69
Drake, Sir Francis 16
Dreadnought (Br) 26, 67*ill*, 68–70, 205
Driant, Emile Cyprien, *La Guerre de Demain* 43
drifters 124
drugs: DORA regulations on 115
Dryad (Br) 198, 198*ill*, 199, 199*n*
Dryer, Captain Frederick 158
Dublin: Easter Rising 202*ill*
Dublin Metropolitan Police 188
Duffield, Alice 147
Duke of Edinburgh (Br) 82–3*ill*, 84
Duke of Wellington (Br) 25, 25*ill*
Dymchurch 18

East Indies Station 32
Eastbourne 18

Eastern Coast Defence Force 269
Eastern Daily Press 186–7
Eastern District Defence Scheme 112
Eastney Point Fort 18
Edgar, King 14
Edinburgh: air raids on 261
Edward 1, King 15
Edward VII, King 64, 68
Edward the Confessor, King 14–15
Edward Warlledge School 243
Eisenhart, Karl, *Die Abrechnung mit England* 43
Elco Company, New Jersey 126
Elgar, Edward 118
Ellis Island 95
Ellwood, Tobias 302
Elmwood House 229
Elswick Ordnance Company 286
Emden docks 105, 296
Entente Cordiale (1904) 64, 300
Erebus (Br) 236
Essex: plans for potential invasion 172–3, 173*n*; raids on 270
Eton Officer Training Corps 269
Ettrick (Br) 267
Evans, Commander Edward Ratcliffe Garth Russell 'Teddy' 231–4
Evans, Sir Samuel 199*n*
Ewing, Sir Alfred 279–80
Excellent (Br) 236
Expédition d'Irlande 188

F D Lambert (Br) 199, 199*n*
Faithful (Br) 138
Falmouth (Br) 145, 158
Farley, Edwin 115–16
Felixstowe: air raid on 266–7
Ferguson, Niall 91
Ferris, Lurana Sheldon 176
Festubert, Battle of (1915) 184
Firedrake (Br) 146, 200
Firfield (Br) 156
First World War: 89–92; recruitment poster 93*ill*
Firth of Forth 85, 192, 207, 282
Fisher, Admiral Sir John 'Jacky' 26, 62–3, 63*port*, 136, 158, 193, 280, 293, 299–300; relations with Churchill 178–9; reorganisation of RN by 10, 66–70, 177; resignation of 179; views on air defence 253; views on Army 77–8; views on submarines 72–3, 76–7
Fishguard 18, 27
fishing boats 120–5; badges for crews of 122–3

Fitzherbert, Rear Admiral Edward 131
Flamborough Head 141, 146, 159, 296
flotilla defence theory 10, 73
Foch, General Ferdinand 245
food production: DORA rules on 226–7
food rationing 226–7, 226*n*
food supplies 32, 40, 77, 226
Formidable (Br) 166, 166*ill*, 167*ill*, 180
Fort Albert, Isle of Wight 36
Fort Ricasoli, Malta 36
Forward (Br) 150–1
Fox, Captain Cecil H 105*port*, 105–6
Frampton, George 97
France: fear of invasion from 15, 18; invasion of Ireland by (1798) 188; relations with Britain 64; relations with Russia 60
Franco-Prussian War (1870–1) 20, 37, 60
Franco-Russian Alliance 38, 62
Franco-Spanish War (1756) 17
Franz-Ferdinand, Emperor of Austria: assassination of 89
Fraser, Lieutenant Commander Harry MacLeod 150
Fraser, Simon Joseph, Lord Lovat 55–6
Freeman, George 188
Freeman's Journal 188
French, Sir John 184, 186
French Navy 22, 292–3
French Revolutionary Wars 9, 19, 26–7
Fritz, *Kapitänleutnant* Hans 254
Frobisher, Sir Martin 16
Fürbringer, Werner 'Fips' 211
Furieux (Fr) 292

Gadfly (Br) 74*ill*
Galatea (Br) 200
Gallipoli campaign 184, 204, 228
Garrison Point 36
Gautier, *Korvettenkapitän* 231
Gazely, Alice Maud 257
Geddes, Eric Campbell 239
Gedge, Staff Paymaster Joseph 106, 106*n*
'George', Operation 245
George V, King 70, 114, 201, 294
German Air Force: Gotha bomber G-V: 265*ill*, 265–8, 299; *Kagohl 3*: 264–7
German Navy 70–1
  1st Scouting Group 167, 192, 211; 2nd Scouting Group 192, 249; 2nd Torpedo Boat Flotilla 249; East Asia Squadron 136; Flanders Destroyer Half Flotilla 222, 229, 231, 249; Flanders Fleet (*Marinekorps Flandern*) 221; Flanders Flotilla 229–30; Flanders Torpedo Boat Flotilla 222, 229–30; Fleet Laws (*Flottengesetze*) 70;
High Seas Fleet (*Hochseeflotte*) 136, 139–40, 145, 167, 191, 248; Imperial Germany Navy (*Kaiserliche Marine*) 65, 71, 289, 298; Risk Fleet (*Risikoflotte*) 71; raids on British towns by 7*map*, 323; rebellions in 249; secret codes (HVB, SKM, VB) 145
German spies 57–8, 98–9, 104, 117, 135, 141–2, 174–5, 183, 258, 270, 297–8; theme in fiction 41–2
Germany: declares unrestricted submarine warfare 170, 225–6; fear of invasion from 9–10, 297; First Naval Law (1898) 295; food rationing in 225*n*; seeks armistice 249; support from Irish Republican movement 188–90
Gibb, Sir Alexander 284
Gibraltar 66–7, 82–3
Girl Guide movement 273–4
Gladstone, Willliam 12, 20
Glatton (Br) 285, 288*ill*, 289
Gneisenau (Ger) 136
Golz, Lieutenant General Colmar, Baron von der 296
Good Hope (Br) 135
Goodenough, Commodore William 145, 157–8, 167–8
Gorgon (Br) 287, 289
Gorleston, Norfolk 137, 138, 243
Graham, James, Marquis of Graham 52
Grand Hotel, Scarborough 144, 147, 148*ill*
Granville Hotel, Scarborough 147
Graudenz (Ger) 137, 144
Gravelines (1588), Battle of 16
Great Eastern Hotel, Harwich 116*ill*, 117
Great Eastern Railway Company 105, 105*n*, 117
Great Yarmouth 132, 136, 187; air raid on 254–8, 255*ill*, 256*ill*; raid on (1915) 11, 136–42, 192–201, 196; (1918) 242–5
Greatorex, Rear Admiral Clement 245–6
Grey, Sir Edward 8, 51, 65–6, 65*port*, 71–2, 78, 81, 83, 90–1, 300
Greypoint (Br) 230
Griffith, George 188; *Angel of the Revolution* 38
Grimsby 110, 123, 132
Gripper, Herbert 118
Grosvenor, Hugh Richard Arthur, Duke of Westminster 219
Guiding Light (anti-submarine vessel) 199
Gulf War (1990) 302
guns and gunnery 22, 29, 34–5, 49–50, 310; 303 Lewis gun 263; 9.2in gun 49*ill*, 50; BL 6in VII: 246*ill*, 276*ill*; Brock bullets 264; Hotchkiss guns 36*ill*; mixed armaments

69; Mk VII coast defence gun 276*ill*; QF gun 86, 248, 248*ill*; Pomeroy bullets 260, 264
Gyles, Donald 233–5

Hague Conference (1899) 250
Hague Conventions 98, 108, 162–3, 320; VIII on submarine mines 105, 298
Hague Treaty (1907) 105
Haig, Field Marshal Douglas 184, 245
Haigh, Signalman G E 230
Halcyon (Br) 122, 137–9
Haldane, Captain John Burdon Sanderson 270
Haldane, Richard Burdon 53, 53*n*, 55, 57–8, 97, 298, 300
Hall, John 149
Halliday, George B 149, 158–9
Hamilton, Sir Frederick 88
Hamilton, Lord George 61
Hampshire (Br) 209
Hankey, Maurice 45–6, 95, 99–101, 298
Harcourt, Lewis Vernon, Viscount 78
Hardinge, Arthur Henry 65
Hardinge, Sir Charles 66
Hardy, Thomas, *The Trumpet Major* 18
Harrington Coke Oven Company 180–1
Hartlepool 86, 144, 299, 301; raid on 11, 150–6, 153*ill*, 154*ill*, 158–9
Harwich 51, 95, 112, 132, 139, 157, 183, 198, 200, 209–10, 281–2, 294; air raid on 115, 266–7; impact of DORA on 115, 117
Harwich Force 139, 203–4, 230, 244; and Battle of Jutland 207–10; and raids on Great Yarmouth and Lowestoft 192–3, 197–8, 200, 244; and raids on London 259, 261
Hastings 15
Hawkcraig Research Station 281
Hawke (Br) 135
Hawke, Admiral Edward 17–18, 18*n*
Hecate (Br) 287
Hegel, Georg 184
Heligoland Bight 85
Heligoland Bight, Battle of (1914) 135–6, 140
Heneage, Admiral Algernon Charles Fieschi 'Pompo' 29
Henrey, Robert, *The Siege of London*, 38
Henri IV (Fr) 293
Henrician Castles 16, 307
Henry VII, King 15
Henry VIII, King 15–16
Herbert, Commander Godfrey 138
Herm Island 98

Hermes (Br) 135
Hersing, *Kapitänleutnant* Otto 171–2, 171*n*
Herwig, Holger 191*n*
Hill, Headon, *The Spies of Wight* 41
Hipper, Admiral Franz von 146, 159*port*, 207, 249 ; and Battle of Dogger Bank 167–8; raid on Great Yarmouth 137–40, 157–8
Hippersley, Richard John Bayntun 279–80
Hirta wireless station 247, 248*ill*
Hobday, John William 236
Hogue (Br) 135
Holmes, Joseph, *The Bombardment of the Cumberland Coast* (poem) 181–2
Home Ports Defence Committee 51, 95
Home Rule Bill (1886) 12; (1912) 189
Home Service Garrison Battalions 186
Homeland (Br) 138
Hood (Br) 10, 109*ill*, 110, 145
Hood, Rear Admiral Horace 100
Hope, Acting Bombardier 159
Hopgood, Edward George 156
Hornby, Admiral Sir Geoffrey Phipps 60
Horton, Admiral Max 17
Hotspur (Br) 289
House of Commons Defence Committee 302
Houston, Sir Robert 244
Houston, William Stephen 156
Hucks, Beatfield Charles 251
Hull 27, 123
Humber 51, 87, 95, 111–12, 132, 141 159, 296
hunting patrols 132
Hydra (Br) 287
hydrophones 11, 281
Hythe 15

Illustrated Mail 58
Illustrious (Br) 110, 294, 295*ill*
Immortalité (Br) 35
Indefatigable (Br) 84
indicator loops 11, 281–2, 322
Indomitable (Br) 69*ill*, 70, 84
industrial unrest 184, 240–2, 321
Inflexible (Br) 32, 70, 84, 136
Ingenohl, Admiral Friedrich von 136, 142, 144, 145–6, 157, 170
Ingleby, Holcombe, *The Zeppelin Raid in West Norfolk* 258
Inglefield, Vice Admiral Sir Frederick Samuel 125
Ingleson, Able Seaman Ernest Ramsden 235
Ingrid II (Br) 156
Invasion of England, The (novel) 38
invasions 13–14, 41–5, 297; mock invasion (1913) 42, 228; preparations for 172–5; theme in fiction 37–40

Inverboyndie (Br) 122*ill*
Invergordon 85
Invincible (Br) 70, 84, 136
Ipswich: raid on 192
Ireland 187–91; Easter Rising (1916) 191, 201–2; invasion by France (1798) 188
Irish Independent 188
Irish Republican Brotherhood (IRB) 188
Irish Times 188
Italian Navy motor boats: *MAS-9*: 291; *MAS-13*: 291

Jackson, Admiral Sir Henry 85, 179
Jackson, Captain Thomas 87
Jackson, William 238
Jagow, Gottlieb von 190
James I, King 17
James II, King 17
James, Colonel Lionel, *The Boy Galloper* 38–9
James, William, *The Moral Equivalent of War* 275–6
Jameson, Admiral William 66–7
Jane's Fighting Ships 235
Jellicoe, Admiral John 11, 102, 104, 109, 132, 139, 145, 157, 199, 205–6, 202–3, 209–10, 215–17, 216*port*, 227–8, 270; and Battle of Heligoland Bight 135; Battle of Jutland 207–9; and raid on Scarborough 145–6, 162; and raid on Southwold 223; relations with Lloyd George 239
Jemappes (Fr) 293
Jericho (Br) 261
Jervis, Admiral John 8
Jeune École 73
Jobling, George 156
John, Augustus 99
John Mitchell (Br) 121*ill*
Jones, Major General Henry David 'Harry' 23
Jones, Commander John Paul 179–80
Jones, Private Theophilus 156
Joynson-Hicks, William 141–2
Jutland, Battle of (1916) 70, 207–9

Kale (Br) 74*ill*
Kearley, Hudson Ewbanke, Viscount Devonport 226, 226*n*
Kell, Reginald 58
Kent: raids on 228–31; propaganda postcard 77*ill*, 111*ill*
Keyes, Admiral Sir Roger 146, 209, 227–8
Kilcoan (Br) 172
Kilnsea Acoustic Mirror 283*ill*
King Edward VII class (Br) 205, 205*ill*
King George V (Br) 145
King Stephen (Br) (later *Ledger*) 198–9

King-Hall, Lieutenant Stephen 160
King's Lynn, Norfolk 256–7
Kingfisher (Br) 261
Kitchener, Herbert, Earl Kitchener 91, 96, 101, 108, 111, 184, 209, 251, 299–300
Knight, Laura 99
Knorr, Admiral Eduard von: plan for pre-emptive strike on RN 295–6
Knox, General Alfred 240
Kolberg (Ger) 137, 144, 146, 168
Königin Luise (Ger) 105–6
Kroell, Theodore 98
Kronprinz Erzherzog Rudolf (Austro-Hungary) 290–1

La Gloire (Fr) 21*ill*, 22, 26
Laertes (Br) 197
Laforey (Br) 230
Lamb, Captain 199*n*
Lambert, Andrew 66, 299
Lambert, George 244
Lambert, Nick 72–3
Lance (Br) 105
Landrail (Br) 105
Lansing, Robert 225
Lark (Br) 105–6, 106*ill*
Laverock (Br) 229
Lavery, John 97, 99
Law of Angary 134
Le Queux, William, *German Spies in England* 174; *The Great War in England in 1897* 39*ill*; *The Invasion of 1910* 3; *Weekly News* 41–2
Ledger (Br) (formerly *King Stephen*) 198–9
Lee, Georgina 94, 109, 160–1, 179, 227, 267, 274, 294
Legion of Frontiersmen 58–9
Leith: air raids on 27, 261–2
Leitrim Observer 188
Leopard (Br) 137
Lerwick 245–6
Leybourne, William 15
Liberal Party 12, 55
Lightfoot (Br) 193, 212, 214
Linda Blanche (Br) 172, 172*ill*
Linnet (Br) 105–6
Lion (Br) 102, 145, 168*ill*, 169
Lively (Br) 137
Llewellyn (Br) 230
Lloyd George, David 80, 216, 232, 240, 298, 299; and conscription 187, 294; and the People's Budget 71–2; relations with Jellicoe 239; views on alcohol 114
Llywelyn ap Gruffudd 15
Loch na Keal 104, 110

Loch Swilly, Ireland 102, 141
Locker-Lampson, Oliver Stillingfleet 219
Loder-Symonds, Captain 236
Lodge Hill depot 86
London: air raids on 258–68
London, Treaty of (1915) 20, 226
London Hospital 253–4
Loos, Battle of (1915) 184
Lord Nelson (Br) 76*ill*
Louis, Captain Prince of Battenberg 46, 58, 89, 90, 136*n*, 300
Louis Philippe, King of France 20–1
Lowca, Cumbria 180
Lowestoft 123, 138; bombers' route to 194*map*; raid on 11, 191–200, 195*ill*, 195*ill*
Loxley, Captain Arthur 166, 167*port*
Lurcher (Br) 146
Lusitania (Br) 70, 126, 234; sinking of 176–8, 177*ill*
Lüttwitz, Captain Baron von 295
Lützow (Ger) 192, 196
Luxmoore, Henry 236

M-N Scheme 283–4
Macdonogh, Major General Sir George 240
Macnamara, Dr Thomas 141, 244–5
Magdala (Br) 287
Maidstone, Kent 111
Maitland, Lieutenant Arthur 269
Mallin, Bombardier F W 159
Maltzahn, Baron Curt von 207
Manley (Br) 198
Manning Committee 27, 51–2
Manual of Coast Fortresses 282
Marconi, Guglielmo 277
Marconi Station, Hunstanton 279*ill*
Marder, Arthur 30–1, 95–6, 200
Margate: raid on 228–31, 267
Marlborough (Br) 208
Marne, Battle of the (1914) 99
'Mars', Operation 245
Marshal Ney (Br) 235–6, 267
Marshal Soult (Br) 235
Martello towers 9, 18–19, 19*ill*, 111
Martin, Rudolf, *Berlin-Bagdad* 43
Maunsell, Guy 284
Maurice Debate (1918) 240*n*
Maurice-Jones, Colonel 35, 92
Max, Prince of Baden 249
Maxwell, Gordon 129
McClaren, Hamish 261–2
McKenna, Admiral Reginald 72, 81, 98
Mediterranean Stations 32, 66, 82, 84
Melville, William 57
Menace (Br) 226

Mercantile Marine Reserve (MMR) 130
merchant shipping 133–4, 224–5
Meteor (Br) 285
'Michael', Operation 245
Military Service Act (1916) 187, 190
Mill, John Stuart, *Principles of Political Economy* 8
mines and mining 10, 104–5, 107, 159; observation minefields 36, 51
minesweeping 131, 159
Ministry of Munitions 137, 241
Minotaur (Br) 32
Mitchell, Alexander Crichton 282
Mitchell, Dr Charles 286
Mitchison, Naomi 270
Moltke (Ger) 137, 144, 146, 152, 165, 163, 167, 192, 192*ill*, 211, 248
Moltke, General Helmut von 99*n*
Monarch (Austro-Hung) 291
Monarch (Br) 145
Monmouth (Br) 135
Montagu, Charles, Marquess of Halifax 8
Montrose (Br) 110
Mordaunt, Penny 303
Morley, John 91–2
Morocco 79
Mortinson, Carl 210
Moss (Br) 199, 199*n*
motor boats 125–6
motor launches (MLs) 126–9; *ML-247*: 128; *ML-463*: 127*ill*; *ML51–500*: 128; *ML524*: 127*ill*; *ML1–50*: 128
Moy (Br) 150–1
Munich (Br) 117
Munificent (Br) 156
Munitions of War Act (1915) 241

Nab Tower (M-N scheme) 284*ill*
Napoleon 1, Emperor of the French 18
Napoleonic Wars 300
National Reserve 59, 186
National Service League (NSL) 55–6, 187, 243
Naval Defence Act (1889) 60–2
Naval Discipline Act (1957) 27, 52, 121
Naval Estimates 287; (1905) 66; (1912) 82
Naval Expenditure (1910–13) 66, 313
Naval Forces Act (1903) 52
Naval Staff Appreciation (1921) 209
Navy League 72
Nelson, Admiral Lord Horatio 18, 27
Netherlands 20
Neuve Chapelle, Battle of (1915) 184
New Romney 15
New York Times 140, 176
New Zealand (Br) 145

Newbolt, Henry 28
Newcastle-upon-Tyne 87
Newmarket (Br) 117
Nicholson, William 97
Nidaros (Nor) 289
Niemann, August, *Der Weltkrieg* 43
Nimrod (Br) 193
Nine Years War (1688–97) 188
Norfolk: preparations for invasion 173
Norman Conquest 14–15
Norse invasion 14
North America and West Indies Station 32–3, 66
North Sea 10, 38–9, 65–7, 73, 84–5, 95–6, 102–10, 145, 216; declaration as prohibited area 107–8; mining of 161, 107–8
Northampton (Br) 32
Northcliffe, Alfred Harmsworth, Lord Northcliffe 39, 55, 229
Northern Daily Mail 155–6
Norwich 173, 192
Nottingham (Br) 145, 158, 213

O'Brien, Edward Conor Marshall 128
O'Heugh, John 155–6
Oban 87
Odin (Ger) 290, 290*ill*
Official History of the Royal Navy 107, 134, 163, 180
Ohlson, Oscar 181
Oliver, Vice Admiral Henry 144, 161–2, 202, 209, 278–9
Oppenheim, E Phillips, *A Maker of History* 41
Orion (Br) 145, 158, 158*ill*
Ostend 19–20
Owen, General John 10, 48–51, 95, 152

Pacific Squadron 33, 66
Pakefield, Suffolk 201
Pakenham, Rear Admiral William 146, 217
Palmer, Admiral William, Lord Selborne 44–5, 51
Panther (Ger) 79, 79*ill*
Paragon (Br) 230
Paramount (Br) 230
Paris, Treaty of (1856) 84*n*
Parker, Martin, *Armada* 8
Parker, Admiral William 27
Parkestone Quay 112, 117, 281
Parry, Lance Corporal J W 238
Pathfinder (Br) 135, 171*n*
Patrol (Br) 150–1, 151*ill*
Pead, William 297
Peck, Commander Ambrose Maynard 231, 233–4

Pembroke (Br) 267
Penelope (Br) 193, 198
People's Budget (1908) 71–2
Petty-Fitzmaurice, Marquess of Lonsdale 65
Phoebe (Br) 156
Pickup, Thomas Temple 238
Pieper, Captain 140
pigeons as message carriers 99
Piscatorial (Br) 256
Pitt, William, the Elder 32
Plantagenet Dynasty 17
Platen-Hallermund, *Kapitänleutnant* Count von 254, 257
Player's Navy Cut cigarettes 28*n*
Plunkett, Commander Reginald 121, 125
Plymouth 15, 24, 96
Pocock, Henry Roger Ashwell 58
Pohl, Admiral Hugo von 170, 191
Poignand, Lieutenant Commander Charles 226
police force 118–19, 119*ill*; strike by 242
Poore, Admiral Sir Richard 144
Port Minesweeping Offices 131
Port War Signal Station 93, 150
Porthcawl Volunteer Coast Intelligence 183
Portsmouth 9, 15, 24, 35, 49, 96, 132
Poynter, Edward 97
Preston, Captain Lionel 131–4
Prince Albert (Br) 287
Prince Rupert (Br) 162, 162*ill*
Princess Royal (Br) 136
Prize Rules 226
Prondzynski, Pilot Lieutenant von 251
propaganda posters 93*ill*, 96*ill*, 97*ill*, 111*ill*, 112*ill*, 160*ill*, 161*ill*, 226*ill*

Queen (Br) 166
Queen Elizabeth Medal 274*n*
Queen Mary (Br) 145
Queen Mary's Army Auxiliary Corps (QMAAC) 272
Queenstown, Ireland 27, 103, 133
Quiberon Bay, Battle of (1759) 17

'Race for the Sea' 99
Raleigh, Sir Walter 16
Ramsgate: raid on 228, 230–1, 235–7
Ranger (US) 180
Rawles, Able Seaman 235
Redmond, John 189, 189*port*
Redwald (Br) 230
Reinsurance Treaty (1887–90) 60
Remy, *Kapitänleutnant* Walter 247–8
Rendel, George 286
Rendel gunboats 285–7

Renown (Br) 31*ill*
Repington, Charles à Court 55, 101
Report of a Committee on Armament of Home Ports (Owen Report 1905) 49, 152
Reydon School, Southwold 224
Richard 1, King 15
Richmond, Captain Herbert 100, 163, 205
Ridley, Jane 64
Rinaldo (Br) 144
River Fencibles 27
Rizzo, Commander Luigi 291
Robeck, Rear Admiral John Michael de 89, 141
Roberts (Br) 243–4, 243*ill*
Roberts, Field Marshal Frederick 44, 55*port*, 55–6, 58–9
Robertson-Scott, Commander Charles A 289
Robida, Albert, *La Guerre au Vingtième Siècle* 43
Robson, Lieutenant Colonel Lancelot 152, 152*port*, 159
Roman Britain 13
Rona (Br) 129*ill*
Room 40: 145, 161, 193, 202, 208, 211–12, 253, 278–80, 298
Roosevelt, Theodore 176
Rostock (Ger) 193*ill*, 194
Rosyth 85, 95–6, 216
Round Towers 15
Roway Iron and Steel Works 242
Roxburgh (Br) 146
Royal Artillery 9, 34
Royal Citadel, Plymouth 33, 33*ill*, 34*ill*, 36*ill*
Royal Commission on the Defence of the United Kingdom (1859) 23, 27
Royal Defence Corps 186, 186*n*
Royal Engineers 9, 36, 93, 284
Royal Engineers Defence Electric Light (DEL) 50*ill*, 51
Royal Flying Corps (RFC) 12, 250
Royal Garrison Artillery (RGA) 10, 34, 34*ill*, 35*ill*, 92–3, 112–3, 120, 171–2, 299–300
Royal Garrison Artillery Volunteers 35, 54, 159
Royal Hospital, Chelsea 267
Royal Hotel, Scarborough 147
Royal Hotel, Whitby 149
Royal Marines 11, 95, 100, 104
Royal Military Canal, Kent 13
Royal Naval Air Service (RNAS) 12, 218, 228, 244, 251, 257, 262, 265
Royal Naval Armoured Car Division (RNACD) 219–20
Royal Naval Artillery Volunteers (RNAV) 27, 52
Royal Naval Coast Volunteers (RNCV) 27, 52
Royal Naval Division 100
Royal Naval Motor Boat Reserve (RNMBR) 125–6
Royal Naval Reserve (RNR) 27, 120, 128
Royal Naval Reserve-Trawler Section (RNR-T) 121, 123
Royal Naval Reserves Act (1859) 120; (1903) 52
Royal Naval Volunteer Reserve (RNVR) 52–3, 120, 128, 300
Royal Navy 9, 11, 28–9, 301–3; fleet distribution (1907–12) 315–17; image of 28; location of fleet stations 32–3, 308; outdated condition of 29–32; recruitment and education of cadets by 63; reorganisation of 66–70, 88; Secret Fleet Orders 203; 1st Battle Cruiser Squadron 145; 2nd Battle Cruiser Squadron 84; 2nd Battle Squadron 104, 145, 157; 3rd Battle Squadron 96, 141, 162, 204, 210; 5th Battle Squadron 99, 141, 204; 1st Cruiser Squadron 84; 2nd Cruiser Squadron 248; 3rd Cruiser Squadron 146; 10th Cruiser Squadron 92, 241; 6th Battle Squadron 165, 204; 3rd Destroyer Flotilla 105; 7th Flotilla 141; 9th Flotilla 141; 1st Light Cruiser Squadron 145; 5th Light Cruiser Squadron 212; Atlantic Fleet 66–8; Battlecruiser Fleet 203; Channel Fleet 66–7, 141, 165; Channel Squadron 33, 38; Flotilla Defence 72–3; Grand Fleet 90, 102, 120, 248, 298, 301; Grand Fleet Battle Orders 209–10; Home Fleet reorganisation 66–7, 88; Minesweeping Division 131; Nore Command 33, 85; Pacific Squadron 66; Plymouth Command 33; Portsmouth Command 33; 'Red Fleet' 85; Training Department 223
Royal Review, Spithead (1914) 302
Royal Sovereign (Br) 61*ill*, 62, 62*n*, 69
Royal Yacht Squadron 130
Rupert (Br) 289
Russell, Alice 272–3
Russia 60–2, 64–5, 90
Russian Revolution 240
Russian-French alliance (1891–4) 44
Russo-German Armistice (1918) 240
Russo-Japanese War (1904–5) 58, 64–5, 69, 95
Russo-Turkish War (1878) 288
Ryalls, John Shields 156
Ryan, Captain Cyril 281
Rye 15

Sagama River (Br) 156
St George (Br) 88*ill*, 89
St Kilda: raid on 11, 247–8
St Petersburgh (Br) 117
Saki (Hector Hugh Munro), *When William Came* 40
Salamis (Greece) 243*n*
Salisbury, Robert, Lord Salisbury 12, 42*n*, 45, 45*n*, 60–1, 299
Samson, Commander Charles 218
Samuel, Herbert 101
Sanders, Sir Patrick 303
Sanderson, Louis Norman 149
Sandringham House 258
Sandwich 15
Sandys, George 57
Saracen (Br) 133*ill*
Saxon Shore forts 13, 305
Scapa Flow 51, 85, 95, 120; raid on 102–4
Scarborough 144; commemorative medal 163–4; raid on (1914) 11, 146–9, 148*ill*, 149*ill*, 158–62, 301; (1917) 237–8, 237*n*
Scarborough Lighthouse 147*ill*
Scarborough Mercury 146*n*, 163
Scharnhorst (Ger) 136
Scheer, Vice Admiral Friedrich Heinrich 191, 191*port*, 191*n*, 207, 209–14, 249
Schiemann, Theodor 188
Schlieffen, Alfred von 296
Schmidt's Delicatessen, London 41, 41*n*
Schneider, *Kapitänleutnant* Rudolph 165–6, 180–1
Schoemann, Hermann 222
Schofield, Lieutenant Brian 198
Schröder, Admiral Ludwig von 220–3, 220*port*
Schwab, Charles M 243*n*
Schweiger, *Kapitänleutnant* Walther 177
Scientific American, 'The United States: An Undefended Treasure Land' 176
Scotland: air raids on 261–2; designated Special Military Area 117–18
Scotney, Able Seaman Harry 138
Scott, Elizabeth 238
Scott, Admiral Sir Percy Moreton 29–30, 259–60, 260*port*
Scott, Captain Robert Falcon 231–2
Scouts Active Service Book, The 183*ill*
Sea Fencibles 9, 27
Sea Palling, Norfolk 187
seagulls: as anti-submarine device 281
Seaham, County Durham 210–11
seaplanes
  British: Curtiss H-12 flying boat 266; Wright seaplane 251–2
  German: Friedrichshafen FF-19 251, 252*ill*
Secret Service Bureau (SSB) 58, 87, 297
Seeley, Colonel John 'Jack' 298
Serbia 90
Seven Years War (1756–63) 17–18, 32
Seydlitz (Ger) 137, 143*ill*, 144, 146, 152, 167, 169, 192, 200, 207, 211
Seymour, Lieutenant Commander Ralph 158
Shakespeare, William, *King John* 8; *Richard II* 13
Sheehy-Skeffington, Frances 188–9
Sheerness 11, 66, 86, 141, 204, 267
Sheerness Royal Dockyards 85
Sheringham, Norfolk 187, 256
Sheringham Golf Links 183
Shiel, M P, *The Yellow Danger* 38
Ship Money tax 17
shore defences 33–6
Shreeve, Skipper Percy 199
Siegfried class (Ger) 289–90
Simnel, Lambert 187–8
Simon, Sir John 92, 135
Sir John French (Br) 261
Slaughter, Mary 210–11
Smith, Catherine O'May Campbell Raida 262
Smith, George 270–1
Smith, Samuel 255
Sole Bay, Battle of (1672) 219
South America Station 33, 66
Southampton (Br) 145, 157, 160, 168
Southend 258, 258*n*
Southern Ship Channel 110
Southern Star (newspaper) 188
Southsea Castle 15
Southwold 219–21, 223–4
Spanish Armada (1588) 16, 188
Sparks, Mary Ann and Arthur 242
Sparrowhawk (Br) 232
Special Branch 98*n*
Spectator, The 56–7, 59, 99, 108, 187, 201, 204, 303
Spee, Vice Admiral Maximilian von 136
Spence, Robert 156
Spiers, Able Seaman Joe 137, 138
Square Towers 15
Stack Rock Fort 21*ill*, 23, 23*n*
Standard Motor Construction Company 128
Stanford, Charles Villiers 28, 28*n*
steam yachts 129–31
Steinhauer, Gustav 57, 297
Stockton, Frank P, *The Great War Syndicate* 42–3
Stone, Charles John, *What Happened after the Battle of Dorking* 38
Stralsund (Ger) 137, 138, 143*ill*, 144

Strand Magazine 40
Strassburg (Ger) 137, 143*ill*, 144
Strasser, *Korvettenkäpitan* Peter 254
strikes 240–2, 321
Stuart, Major General John Spencer 42
submarine cables 277–8, 278*n*
submarine warfare: Germany declares unrestricted warfare 170, 225–6
submarines 72–3, 76–7
 British: Holland-type 76; *C-9*: 151; *C-35*: 75*ill*; *D-3*: 138; *D-5*: 138; *E-10*: 138; *E-22*: 199; *E-23*: 215
 German: *U-17*: 142; *U-20*: 177, 178*ill*; *U-21*: 171–2; *U-24*: 165–6, 180–1; *U-27*: 180; *U-38*: 180; *U-90*: 247; *UB-13*: 200; *UB-18*: 199; *UB-21*: 237; *UB-29*: 198; *UB-39*: 210–11; *UB-116*: 282; *UC-5*: 200
Success (Br) 138
Sueter, Captain Murray 253
Suez Canal 32, 84
Suffolk: plans for potential invasion 175
Sunday Times 302–3
Sunderland 207–15
Supernumerary Companies 186
Surrey: plans for potential invasion 173–4
Surrey Comet 173–4
Sussex (Br) 185, 207
Swift (Br) 102, 230, 231–5
Sydney Morning Herald 244

Tarlair (Br) 281, 282
Taureau (Fr) 292
Taylor, Martha 255
Temeraire (Br) 76*ill*
Tempêtes (Fr) 292
Tennant, Harold 258
Tennent, Josephine 271–2
Terra Nova (Br) 231
Territorial (Br) 78*ill*
Territorial and Reserve Force Bill (1907) 53
Territorial Force (TF) 53–4, 57, 59, 92, 120, 269, 300
terrorism: theme in fiction 38
Terschelling Island 139, 146
Test (Br) 150
Thompson, David Couper, *Spies of the Kaiser: Plotting the Downfall of England* 41
Thomson, Basil 98*n*, 98–9
Thorncroft, Ivy Edith 236
Thunder (Br) 285
Thwaites, Major William 42
Tiger (Br) 145
Times, The 20, 26, 55, 60, 101, 161, 183, 201, 258, 285
Tirpitz, Admiral Alfred von 65, 70–1, 296

Tonnant (Fr) 292
Tonnerres (Fr) 292
torpedo boat destroyers (TBDs) 75
torpedo boats
 British
 TB-4: 230
 German 221*ill*, 222*il*.; *V-47*: 222; *V-67*: 222; *V-68*: 222
torpedoes 35–6
Touchstone (Br) 267
Trafalgar, Battle of (1805) 18, 61
trawlers 121–5; anti-submarine trawlers 124; patrol trawlers 124
trench warfare 111, 113, 144, 107, 201, 219, 240
Trevelyan, Charles 92*n*
Trieste: raid on 291
Trusty (Br) 285
Tsushima, Battle of (1905) 65, 65*n*, 72
Tucker, William Sansome: microphones 283, 283*n*
'*Türkenkreuz*' (Turk's Cross), Operation 264
Turner, Alfred 194–5, 197
Turner, Lieutenant Commander Robert Ross 215
Turner, Captain William 177
Twentyman, William 181
Two Power Standard 61–2, 72
Tyne Turrets 294
Tyrwhitt, Admiral Sir Reginald 139, 139*port*, 145–6, 157, 294, 259 205, 207–9, 212–5, 294; and Battle of Jutland 208–9; and raid on Great Yarmouth 139, 157, 193–4, 196–8, 200–3; and raid on Dogger Bank 167–9; and raid on Sunderland 212–5

Ulster Volunteer Force 219
Undaunted (Br) 139, 146, 168
United Arts Force (UAF) 97–8
United Irishman 188
United States: 'Black Tom' explosion (1916) 298; conscription in 237*n*; declares war on Germany (1917) 237; Espionage Act (1917) 237*n*; fears of invasion 175–6; potential war with Britain 42*n*; Sedition Act (1918) 237*n*; support for Irish republican movement 189–90

Valmy (Fr) 293
Vane-Tempest, Edith, Marchioness of Londonderry 272
Verdun, Battle of (1916) 43, 207
Vickers Company 171; strikes at 241
Victoria, Queen 60; Diamond Jubilee Fleet (1897) 31, 63, 63; Golden Jubilee (1887) 31

Victoria and Albert (Br) 30*ill*
Victory (Br) 25, 68
Viking longships 14
Vincent, Colonel Sir Howard 47
Vivid (Br) 144
Voluntary Aid Detachments (VAD) 273
Volunteer Corps 174
Volunteer Training Corps (VTC) 97–8, 274–5
volunteers 26–8, 34, 52–3, 120–34, 271–6, 300–1, 303; opposition to 27, 52; psychology of 274–6
Von der Tann (Ger) 137, 142*ill*, 144, 146, 192, 196

Wales 15
Walney Island 170–1, 299
Walther, Commander Franz 237–8
War Cabinet 227, 266–7, 298
War Channel 10, 107
War Council 253
War Illustrated 163, 234, 257
War Office 12, 46–7, 51–2, 86–7, 93, 186–7, 250–1, 260, 299
Wardle, Commander Thomas 247
Warneford, Sub Lieutenant Reginald 'Rex' 263–4
Warrender, Admiral Sir George 145, 157
Warrior (Br) 22*ill*, 23, 26–7, 84
Watkin, Captain H S 50
Watson, Commander Reginald James 236
Waveney (Br) 150–1
Weil, Patrick 175–6
Wells, H G 10, 250; *The War in the Air* 11, 39–40
Western Front 113, 179, 184, 245, 249, 294
Westfalen (Ger) 214*ill*, 215
Weybourne 183, 187
Whale Island, mock invasion of 42*ill*
Whitby 144, 149–50
Whitehaven 179–80
Wien (Austro-Hungary) 291, 291*ill*
Wilde, Oscar 217
Wilhelm II, Kaiser 99, 136, 253, 297; *My Early Life* 65; war poster 96*ill*

William I, William the Conqueror 14–15
Williams, Ordinary Seaman William David 197
Williamson, Commander Frederick Vere 244*n*
Willoughby de Broke, Lord John Vernon 57–8
Wilson, Admiral Sir Arthur Knyvet 81
Wilson, General Sir Henry 80–2, 81*port*, 96
Wilson, Woodrow 185, 249
Winchelsea 15
Wintour, Captain Charles John 102
wireless telegraphy 277
Wodehouse, P G, *The Swoop!* 43
women: employment of 271–4, 301; volunteering by 273
Women's Auxiliary Army Corps (WAAC) 271–2
Women's Legion 272
Women's Royal Naval Service (WRNS) 272–4
Wood, Leonard 176
Wood, Walter, *The Enemy in our Midst* 41
Woolwich Arsenal 263
Wyllie, W L 52

Y-system wireless listening posts 11, 280, 298
Yachting Monthly 130–1
Yellow Sea, Battle of the (1904) 64–5
Yorck (Ger) 139–40, 140*ill*
Yorke, Charles Philip 18
Ypres, 2nd Battle of (1915) 184

Zarefah (Br) 131
Zaza (Br) 138, 138*n*
Zeebrugge 19–20
Zeppelin, Graf Ferdinand von 250
Zeppelins 11, 252–68, 270, 299; *L-1*: 250; *L-3*: 254, 256–7; *L-4*: 254, 256–7; *L-6*: 254; *L-14*: 261; *L-19*: 199; *L-22*: 261; *L-48|*: 266; *L-64*: 255*ill*; *LZ-31*: 258; *LZ-37*: 263 *LZ-38*: 258
Zimmermann, Arthur 190